the WINGS to AWAKENING

An Anthology from the Pali Canon

Translated and Explained by

Thanissaro Bhikkhu
(Geoffrey DeGraff)

Printed for free distribution

Dhamma Dana Publications
Barre Center for Buddhist Studies
Barre, Massachusetts

•

The Dhamma Dana Publication Fund

is dedicated to bringing a long-standing Buddhist tradition to America by making high-quality books on Buddhist teachings available for free distribution.

For further information, write:

The Dhamma Dana Publication Fund
Barre Center for Buddhist Studies
149 Lockwood Road
Barre, MA 01005 USA

•

Printed in the United States of America

Library of Congress Cataloging-in-Publication Data pending.

So this is what you think of me: "The Blessed One, sympathetic, seeking our well-being, teaches the Dhamma out of sympathy." Then you should train yourselves—harmoniously, cordially, and without dispute—in the qualities I have pointed out, having known them directly: the four frames of reference, the four right exertions, the four bases of power, the five faculties, the five strengths, the seven factors of Awakening, the noble eightfold path.

—*M.103*

Contents

Acknowledgments

This book has been several years in the making. In the course of assembling it, I have used some of the material it contains to lead study courses at the Barre Center for Buddhist Studies, Barre, Massachusetts; at Awareness Grove, Laguna Beach, California; with the Insight Meditation Society of Orange County; with the San Diego Vipassana Community; and with the Open Door Sangha of Santa Barbara. The feedback coming from the participants in these courses has been very helpful in forcing me to clarify the presentation and to make explicit the connections between the words and their application in practice. It has been encouraging to see that people in America—contrary to their reputation in other parts of the world—are interested in learning authentic Buddhist teachings and integrating them into their lives. This encouragement is what has given me the impetus to turn this material into a book.

In addition to the participants at the above courses, many people have read and offered valuable comments on earlier incarnations of the manuscript. Ven. Bhikkhu Bodhi kindly read through and suggested corrections in the translations from the Pali Canon. Dorothea Bowen, John Bullitt, Jim Colfax, Charles Hallisey, Karen King, Mu Soeng, Andrew Olendzki, Gregory M. Smith, and Jane Yudelman read through translations and earlier versions of the essays. John Bullitt also helped with the Index. The finished book owes a great deal to comments and suggestions of all of these people. Any mistakes that remain, of course, are my own responsibility.

I dedicate this book to all of my teachers, and in particular to Phra Ajaan Lee Dhammadharo, the teacher of my primary teacher, Phra Ajaan Fuang Jotiko. The example of Ajaan Lee's life has had a large influence on my own, in more ways than I can ever really repay. His teaching of the Buddhist path as a skill—as expressed in the Wings to Awakening and embodied in the practice of breath meditation—provided the original and on-going inspiration for writing this book. I offer it to his memory with the highest respect.

Ṭhānissaro Bhikkhu

Metta Forest Monastery
P. O. Box 1409
Valley Center, CA 92082
October, 1996

Abbreviations

Pali Buddhist Texts

A	Aṅguttara Nikāya
D	Dīgha Nikāya
DHP	Dhammapada
ITI	Itivuttaka
M	Majjhima Nikāya
MV	Mahāvagga
S	Saṁyutta Nikāya
THIG	Therīgāthā
UD	Udāna

References to D, ITI, and M are to discourse *(sutta).* References to DHP are to verse. The reference to MV is to chapter, section, and subsection. References to other texts are to section *(saṁyutta, nipāta,* or *vagga)* and discourse.

All translations are the author's own, and are based on the Royal Thai Edition of the Pali Canon (Bangkok: Mahamakut Rajavidyalaya, 1982).

Other Abbreviations

Comm	Commentary
lit	literal meaning
PTS	Pali Text Society
vl	variant reading

In the translated passages, parentheses ( ) enclose alternative renderings and material summarized from longer passages in the text. Square brackets [ ] enclose explanatory information, cross-references, and other material not found in the original text. Fancy brackets { } enclose material interpolated from other passages in the Canon; the source of this material is indicated in fancy brackets as part of the citation at the end of the passage.

Because Pali has many ways of expressing the word "and," I have—to avoid monotony—used the ampersand (&) to join lists of words and short phrases, and the word "and" to long long phrases and clauses.

In passages where no speaker is identified, the words are the Buddha's.

Preface:

HOW TO READ THIS BOOK

Many anthologies of the Buddha's teachings have appeared in English, but this is the first to be organized around the set of teachings that the Buddha himself said formed the heart of his message: the Wings to Awakening *(bodhi-pakkhiya-dhamma).* The material is arranged in three parts, preceded by a long Introduction. The Introduction tries to define the concept of Awakening so as to give a clear sense of where the Wings to Awakening are headed. It does this by discussing the Buddha's accounts of his own Awakening, with special focus on the way in which the principle of skillful kamma (in Sanskrit, *karma)* formed both the "how" and the "what" of that Awakening: The Buddha was able to reach Awakening only by developing skillful kamma—this is the "how"; his understanding of the process of developing skillful kamma has what sparked the insights that constituted Awakening—this is the "what."

With this background established, the remainder of the book focuses in detail on the Wings to Awakening as a detailed analysis of the "how." Part One focuses on aspects of the principle of skillful kamma that shaped the way the Wings to Awakening are formulated. Part Two goes through the seven sets that make up the Wings to Awakening themselves: the four foundations of mindfulness (here called the four frames of reference), the four right exertions, the four bases for power, the five faculties, the five strengths, the seven factors of Awakening, and the noble eightfold path. Part Three reduces all the terms in the seven sets to the five faculties, and then deals with those faculties in detail. With the fifth and final faculty, discernment, the book concludes by returning to the "what" of Awakening, showing how discernment focuses on the Wings themselves as topics to be observed in such a way that they will spark the insights leading to total release.

Thus the organization of the book is somewhat circular. As with any circle, there are several points where the book can be entered. I would recommend two to begin with. The first is to read straight through the book from beginning to end, gaining a systematic framework for the material from Parts One and Two, which explain why the seven sets are organized as they are, and then focusing more on individual elements in the sets in Part Three. This way of approaching the material has the advantage of giving an overall perspective on the topic before going into the details, making the role and meaning of the details clear from the start. However, this approach is the reverse of what actually happens in the practice. A practicing meditator must learn first to focus on individual phenomena in and of themselves, and then, through observation and experimentation, to discover their inter-relationships. For this reason, some readers—especially those who find the discussion of causal relationships in Parts One and Two too abstract to be helpful—may prefer to skip from the Introduction straight to sections A through E of Part Three, to familiarize themselves with teachings that may connect more directly with their own experience. They may then return later to Parts One and Two to gain a more overall perspective on how the practice is meant to deal with those experiences.

Regardless of which approach you take to the material, you should discover fairly quickly that the relationships among the overall patterns and individual elements in the Wings are very complex. This complexity reflects the non-linear nature of the Buddha's teachings on causal relationships, and is reflected in the many cross-references among the various parts of the book. In this way, the structure of this book, instead of being a simple circle, is actually a pattern of many loops within loops. Thus a third way to read it—for those familiar enough with the material to want to explore unexpected connections—would be to follow the cross-references to see where they lead.

Parts One through Three of the book are each divided into sections consisting of passages translated from discourses in the Pali Canon, which is apparently the earliest extant record of the Buddha's teachings. Each section is introduced, where necessary, with an essay. These essays are printed in sans serif type to distinguish them clearly from the translated passages. They are attempts to provide context—and thus meaning—for the passages, to show how they relate to one another, to specific issues in the practice, and to the path of practice as a whole. They are not meant to anticipate or answer every possible question raised by the passages. Instead, they are aimed at giving an idea of the kinds of questions that can be most fruitfully brought to the passages, so that the lessons contained in the passages can properly be applied to the practice. As the Buddha has pointed out, the attitude of "appropriate attention" *(yoniso manasikāra)*, the ability to focus on the right questions, is one of the most important skills to develop in the course of the practice. This skill is much more fruitful than an attitude that tries to come to the practice armed with all the right answers in advance.

The context provided by the essays is threefold: *doctrinal*, i.e., placing the passages within the structure of the Buddha's teachings taken as a whole; *historical*, i.e., relating them to what is known of the intellectual and social history of the Buddha's time; and *practical,* i.e., applying them to the actual practice of the Buddhist path in the present.

The first and foremost sources for the doctrinal context are the discourses in the Canon itself. The Buddha and his noble disciples are by far the most reliable guides to the meaning of their own words. Often a teaching that seems vague or confusing when encountered on its own in a single discourse becomes clearer when viewed in the context of several discourses that treat it from a variety of angles, just as it is easier to get a sense of a building from a series of pictures taken from different perspectives than from a single snapshot. This approach to understanding the discourses is instructive not only when discourse *x* explicitly defines a term mentioned in discourse *y,* but also when patterns of imagery and terminology permeate many passages. Two cases in point: In separate contexts, the discourses compare suffering to fire, and the practice of training the mind in meditation to the art of tuning and playing a musical instrument. In each case, technical terms—from physics in the first instance, from music theory in the second—are applied to the mind in a large number of contexts. Thus it is helpful to understand where the terms are coming from in order to grasp their connotations and to gain an intuitive sense—based on our own familiarity with fire and music—of what they mean.

In a few instances, I have cited alternative versions of the discourses—such as those contained in the Sarvastivadin Canon preserved in Chinese translation—to throw light on passages in the Pali. Although the Sarvastivadin Canon as a whole seems to be later than the Pali, there is no way of knowing whether particular Sarvastivadin discourses are earlier or later than their Pali counterparts, so the comparisons drawn between the two are intended simply as food for thought.

I have also drawn occasionally on the Pali Abhidhamma and commentaries, which postdate the discourses by several centuries. Here, however, I have had to be selective. These texts employ a systematic approach to interpreting the discourses that fits some teachings better than others. There are instances where a particular teaching has one meaning in terms of this system, and another when viewed in the context of the discourses themselves. Thus I have taken specific insights from these texts where they seem genuinely to illumine the meaning of the discourses, but without adopting the overall structure that they impose on the teachings.

To provide historical context, I have drawn on a variety of sources. Again, the foremost source here is the Pali Canon itself, both in what it has to say explicitly about the social and intellectual milieu of the Buddha's time, and in what it says implicitly about the way the intellectual disciplines of the Buddha's time—such as science, mathematics, and music theory—helped to shape the way the Buddha expressed his thought. I have also drawn on secondary sources where these do a useful job of fleshing out themes present in the Pali Canon. These secondary sources are cited in the Bibliography.

Because the Pali tradition is still a living one, the doctrinal and historical contexts do not account for the full range of meanings that practicing Buddhists continue to find in the texts. To provide this living dimension, I have drawn on the teachings of modern practice traditions where these seem to harmonize with the message of the Canon and add an illuminating perspective. Most of these teachings are drawn from the Thai Forest Tradition, but I have also drawn on other traditions as well. I have followed a traditional Buddhist practice in not identifying the sources for these teachings, and for two reasons: first, in many ways I owe every insight offered in this book to the training I have received from my teachers in the Forest Tradition, and it seems artificial to credit them for some points and not for others; second, there is the possibility that I have misunderstood some of their teachings or taken them out of context, so I don't want to risk crediting my misunderstandings to them.

In providing a more modern context for the passages presented in this book, however, I have not tried to interpret the teachings in terms of modern psychology or sociology. The Buddha's message is timeless and direct. It does not need to be translated into the passing fashions of disciplines that are in many ways more removed than it is from the realities of direct experience, and more likely to grow out of date. However, there are two modern disciplines that I have drawn on to help explain some of the more formal aspects of the Buddha's mode of speech his and analysis of causal principles.

The first discipline is phenomenology, the branch of philosophy that deals with phenomena as they are directly experienced, in and of themselves. There are many schools of modern phenomenology, and it is not my purpose to try to equate the Buddha's teachings with any one of them. However, the Buddha does recommend a mode of perception that he calls "entry into emptiness *(suññatā)*" [see. M.121], in which one simply notes the presence or absence of phenomena, without making any further assumptions about them. This approach resembles what in modern philosophy could be called "radical phenomenology," a mode of perception that looks at experiences and processes simply as events, with no reference to the question of whether there are any "things" lying behind those events, or of whether the events can be said really to exist [see passages §230 and §186]. Because of this resemblance, the word "phenomenology" is useful in helping to explain the source of the Buddha's descriptions of the workings of kamma and the process of dependent co-arising in particular. Once we know where he is coming from, it is easier to make sense of his statements and to use them in their proper context.

I have made similar use of modern science—chaos theory in particular. There are many parallels between Buddhist theories of causation and modern deterministic chaos theory. Examples and terminology drawn from the latter—such as feedback, scale invariance, and fluid turbulence—are very useful in explaining the former. Again, in using these parallels I am not trying to equate Buddhist teachings with chaos theory or to engage in pseudo-science. Fashions in science change so rapidly that we do the Buddha's teachings no favor in trying to "prove" them in light of current scientific paradigms. Here I am simply pointing out similarities as a way of helping to make those teachings intelligible in modern terms. Deterministic chaos theory is the only modern body of knowledge that has worked out a vocabulary for the patterns of behavior described in Buddhist explanations of causality, and so it seems a natural source to draw on, both to describe those patterns and to point out some of their less obvious implications.

In doing so, I realize that I run the risk of alienating non-scientists who feel intimidated by scientific terminology, as well as scientists who resent the application of terminology from their disciplines to "non-scientific" fields. To both groups I can say only that the terms in and of themselves are not "scientific." Much of our current everyday terminology for explaining causal relations is derived from the science of the eighteenth century; I expect that it will only be a matter of time before the terminology of more recent science will percolate into everyday language. For the purpose of this book, it is important to point out that when the Buddha talked about causality, his notion of causal relations did not correspond to our ordinary, linear, picture of causal chains. If this point is not grasped, the common tendency is to judge the Buddha's descriptions of causality against our own and to find them either confusing or confused. Viewing them in the light of deterministic chaos theory, however, helps us to see that they are both coherent and of practical use.

Another example of an analogy drawn from modern science is the term "holographic," which I have used to describe some formulations of the Buddhist path. When a hologram is made of an object, an image of the entire object—albeit fairly fuzzy—can be made from even small fragments of the hologram. In the same way, some formulations of the path contain a rough version of the entire path complete in each individual step. In my search for an adjective to describe such formulations, "holographic" seemed the best choice.

If you are unfamiliar with the terminology of phenomenology, chaos theory, and holograms, read section I/A, on skillfulness, to find the doctrinal context in which these terms can be related to an immediate experience: the process of developing a skill. The approach of phenomenology relates to the fact that, on the night of his Awakening, the Buddha focused his attention directly on the mental process of developing skillful states in the mind, without referring to who or what was developing the skill, or to whether there was a substratum of some sort underlying the process. Chaos theory relates to the patterns of causality that the Buddha discerned while observing this process, whereby the effects of action can in turn become causal factors influencing new action. Holography relates to his discovery that skillfulness is developed by taking clusters of good qualities already present in the mind and using them to strengthen one another each step along the way. Once these familiar reference points are understood, the abstract terms describing them should become less foreign and more helpful.

In providing doctrinal, historical, and practical context based on all the above-mentioned sources, the essays are meant to give an entry into the mental horizons and landscape of the texts they introduce. They are also meant to suggest how the texts may be used for their intended purpose: to help eliminate obstacles to the release of the mind. Although some of the essays address controversial questions, the textual passages are not meant to prove the points made in the essays. In assembling this anthology, I first gathered and translated the passages from the Canon, and then provided the essays after contemplating what I had gathered. For this reason, any reader who disagrees with the positions presented in the essays should still find the translations useful for his/her own purposes. I am painfully aware that some of the essays, especially those in Part I, tend to overpower the material they are designed to introduce, but this is because the themes in Part I play a pervasive role in the Buddha's teachings as a whole. Thus I had to deal with them in considerable detail to point out how they relate not only to the passages in Part I, but also to themes raised in the rest of the book.

Although the essays should go far toward familiarizing the reader with the conceptual world and relevance of the textual passages, there are other aspects of the passages that might prove daunting to the uninitiated, and so I would like to deal with them here.

To begin with, the teachings on the Wings to Awakening are interrelated in very complex ways. Because books must be arranged in linear sequence, taking one thing at a time in a row, this means that no book can do justice to all the side avenues and underground passageways that connect elements in one set of teachings to those in another. For this reason, I have organized the material in line with the order of the sets as given in the Canon, but—as mentioned above—have extensively cross-referenced it for the sake of readers who want to explore connections that fall outside the linear pattern. Cross-references are given in brackets [ ], and take three forms. An example that looks like this—[§123]—is a reference to a passage from the Pali Canon translated in this book. One that looks like this—[III/E]—is a reference to an essay introducing a section, in this case Section E in Part III. One that looks like this—[M.107]—is a reference to a passage from the Pali Canon not translated here. The abbreviations used in these last references are explained on the Abbreviations page. Many passages falling in this last category are translated in my book, *The Mind Like Fire Unbound,* in which case the reference will include the abbreviation MFU followed by the number of the page on which the passage is located in that book. My hope is that these cross-references will open up useful lines of thought to whoever takes the time to explore them.

Another potential difficulty for the uninitiated reader lies in the style of the passages. The Pali Canon was, for 500 years, an entirely oral tradition. As a result, it tends to be terse in some areas and repetitive in others. I've made an effort to cut out as many of the repetitions as possible, but I'll have to ask your patience for those that remain. Think of them as the refrains in a piece of music. Also, when the Buddha is referring to monks doing this and that, keep in mind that his audience was frequently composed entirely of monks. The commentaries state that the word "monk" includes anyone—male or female, lay or ordained—who is serious about the practice, and this meaning should always be kept in mind. I apologize for the gender bias in the translations. Although I have tried to figure out ways to minimize it, I find myself stymied because it is so thoroughly embedded in a literature originally addressed to monks.

I trust, however, that none of these difficulties will prove insurmountable, and that you will find, as I have, that the teachings of the Pali Canon more than reward the effort put into exploring them. The reality of the Wings to Awakening lies in the qualities of the mind. The words with which they are expressed in the Pali Canon are simply pointers. These pointers have to be tested in the light of serious practice, but my conviction is that, of all the meditation teachers the human race has ever seen, the Buddha is still the best. His words should be read repeatedly, reflectively, and put to test in the practice. My hope in gathering his teachings in this way is that they will give you useful insights for training the mind so that someday you won't have to read about Awakening, but will be able to know it for yourself.

A Table of the Wings to Awakening

I. The Seven Sets

The Four Frames of Reference (satipaṭṭhāna)

1. Remaining focused on the body in & of itself—ardent, alert, & mindful—putting aside greed & distress with reference to the world.

2. Remaining focused on feelings in & of themselves—ardent, alert, & mindful—putting aside greed & distress with reference to the world.

3. Remaining focused on the mind in & of itself—ardent, alert, & mindful—putting aside greed & distress with reference to the world.

4. Remaining focused on mental qualities in & of themselves—ardent, alert, & mindful—putting aside greed & distress with reference to the world.

The Four Right Exertions (sammappadhāna)

1. Generating desire, endeavoring, arousing persistence, upholding & exerting one's intent for the sake of the non-arising of evil, unskillful qualities that have not yet arisen.

2. Generating desire, endeavoring, arousing persistence, upholding & exerting one's intent for the sake of the abandoning of evil, unskillful qualities that have arisen.

3. Generating desire, endeavoring, arousing persistence, upholding & exerting one's intent for the sake of the arising of skillful qualities that have not yet arisen.

4. Generating desire, endeavoring, arousing persistence, upholding & exerting one's intent for the maintenance, non-confusion, increase, plenitude, development, & culmination of skillful qualities that have arisen.

The Four Bases of Power (iddhipāda)

1. Developing the base of power endowed with concentration founded on desire & the fabrications of exertion.

2. Developing the base of power endowed with concentration founded on persistence & the fabrications of exertion.

3. Developing the base of power endowed with concentration founded on intent & the fabrications of exertion.

4. Developing the base of power endowed with concentration founded on discrimination & the fabrications of exertion.

The Five Faculties (indrīya)

1. The faculty of conviction *(saddhindrīya).*
2. The faculty of persistence *(viriyindrīya).*
3. The faculty of mindfulness *(satindrīya).*
4. The faculty of concentration *(samādhindrīya).*
5. The faculty of discernment *(paññindrīya).*

The Five Strengths (bala)

1. The strength of conviction *(saddhā-bala).*
2. The strength of persistence *(viriya-bala).*
3. The strength of mindfulness *(sati-bala).*
4. The strength of concentration *(samādhi-bala).*
5. The strength of discernment *(paññā-bala).*

The Seven Factors of Awakening (bojjhaṅga)

1. Mindfulness as a factor of awakening *(sati-sambojjhaṅga).*
2. Analysis of qualities as a factor of awakening *(dhamma-vicaya-sambojjhaṅga).*
3. Persistence as a factor of awakening *(viriya-sambojjhaṅga).*
4. Rapture as a factor of awakening *(pīti-sambojjhaṅga).*
5. Serenity as a factor of awakening *(passaddhi-sambojjhaṅga).*
6. Concentration as a factor of awakening *(samādhi-sambojjhaṅga).*
7. Equanimity as a factor of awakening *(upekkhā-sambojjhaṅga).*

The Noble Eightfold Path (ariya-magga)

1. Right view *(sammā-diṭṭhi).*
2. Right resolve *(sammā-saṅkappa).*
3. Right speech *(sammā-vācā).*
4. Right action *(sammā-kammanta).*
5. Right livelihood *(sammā-ājīva).*
6. Right effort *(sammā-vāyāma).*
7. Right mindfulness *(sammā-sati).*
8. Right concentration *(sammā-samādhi).*

II. The Factors of the Seven Sets classed under the Five Faculties

Conviction

Right Speech (Eightfold Path)
Right Action (Eightfold Path)
Right Livelihood (Eightfold Path)
Desire (Bases of Power)

Persistence

Right Effort (Eightfold Path)
Four Right Exertions
Persistence (Bases of Power)
Persistence (Factors of Awakening)

Mindfulness

Four Frames of Reference
Right Mindfulness (Eightfold Path)
Intent (Bases of Power)
Mindfulness (Factors of Awakening)

Concentration

Four Bases of Power
Right Concentration (Eightfold Path)
Rapture (Factors of Awakening)
Serenity (Factors of Awakening)
Concentration (Factors of Awakening)
Equanimity (Factors of Awakening)

Discernment

Right View (Eightfold Path)
Right Aspiration (Eightfold Path)
Analysis of Qualities (Factors of Awakening)
Discrimination (Bases of Power)
Equanimity (Factors of Awakening)

Introduction

The Wings to Awakening are the Buddha's own list of his most important teachings. Toward the end of his life, he stated several times that as long as the teachings in this list were remembered and put into practice, his message would endure. Thus the Wings constitute, in the Buddha's eyes, the words and skills most worth mastering and passing along to others.

THE BUDDHA'S AWAKENING

When discussing the Buddha's teachings, the best place to start is with his Awakening. That way, one will know where the teachings are coming from and where they are aimed. To appreciate the Awakening, though, we have to know what led Prince Siddhattha Gotama—the Buddha before his Awakening—to seek it in the first place. According to his own account, the search began many lifetimes ago, but in this lifetime it was sparked by the realization of the inevitability of aging, illness, and death. In his words:

> I lived in refinement, utmost refinement, total refinement. My father even had lotus ponds made in our palace: one where red-lotuses bloomed, one where white lotuses bloomed, one where blue lotuses bloomed, all for my sake. I used no sandalwood that was not from Vārāṇasī. My turban was from Vārāṇasī, as were my tunic, my lower garments, & my outer cloak. A white sunshade was held over me day & night to protect me from cold, heat, dust, dirt, & dew.
>
> I had three palaces: one for the cold season, one for the hot season, one for the rainy season. During the four months of the rainy season I was entertained in the rainy-season palace by minstrels without a single man among them, and I did not once come down from the palace. Whereas the servants, workers, & retainers in other people's homes are fed meals of lentil soup & broken rice, in my father's home the servants, workers, & retainers were fed wheat, rice, & meat.
>
> Even though I was endowed with such fortune, such total refinement, the thought occurred to me: "When an untaught, run-of-the-mill person, himself subject to aging, not beyond aging, sees another who is aged, he is horrified, humiliated, & disgusted, oblivious to himself that he too is subject to aging, not beyond aging. If I—who am subject to aging, not beyond

aging—were to be horrified, humiliated, & disgusted on seeing another person who is aged, that would not be fitting for me." As I noticed this, the [typical] young person's intoxication with youth entirely dropped away.

Even though I was endowed with such fortune, such total refinement, the thought occurred to me: "When an untaught, run-of-the-mill person, himself subject to illness, not beyond illness, sees another who is ill, he is horrified, humiliated, & disgusted, oblivious to himself that he too is subject to illness, not beyond illness. And if I—who am subject to illness, not beyond illness—were to be horrified, humiliated, & disgusted on seeing another person who is ill, that would not be fitting for me." As I noticed this, the healthy person's intoxication with health entirely dropped away.

Even though I was endowed with such fortune, such total refinement, the thought occurred to me: "When an untaught, run-of-the-mill person, himself subject to death, not beyond death, sees another who is dead, he is horrified, humiliated, & disgusted, oblivious to himself that he too is subject to death, not beyond death. And if I—who am subject to death, not beyond death—were to be horrified, humiliated, & disgusted on seeing another person who is dead, that would not be fitting for me." As I noticed this, the living person's intoxication with life entirely dropped away.

A.III.38

Before my Awakening, when I was still an unawakened Bodhisatta (Buddha-to-be), being subject myself to birth, aging, illness, death, sorrow, & defilement, I sought (happiness in) what was subject to birth, aging, illness, death, sorrow, & defilement. The thought occurred to me: "Why am I, being subject myself to birth...defilement, seeking what is subject to birth...defilement? What if I...were to seek the unborn, unaging, unailing, undying, sorrowless, undefiled, unsurpassed security from bondage: Unbinding."

So at a later time, when I was still young, black-haired, endowed with the blessings of youth in the first stage of life, I shaved off my hair & beard—though my parents wished otherwise and were grieving with tears on their faces—and I put on the ochre robe and went forth from the home life into homelessness.

M.26

These passages are universal in their import, but a fuller appreciation of why the young prince left home for the life of a homeless wanderer requires some understanding of the beliefs and social developments of his time.

Prince Siddhattha lived in an aristocratic republic in northern India during the sixth century B.C.E., a time of great social upheaval. A new monetary economy was replacing the older agrarian economy. Absolute monarchies, in alliance with the newly forming merchant class, were swallowing up the older aristocracies. As often happens when an aristocratic elite is being disenfranchised, people on all levels of society were beginning to call into question the beliefs that had supported the older order, and were looking to science and other alternative modes of knowledge to provide them with a new view of life.

The foremost science in North India at that time was astronomy. New, precise observations of planetary movements, combined with newly developed means of calculation, had led astronomers to conclude that time was measured in aeons, incomprehensibly long cycles that repeat themselves endlessly. Taking up these conclusions, philosophers of the time tried to work out the implications of this vast temporal frame for the drama of human life and the quest for ultimate happiness. These philosophers fell into two broad camps: those who conducted their speculations within the traditions of the Vedas, early Indian religious and ritual texts that provided the orthodox beliefs of the old order; and other, unorthodox groups, called the Samaṇas (contemplatives), who questioned the authority of the Vedas. Modern etymology derives the word Samaṇa from "striver," but the etymology of the time derived it from *sama*, which means to be "on pitch" or "in tune." The Samaṇa philosophers were trying to find a way of life and thought that was in tune, not with social conventions, but with the laws of nature as these could be directly contemplated through scientific observation, personal experience, reason, meditation, or shamanic practices, such as the pursuit of altered states of consciousness through fasting or other austerities. Many of these forms of contemplation required that one abandon the constraints and responsibilities of the home life, and take up the life of a homeless wanderer. This was the rationale behind Prince Siddhattha's decision to leave the home life in order to see if there might be a true happiness beyond the sway of aging, illness, and death.

Already by his time, philosophers of the Vedic and Samaṇa schools had developed widely differing interpretations of what the laws of nature were and how they affected the pursuit of true happiness. Their main points of disagreement were two:

1) Survival beyond death. Most Vedic and Samaṇa philosophers assumed that a person's identity extended beyond this lifetime, aeons before birth back into the past and after death on into the future, although there was some disagreement as to whether one's identity from life to life would change or remain the same. The Vedas had viewed rebirth in a positive light, but by the time of Prince Siddhattha the influence of the newly discovered astronomical cycles had led those who believed in rebirth to regard the cycles as pointless and restrictive, and release as the only possibility for true happiness. There was, however, a Samaṇa school of hedonist materialists, called Lokayatans, who denied the existence of any identity beyond death and insisted that happiness could be found only by indulging in sensual pleasures here and now.

2) Causality. Most philosophers accepted the idea that human action played a causative role in providing for one's future happiness both in this life and beyond. Views about how this causal principle worked, though, differed from school to school. For some Vedists, the only effective action was ritual. The Jains, a Samaṇa school, taught that all action fell under linear, deterministic causal laws and formed a bond to the recurring cycle. Present experience, they said, came from past actions; present actions would shape future experience. This linear causality was also materialistic: physical action created *āsavas* (effluents, fermentations)—sticky substances on the soul that kept it attached to the cycle. According to them, the only escape from the cycle lay in a life of non-violence and inaction, culminating in a slow suicide by starvation, which would burn the asavas away, thus releasing the soul. Some *Upanishads*—post-Vedic speculative texts—expressed causality as a morally neutral, purely physical process of evolution. Others stated that moral laws were intrinsic to the nature of causality, rather than being mere social conventions, and that the morality of an action determined how it affected one's future course in the round of rebirth. Whether these last texts were composed before or after the Buddha taught this view, though, no one knows. At any rate, all pre-Buddhist thinkers who accepted the principle of causality, however they expressed it, saw it as a purely linear process.

On the other side of the issue, the Lokayatans insisted that no causal principle acted between events, and that all events were spontaneous and self-caused. This meant that actions had no consequences, and one could safely ignore moral rules in one's pursuit of sensual pleasure. One branch of another Samaṇa school, the Ājīvakas, insisted that causality was illusory. The only truly existent things, they said, were the unchanging substances that formed the building blocks of the universe. Because causality implied change, it was therefore unreal. As a result, human action had no effect on anything of any substance—

including happiness—and so was of no account. Another branch of the same school, which specialized in astrology, insisted that causality was real but totally deterministic. Human life was entirely determined by impersonal, amoral fate, written in the stars; human action played no role in providing for one's happiness or misery; morality was purely a social convention. Thus they insisted that release from the round of rebirth came only when the round worked itself out. Peace of mind could be found by accepting one's fate and patiently waiting for the cycle, like a ball of string unwinding, to come to its end.

These divergent viewpoints formed the intellectual backdrop for Prince Siddhattha's quest for ultimate happiness. In fact, his Awakening may be seen as his own resolution of these two issues.

The Pali Canon records several different versions of the Buddha's own descriptions of his Awakening. These descriptions are among the earliest extended autobiographical accounts in human history. The Buddha presents himself as an explorer and experimenter—and an exceedingly brave one at that, putting his life on the line in the search for an undying happiness. After trying several false paths, including formless mental absorptions and physical austerities, he happened on the path that eventually worked: bringing the mind into the present by focusing it on the breath, and then making a calm, mindful analysis of the processes of the mind as they presented themselves directly to his immediate awareness. Seeing these processes as inconstant, stressful, and not-self, he abandoned his sense of identification with them. This caused them to disband, and what remained was Deathlessness *(amata-dhamma)*, beyond the dimensions of time and space. This was the happiness for which he had been seeking.

In one passage of the Pali Canon [§188], the Buddha noted that what he had come to realize in the course of his Awakening could be compared to the leaves of an entire forest; what he taught to others was like a mere handful of leaves. The latter part comprised the essential points for helping others to attain Awakening themselves. The part he had kept back would have been useless for that purpose. Thus, when we discuss the Buddha's Awakening, we must keep in mind that we know only a small sliver of the total event. However, the sliver we do know is designed to aid in our own Awakening. That is the part we will focus on here, keeping the Buddha's purpose for teaching it constantly in mind.

When the Buddha later analyzed the process of Awakening, he stated that it consisted of two kinds of knowledge:

> "First there is the knowledge of the regularity of the Dhamma, after which there is the knowledge of Unbinding."
>
> S.XII.70

The regularity of the Dhamma, here, denotes the causal principle that underlies all "fabricated" *(saṅkhata)* experience, i.e., experience made up of causal conditions and influences. Knowing this principle means mastering it: One can not only trace the course of causal processes but also escape from them by skillfully letting them disband. The knowledge of Unbinding is the realization of total freedom that comes when one has disbanded the causal processes of the realm of fabrication, leaving the freedom from causal influences that is termed the "Unfabricated." The Buddha's choice of the word Unbinding *(nibbāna)*—which literally means the extinguishing of a fire—derives from the way the physics of fire was viewed at his time. As fire burned, it was seen as clinging to its fuel in a state of entrapment and agitation. When it went out, it let go of its fuel, growing calm and free. Thus when the Indians of his time saw a fire going out, they did not feel that they were watching extinction. Rather, they were seeing a metaphorical lesson in how freedom could be attained by letting go.

The first knowledge, that of the regularity of the Dhamma, is the describable part of the process of Awakening; the second knowledge, that of Unbinding, though indescribable, is what guarantees the worth of the first: When one has been totally freed from all suffering and stress, one knows that one has properly mastered the realm of fabrication and can vouch for the usefulness of the insights that led to that freedom. Truth, here, is simply the way things work; true knowledge is gauged by how skillfully one can manipulate them.

There are many places in the Pali Canon where the Buddha describes his own act of Awakening to the first knowledge as consisting of three insights:

- recollection of past lives,
- insight into the death and rebirth of beings throughout the cosmos, and
- insight into the ending of the mental effluents or fermentations *(āsava)* within the mind [§1]. (As we will see below, the Buddha's Awakening gave a new meaning to this term borrowed from the Jains.)

The first two insights were not the exclusive property of the Buddhist tradition. Shamanic traditions throughout the world have reported seers who have had similar insights. The third insight, however, went beyond shamanism into a phenomenology of the mind, i.e., a systematic account of phenomena as they are directly experienced. This insight was exclusively Buddhist, although it was based on the previous two. Because it was multi-faceted, the Canon describes it from a variety of standpoints, stressing different aspects as they apply to specific contexts. In the course of this book, we too will explore specific facets of this insight from different angles. Here we will simply provide a general outline to show how the principle of skillful kamma underlay the main features of this insight.

The Bodhisatta's realization in his second insight that kamma determines how beings fare in the round of rebirth caused him to focus on the question of kamma in his third insight. And, because the second insight pointed to right and wrong views as the factors determining the quality of kamma, he looked into the possibility that kamma was primarily a mental process, rather than a physical process, as the Vedists and Jains taught. As a result, he focused on the mental kamma that was taking place at that very moment in his mind, to understand the process more clearly. In particular, he wanted to see if there might be a type of right view that, instead of continuing the round of rebirth, would bring release from it. To do this, he realized that he would have to make his powers of discernment more skillful; this meant that the process of developing skillfulness would have to be the kamma that he would observe.

Now, in the process of developing a skill, two major assumptions are made: that there is a causal relationship between acts and their results, and that good results are better than bad. If these assumptions were not valid, there would be no point in developing a skill. The Bodhisatta noticed that this point of view provided two variables—causes and results, and favorable and unfavorable—that divided experience into four categories, which he later formulated as **the four noble truths** *(ariya-sacca):* stress, its origination, its cessation, and the path to its cessation [§189]. Each category, he further realized, entailed a duty. Stress had to be comprehended, its cause abandoned, its disbanding realized, and the path to its cessation developed [§195].

In trying to comprehend stress and its relationship to kamma, the Bodhisatta discovered that, contrary to the teachings of the Jains, kamma was not something extrinsic to the cycle of rebirth that bound one to the cycle. Rather, (1) the common cycle of kamma, result, and reaction was the cycle of rebirth in and of itself, and (2) the binding agent in the cycle was not kamma itself, but rather an optional part of the reaction to the results of kamma. The Bodhisatta analyzed the cycle of kamma, result, and reaction into the following terms: kamma is intention; its result, feeling; the reaction to that feeling, perception and attention—i.e., attention to perceptions about the feeling—which together form the views that color further intentions. If perception and attention are clouded by ignorance, craving, and clinging, they lead to stress and further ignorance, and form the basis for intentions that keep the cycle in motion. In his later teachings, the Buddha identified these clouding factors—forms of clinging, together with their resultant states of becoming and ignorance [§227]—as the asavas or effluents that act as binding agents to the cycle. In this way, he took a Jain term and gave it a new meaning, mental rather than physical. At the same time, his full-scale analysis of the interaction between kamma and the effluents formed one of the central points of his teaching, termed **dependent co-arising** *(paṭicca-samuppāda)* [§211, 218, 231].

The fact that it is possible to develop a skill suggested to the Bodhisatta, while he was developing his third insight, that the craving and clinging that cloud one's perceptions and attention did not necessarily follow on the feeling that resulted from kamma. Otherwise, there would be no way to develop skillful intentions. Thus craving and clinging could be abandoned. This would require steady and refined acts of attention and intention, which came down to well-developed concentration and discernment, the central qualities in the path to the cessation of stress. Concentration gave discernment the focus and solidity it needed to see clearly, while discernment followed the two-fold pattern that attention must play in the development of any skill: sensitivity to the context of the act, formed by pre-existing factors coming from the past, together with sensitivity to the act itself, formed by present intentions. In other words, discernment had to see the results of an action as stemming from a combination of past and present causes.

As the more blatant forms of craving, clinging, and ignorance were eradicated with the continued refinement of concentration and discernment, there came a point where the only acts of attention and intention left to analyze were the acts of concentration and discernment in and of themselves. The feedback loop that this process entailed—with concentration and discernment shaping one another in the immediate present—brought the investigation into such close quarters that the terms of analysis were reduced to the most basic words for pointing to present experiences: "this" and "that." The double focus of discernment, in terms of past and present influences, was reduced to the most basic conditions that make up the experience of "the present" (and, by extension, "space") on the one hand, and "time" on the other: Attention to present participation in the causal process was reduced to the basic condition for the experience of the present, i.e., mutual presence ("When this is, that is; when this isn't, that isn't"), while attention to influences from the past was reduced to the basic condition for the experience of time, i.e., the dependence of one event on another ("From the arising of this comes the arising of that; from the cessation of this comes the cessation of that"). These expressions later formed the basic formula of the Buddha's teachings on causality, which he termed **this/that conditionality** *(idappaccayatā)* [§211] to emphasize that the formula described patterns of events viewed in a mode of perception empty of any assumptions outside of what could be immediately perceived.

After reaching this point, there was nothing further that concentration and discernment—themselves being conditioned by time and the present—could do. When all residual attachments even to these subtle realizations were let go, there thus followed a state called non-fashioning, in which the mind made absolutely no present input into experience. With no present input to maintain experience of time and the present, the cycle of fabricated experience disbanded. This formed an opening to the Unfabricated, the undying happiness that the Bodhisatta, now the Buddha, had sought. This was the knowledge of Unbinding, or total release.

THE BUDDHA'S TEACHINGS

The texts say that the Buddha spent a total of 49 days after his Awakening, sensitive to the bliss of release, reviewing the implications of the insights that had brought about his Awakening. At the end of this period, he thought of teaching other living beings. At first the subtlety and complexity of his Awakening made him wonder if anyone would be able to understand and benefit from his teachings. However, after he ascertained through his new powers of mind that there were those who would understand, he made the decision to teach, determining that he would not enter total Unbinding until he had established his teachings—his doctrine and discipline (Dhamma-Vinaya)—on a solid basis for the long-term benefit of human and divine beings.

The two primary knowledges that constituted the Awakening—knowledge of the regularity of the Dhamma and knowledge of Unbinding—played a major role in shaping what the Buddha taught and how he taught it. Of the two, the knowledge of Unbinding was the more important. It not only guaranteed the truth of the other knowledge, but also constituted the Buddha's whole purpose in teaching: he wanted others to attain this happiness as well. However, because the first knowledge was what led to the second, it provided the guidelines that the Buddha used in determining what would be useful to communicate to others so that they too would arrive at the knowledge of Unbinding of their own accord. These guidelines were nothing other than the three insights of which this knowledge was composed: recollection of past lives, insight into the death and rebirth of beings, and insight into the ending of the mental effluents. As became clear during the Buddha's teaching career, not all those who would reach the knowledge of Unbinding would need to gain direct insight into previous lifetimes or into the death and rebirth of other beings, but they would have to gain direct insight into the ending of the mental effluents. The mastery of causality that formed the heart of this insight thus formed the heart of his teaching, with the first two insights providing the background against which the teachings were to be put into practice.

As we noted above, the three insights taken together provided answers to the questions that had provoked Prince Siddhattha's quest for Awakening in the first place. His remembrance of previous lives showed on the one hand that death is not annihilation, but on the other hand that there is no core identity that remains unchanged or makes steady, upward progress through the process of rebirth. One life follows another as one dream may follow another, with similar wide swings in one's sense of who or where one is. Thus there is no inherent security in the process.

The second insight—into the death and rebirth of beings throughout the cosmos—provided part of the answer to the questions surrounding the issue of causality in the pursuit of happiness. The primary causal factor is the mind, and in particular the moral quality of the intentions comprising its thoughts, words, and deeds, and rightness of the views underlying them. Thus moral principles are inherent in the functioning of the cosmos, rather than being mere social conventions. For this reason, any quest for happiness must focus on mastering the quality of the mind's views and intentions.

The third insight—into the ending of the mental effluents—showed that escape from the cycle of rebirth could be found, not through ritual action or total inaction, but through the skillful development of a type of right view that abandoned the effluents that kept the cycle of kamma, stress, and ignorance in motion. As we have seen, this type of right view went through three stages of refinement as the third insight progressed: the four noble truths, dependent co-arising, and this/that conditionality. We will discuss the first two stages in detail elsewhere in this book [III/H/i and III/H/iii]. Here we will focus on this/that conditionality, the most radical aspect of the Buddha's third insight. In terms of its content, it explained how past and present intentions underlay all experience of time and the present. The truth of this content was shown by its role in disbanding all experience of time and the present simply by bringing present intentions to a standstill. Small wonder, then, that this principle provided the most fundamental influence in shaping the Buddha's teaching.

The Buddha expressed this/that conditionality in a simple-looking formula:

> "(1) When this is, that is.
> (2) From the arising of this comes the arising of that.

(3) When this isn't, that isn't.
(4) From the stopping of this comes the stopping of that."

A.X.92

There are many possible ways of interpreting this formula, but only one does justice both to the way the formula is worded and to the complex, fluid manner in which specific examples of causal relationships are described in the Canon. That way is to view the formula as the interplay of two causal principles, one linear and the other synchronic, that combine to form a non-linear pattern. The linear principle—taking (2) and (4) as a pair—connects events, rather than objects, over time; the synchronic principle—(1) and (3)—connects objects and events in the present moment. The two principles intersect, so that any given event is influenced by two sets of conditions: input acting from the past and input acting from the present. Although each principle seems simple, the fact that they interact makes their consequences very complex [§10]. To begin with, every act has repercussions in the present moment together with reverberations extending into the future. Depending on the intensity of the act, these reverberations can last for a very short or a very long time. Thus every event takes place in a context determined by the combined effects of past events coming from a wide range in time, together with the effects of present acts. These effects can intensify one another, can coexist with little interaction, or can cancel one another out. Thus, even though it is possible to predict that a certain type of act will tend to give a certain type of result—for example, acting on anger will lead to pain—there is no way to predict when or where that result will make itself felt [§11].

The complexity of the system is further enhanced by the fact that both causal principles meet at the mind. Through its views and intentions, the mind takes a causal role in keeping both principles in action. Through its sensory powers, it is affected by the results of the causes it has set in motion. This creates the possibility for the causal principles to feed back into themselves, as the mind reacts to the results of its own actions. These reactions can take the form of positive feedback loops, intensifying the original input and its results, much like the howl in a speaker placed next to the microphone feeding into it. They can also create negative feedback loops, counteracting the original input, much like the action of a thermostat that turns off a heater when the temperature in a room is too high, and turns it on again when it gets too low. Because the results of actions can be immediate, and the mind can then react to them immediately, these feedback loops can at times quickly spin out of control; at other times, they may act as skillful checks on one's behavior. For example, a man may act out of anger, which gives him an immediate sense of dis-ease to which he may react with further anger, thus creating a snowballing effect. On the other hand, he may come to understand that the anger is causing his dis-ease, and so immediately does what he can to stop it. However, there can also be times when the results of his past actions may obscure the dis-ease he is causing himself in the present, so that he does not immediately react to it one way or another.

In this way, the combination of two causal principles—influences from the past interacting with those in the immediate present—accounts for the complexity of causal relationships as they function on the level of immediate experience. However, the combination of the two principles also opens the possibility for finding a systematic way to break the causal web. If causes and effects were entirely linear, the cosmos would be totally deterministic, and nothing could be done to escape from the machinations of the causal process. If they were entirely synchronic, there would be no relationship from one moment to the next, and all events would be arbitrary. The web could break down totally or reform spontaneously for no reason at all. However, with the two modes working together, one can learn from causal patterns observed from the past and apply one's insights to disentangling the same causal patterns acting in the present. If one's insights are true, one can then gain freedom from those patterns.

For this reason, the principle of this/that conditionality provides an ideal foundation, both theoretical and practical, for a doctrine of release. And, as a teacher, the Buddha took full advantage of its implications, using it in such a way that it accounts not only for the presentation and content of his teachings, but also for their organization, their function, and their utility. It even accounts for the need for the teachings and for the fact that the Buddha was able to teach them in the first place. We will take up these points in reverse order.

The fact of the teaching: As noted above, this/that conditionality is a combination of two causal modes: linear activity, connecting events over time; and synchronic causality, connecting objects in the present. The fact that the causal principle was not totally linear accounts for the fact that the Buddha was able to break the causal circle as soon as he had totally comprehended it, and did not have to wait for all of his previous kamma to work itself out first. The fact that the principle was not totally synchronic, however, accounts for the fact that he survived his Awakening and lived to tell about it. Although he created no new kamma after his Awakening, he continued to live and teach under the influence of the kamma he had created before his Awakening, finally passing away only when those kammic influences totally worked themselves out. Thus the combination of the two patterns allowed for an experience of the Unfabricated that could be survived, opening the opportunity for the Buddha to teach others about it before his total Unbinding.

The need for the teachings: This/that conditionality, even though it can be expressed in a simple formula, is very complex in its working-out. As a result, the conditions of time and the present are bewildering to most people. This is particularly true in the process leading up to suffering and stress. As §189 states, beings react to suffering in two ways: bewilderment and a search for a way out. If the conditions for suffering were not so complex, it would be the result of a simple, regular process that would not be so confusing. People would be able to understand it without any need for outside teachings. The fact of its actual complexity, however, explains why people find it bewildering and, as a result of their bewilderment, have devised a wide variety of unskillful means to escape from it: recourse to such external means as magic, ritual, revenge, and force; and to such internal means as denial, repression, self-hatred, and prayer. Thus the complexity of this/that conditionality accounts for the lack of skill that people bring to their lives—creating more suffering and stress in their attempts to escape suffering and stress—and shows that this lack of skill is a result of ignorance. This explains the need for a teaching that points out the true nature of the causal system operating in the world, so that proper understanding of the system can lead people to deal with it skillfully and actually gain the release they seek.

The utility of the teachings: The fact that this/that conditionality allows for causal input from the present moment means that the causal process is not totally deterministic. Although linear causality places restrictions on what can be done and known in any particular moment, synchronic causality allows some room for free will. Human effort can thus make a difference in the immediate present. At the same time, the fact that the principle of this/that conditionality is expressed in impersonal terms means that the Buddha's insights did not depend on any power peculiar to him personally. As he noted in recounting his experience, the realizations he attained were such that anyone who developed the mind to the same pitch of heedfulness, ardency, and resolution and then directed it to the proper task would be able to attain them as well [§1]. For these reasons, the act of teaching would not be futile, because the mental qualities needed for the task of Awakening were available to other people, who would have the freedom to develop them if they wanted to.

The function of the teachings: As chaos theory has shown in graphic terms, any causal system that contains three or more feedback loops can develop into incredible complexity, with small but well-placed changes in input tipping the balance from complex order to seeming chaos, or from chaos to order in the twinkling of an eye. A similar observation applies to this/that conditionality. Given the inherent complexity and instability of such a system, a simple description of it would be futile: the complexity would boggle the mind, and the instability would insure that any such description would not be helpful for long. At the same time, the instability of the system makes it imperative for anyone immersed in such a system to find a way out, for instability threatens any true chance for lasting peace or happiness. The complexity of the system requires that one find a reliable analysis of the sensitive points in the system and how they can be skillfully manipulated in a way that brings the system down from within. All of these considerations play a role in determining the function for which the Buddha designed his teachings. They are meant to act as a guide to skillful ways of understanding the principles underlying the causal system, and to skillful ways of manipulating the causal factors so as to gain freedom from them. The concept of skillful and unskillful thoughts, words, and deeds thus plays a central role in the teaching.

In fact, the teachings themselves are meant to function as skillful thoughts toward the goal of Awakening. The Buddha was very clear on the point that he did not mean for his teachings to become a metaphysical system, or for them to be adhered to simply for the sake of their truth value. He discussed metaphysical topics only when they could play a role in skillful behavior. Many metaphysical questions—such as whether or not there is a soul or self, whether or not the world is eternal, whether or not it is infinite, etc.—he refused to answer, on the grounds that they were either counterproductive or irrelevant to the task at hand: that of gaining escape from the stress and suffering inherent in time and the present.

Although the Buddha insisted that all of his teachings were true—none of his skillful means were useful fictions—they were to be put aside when one had fully benefited from putting them into practice. In his teachings, true but conditioned knowledge is put into service to an unconditioned goal, that of release in which the mind itself becomes true. Because a meditator has to use causal factors in order to disband the causal system, he/she has to make use of factors that eventually have to be transcended. This pattern of developing qualities in the practice that one must eventually let go as one attains the Unfabricated is common throughout the Buddha's teachings. Eventually even skillfulness itself has to be transcended.

The organization of the teachings: The fact that the causal system contains many feedback loops means that a particular causal connection—either one that continues the system or one designed to disband it—can follow one of several paths. Thus there is a need for a variety of explanations for people who find themselves involved in these different paths. This need explains the topical organization of the Buddha's teachings in his discourses. In talking to different people, or to the same people at different times, he gave different accounts of the causal links leading up to stress and suffering, and to the knowledge that can bring that stress and suffering to an end. Those who have tried to form a single, consistent account of Buddhist causal analyses have found themselves stymied by this fact, and have often discounted the wide variety of analyses by insisting that only one of them is the "true" Buddhist analysis; or that only the general principle of mutual causality is important, the individual links of the analyses being immaterial; or that the Buddha did not really understand causality at all. None of these positions do justice to the Buddha's skill as a teacher of this person and that, each caught at different junctures in the feedback loops of this/that conditionality.

As we will see when we consider the Wings to Awakening in detail, the Buddha listed different ways of envisioning the causal factors at work in developing the knowledge needed to gain release from the realm of fabrication. Although the lists follow different lines of this/that conditionality, he insisted that they were equivalent. Thus any fair account of his teachings must make room for the variety of paths he outlined, and for the fact that each is helpfully specific and precise.

The content of the teachings: Perhaps one of the most radical aspects of the Buddha's teachings is the assertion that the factors at work in the cosmos at large are the same as those at work in the way each individual mind processes experience. These processes, rather than the sensory data that they process, are primary in one's experience of the cosmos. If one can disband the act of processing, one is freed from the cosmic causal net.

What this means in the case of the individual mind—engaged in and suffering from the processes of time and the present—is that the way out is to be found by focusing directly on the processing of present experience, for that is where the crucial issues play themselves out most clearly. Here and now is where everything important is happening, not there and then. At the same time, the skills that are needed to deal with these issues are skills of the mind: proper ways of analyzing what one experiences and proper qualities of mind to bring to the analysis to make it as clear and effective as possible. This boils down to the proper frame of reference, the proper quality of awareness, and the proper mode of analysis. These are precisely the topics covered in the Wings to Awakening, although as one's skill develops, they coalesce: The quality of awareness itself becomes the frame of reference and the object to which the analysis is applied.

The presentation of the teaching: Because the Buddha's listeners were already caught in the midst of the web of this/that conditionality, he had to present his message in a way that spoke to their condition. This meant that he had to be sensitive both to the linear effects of past kamma that might either prevent or support the listener's ability to benefit from the teaching, and to the listener's current attitudes and concerns. A person whose adverse past kamma prevented Awakening in this lifetime might benefit from a more elementary teaching that would put him/her in a better position to gain Awakening in a future lifetime. Another person's past kamma might open the possibility for Awakening in this lifetime, but his/her present attitude might have to be changed before he/she was willing to accept the teaching.

A second complication entailed by the principle of this/that conditionality is that it has to be known and mastered at the level of direct experience in and of itself. This mastery is thus a task that each person must do for him or herself. No one can master direct experience for anyone else. The Buddha therefore had to find a way to induce his listeners to accept his diagnosis of their sufferings and his prescription for their cure. He also had to convince them to believe in their own ability to follow the instructions and obtain the desired results. To use a traditional Buddhist analogy, the Buddha was like a doctor who had to convince his patients to administer a cure to themselves, much as a doctor has to convince his patients to follow his directions in taking medicine, getting exercise, and changing their diet and lifestyle, and so forth. The Buddha had an additional difficulty, however, in that his definition of health—Unbinding—was something that none of his listeners had yet experienced for themselves. Hence the most important point of his teaching was something that his listeners would have to take on faith. Only when they had seen the results of putting the teachings into practice for themselves would faith no longer be necessary.

Thus, for every listener, faith in the Buddha's Awakening was a prerequisite for advanced growth in the teaching. Without faith in the fact of the Buddha's knowledge of Unbinding, one could not fully accept his prescription. Without faith in the regularity of the Dhamma—including conviction in the principle of kamma and the impersonality of the causal law, making the path open in principle to everyone—one could not fully have faith in one's own ability to follow the path. Of course, this faith would then be confirmed, step by step, as one followed the teaching and began gaining results, but full confirmation would come only with an experience of Awakening. Prior to that point, one's trust, bolstered only by partial results, would have to be a matter of faith [M.27]. Acquiring this faith is called "going for refuge" in the Buddha. The "refuge" here derives from the fact that one has placed trust in the truth of the Buddha's Awakening and expects that by following his teachings—in particular, the principle of skillful kamma—one protects oneself from creating further suffering for oneself or others, eventually reaching true, unconditioned happiness. This act of going for refuge is what qualifies one as a Buddhist—as opposed to someone simply interested in the Buddha's teachings—and puts one in a position to benefit fully from what the Buddha taught.

The Buddha employed various means of instilling faith in his listeners, but the primary means fall into three classes: his character, his psychic powers, and his powers of reason. When he gave his first sermon—to the Five Brethren, his former compatriots—he had to preface his remarks by reminding them of his honest and responsible character before they would willingly listen to him. When he taught the Kassapa brothers, he first had to subdue their pride with a dazzling array of psychic feats. In most cases, however, he needed only to reason with his listeners and interlocutors, although here again he had to be sensitive to the level of their minds so that he could lead them step by step, taking them from what they saw as immediately apparent and directing them to ever higher and more subtle points. The typical pattern was for the Buddha to begin with the immediate joys of generosity and virtue; then go on to the longer-term sensual rewards of these qualities, in line with the principle of kamma; then the ultimate drawbacks of those sensual rewards; and finally the benefits of renunciation. If his listeners could follow his reasoning this far, they would be ready for the more advanced teachings.

We often view reason as something distinct from faith, but for the Buddha it was simply one way of instilling faith or conviction in his listeners. At several points in the Pali Canon [e.g., D.1] he points out the fallacies that can result when one draws reasoned conclusions from a limited range of experience, from false analogies, or from inappropriate modes of analysis. Because his teachings could not be proven prior to an experience of Awakening, he recognized that the proper use of reason was not in trying to prove his teachings, but simply in showing that they made sense. People can make sense of things when they see them as similar to something they already know and understand. Thus the main function of reason in presenting the teachings is in finding proper analogies for understanding them: hence the many metaphors and similes used throughout the texts. Faith based on reason and understanding, the Buddha taught, was more solid than unreasoned faith, but neither could substitute for the direct knowledge of the regularity of the Dhamma and of Unbinding, for only the experience of Unbinding was a guarantee of true knowledge. Nevertheless, faith was a prerequisite for attaining that direct knowledge. Only when the initial presentation of the teaching had aroused faith in the listener, would he/she be in a position to benefit from a less-adorned presentation of the content and put it into practice.

The need for various ways of presenting his points on a wide range of levels meant that the body of the Buddha's teachings grew ever more varied and immense with time. As his career drew to a close, he found it necessary to highlight the essential core of the teaching, the unadorned content, so that the more timeless aspects of his message would remain clear in his followers' minds. Societies and cultures inevitably change, so that what counts as effective persuasion in one time and place may be ineffective in another. The basic structure of this/that conditionality does not change, however; the qualities of the mind needed for mastering causality and realizing the Unfabricated will always remain the same. The Buddha thus presented the Wings to Awakening as the unadorned content: the timeless, essential core.

Even here, however, the principle of this/that conditionality affected his presentation. He needed to find principles that would be relatively immune to changes in society and culture. He needed a mode of presentation that was simple enough to memorize, but not so simplistic as to distort or limit the teaching. He also needed words that would point, not to abstractions, but to the immediate realities of awareness in the listener's own mind. And, finally, he needed a useful framework for the teaching as a whole, so that those who wanted to track down specific points would not lose sight of how those points fit into the larger picture of the practice.

His solution was to give lists of personal qualities, as we noted above, rather than any of the more abstruse, philosophical doctrines that are often cited as distinctively Buddhist. These personal qualities are immediately present, to at least some extent, in every human mind. Thus they retain a constant meaning no matter what changes occur in one's mental landscape or cultural horizons. The Buddha presents them in seven alternative, interconnected lists (see Table I). Each list—when all of its implications are worked out—is equivalent to all of the others in its effects, but each takes a distinctive approach to the practice. Thus the lists provide enough variety to meet the needs of people caught in different parts of the causal network. As one searches the texts for explanations of the meaning of specific terms and factors in the lists, one finds that the lists connect—directly or indirectly—with everything there. At the same time, the categories of the lists, because they point to qualities in the mind, encourage the listener to regard the teachings not as a system in and of themselves, but as tools for looking directly into his/her own mind, where the sources and solutions to the problem of suffering lie.

As a result, although the lists are short and simple, they are an effective introduction to the teaching and a guide to its practice. From his experience with this/that conditionality on the path, the

Buddha had seen that if one develops the mental qualities listed in any one of these seven sets, focuses them on the present, keeping in mind the four frames of reference and analyzing what appears to one's immediate awareness in terms of the categories of the four noble truths, one will inevitably come to the same realizations that he did: the regularity of the Dhamma and the reality of Unbinding. This was the happiness he himself sought and found, and that he wanted others to attain.

In addition to the seven lists, the Buddha left behind a monastic order designed not only so that the teachings would be memorized from generation to generation, but also so that future generations would have living examples of the teaching to learn from, and a conducive social environment in which to put them into practice. This environment was intended as a gift not only for those who would ordain, but also for those lay people who associated with the order, taking the opportunity to develop their own generosity, morality, and mindfulness in the process. Associating with others who are following a sensitive disciplinary code forces one to become more sensitive and disciplined oneself. Although our concern in this book is with the Dhamma, or the teaching of the Wings to Awakening, we should not forget that the Buddha named his teaching Dhamma-Vinaya. The Vinaya was the set of rules and regulations he established for the smooth running of the order. Dhamma is the primary member of the compound, but the Vinaya forms the context that helps keep it alive. They meet in a common focus on the factor of intention. The Vinaya uses its rules not only to foster communal order, but also to sensitize individual practitioners to the element of intention in all their actions. The Dhamma then makes use of this sensitivity as a means of fostering the insights that lead to Awakening.

After he had placed the Dhamma-Vinaya on a sure footing, the Buddha passed away into total Unbinding. This event has provoked a great deal of controversy within and without the Buddhist tradition, some people saying that if the Buddha was truly compassionate, he should have taken repeated rebirth so that the rest of humanity could continue to benefit from the excellent qualities that he had built into his mind. His total Unbinding, however, can be seen as one of his greatest kindnesses to his followers. By example he showed that, although the path to true happiness entails generosity and kindness to others, the goal of the path needs no justification in terms of anything else. The limitless freedom of Unbinding is a worthy end for its own sake. Society's usual demand that people must justify their actions by appeal to the continued smooth functioning of society or the happiness of others, has no sway over the innate worth of this level. The Buddha made use of the kammic residue remaining after his Awakening to make a free gift of the Dhamma-Vinaya to all who care about genuine happiness and health, but when those residues were exhausted, he took the noble way of true health as an example and challenge to us all.

Thus the Dhamma-Vinaya can be seen as the Buddha's generous gift to posterity. The rules of the Vinaya offer an environment for practice, while the Wings to Awakening are an invitation and guide to that practice, leading to true happiness. Anyone, anywhere, who is seriously interested in true happiness is welcome to focus on the qualities listed here, to see if this/that conditionality is indeed the causal principle governing the dimensions of time and the present, and to test if it can be mastered in a way that leads to the promised result: freedom transcending those dimensions, totally beyond measure and unbound.

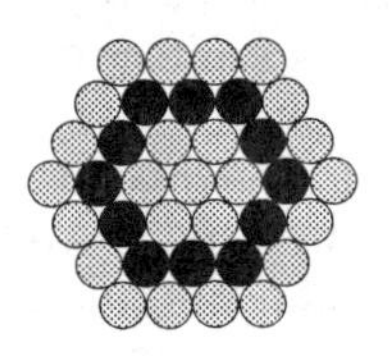

I. Basic Principles

A. SKILLFULNESS

The Buddha's teachings, like the principles they describe, are interrelated in complex ways. It is difficult to point out any one teaching that underlies everything else, as all the teachings are mutually dependent. Nevertheless, there are a number of possible entry points into their pattern, and one of those points is the Buddha's observation that it is possible to master a skill.

Unlike many of his contemporaries—and many thinkers before and since—the Buddha did not try to reason from abstract principles down to direct experience. As we noted in the Introduction, the Buddha's contemporaries were influenced by the premier science of their time—astronomy—in the way they viewed experience, and it is easy to see prejudices derived from astronomy at work in their thought: that the universe is composed of discrete bodies acting in line with regular, linear causes; and that human knowledge of these processes has no impact on the way they behave. These prejudices, when applied to human experience, resulted in what the Buddha called theories of being, or what we today would call theories of order: that the processes of the universe can be totally explained in terms of physical principles that follow linear causal patterns unaffected by human intervention. The various conclusions that developed out of this approach differed primarily in how one's soul—viewed in various ways either as a discrete thing or as a more abstract principle—was to look for release from this vast cosmic machine. Some insisted that action was illusory; others, that action was real but totally determined by fixed rules, serving only to bind one to the impersonal cycle.

In reaction to the theories of being, the Lokayatans proposed a theory of non-being or absolute chaos that, like all reactionary ideologies, was defined largely by what it denied. Although it admitted the primacy of the physical universe, it denied that any causal laws operated on the observable, human level. Everything, the Lokayatans said, was totally spontaneous, random, and chaotic. No personal souls were observable, and thus human identity was composed only of the temporary conjunction of elements that made up the body, terminating when those elements separated at death.

In a manner typical of his approach to problems, the Buddha avoided both sides of this argument by focusing directly on the level of immediate experience and exploring the implications of truths that both sides overlooked. Instead of fixing on the content of the views expressed, he considered the actions of those who were expressing the views. The logic either of total determinism or of total chaos must end in the conclusion that purposeful action is pointless, and yet adherents of both schools continued to act in purposeful ways. The fact that each side advanced an interpretation of reality implied that both agreed that there were skillful and unskillful ways of approaching the truth, for each insisted that the other used unskillful forms of observation and argumentation to advance its views. Thus the Buddha looked directly at skillful action in and of itself, worked out its implications in viewing knowledge itself as a skill—rather than a body of facts—and found that those implications carried him all the way to release.

We have already touched on how implications drawn from the fact of skillful action shaped the major outlines of the Buddha's teachings. It will be useful to review those implications here. To begin with, the fact that skills can be developed implies that action is not illusory, that it actually gives results. Otherwise, there would be no such thing as skill, for no actions would be more effective than others. The fact of skillfulness also implies that some results are preferable to others, for otherwise there would be no point in trying to develop skills. In addition, the fact that it is possible to learn from mistakes in the course of developing a skill, so that one's future actions may be more skillful, implies that the cycle of action, result, and reaction is not entirely deterministic, and that acts of perception, attention, and intention can actually provide new input as the cycle goes through successive turns.

The important element in this input is attention. Anyone who has mastered a skill will realize that the process of attaining mastery requires attention to three things: (1) to pre-existing conditions, (2) to what one is doing in relation to those conditions, and (3) to the results that come from one's actions. This threefold focus enables one to monitor one's actions and adjust them accordingly. In this way, one's attention to conditions, actions, and effects allows the results of an action to feed back into future action, thus allowing for refinement in one's skill. By working out the implications of these requirements, the Buddha arrived at the principle of this/that conditionality, in which multiple feedback loops—sensitive to pre-existing conditions, to present input, and to their combined outcome—account for the incredible complexity of the world of experience in a way similar to that of modern theories of "deterministic chaos." In this sense, even though this/that conditionality may seem somewhat alien when viewed in the abstract, it is actually a very familiar but overlooked assumption that underlies all conscious, purposeful action. The Buddha simply explored the implications of this assumption much further than anyone else, all the way to the disbanding of space, time, and the present, together with their inherent stress.

These implications of the fact of skillfulness account for the main framework of the Buddha's doctrine as expressed in the teachings on the four noble truths, dependent co-arising, and this/that conditionality. Other facets of skillful action also account for more detailed points within this framework. For instance, the Buddha's exploration of stress and its origination, in the light of skillful action, provided the analysis of mental and physical events ("name-and-form," *nama-rupa)* that plays a central role in the second noble truth as expressed in terms of dependent co-arising. The first lesson of skillfulness is that the essence of an action lies in the intention motivating it: an act motivated by the intention for greater skillfulness will give results different from those of an act motivated by greed, aversion, or delusion. Intention, in turn, is influenced by the appropriateness or inappropriateness of the act of attention to one's circumstances. The less an act of attention is clouded by delusion, the more clearly it will see things in appropriate terms. The combination of attention and intention in turn determines the quality of the feeling and the physical events that result from the act. The more skilled the action, the more refined the feelings and physical events that result. Perceptions arise with regard to those results, some more appropriate than others. The act of attention selects which ones to focus on, thus feeding back into another round in the cycle of action, with all its inherent instabilities and uncertainties. Underlying the entire cycle is the fact that all its factors are in contact with consciousness. This constellation of factors came to form the central causal connection in one of the Buddha's most basic formulations of dependent co-arising, in which the mutual dependence of "name" (attention, intention, feeling, perception, and contact) and "form" (physical events) on the one hand, and consciousness on the other, accounts for the arising of all stress [§§218, 228].

The interplay of name, form, and consciousness also plays a role in the formulation of the third and fourth noble truths, providing an answer to the quandary of how the stress and suffering inherent in the cycle of action can be ended. If one tried simply to stop the cycle through a direct intention, the intention itself would count as a factor to keep the cycle going. This double bind can be dissolved, however, if one can watch as the contact between consciousness and the cycle naturally falls away. This possibility requires, not an attempt at inaction, but even greater skillfulness in all the factors of action. Convinced that the only way to true happiness would be to find a way out of the cycle, that there had to be such a way, and that was it, the Bodhisatta developed each of the factors of skillful action to an even higher degree of skill. The most skillful form of attention, he discovered, was to view all of experience in terms of the four noble truths: stress, its origination, its cessation, and the path of practice leading to its cessation. These truths not only formed his most basic teaching [§188], but also played a role in the path of practice leading to the cessation of stress, as the factor of right view. The most skillful form of intention was to engage in the directed thought and evaluation that would lead the mind to the stillness of mental absorption. These factors played a role both as aspects of the path factor of right concentration and as the highest form of the path factor of right resolve [§106]. The most refined forms of feeling and perception were the feelings of pleasure and equanimity and their accompanying levels of perception in the highest states of mental absorption [D.9; §164], later included in the path factor of right concentration as well [§102].

The Wings to Awakening—as alternate expressions of the path to the cessation of stress—are also shaped by the implications of the fact of skillfulness. These implications account directly for the main factors in the Wings—the qualities of equanimity, concentration, and discernment that are needed to develop skillfulness—and indirectly for all the other qualities on which these qualities depend. As expressed in the non-linear pattern of this/that conditionality, these implications also account for the way in which the factors in the Wings must act as supports for one another in a pattern of mutual feedback. And, in the most general terms, the fact that skillfulness leads ultimately to a dimension where skillfulness is transcended, accounts for a paradoxical dynamic common to all seven sets that form the Wings: the meditator must intentionally make use of qualities from which he/she wants to escape, gaining familiarity with them in the course of mastering them to the point where they are naturally stilled. There the transcendent paths and their fruitions take over. This is the sense in which even the path of right practice must eventually be abandoned, but only after it has been brought to the culmination of its development. Many people have misunderstood this point, believing that the Buddha's teachings on non-attachment require that one relinquish one's attachment to the path of practice as quickly as possible. Actually, to make a show of abandoning the path before it is fully developed is to abort the entire practice. As one teacher has put it, a person climbing up to a roof by means of a ladder can let go of the ladder only when safely on the roof. In terms of the famous raft simile [§§113-114], one abandons the raft only after crossing the ocean. If one were to abandon it in mid-ocean, to make a show of going spontaneously with the flow of the ocean's many currents, one could drown.

When the factors of the path *are* mutually brought to a state of consummation, however, there occurs a point of equipoise called "non-fashioning" *(atammayata)* [§179], in which their contact with consciousness—still fully conscious—naturally becomes disengaged. One modern teacher has compared this disengagement to that of a fruit naturally falling, when fully ripened, from the tree. This is how the cycle of action is brought to an end. And, as the Buddha discovered, this is how all experience of stress, suffering, and the entire cosmos conditioned by time and the present can be brought to an end as well, leaving the limitless freedom of "consciousness without feature" [§235], the endpoint of all human striving.

Thus we can say that the Dhamma—in terms of doctrine, practice, and attainment—derives from the fully explored implications of one observation: that it is possible to master a skill. This point is reflected not only in the content of the Buddha's teachings, but also in the way they are expressed. The Buddha used many metaphors, explicit and implicit, citing the skills of craftsmen, artists, and athletes to illustrate his points. The texts abound with explicit similes referring to acrobats, archers, bathmen, butchers, carpenters, farmers, fletchers, herdsmen, musicians, painters, etc., pointing out how their skills correspond either to the way the mind fashions stress and suffering for itself, or to the skills a meditator needs to develop in order to master the path to release. On the implicit level, the passages dealing with meditation are filled with terms derived from music theory. In his younger days as a prince, the Bodhisatta—like other young aristocrats of his time—was undoubtedly a connoisseur of the musical arts, and so was naturally familiar with the theory that lay behind them. Because the terminology of this theory is so pervasive in the teachings he formulated as a Buddha, it will be useful to discuss it here briefly.

Unfortunately, we do not have a full treatise on the theory of musical performance as practiced during the Buddha's time, but there are enough references to music scattered through the texts for us to piece together the outlines of that theory. The first step in performance was to tune one's instrument, "establishing" one's tonic note (literally, "base," *thana)* to make it on-pitch ("even," or *sama),* then to fine-tune or attune ("ferret out" or "penetrate") the remaining notes (again, "bases") of the scale in relation to the tonic. This required a great deal of skill, sensitivity, and some mathematical knowledge, as the well-tempered scale had not yet been developed, and many different ways of calculating the scale were in use, each appropriate to a different emotion. The musician then picked up the theme *(nimitta)* of the composition. The theme functioned in several ways, and thus the word "theme" carried several meanings. On the one hand it was the essential message of the piece, the image or impression that the performer wanted to leave in the listener's mind. On the other hand, it was the governing principle that determined what ornamentation or variations would be suitable to the piece.

These musical terms recur throughout the Buddha's discussion of meditation [§§66, 74, 86, 150, 161, etc.]. For instance, in one context the Buddha says that one should establish one's persistence to the right pitch, attune the remaining faculties to that pitch, and then pick up one's theme. In other contexts, he says that one should become attuned to a particular theme, or that one should develop meditation in tune with a particular object. Impossibilities are said to be "non-base," analogous to tones that cannot function as musical notes. There are enough passages to show that the Buddha used this terminology conscious of its musical connotations, and that he wanted to make the point that the practice of meditation was similar to the art of musical performance. We should thus try to be sensitive to these terms and their implications, for the comparison between music and meditation is a useful one.

In the most general sense, this comparison underlines the fact that the knowledge needed for release from suffering is the same sort as that involved in mastering a skill—a continued focus on the present, a sensitivity to one's context, one's own actions, and their combined consequences, rather than a command of an abstract body of facts. To develop the path is to become more and more sensitive to the present—in particular, more sensitive to one's own sensitivity and its consequences. This is similar to the way in which a musician must learn to listen to his/her own performance, a process that ultimately involves listening to the quality of one's listening itself. The greater one's sensitivity in listening, the more profound one's performances become. In the same way, the greater one's sensitivity to one's own mind in the development of skillful qualities, the more one abandons the causes of suffering and realizes its cessation.

In addition to this general observation, the comparison between music and meditation highlights a number of practical points in the development of meditative skill. First, it underscores the need for flexibility and ingenuity in the practice, tempered by an awareness of the limits of how far that flexibility can go. A skilled musician in the Buddha's time had to master not one but many tuning systems so as to handle a full range of musical themes, while simultaneously knowing which ways of tuning were unworkable. In the same way, a skilled meditator should know of many valid ways of tuning the mind to the theme of its meditation—and should have a command of them all so as to deal with various contingencies as they arise—but at the same time must be aware that some varieties of meditation simply do not lead to Awakening. In this light, the seven sets of the Wings to Awakening can be viewed as the Buddha's complete list of workable systems for tuning the mind. (There is evidence suggesting that seven is the number of musical tuning systems *(gramaraga)* recognized in the Buddha's time.) The implication here is that any path of practice deviating from these systems would be like an instrument tuned to a discordant scale, and would not be in harmony with the way of the contemplative *(samana)* who aims at a life in tune *(sama)* with the Dhamma.

A second point is that the musical analogy makes vivid the need for balance in meditative practice, a lesson that appears repeatedly in the texts [§§66, 86, 97, 161]. Just as a musical instrument should neither be too sharp nor too flat, the mind on the path has to find a balance between excessive energy and excessive stillness. At the same time, it must constantly watch out for the tendency for its energy to slacken in the same way that stringed instruments tend to go flat. The "rightness" of right view and other factors of the path thus carries the connotation not only of being correct, but also of being "just right."

A third point is that this analogy helps clarify passages in the texts that speak of attaining the goal without effort [§62]. Taken out of context, these passages seem to contradict or totally negate the many other passages that focus on the need for effort in the practice. Viewed in context of the music analogy, however, they make perfect sense. Like a musical virtuoso, one develops skill to the point where it becomes effortless, but the perfection of the skill does not negate the fact that it took a great deal of effort to reach that level of mastery.

In fact, the Buddha's path is a meta-skill—the full art or science of skillfulness, in and of itself—in which one focuses on the mind as the source of what is skillful and unskillful, learns to deal skillfully with unskillful states of mind, then to deal more skillfully even with skillful states to the point of focusing not on the skill, but on the skill of acquiring a skill, so that one ultimately sees what lies both in the skillfulness and beyond [§61].

* * *

The passages included in this first section cover three themes: (1) how the distinction between what is skillful and not is fundamental to the practice; (2) how to determine what is skillful and not; and (3) how to become skillful in developing skillful states of mind. Because these issues are so basic, the passages are fairly self-explanatory. A few of their facets, however, are easy to overlook.

First, it is important to note that the definition of skillful states of mind as free of greed, aversion, and delusion, provides a convenient rule of thumb for distinguishing between intentions that are merely good and those that are actually skillful. Sometimes good intentions are colored by ignorance, as when one tries to help another person without knowing the true source of that person's problem. This would qualify as a good but not a skillful intention. As we have noticed, the processes of causality are sensitive and complex. Thus there is no getting by on well-meaning intentions alone. One must monitor one's actions continually to make sure that they are in fact appropriate to the present situation, and that one is not acting out of ignorance. Delusion, even well-meaning delusion, is a source for unskillful acts. For this reason, one needs to be constantly observant of one's actions and their effects [§6] so that one's good intentions can truly become skillful, and one's actions can actually do justice to the specific conditions in the here and now produced by the process of this/that conditionality.

Second, the distinction between skillful and unskillful provides an insightful explanation for the causes for good and evil behavior. This distinction is not limited to the values of any particular society, and it avoids the issue of whether beings are inherently good or bad. When people act in evil ways, it is because they lack skill in the way they think; when they think in skillful ways, they naturally will do good. Because skill is something that can be acquired, the way to goodness is open for all people who want to be good, no matter how badly they have behaved in the past. The Canon tells of people who had committed misdeeds and, upon realizing their mistakes, confessed them to the Buddha. The most striking instance was King Ajatasattu [D.2], who had killed his father in order to secure his position on the throne. In spite of the gross nature of the deed, the Buddha approved of the king's confession, and—instead of playing on any feelings of guilt the king might have had—encouraged him in his determination to mend his ways, adding that it is a cause for progress in the noble way if one realizes one's mistakes as such and resolves not to repeat them. Thus it is always possible to make a fresh start in life, aware of one's past bad kamma and resolving to mend one's ways, unburdened with any feelings that one might be inherently unworthy or bad.

Third, it is important to note the two basic factors, internal and external, that enable one to tell what is skillful and unskillful. The main internal factor is "appropriate attention," [§53] which is well illustrated in §1. One learns to view one's thoughts objectively, without partiality, in terms of their actual consequences. As this factor develops from a sense of conviction in the principle of kamma [§§9-17], it turns into the ability to view all of experience in terms of the four noble truths [§51]. The main external factor is friendship with admirable people [§54], defined as those who live by the principle of kamma. From their teachings, one can learn the advisability of trying to develop skillfulness in the first place; in their behavior, one can see skillfulness in action. These internal and external factors reinforce one another, in that skillful attitudes lead one to seek out admirable people to begin with, and admirable people lead one by word and example to see the less obvious advantages of skillful attitudes. Fortunately, every human being alive has some skillful qualities in his or her mind, as well as access to people who are admirable on at least some level. Thus no one consciously starting on the Buddhist path is starting from scratch. Rather, each person is advised to make the most of opportunities that have already been present and to search for further opportunities to develop the mind in a skillful direction.

The two prerequisites for skillfulness are amplified in §2. The discourse from which this passage comes—the Discourse to the Kalamas—is often referred to as the Buddha's charter of free inquiry, because of the emphasis it lays on seeing the truth for oneself, without reliance on outside authority. This interpretation, however, misses one of the important clauses in the discourse, where the Buddha says that one must take note of what wise people censure and praise. In other words, one must check one's own perceptions against those of people of upright character and solid experience, for until one gains Awakening, one's perceptions are bound to be partial and biased. This is why the Buddha says [§115] that friendship with admirable people—which begins with the ability to recognize admirable people—is the whole of the life of practice.

The interaction between appropriate attention and friendship with admirable people in mastering skillful mental qualities is well-illustrated in §6. This passage, in which the Buddha shortly after his Awakening is instructing his seven-year-old son (who was born just before Prince Siddhattha left home), shows very explicitly how one develops appropriate attention by reflecting on the consequences of one's actions before, while, and after acting. If one realizes, after acting, that what looked like a proper action before and while acting actually turned out to have unfavorable consequences, one should confess the mistake to one's experienced friends on the path. This allows one to benefit from their counsel and also to make public one's resolve not to make the same mistake again. In this way, although one is responsible for treading the path oneself, one can benefit from the wisdom and encouragement of those already familiar with the way.

§ 1. Before my self-awakening, when I was still just an unawakened Bodhisatta, the thought occurred to me: 'Why don't I keep dividing my thinking into two classes?' So I made thinking imbued with sensuality, thinking imbued with ill will, & thinking imbued with harmfulness one class, and thinking imbued with renunciation, thinking imbued with non-ill will, & thinking imbued with harmlessness another class.

And as I remained thus heedful, ardent, & resolute, thinking imbued with sensuality arose. I discerned that 'Thinking imbued with sensuality has arisen in me; and that leads to my own affliction or to the affliction of others or to the affliction of both. It obstructs discernment, promotes vexation, & does not lead to Unbinding.'

As I noticed that it leads to my own affliction, it subsided. As I noticed that it leads to the affliction of others...to the affliction of both...it obstructs discernment, promotes vexation, & does not lead to Unbinding, it subsided. Whenever thinking imbued with sensuality had arisen, I simply abandoned it, destroyed it, dispelled it, wiped it out of existence. (Similarly with thinking imbued with ill will & harmfulness.)

Whatever a monk keeps pursuing with his thinking & pondering, that becomes the inclination of his awareness. If a monk keeps pursuing thinking imbued with sensuality, abandoning thinking imbued with renunciation, his mind is bent by that thinking imbued with sensuality. (Similarly with thinking imbued with ill will & harmfulness.)

Just as in the last month of the Rains, in the autumn season when the crops are ripening, a cowherd would look after his cows: He would tap & poke & check & curb them with a stick on this side & that. Why is that? Because he foresees flogging or imprisonment or a fine or public censure arising from that [if he let his cows wander into the crops]. In the same way I foresaw in unskillful qualities drawbacks, degradation, & defilement, and I foresaw in skillful qualities rewards related to renunciation & promoting cleansing.

And as I remained thus heedful, ardent, & resolute, thinking imbued with renunciation arose. I discerned that 'Thinking imbued with renunciation has arisen in me; and that leads neither to my own affliction, nor to the affliction of others, nor to the affliction of both. It fosters discernment, promotes lack of vexation, & leads to Unbinding. If I were to think & ponder in line with that even for a night...even for a day...even for a day & night, I do not envision any danger that would come from it, except that thinking & pondering a long time would tire the body. When the body is tired, the mind is disturbed; and a disturbed mind is far from concentration.' So I steadied my mind right within, settled, unified, & concentrated it. Why is that? So that my mind would not be disturbed. (Similarly with thinking imbued with non-ill will & harmlessness.)

Whatever a monk keeps pursuing with his thinking & pondering, that becomes the inclination of his awareness. If a monk keeps pursuing thinking imbued with renunciation, abandoning thinking imbued with sensuality, his mind is bent by that thinking imbued with renunciation. (Similarly with thinking imbued with non-ill will & harmlessness.)

Just as in the last month of the hot season, when all the crops have been gathered into the village, a cowherd would look after his cows: While resting under the shade of a tree or out in the open, he simply keeps himself mindful of 'those cows.' In the same way, I simply kept myself mindful of 'those mental qualities.'

Unflagging persistence was aroused in me, and unmuddled mindfulness established. My body was calm & unaroused, my mind concentrated & single. Quite withdrawn from sensuality, withdrawn from unskillful mental qualities, I entered & remained in the *first jhāna:* rapture & pleasure born from withdrawal, accompanied by directed thought & evaluation. With the stilling of directed thought & evaluation, I entered & remained in the *second jhāna:* rapture & pleasure born of composure, unification of awareness free from directed thought & evaluation—internal assurance. With the fading of rapture I remained in equanimity, mindful & alert, and physically sensitive of pleasure. I entered & remained in the *third jhāna,* of which the Noble Ones declare, 'Equanimous & mindful, he has a pleasurable abiding.' With the abandoning of pleasure & pain—as with the earlier disappearance of elation & distress—I entered & remained in the *fourth jhāna:* purity of equanimity & mindfulness, neither pleasure nor pain.

When the mind was thus concentrated, purified, bright, unblemished, rid of defilement, pliant, malleable, steady, & attained to imperturbability, I directed it to the *knowledge of recollecting my past lives.* I recollected my manifold past lives, i.e., one birth, two...five, ten...fifty, a hundred, a thousand, a hundred thousand, many aeons of cosmic contraction, many aeons of cosmic expansion, many aeons of cosmic contraction & expansion: 'There I had such a name, belonged to such a clan, had such an appearance. Such was my food, such my experience of pleasure & pain, such the end of my life. Passing away from that state, I re-arose there. There too I had such a name, belonged to such a clan, had such an appearance. Such was my food, such my experience of pleasure & pain, such the end of my life. Passing away from that state, I re-arose here.' Thus I remembered my manifold past lives in their modes & details.

This was the first knowledge I attained in the first watch of the night. Ignorance was destroyed; knowledge arose; darkness was destroyed; light arose—as happens in one who is heedful, ardent, & resolute.

When the mind was thus concentrated, purified, bright, unblemished, rid of defilement, pliant, malleable, steady, & attained to imperturbability, I directed it to the *knowledge of the passing away & reappearance of beings.* I saw—by means of the divine eye, purified & surpassing the human—beings passing away & re-appearing, and I discerned how they are inferior & superior, beautiful & ugly, fortunate & unfortunate in accordance with their kamma: 'These beings—who were endowed with bad conduct of body, speech & mind, who reviled the Noble Ones, held wrong views and undertook actions under the influence of wrong views—with the break-up of the body, after death, have re-appeared in the plane of deprivation, the bad destination, the lower realms, in hell. But these beings—who were endowed with good conduct of body, speech, & mind, who did not revile the Noble Ones, who held right views and undertook actions under the influence of right views—with the break-up of the body, after death, have re-appeared in the good destinations, in the heavenly world.' Thus—by means of the divine eye, purified & surpassing the human—I saw beings passing away & re-appearing, and I discerned how they are inferior & superior, beautiful & ugly, fortunate & unfortunate in accordance with their kamma.

This was the second knowledge I attained in the second watch of the night. Ignorance was destroyed; knowledge arose; darkness was destroyed; light arose—as happens in one who is heedful, ardent, & resolute.

When the mind was thus concentrated, purified, bright, unblemished, rid of defilement, pliant, malleable, steady, & attained to imperturbability, I directed it to the *knowledge of the ending of the effluents.* I discerned, as it was actually present, that 'This is stress... This is the origination of stress...This is the cessation of stress...This is the way leading to the cessation of stress...These are effluents... This is the origination of effluents...This is the cessation of effluents... This is the way leading to the cessation of effluents.' My heart, thus knowing, thus seeing, was released from the effluent of sensuality, released from the effluent of becoming, released from the effluent of ignorance. With release, there was the knowledge, 'Released.' I discerned that 'Birth is ended, the holy life fulfilled, the task done. There is nothing further for this world.'

This was the third knowledge I attained in the third watch of the night. Ignorance was destroyed; knowledge arose; darkness was destroyed; light arose—as happens in one who is heedful, ardent, & resolute.

M.19

§ 2. As they were sitting to one side, the Kalamas of Kesaputta said to the Blessed One, 'Venerable sir, there are some priests & contemplatives who come to Kesaputta. They expound & glorify their own doctrines, but as for the doctrines of others, they deprecate them, revile them, show contempt for them, & disparage them. And then other priests & contemplatives come to Kesaputta. They expound & glorify their own doctrines, but as for the doctrines of others, they deprecate them, revile them, show contempt for them, & disparage them. They leave us simply uncertain & doubtful: Which of these venerable priests & contemplatives are speaking the truth, and which ones are lying?'

'Of course you are uncertain, Kalamas. Of course you are doubtful. When there are reasons for doubt, uncertainty is born. So in this case, Kalamas, don't go by reports, by legends, by traditions, by scripture, by conjecture, by inference, by analogies, by agreement with your views, by probability, or by the thought, "This contemplative is our teacher." When you know *for yourselves* that, "These qualities are unskillful; these qualities are blameworthy; these qualities are criticized by the wise; these qualities, when undertaken & carried out, lead to harm & to suffering"—then you should abandon them...

'What do you think, Kalamas? When greed arises in a person, does it arise for welfare or for harm?'

'For harm, lord.'

'And this greedy person, overcome by greed, his mind possessed by greed: Doesn't he kill living beings, take what is not given, go after another person's wife, tell lies, and induce others to do likewise, all of which is for long-term harm & suffering?'

'Yes, lord.'

(Similarly for aversion & delusion.)

So what do you think, Kalamas: Are these qualities skillful or unskillful?'

'Unskillful, lord.'

'Blameworthy or blameless?'

'Blameworthy, lord.'

'Criticized by the wise or praised by the wise?'

'Criticized by the wise, lord.'

'When undertaken & carried out, do they lead to harm & to suffering, or not?'

'When undertaken & carried out, they lead to harm & to suffering...'

'...Now, Kalamas, don't go by reports, by legends, by traditions, by scripture, by conjecture, by inference, by analogies, by agreement with your views, by probability, or by the thought, "This contemplative is our teacher." When you know for yourselves that, "These qualities are skillful; these qualities are blameless; these qualities are praised by the wise; these qualities, when undertaken & carried out, lead to welfare & to happiness"—then you should enter & remain in them.

'What do you think, Kalamas? When lack of greed arises in a person, does it arise for welfare or for harm?'

'For welfare, lord.'

'And this ungreedy person, not overcome by greed, his mind not possessed by greed: He doesn't kill living beings, take what is not given, go after another person's wife, tell lies, or induce others to do likewise, all of which is for long-term welfare & happiness—right?'

'Yes, lord.'

(Similarly for lack of aversion & lack of delusion.)

So what do you think, Kalamas: Are these qualities skillful or unskillful?'

'Skillful, lord.'

'Blameworthy or blameless?'

'Blameless, lord.'

'Criticized by the wise or praised by the wise?'

'Praised by the wise, lord.'

'When undertaken & carried out, do they lead to welfare & to happiness, or not?'

'When undertaken & carried out, they lead to welfare & to happiness...'

A.III.65

§ 3. Now what is unskillful? Taking life is unskillful, taking what is not given...sexual misconduct...lying...abusive speech...divisive tale-bearing...idle chatter is unskillful. Covetousness...ill will...wrong views are unskillful. These things are termed unskillful.

And what are the roots of unskillful things? Greed is a root of unskillful things, aversion is a root of unskillful things, delusion is a root of unskillful things. These are termed the roots of unskillful things.

And what is skillful? Abstaining from taking life is skillful, abstaining from taking what is not given...from sexual misconduct...from lying...from abusive speech...from divisive tale-bearing...abstaining from idle chatter is skillful. Lack of covetousness...lack of ill will... right views are skillful. These things are termed skillful.

And what are the roots of skillful things? Lack of greed is a root of skillful things, lack of aversion is a root of skillful things, lack of delusion is a root of skillful things. These are termed the roots of skillful things.

M.9

§ 4. The Tathagata, the Worthy one, the Rightly Self-awakened One has two Dhamma discourses given in sequence. Which two? 'See evil as evil.' This is the first Dhamma discourse. 'Having seen evil as evil, become disenchanted with it, dispassionate toward it, freed from it.' This is the second Dhamma discourse....

...,.See evil
Be dispassionate toward evil.
With a mind dispassionate toward evil
You will make an end of stress.

Iti.39

§ 5. Abandon what is unskillful, monks. It is possible to abandon what is unskillful. If it were not possible to abandon what is unskillful, I would not say to you, 'Abandon what is unskillful.' But because it is possible to abandon what is unskillful, I say to you, 'Abandon what is unskillful.' If this abandoning of what is unskillful were conducive to harm and pain, I would not say to you, 'Abandon what is unskillful.' But because this abandoning of what is unskillful is conducive to benefit and pleasure, I say to you, 'Abandon what is unskillful.'

Develop what is skillful, monks. It is possible to develop what is skillful. If it were not possible to develop what is skillful, I would not say to you, 'Develop what is skillful.' But because it is possible to develop what is skillful, I say to you, 'Develop what is skillful.' If this development of what is skillful were conducive to harm and pain, I would not say to you, 'Develop what is skillful.' But because this development of what is skillful is conducive to benefit and pleasure, I say to you, 'Develop what is skillful.'

A.II.19

§ 6. The Buddha: How do you construe this, Rahula: What is a mirror for?

Rahula: For reflection, sir.

The Buddha: In the same way, Rāhula, bodily acts, verbal acts, & mental acts are to be done with repeated reflection.

Whenever you want to perform a bodily act, you should reflect on it: 'This bodily act I want to perform—would it lead to self-affliction, to the affliction of others, or to both? Is it an unskillful bodily act, with painful consequences, painful results?' If, on reflection, you know that it would lead to self-affliction, to the affliction of others, or to both; it would be an unskillful bodily act with painful consequences, painful results, then any bodily act of that sort is absolutely unfit for you to do. But if on reflection you know that it would not cause affliction...it would be a skillful bodily act with happy consequences, happy results, then any bodily act of that sort is fit for you to do.

(Similarly with verbal acts & mental acts.)

While you are performing a bodily act, you should reflect on it: 'This bodily act I am doing—is it leading to self-affliction, to the affliction of others, or to both? Is it an unskillful bodily act, with painful consequences, painful results?' If, on reflection, you know that it is leading to self-affliction, to affliction of others, or both...you should give it up. But if on reflection you know that it is not...you may continue with it.

(Similarly with verbal acts & mental acts.)

Having performed a bodily act, you should reflect on it....If, on reflection, you know that it led to self-affliction, to the affliction of others, or to both; it was an unskillful bodily act with painful consequences, painful results, then you should confess it, reveal it, lay it open to the Teacher or to a knowledgeable companion in the holy life. Having confessed it...you should exercise restraint in the future. But if on reflection you know that it did not lead to affliction...it was a skillful bodily act with happy consequences, happy results, then you should stay mentally refreshed & joyful, training day & night in skillful mental qualities.

(Similarly with verbal acts.)

Having performed a mental act, you should reflect on it....If, on reflection, you know that it led to self-affliction, to the affliction of others, or to both; it was an unskillful mental act with painful consequences, painful results, then you should feel horrified, humiliated, & disgusted with it. Feeling horrified... you should exercise restraint in the future. But if on reflection you know that it did not lead to affliction...it was a skillful mental act with happy consequences, happy results, then you should stay mentally refreshed & joyful, training day & night in skillful mental qualities.

Rahula, all the priests & contemplatives in the course of the past who purified their bodily acts, verbal acts, & mental acts, did it through repeated reflection on their bodily acts, verbal acts, & mental acts in just this way.

All the priests & contemplatives in the course of the future...All the priests & contemplatives at present who purify their bodily acts, verbal acts, & mental acts, do it through repeated reflection on their bodily acts, verbal acts, & mental acts in just this way.

Therefore, Rahula, you should train yourself: 'I will purify my bodily acts through repeated reflection. I will purify my verbal acts through repeated reflection. I will purify my mental acts through repeated reflection.' Thus you should train yourself.

That is what the Blessed One said. Pleased, Ven. Rahula delighted in the Blessed One's words.

M.61

§ 7. The non-doing of any evil,
the performance of what is skillful,
the cleansing of one's own mind:
This is the Buddhas' teaching.

Not reviling, not injuring,
restraint in line with the Paṭimokkha,
moderation in food,
dwelling in seclusion,
devotion to the heightened mind:
This is the Buddhas' teaching.

DHP.183, 185

B. KAMMA & THE ENDING OF KAMMA

The Buddha's doctrine of kamma takes the fact of skillful action, which can be observed on the ordinary sensory level, and gives it an importance that, for a person pursuing the Buddhist goal, must be accepted on faith. According to this doctrine, skillful action is not simply one factor out of many contributing to happiness: it is the primary factor. It does not lead simply to happiness within the dimensions of time and the present: if developed to the ultimate level of refinement, it can lead to an Awakening totally released from those dimensions. These assertions cannot be proven prior to an experience of that Awakening, but they must be accepted as working hypotheses in the effort to develop the skillfulness needed for Awakening. This paradox—which lies at the heart of the act of taking refuge in the Triple Gem—explains why the serious pursuit of the Buddhist path is a sustained act of faith that can become truly firm only with the first glimpse of Awakening, called stream-entry. It also explains why a strong desire to gain release from the stress and suffering inherent in conditioned existence is needed for such a pursuit, for without that desire it is very difficult to break through this paradox with the necessary leap of faith.

The basic context for the doctrine of kamma was provided by the first two insights on the night of the Buddha's Awakening—remembrance of previous lives, and insight into the death and rebirth of beings throughout the cosmos [§1]. This context was expressed in terms of personal narrative (the story of the Bodhisatta's own journey from life to life) and cosmology (general principles underlying the workings of the cosmos as a whole). The possibility of rebirth accounted for the way in which kamma could shape experiences in life, such as the situation into which a young child is born, for which no kammic cause in the present lifetime could be found. The pattern of death and rebirth for all beings, in which the quality of the state of rebirth depends on the moral quality of actions performed in previous lifetimes, presented the possibility that moral standards, instead of being mere social conventions, were intrinsic to the workings of any and all experience of the cosmos.

Essential to the Buddha's second insight was his realization of the mind's role in determining the moral quality of actions. His analysis of the process of developing a skill showed him that skillfulness depended not so much on the physical performance of an act as on the mental qualities of perception, attention, and intention that played a part in it. Of these three qualities, the intention formed the essence of the act [§10]—as it constituted the decision to act—while attention and perception informed it. Thus the skillfulness of these mental phenomena accounted for the act's kammic consequences. The less greed, aversion, and delusion motivating the act, the better its results. Unintentional acts would have kammic consequences only when they resulted from carelessness in areas where one would reasonably be held responsible. Intentional actions performed under the influence of right view—which on this level means conviction in the principle of kamma [II/E; III/A; §106]—led inherently to pleasant states of rebirth, while those performed under the influence of wrong view led to unpleasant states. Thus the quality of the views on which one acts—i.e., the quality of the perception and attention informing the intention—is a major factor in shaping experience. This observation undercuts the radical distinction between mind and material reality that is taken for granted in our own culture and that was also assumed by many of the Samana schools of the Buddha's time. From the Buddha's viewpoint, mental and physical phenomena are two sides of a single coin, with the mental side of prior importance [§8].

Most descriptions of the Buddha's teachings on kamma tend to stop here, but there are many passages on kamma in the Canon—and included in this section—that do not fit into the neat picture based merely the first two insights on the night of the Awakening. The only way to account for these passages is to note the simple fact that Buddha's teachings on kamma were shaped not only by these two insights, but also by the third insight and the resulting knowledge of Unbinding. The third insight explored the possibility of a fourth kind of kamma—in addition to good, bad, and a mixture of the two—that was skillful enough to bring about the ending of kamma [§§16-17]. At the same time, in the course of developing the level of skillfulness needed to bring kamma to an end, the Buddha learned a great deal about the nature of action that forced him to recast his understanding of kamma in much more subtle terms. The knowledge of Unbinding—which followed on the full development of this fourth type of kamma and the realizations that accompanied it—acted as the proof that the understandings comprising the three insights were true. To explore these points will not only help give us a more complete understanding of the Buddha's teachings on kamma, but will also show why conviction in the principle of skillful kamma is essential to Buddhist practice.

In his effort to master kamma in such a way as to bring kamma to an end, the Buddha discovered that he had to abandon the contexts of personal narrative and cosmology in which the issue of kamma first presented itself. Both these forms of understanding deal in categories of being and non-being, self and others, but the Buddha found that it was impossible to bring kamma to an end if one thought in such terms. For example, narrative and cosmological modes of thinking would lead one to ask whether the agent who performed an act of kamma was the same as the person experiencing the result, someone else, both, or neither. If one answered that it was the same person, then the person experiencing the result would have to identify not only with the actor, but also with the mode of action, and thus would not be able to gain release from it. If one answered that it was another person, both oneself and another, or neither, then the person experiencing the result would see no need to heighten the skill or understanding of his/her own kamma in the present, for the experience of pleasure and pain was not his or her own full responsibility. In either case, the development of the fourth type of kamma would be aborted [§§228-229].

To avoid the drawbacks of the narrative and cosmological mind-sets, the Buddha pursued an entirely different tack—what he called "entry into emptiness," and what modern philosophy calls radical phenomenology: a focus on the events of present consciousness, in and of themselves, without reference to questions of whether there are any entities underlying those events. In the Buddha's case, he focused simply on the process of kammic cause and result as it played itself out in the immediate present, in the process of developing the skillfulness of the mind, without reference to who or what lay behind those processes. On the most basic level of this mode of awareness, there was no sense even of "existence" or "non-existence" [§186], but simply the events of stress, its origination, its cessation, and the path to its cessation, arising and passing away. It was in this mode that he was able to pursue the fourth type of kamma to its end, at the same time gaining heightened insight into the nature of action itself and its many implications, including questions of rebirth, the relationship of mental to physical events, and the way kamma constructs all experience of the cosmos.

Because the Buddha gained both understanding of and release from kamma by pursuing the phenomenological mode of attention, his full-dress systematic analysis of kamma is also expressed in that mode. This analysis is included in his teachings on this/that conditionality, dependent co-arising, and the four noble truths: the three levels of refinement in the type of right view without effluents that underlay his mastery of the fourth type of kamma. Here we will consider, in turn, how each of these teachings shaped the Buddha's teachings on kamma, how the knowledge of Unbinding confirmed those teachings, and how the success of the phenomenological mode of analysis shaped the Buddha's use of narrative and cosmological modes in instructing others. We will conclude with a discussion of how these points show the need for conviction in the principle of kamma as a working hypothesis for anyone who wants to gain release from suffering and stress.

To begin with **this/that conditionality:** This principle accounts not only for the complexity of the kammic process, but also for its being regular without at the same time being rigidly deterministic. The non-linearity of this/that conditionality also accounts for the fact that the process can be successfully dismantled by radical attention to the present moment.

Unlike the theory of linear causality—which led the Vedists and Jains to see the relationship between an act and its result as predictable and tit-for-tat—the principle of this/that conditionality gives an inherent complexity to that relationship. The results of kamma experienced at any one point in time come not only from past kamma, but also from present kamma. This means that, although there are general patterns relating habitual acts to corresponding results [§9], there is no set one-for-one, tit-for-tat, relationship between a particular action and its results. Instead, the results are determined by the context of the act, both in terms of actions that preceded or followed it [§11] and in terms one's state of mind at the time of acting or experiencing the result [§13]. As we noted in the Introduction, the feedback loops inherent in this/that conditionality mean that the working out of any particular cause-effect relationship can be very complex indeed. This explains why the Buddha says in §12 that the results of kamma are imponderable. Only a person who has developed the mental range of a Buddha—another imponderable itself—would be able to trace the intricacies of the kammic network. The basic premise of kamma is simple—that skillful intentions lead to favorable results, and unskillful ones to unfavorable results—but the process by which those results work themselves out is so intricate that it cannot be fully mapped. We can compare this with the Mandelbrot set, a mathematical set generated by a simple equation, but whose graph is so complex that it will probably never be completely explored.

Although the precise working out of the kammic process is somewhat unpredictable, it is not chaotic. The relationship between kammic causes and their effects is entirely regular: when an action is of the sort that it will be felt in such and such a way, that is how its result will be experienced [§13]. Skillful intentions lead to favorable results, unskillful ones to unfavorable results. Thus, when one participates in the kammic process, one is at the mercy of a pattern that one's actions put into motion, but that is not entirely under one's present control. Despite the power of the mind, one cannot reshape the basic laws of cosmic causality at whim. These laws include the physical laws, within which one's kamma must ripen and work itself out. This is the point of passage §14, in which the Buddha explains that present pain can be explained not only by past kamma but also by a host of other factors; the list of alternative factors he gives comes straight from the various causes for pain that were recognized in the medical treatises of his time. If we compare this list with his definition of old kamma in §15, we see that many if not all of the alternative causes are actually the result of past actions. The point here is that old kamma does not override other causal factors operating in the universe—such as those recognized by the physical sciences—but instead finds its expression within them.

However, the fact that the kammic process relies on input from the present moment means that it is not totally deterministic. Input from the past may place restrictions on what can be done and known in any particular moment, but the allowance for new input from the present provides some room for free will. This allowance also opens the possibility for escape from the cycle of kamma altogether by means of the fourth type of kamma: the development of heightened skillfulness through the pursuit of the seven factors of Awakening and the noble eightfold path—and, by extension, all of the Wings to Awakening [§16-17].

The non-linearity of this/that conditionality explains why heightened skillfulness, when focused on the present moment, can succeed in leading to the end of the kamma that has formed the experience of the entire cosmos. All non-linear processes exhibit what is called scale invariance, which means that the behavior of the process on any one scale is similar to its behavior on smaller or larger scales. To understand, say, the large-scale pattern of a particular non-linear process, one need only focus on its behavior on a smaller scale that is easier to observe, and one will see the same pattern at work. In the case of kamma, one need only focus on the process of kamma in the immediate present, in the course of developing heightened skillfulness, and the large-scale issues over the expanses of space and time will become clear as one gains release from them.

The teaching on **dependent co-arising** helps to provide more detailed instructions on this point, showing precisely where the cycle of kamma provides openings for more skillful present input. In doing so, it both explains the importance of the act of attention in developing the fourth type of kamma, and acts as a guide for focusing attention on present experience in appropriate ways [III/H/iii].

Dependent co-arising shows how the cosmos, when viewed in the context of how it is directly experienced by a person developing skillfulness, is subsumed entirely under factors that are immediately present to awareness: the five aggregates of form, feeling, perception, mental fabrication, and consciousness, and the six sense media [§§212-213]. Included in this description is the Buddha's ultimate analysis of kamma and rebirth. The nexus of kamma, clinging, becoming, and birth accounts for the realm in which birth takes place [§220], whereas the nexus of name-and-form with consciousness accounts for the arising and survival of the kammically active organism within that realm [§231]. Also included in dependent co-arising is a detailed analysis of the way in which kamma can—but does not necessarily have to—lead to bondage to the cycle of rebirth. Unlike the Jains, the Buddha taught that this bondage was mental rather than physical. It was caused not by sticky substances created by the physical violence of an act, but by the fact that, when there is ignorance of the four noble truths [III/H/i] (a subtle form of delusion, the most basic root of unskillfulness), the feeling that results from kamma gives rise to craving (a subtle form of greed and aversion), clinging, and becoming; and these, in turn, form the conditions for further kamma. Thus the results of action, in the presence of ignorance, breed the conditions for more action, creating feedback loops that keep the kammic processes in motion. For this reason, the Buddha defined the effluents as clinging—expressed in some lists as sensuality, in others as sensuality and views—together with becoming and the ignorance that underlies them all. If ignorance of the four truths can be ended, however, feeling does not form a condition for craving or clinging, and thus there is no becoming to provide a realm for further kamma. Thus the mastery of the fourth type of kamma requires discernment of the four noble truths.

It is important to note that dependent co-arising makes no statements as to the existence or lack of existence of any entity to which these events pertain or to whom they belong [§230]. As we noted above, such terms of analysis as "being," "non-being," "self," or "other," pertain properly to the modes of cosmology and personal narrative, and have no place in a radically phenomenological analysis. Questions and terms that derive from the conventions of narrative and the construction of a world view have no place in the direct awareness of experience in and of itself. This is one reason why people who have not mastered the path of practice, and who thus function primarily in terms of a world view or a sense of their own personal story, find the teaching of dependent co-arising so inscrutable. Even though the Buddha's phenomenological approach answered his questions as to the nature of kamma, it also reshaped his questions so that they had little in common with the questions that most people bring to the practice. As with all insights gained on the phenomenological level, dependent co-arising is expressed in terms closest to the actual experience of events. Only when a person has become thoroughly familiar with that level of experience is the analysis fully intelligible. Thus, although the detailed nature of dependent co-arising is one of its strengths, it is also one of its weaknesses as a teaching tool, for the subtlety and complexity of the analysis can be intimidating even to advanced practitioners.

For this reason, the Buddha most often expressed the right view underlying the fourth type of kamma in terms of **the four noble truths.** These truths provide a more congenial entry point into the phenomenological mode of awareness for they focus the analysis of kamma directly on the question of stress and suffering: issues that tie in immediately with the narratives that people make of their own life experiences. As the Buddha noted in his second insight, his memory of previous lives included his experience of pleasure and pain in each life, and most people—when recounting their own lives—tend to focus on these issues as well. The four truths, however, do not stop simply with tales about stress: they approach it from the problem-solving perspective of a person engaged in developing a skill. What this means for the meditator trying to master the fourth type of kamma is that these truths cannot be fully comprehended by passive observation. Only by participating sensitively in the process of developing skillfulness and gaining a practical feel for the relationship of cause and effect among the mental factors that shape that process, can one eradicate the effluents that obstruct the ending of kamma [II/B; III/E; III/H]. This point is underscored by a fact noted above: the ignorance and craving that are needed to keep the cycle of kamma in motion are subtle forms of the roots of unskillfulness. Thus, only through developing skillfulness to the ultimate degree can the cycle be brought to equilibrium and, as a result, disband.

The truth of the Buddha's understanding of the processes of kamma—as informed by this/that conditionality, dependent co-arising, and the four noble truths—was proven by **the knowledge of Unbinding** that followed immediately on his mastery of the fourth type of kamma. He found that when skillfulness is intentionally brought to a point of full consummation, as expressed in the direct awareness of this/that conditionality, it leads to a state of non-action, or non-fashioning, that forms the threshold to a level of consciousness in which all experience of the cosmos has fallen away. When one's experience of the cosmos resumes after the experience of Awakening, one sees clearly that it is composed entirely of the results of old kamma; with no new kamma being added to the process, all experience of the cosmos will eventually run out—or, in the words of the texts [§225], "will grow cold right here." This discovery proved the basic premise that kamma not only plays a role in shaping experience of the cosmos, it plays the primary role. If this were not so, then even when kamma was ended there would still remain the types of experience that came from other sources. But because no experience of the cosmos remained when all present kamma disbanded, and none would resume after all old kamma ran out, kamma would have to be the necessary factor accounting for all such experience. This fact implies that even the limiting factors that one encounters in terms of sights, sounds, etc., are actually the fruit of past kamma in thought, word, and deed—committed not only in this, but also in many preceding lifetimes. Thus, even though the Buddha's development of the fourth type of kamma focused on the present moment, the resulting Awakening gave insights that encompassed not only the present but also all of time.

Having used the phenomenological mode to solve the problem of kamma and reach Unbinding, however, the Buddha was not limited to that mode. After his Awakening, he was free to return at will to the narrative and cosmological modes of thought and speech, without being caught up in their presuppositions [D.9]. For most people, he found, even the four noble truths were too alien to form an entry point into the teaching. Thus he had to use the narrative and cosmological modes of discourse to bring such people, step by step, to the point where they were ready to comprehend those truths. What he had learned in the final stage of his Awakening did not negate the validity of the first and second insights into kamma and rebirth; instead, it perfected them. The main change that the experience of Awakening made in his view of personal narrative and cosmology is that it opened them both to the dimension of release. The drama of kamma in the cosmos is not a closed cycle; the principles of kamma can be mastered to the point where they open to the way out. The narrative of a person's course through the cosmos is not doomed to aimless and endlessly repeated death and rebirth; the person can tread the path of practice to Unbinding and so bring the narrative to an end. Thus the Buddha used narrative and cosmological explanations to persuade his listeners to explore the phenomenology of skillful action so that they too might gain release; his descriptions of the role of action in shaping the vast expanses of space, time, and existence was designed to focus the listener's attention on the liberating potential of what he/she was doing in the here and now. Some of his most poignant teachings are narratives devoted to just this purpose:

> How do you construe this, monks: Which is greater, the tears you have shed while transmigrating & wandering this long time—crying & weeping from being joined with what is displeasing, from being separated from what is pleasing—or the water in the four great oceans?...This is the greater: The tears you have shed....Why is that? From an inconceivable beginning, monks, comes transmigration. A beginning point is not evident, although beings hindered by ignorance and fettered by craving are transmigrating & wandering on. Long have you thus experienced stress, experienced pain, experienced loss, swelling the cemeteries—long enough to become disenchanted with all fabrications, enough to become dispassionate, enough to be released.
>
> S.XV.3

The cosmological discourses—such as D.26, D.27, M.129, and M.130—are aimed at a similar point. D.26 describes how the evolution and devolution of the cosmos derives from the skillful and unskillful kamma of the beings who inhabit it, and ends with the admonition that one should make an island for oneself, safe from the process of the ups and downs of the cosmos. This island is nothing other than the practice of the four frames of reference, which, as we will see in II/B, are precisely the training aimed at familiarizing oneself with the phenomenology of skillful action. D.27 shows how kamma accounts for the evolution of human society, and ends with the statement that the most exalted member of society is the Arahant who has gained release through highest discernment. M.129 and M.130 give graphic descriptions of the levels of heaven and hell into which beings may be reborn after death through the power of good and bad kamma, M.130 ending with a verse on the need to practice the path to non-clinging to escape the dangers of birth and death entirely.

Thus the experience of his Awakening gave a new purpose to narrative and cosmology in the Buddha's eyes: they became tools for persuading his listeners to adopt the training that would lead them to the phenomenological mode. This accounts for the ad hoc and fragmentary nature of the narratives and cosmological sketches in his teachings. They are not meant to be analyzed in a systematic way. It is a mistake to tease out their implications to see what they may say about such metaphysical questions as the existence or lack of existence of entities or identities underlying the process of kamma and rebirth, the relationship between the laws of kamma and the laws of the physical sciences, or the nature of the mechanism by which kamma makes its results felt over time [see the discussion of appropriate questions in II/G]. The search for systematic answers to such issues is not only invalid or irrelevant from the Buddhist point of view, it is actually counterproductive in that it blocks one from entering the path to release. And, we should note, none of the modes of discourse—narrative, cosmological, or phenomenological—is capable of describing or even framing proper questions about what happens after Awakening, for such issues, which lie beyond the conditions of time and the present, cannot be properly expressed by the conventions of language and analysis, which are bound by those conditions. Only a person who has mastered the skill of release has the mental skills needed to comprehend such matters [A.IV.173, MFU pp. 31-32]. The Buddha reserved his systematic explanations for the particular phenomenological mode to be used in viewing the process of kamma in its own terms, as it is being mastered, so that the actual problem of kamma and its retribution (as opposed to the theoretical questions about them) will be solved. The right way to listen to the narratives and cosmological sketches, then, is to see what they imply about one's own need to master the kammic process on the level of awareness in and of itself.

From these points it should become clear why kamma, as an article of faith, is a necessary factor in the path of Buddhist practice. The teaching on kamma, in its narrative and cosmological forms, provides the context for the practice, giving it direction and urgency. Because the cosmos is governed by the laws of kamma, those laws provide the only mechanism by which happiness can be found. But because good and bad kamma, consisting of good and bad intentions, simply perpetuate the ups and downs of experience in the cosmos, a way must be found out of the mechanism of kamma by mastering it in a way that allows it to disband in an attentive state of non-intention. And, because there is no telling what sudden surprises the results of one's past kamma may still hold in store, one should try to develop that mastery as quickly as possible.

In its phenomenological mode, the teaching on kamma accounts for the focus and the terms of analysis used in the practice. It also accounts for the mental qualities needed to attain and maintain that level of focus and analysis. In terms of focus, the principle of scale invariance at work in the complexities of kamma means that their essential processes can be mastered by focusing total attention on them right at the mind in the immediate present. This focus accounts for the practice of frames-of-reference meditation [II/B], in which attention is directed at present phenomena in and of themselves. These phenomena are then analyzed in terms of the four noble truths, the phenomenological terms in which appropriate attention and discernment direct and observe the experience of developing the qualities of skillful action. The most immediate skillful kamma that can be observed on this level is the mastery of the very same mental qualities that are supporting this refined level of focus and analysis: mindfulness, concentration, and discernment, together with the more basic qualities on which they are based. Thus, these mental qualities act not only as supports to the focus and analysis, but also as their object. Ultimately, discernment becomes so refined that the focus and analysis take as their object the act of focusing and analyzing, in and of themselves. The cycle of action then short-circuits as it reaches culmination, and Unbinding occurs. These elements of focus, analysis, and mental qualities, together with the dynamic of their development to a point of culmination, are covered by the teachings on the Wings to Awakening, which will be discussed in detail in Parts II and III. Thus the Wings can be viewed as a direct expression of the role of skillful kamma in the path to release.

It is entirely possible that a person with no firm conviction in the principle of kamma can follow parts of the Buddhist path, including mindfulness and concentration practices, and gain positive results from them. For instance, one can pursue mindfulness practice for the sense of balance, equanimity, and peace it gives to one's daily life, or for the sake of bringing the mind to the present for the purpose of spontaneity and "going with the flow." The full practice of the path, however, is a skillful diverting of the flow of the mind from its habitual kammic streams to the stream of Unbinding. As the Buddha said, this practice requires a willingness to "develop and abandon" to an extreme degree [A.IV.28]. The *developing* requires a supreme effort aimed at full and conscious mastery of mindfulness, concentration, and discernment to the point of non-fashioning and on to release. A lack of conviction in the principle of kamma would undercut the patience and commitment, the desire, persistence, intent, and refined powers of discrimination [II/D] needed to pursue concentration and discernment to the most heightened levels, beyond what is needed for a general sense of peace or spontaneity. The *abandoning* involves uprooting the most deeply buried forms of clinging and attachment that keep one bound to the cycle of rebirth. Some of these forms of clinging—such as views and theories about self-identity—are so entrenched in the narrative and cosmological modes in which most people function that only firm conviction in the benefits to be had by abandoning them will be able to pry them loose. This is why the Buddha insisted repeatedly—and we will have occasion to return to this theme at several points in this book [II/E; III/A]—that conviction in the fact of his Awakening necessarily involves conviction in the principle of kamma, and that both forms of conviction are needed for the full mastery of the kamma of heightened skillfulness leading to release.

There are many well-known passages in the Canon where the Buddha asks his listeners not to accept his teachings simply on faith, but these remarks were directed to people just beginning the practice. Such people need only accept the general principles of skillful action on a trial basis, focusing on the input that their actions are putting into the causal system at the present moment, and exploring the connection between skillful intentions and favorable results. The more complex issues of kamma come into play at this level only in forcing one to be patient with the practice. Many times skillful intentions do not produce their favorable results immediately, aside from the sense of well-being—sometimes clearly perceptible, sometimes barely—that comes with acting skillfully. Were it not for this delay, the principle of kamma would be self-evident, no one would dare act on unskillful intentions, and there would be no need to take the principle on faith. As we noted in the Introduction, the complexity of this/that conditionality is the major cause of the confusion and lack of skill with which most people live their lives. The ability to master this process takes time.

As one progresses further on the path, however—and as the process of developing skillfulness in and of itself comes more and more to take center stage in one's awareness—the actual results of one's developing skillfulness should give greater and greater reason for conviction in the principle of kamma. Except in cases where people fall into the trap of heedlessness or complacency, these results can spur and inspire one to hold to the principle of kamma with the increasing levels of firmness, focus, and refinement needed for Awakening.

§ 8. Phenomena are preceded by the heart,
ruled by the heart,
fashioned of the heart.

If one speaks or acts with a corrupted heart,

suffering follows one,
as the wheel of the chariot
follows
the foot of the animal drawing it.

Phenomena are preceded by the heart,
ruled by the heart,
fashioned of the heart.

If one speaks or acts with a bright heart,
happiness follows one,
like a shadow
that never leaves.

DHP.1-2

§ 9. Beings are the owners of their kamma, heir to their kamma, born of their kamma, related through their kamma, and have their kamma as their refuge. Kamma is what creates distinctions among beings in terms of coarseness & refinement....

There is the case where a certain woman or man is one who takes life—brutal, bloody-handed, violent, cruel, merciless to living beings. From performing & undertaking such kamma, then on the break-up of the body, after death, this person re-appears in the plane of deprivation, the bad destination, the lower realms, in hell. Or, if he/she does not reappear in the plane of deprivation...in hell, but instead returns to the human state, then wherever he/she is reborn, he/she is short-lived. This is the way leading to short life, namely being one who takes life....

But there is the case where a certain woman or man, abandoning the taking of life, abstains from the taking of life, dwelling with rod laid down, knife laid down, scrupulous, merciful, compassionate for the welfare of all living beings. From performing & undertaking such kamma, then on the break-up of the body, after death, this person re-appears in the good destinations, in the heavenly world. Or, if he/she does not reappear...in the heavenly world, but instead returns to the human state, then wherever he/she is reborn, he/she is long-lived. This is the way leading to long life, namely being one who, abandoning the taking of life, abstains from the taking of life....

Furthermore, there is the case where a certain woman or man has a tendency to injure living beings with the hand, with a clod, with a stick, or with a knife....On the break-up of the body, after death, this person re-appears in the plane of deprivation....in hell. Or, if he/she...instead returns to the human state, then wherever he/she is reborn, he/she is sickly. This is the way leading to being sickly, namely being one who has a tendency to injure living beings....

But there is the case where a certain woman or man does not have a tendency to injure living beings....This is the way leading to being healthy....

Furthermore, there is the case where a certain woman or man has an angry & irritable nature. Even when lightly criticized, he/she gets offended, provoked, hostile, & resentful, and displays annoyance, aversion, & bitterness....This is the way leading to being ugly....

But there is the case where a certain woman or man does not have an angry & irritable nature. Even when heavily criticized, he/she does not get offended, provoked, hostile, or resentful, and displays no annoyance, aversion, or bitterness....This is the way leading to being beautiful....

Furthermore, there is the case where a certain woman or man has an envious nature—envying, resenting, & begrudging the fortune, honor, respect, reverence, salutations, & veneration received by others....This is the way leading to having little authority....

But there is the case where a certain woman or man does not have an envious nature—neither envying, resenting, nor begrudging the fortune, honor, respect, reverence, salutations, & veneration received by others....This is the way leading to having great authority....

Furthermore, there is the case where a certain woman or man does not give food, drink, clothing, vehicles, garlands, scents, ointments, beds, dwellings, or lamps to priests or contemplatives....This is the way leading to being poor....

But there is the case where a certain woman or man gives food, drink, clothing, vehicles, garlands, scents, ointments, beds, dwellings, & lamps to priests & contemplatives....This is the way leading to being wealthy....

Furthermore, there is the case where a certain woman or man is obstinate & arrogant, not paying homage to those who deserve homage, not rising up for those in whose presence one should rise up, not offering a seat to those who deserve a seat, not making way for those for whom one should make way, not honoring, respecting, revering, or venerating those who should be honored...venerated. This is the way leading to being reborn in a low birth....

But there is the case where a certain woman or man is not obstinate or arrogant, who pays homage to those who deserve homage, rises up for those in whose presence one should rise up, offers a seat to those who deserve a seat, makes way for those for whom one should make way, honors, respects, reveres, & venerates those who should be honored...venerated. This is the way leading to being reborn in a high birth....

Furthermore, there is the case where a certain woman or man, having approached a priest or contemplative, does not ask, "What, venerable sir, is skillful? What is unskillful? What is blameworthy? What is blameless? What is to be cultivated? What is not to be cultivated? What kind of action will lead to my long-term harm & suffering? What kind of action will lead to my long-term welfare & happiness?"....This is the way leading to having weak discernment....

But there is the case where a certain woman or man, having approached a priest or contemplative, asks, "What, venerable sir, is skillful? What is unskillful? What is blameworthy? What is blameless? What is to be cultivated? What is not to be cultivated? What kind of action will lead to my long-term harm & suffering? What kind of action will lead to my long-term welfare & happiness?".... This is the way leading to having great discernment....

Beings are the owners of their kamma, heir to their kamma, born of their kamma, related through their kamma, and have their kamma as their refuge. Kamma is what creates distinctions among beings in terms of coarseness & refinement.

M.135

§ 10. 'Kamma should be known. The cause by which kamma comes into play should be known. The diversity in kamma should be known. The result of kamma should be known. The cessation of kamma should be known. The path of practice for the cessation of kamma should be known.' Thus it has been said. Why was it said?

Intention, I tell you, is kamma. Intending, one does kamma by way of body, speech, & intellect.

And what is the cause by which kamma comes into play? Contact....

And what is the diversity in kamma? There is kamma to be experienced in hell, kamma to be experienced in the realm of common animals, kamma to be experienced in the realm of the hungry shades, kamma to be experienced in the human world, kamma to be experienced in the heavenly worlds. [In the Buddhist cosmology, sojourns in hell or in heaven, as in the other realms, are not eternal. After the force of one's kamma leading to rebirth in those levels has worn out, one is reborn elsewhere.]....

And what is the result of kamma? The result of kamma is of three sorts, I tell you: that which arises right here & now, that which arises later [in this lifetime], and that which arises following that....

And what is the cessation of kamma? From the cessation of contact is the cessation of kamma....

And what is the way leading to the cessation of kamma? Just this noble eightfold path: right view, right resolve, right speech, right action, right livelihood, right effort, right mindfulness, right concentration.

Now when a noble disciple discerns kamma in this way, the cause by which kamma comes into play in this way, the diversity of kamma in this way, the result of kamma in this way, the cessation of kamma in this way, & the path of practice leading to the cessation of kamma in this way, then he discerns this penetrative holy life as the cessation of kamma.

'Kamma should be known. The cause by which stress comes into play...The diversity in kamma...The result of kamma...The cessation of kamma...The path of practice for the cessation of kamma should be known.' Thus it has been said, and this is why it was said.

A.VI.63

§ 11. There are four kinds of person to be found in the world. Which four? There is the case where a certain person takes life, takes what is not given (steals), engages in illicit sex, lies, speaks divisively, speaks harshly, engages in idle chatter; is covetous, has a hostile mind, & holds wrong views. On the break-up of the body, after death, he reappears in the plane of deprivation, the bad destination, the lower realms, in hell.

But there is also the case where a certain person takes life...holds wrong views, [yet] on the break-up of the body, after death, he reappears in the good destinations, in the heavenly world.

And there is the case where a certain person abstains from taking life, abstains from taking what is not given...is not covetous, does not have a hostile mind, & holds right views. On the break-up of the body, after death, he reappears in the good destinations, in the heavenly world.

But there is also the case where a certain person abstains from taking life, abstains from taking what is not given...is not covetous, does not have a hostile mind, & holds right views, [yet] on the break-up of the body, after death, he reappears in the plane of deprivation, the bad destination, the lower realms, in hell....

In the case of the person who takes life...[yet] on the break-up of the body, after death, reappears in the good destinations, in the heavenly world: either earlier he performed fine kamma that is to be felt as pleasant, or later he performed fine kamma that is to be felt as pleasant, or at the time of death he acquired & adopted right views. Because of that, on the break-up of the body, after death, he reappears in the good destinations, in the heavenly world. But as for the results of taking life...holding wrong views, he will feel them either right here & now, or later [in this lifetime], or following that....

In the case of the person who abstains from taking life...but on the break-up of the body, after death, reappears in the plane of deprivation, the bad destination, the lower realms, in hell: either earlier he performed evil kamma that is to be felt as painful, or later he performed evil kamma that is to be felt as painful, or at the time of death he acquired & adopted wrong views. Because of that, on the break-up of the body, after death, he reappears in the plane of deprivation, the bad destination, the lower realms, in hell. But as for the results of abstaining from taking life...holding right views, he will feel them either right here & now, or later [in this lifetime], or following that....

M.136

§ 12. These four imponderables are not to be speculated about. Whoever speculates about them would go mad & experience vexation. Which four? The Buddha-range of the Buddhas [i.e., the range of powers a Buddha develops as a result of becoming a Buddha]... The jhana-range of one absorbed in jhāna [i.e., the range of powers that one may obtain while absorbed in jhāna]...The results of kamma... Speculation about [the first moment, purpose, etc., of] the cosmos is an imponderable that is not to be speculated about. Whoever speculates about these things would go mad & experience vexation.

A.IV.77

§ 13. The Buddha: 'For anyone who says, "In whatever way a person makes kamma, that is how it is experienced," there is no living of the holy life, there is no opportunity for the right ending of stress. But for anyone who says, "When a person makes kamma to be felt in such & such a way, that is how its result is experienced," there is the living of the holy life, there is the opportunity for the right ending of stress.

'There is the case where a trifling evil act done by a certain individual takes him to hell. There is the case where the very same sort of trifling deed done by another individual is experienced in the here & now, and for the most part barely appears for a moment.

'Now, a trifling evil act done by what sort of individual takes him to hell? There is the case where a certain individual is undeveloped in [contemplating] the body, undeveloped in virtue, undeveloped in mind, undeveloped in discernment: restricted, small-hearted, dwelling with suffering. A trifling evil act done by this sort of individual takes him to hell.

'Now, a trifling evil act done by what sort of individual is experienced in the here & now, and for the most part barely appears for a moment? There is the case where a certain individual is developed in [contemplating] the body, developed in virtue, developed in mind, developed in discernment: unrestricted, large-hearted, dwelling with the unlimited. A trifling evil act done by this sort of individual is experienced in the here & now, and for the most part barely appears for a moment.

'Suppose that a man were to drop a salt crystal into a small amount of water in a cup. What do you think? Would the water in the cup become salty because of the salt crystal, and unfit to drink?'

'Yes, lord....'

'Now suppose that a man were to drop a salt crystal into the River Ganges. What do you think? Would the water in the River Ganges become salty because of the salt crystal, and unfit to drink?'

'No, lord....'

'In the same way, there is the case where a trifling evil act done by one individual [the first] takes him to hell; and there is the case where the very same sort of trifling deed done by the other individual is experienced in the here & now, and for the most part barely appears for a moment.'

A.III.99

§ 14. Moliyasıvaka: There are some priests & contemplatives who are of this doctrine, this view: Whatever an individual feels—pleasure, pain, neither-pleasure-nor-pain—is entirely caused by what was done before. Now what does the Ven. Gotama say to that?

The Buddha: There are cases where some feelings arise based on bile [i.e., diseases and pains that come from a malfunctioning gall bladder]. You yourself should know how some feelings arise based on bile. Even the world is agreed on how some feelings arise based on bile. So any priests & contemplatives who are of the doctrine & view that whatever an individual feels—pleasure, pain, neither-pleasure-nor-pain—is entirely caused by what was done before—slip past what they themselves know, slip past what is agreed on by the world. Therefore I say that those priests & contemplatives are wrong.

There are cases where some feelings arise based on phlegm...based on internal winds...based on a combination of bodily humors...from the change of the seasons...from uneven ('out-of-tune') care of the body...from attacks...from the result of kamma. You yourself should know how some feelings arise from the result of kamma. Even the world is agreed on how some feelings arise from the result of kamma. So any priests & contemplatives who are of the doctrine & view that whatever an individual feels—pleasure, pain, neither pleasure-nor-pain—is entirely caused by what was done before—slip past what they themselves know, slip past what is agreed on by the world. Therefore I say that those priests & contemplatives are wrong.

S.XXXVI.21

§ 15. What, monks, is old kamma? The eye is to be seen as old kamma, fabricated & willed, capable of being felt. The ear...The nose...The tongue...The body...The intellect is to be seen as old kamma, fabricated & willed, capable of being felt. This is called old kamma.

And what is new kamma? Whatever kamma one does now with the body, with speech, or with the intellect. This is called new kamma.

And what is the cessation of kamma? Whoever touches the release that comes from the cessation of bodily kamma, verbal kamma, & mental kamma. That is called the cessation of kamma.

And what is the path of practice leading to the cessation of kamma? Just this noble eightfold path....This is called the path of practice leading to the cessation of kamma.

S.XXXV.145

§ 16. These four types of kamma have been understood, realized, & made known by me. Which four? There is kamma that is black with black result; kamma that is white with white result; kamma that is black & white with black & white result; and kamma that is neither black nor white with neither black nor white result, leading to the ending of kamma.

And what is kamma that is black with black result? There is the case where a certain person fabricates an injurious bodily fabrication... an injurious verbal fabrication...an injurious mental fabrication.... He rearises in an injurious world, where he is touched by injurious contacts....He experiences feelings that are exclusively painful, like those of the beings in hell. This is called kamma that is black with black result.

And what is kamma that is white with white result? There is the case where a certain person fabricates an uninjurious bodily fabrication... an uninjurious verbal fabrication...an uninjurious mental fabrication.... He rearises in an uninjurious world, where he is touched by uninjurious contacts....He experiences feelings that are exclusively pleasant, like those of the Ever-radiant Devas. This is called kamma that is white with white result.

And what is kamma that is black & white with black & white result? There is the case where a certain person fabricates a bodily fabrication that is injurious & uninjurious...a verbal fabrication that is injurious & uninjurious...a mental fabrication that is injurious & uninjurious....He rearises in an injurious & uninjurious world, where he is touched by injurious & uninjurious contacts....He experiences injurious & uninjurious feelings, pleasure mingled with pain, like those of human beings, some devas, and some beings in the lower realms. This is called kamma that is black & white with black & white result.

And what is kamma that is neither black nor white with neither black nor white result, leading to the ending of kamma? The intention right there to abandon this kamma that is black with black result, the intention right there to abandon this kamma that is white with white result, the intention right there to abandon this kamma that is black & white with black & white result. This is called kamma that is neither black nor white with neither black nor white result, leading to the ending of kamma.

A.IV.232

[A related discourse repeats most of the above, defining black kamma with black result with the following example: "There is the case of a certain person who kills living beings, steals what is not given, engages in illicit sex, tells lies, and drinks fermented & distilled liquors that are the basis for heedlessness," and white kamma with white result with the following example: "There is the case of a certain person who abstains from killing living beings, abstains from stealing what is not given, abstains from engaging in illicit sex, abstains from telling lies, and abstains from drinking fermented & distilled liquors that are the basis for heedlessness."]

A.IV.234

§ 17. And what is kamma that is neither black nor white with neither black nor white result, leading to the ending of kamma? Right view, right resolve, right speech, right action, right livelihood, right effort, right mindfulness, right concentration.

A.IV.237

[The discourse immediately following this is identical to this except that it replaces the above factors of the noble eightfold path with the following seven factors of Awakening: mindfulness as a factor of awakening, analysis of qualities...persistence...rapture...serenity... concentration...equanimity as a factor of awakening.]

A.IV.238

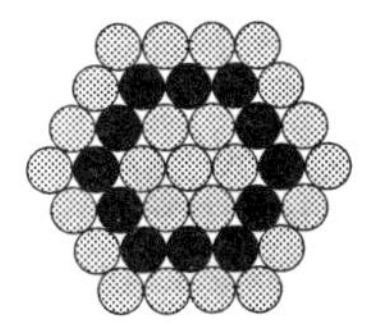

II. The Seven Sets

A. THE TREASURES OF THE TEACHING

Nowhere in the Canon does the Buddha list the seven sets of teachings under the name of Wings to Awakening. He mentions the seven sets as a group many times when he is summarizing his main teachings, but there is no firm evidence one way or the other as to whether he ever actually gave a name to the group. In one passage he applies the term "wings to self-Awakening" to the five faculties [§77]; and in two passages [§§24-25] he makes reference to the seven Wings to Awakening, which may or may not denote the seven sets. Nevertheless, given the fact that the Buddha called the five faculties wings to self-Awakening, and all seven sets are equivalent to the five faculties, the name "Wings to Awakening" for all seven seems appropriate. This was the name that they definitely had in early post-canonical texts, such as the *Petakopadesa,* and that they have maintained ever since.

The seven sets have played an important role throughout the history of Buddhism, in all of its various branches. They provided the framework for the earliest Abhidhamma texts, systematic presentations of the doctrine that were added to the early Canons a few centuries after the Buddha's passing away. They were also part of the first Buddhist text translated into Chinese, and later came to exemplify "Hinayana" teachings in T'ien-t'ai and other Chinese doctrinal systems. Tantric Buddhism features mandalas containing 37 deities, symbolic of the 37 factors making up the seven sets. Tibetan architecture, probably following the treatises of the medieval Indian universities, identifies the various parts of standard stupa design as symbols of the seven sets. Thus the Wings provide one of the few common threads that, in actual or symbolic form, run through all the traditions claiming descent from the Buddha.

One of the peculiarities of the Wings, viewed as a whole, is that two sets are duplicates: the five faculties and the five strengths contain the same five factors. Several theories have been advanced as to why the Buddha included what is essentially the same set twice. One is that he wanted to indicate that the five factors that make up each set could exist in the mind in two distinct levels of intensity, one sufficient for the path to stream-entry, the first level of Awakening, and the other needed for Arahantship, the highest level. This may parallel the passage [§106] where the Buddha makes a similar distinction between the noble eightfold path of stream-entry and the tenfold path of Arahantship. There is some disagreement among later writers as to which of the two sets, the faculties or the strengths, should be considered the more intense, although there is one canonical passage [§85] where the term "faculty" seems to rank on a higher level than "strength."

Another hypothesis—not necessarily at odds with the first—is that the Buddha wanted the number of factors to total 37 because the number had symbolic meaning. In ancient times, before the development of the decimal system, multiplication tables were arranged in hexagonal patterns. The complete table used to calculate the ratios used in tuning musical instruments to reciprocal scales—scales that played the same notes going up as going down—had one member in the middle surrounded by three hexagonal rings containing, in ascending order, six, twelve, and eighteen members, giving a total of 37 members. (See the diagram on the back cover of this book.) The table of whole-number ratios that formed the basis for trigonometry, and thus for the study of astronomy, contained 37 members. Thus the number 37 carried connotations of basic completeness. This principle is at work in Plato's *Laws*, where the ideal city has 37 guardians, and it may also be at work here.

A related consideration may be that the number seven, in the seven sets, was symbolic of treasure. The sea, in the time of the Buddha, was said to have seven treasures [§18], and the universal monarch was said to have seven treasures that formed his spontaneous regalia [M.129]. The Buddha explicitly borrows this number symbolism when he states that the seven sets are the treasures of his teaching.

Another possibility, which we have already noted [I/B], is that musicians in the Buddha's time recognized seven systems for tuning the musical scale—all other systems being rejected as discordant—and the Buddha may have borrowed this numerical symbolism to suggest that his teachings formed a complete guide to all the possible ways in which a Samana—a person in tune *(sama)*—could tune his or her mind to the truth.

From a less historical and more practical point of view, the important question about the seven sets is how they fit into the general plan of Buddhist practice. Their role is most succinctly stated in §25: the development of the seven sets follows on the development of virtue and leads naturally into the development of transcendent discernment, thus filling the role that other passages assign to concentration practice. This suggests—and again, the suggestion is borne out by passages that deal with the issue in more detail—that the seven sets are to be developed in the course of a concentration practice based on a moral life and aimed at the development of discernment. When §23 ends its list of preconditions for the practice of the seven sets with four meditation practices—actually three, as the perception of inconstancy is an integral part of mindfulness of in-and-out breathing—it is simply listing the concentration practices most frequently recommended in the texts as focal points for developing the skills of the seven sets. Nevertheless, although the seven sets focus most specifically on the practice of concentration, the close interconnections among virtue, concentration, and discernment mean that the sets include the factors of virtue and discernment as well, thus encompassing the entire path of Buddhist practice.

A virtuous and moral life is an absolute prerequisite for practicing the sets. This is a point that cannot be overstated, a fact reflected in the large number of canonical passages that hammer it home: far too many to include in this anthology. Some of the sets—the five faculties/strengths and the noble eightfold path—actually include the practice of a virtuous life in their factors, under the faculty/strength of conviction, and under the factors of right speech, right action, and right livelihood in the eightfold path. The remaining sets, the texts tell us, are meant to follow on the development of personal virtue in the same way that sunrise follows on the pre-dawn colors in the eastern sky.

The texts explain the precepts that underline a virtuous life, not as rules imposed by an outside authority, but as guidelines for action that a person would voluntarily undertake when accepting the importance of the principles of kamma and skillful action in shaping the course of one's experiences. Killing, for instance, is obviously an unskillful action when viewed in the full light of its kammic consequences. The same holds true with other actions forbidden by the precepts, such as drinking alcohol, stealing, illicit sex, lying, and abusive language. [For a more complete list, see §§103-104.] Passage §103 shows that the Buddha's teachings on virtue consist not only of the "don't's" of the precepts, but also of the "do's" of such positive standards as sympathy, reliability, and genuine helpfulness. Skillfulness is not simply a matter of avoiding bad consequences; it also actively cultivates the good.

In keeping with the teaching that kamma is essentially intention, the precepts are designed to focus on the state of mind motivating the act. A precept is broken only when one does so intentionally. Thus the practice of observing the precepts requires constant attention to the factor of intention in one's actions; it also requires that one develop the "sublime attitudes" *(brahma-vihara)* of good will, compassion, appreciation, and equanimity [§98], which strengthen one's ability to side with skillful intentions. In this way, the Buddha's approach to morality is to use the realm of personal action as an arena for the comprehensive training of the mind.

These three aspects of the Buddhist approach to morality—the avoidance of bad kamma, the development of skillful mental states, and the purification of intention—follow the pattern of the heart of the Buddha's teachings as presented in the first verse of §7. They also explain why virtue is a necessary foundation for the practice of concentration: A moral life brings about absence of remorse [A.X.1]; people who, in all honesty, have no reason for remorse over their actions or for anxiety over their consequences, feel a natural sense of inner joy. This joy is intensified when they reflect on the positive acts of kindness and generosity that they have performed for others. Thus intensified, this joy then provides the basis for the inner pleasure that allows for concentration. In this way, a healthy sense of self-worth is a necessary precondition for a stable mind [§238].

In addition, the practice of virtue forces one to develop a number of the "concentration" factors in the sets themselves, on a preliminary level of skill, thus making them strong and fit for formal concentration practice. To maintain a precept, one must keep it constantly in mind: this strengthens mindfulness. One must stick to one's determination to abide by one's principles: this strengthens persistence. One must pay attention to the present moment, for that is where the decision to keep or break a precept is made; and one must remain firm in one's cultivation of the sublime attitudes: these factors strengthen concentration. One must be clear about one's motives for acting, and at the same time be sensitive in knowing how to apply a particular precept to one's present situation: e.g., being quick to see how to avoid an issue in which telling the truth might be harmful, yet without telling a lie. This strengthens one's ability to analyze the mind in the present moment, intensifying one's powers of discernment in general. These four factors—mindfulness, effort, concentration, and discernment—are the central elements in all of the seven sets. Thus, the practice of virtue exercises, on a rudimentary level, the qualities of mind needed for concentration practice.

A close look at the seven sets will show that a similar relationship exists between these qualities, as they are developed in concentration practice, and the transcendent discernment toward which they lead. On the one hand, concentration is needed as a basis for discernment; on the other hand, discernment is exercised in developing concentration, becoming more precise and penetrating as a result. To understand how this happens, we must first note that the seven sets fall into two types. The first type consists of the four frames of reference, the four right exertions, and the four bases of power. Each of these sets focuses on a single factor in the "concentration aggregate" [§105] of the noble eightfold path: the frames of reference on mindfulness, the right exertions on effort, and the bases of power on concentration. Their factors are defined in such a way that the proper development of any one set involves the other two sets, together with the factor of discernment. In this sense they point out the "holographic" nature of the path: each part must include the whole, just as every piece of a hologram can reproduce the entire holographic image.

The sets included in the second type are the five faculties, the five strengths, the seven factors of Awakening, and the noble eightfold path. Each of these sets lists its factors in a causal chain progressing through a spiraling loop. The five faculties and strengths start with conviction, which then leads naturally to persistence, mindfulness, concentration, and then discernment. Discernment, in turn, provides a basis for even firmer conviction. Similarly, the seven factors of Awakening start with mindfulness, which develops into an analysis of (present) mental qualities, persistence, rapture, serenity, concentration, and finally equanimity. Equanimity, in turn, provides a steady basis for the further development of mindfulness. The noble eightfold path starts out with right view and right resolve, which together constitute discernment, leading to right speech, right action, right livelihood, right effort, right mindfulness, and right concentration. Concentration, in turn, forms a basis for the clearer development of discernment. In this way the various factors of the path are mutually reinforcing in an upward spiral that leads to Awakening.

Comparing the sets in the second type with one another, however, we find a certain complexity in their feedback loops. In terms of their most important factors, we see that the faculties and strengths depict the causal sequence as:

effort » mindfulness » concentration » discernment;

the factors of Awakening give it as:

mindfulness » discernment » effort » concentration;

and the noble eightfold path:

discernment » effort » mindfulness » concentration.

Although the sequences differ, they have one pattern in common: concentration always follows after right effort and mindfulness. This suggests not only that concentration depends on these two factors, but also that effort and mindfulness, when properly developed, are meant to lead to concentration. This suggestion is borne out in the texts that deal with these factors in detail [§§1, 33-35, 58, 61].

The two factors with the most variegated roles in these lists are mindfulness and discernment. Mindfulness is essential at every step along the way. There are passages [§26] teaching that mindfulness is a prerequisite for virtue, which—together with right view—is in turn a prerequisite for right mindfulness [§27]. Similarly, mindfulness is necessary for concentration, which in turn can be devoted to the development of greater mindfulness [§149], which can lead further to discernment.

As for discernment: If we look at the lists placing discernment after the other factors, we find that certain aspects of discernment are presumed by the earlier factors. In the five faculties, for instance, conviction includes belief in the principle of kamma, which is one of the elements of right discernment. In the lists that place discernment toward the beginning of the process, we find transcendent discernment added on to the end: the seven factors of Awakening, when fully developed, lead to clear knowing (transcendent discernment) and release; when the noble eightfold path reaches the point of full Awakening, it leads to right knowledge (transcendent discernment again) and right release. The implication here is that discernment, functioning on different levels, plays a role adding feedback loops of ever greater sensitivity every step along the way. This point is made explicit in §106.

For this reason, skillfulness—as a constant, sensitive mindfulness and discernment toward one's own actions—lies at the essence of every moment in the continued development of the path. On the one hand it creates the conditions necessary for the path to develop: knowledge of what is skillful and unskillful must necessarily precede right effort and mindfulness, and must help mindfulness lead to concentration. On the other hand, the factors of mindfulness and concentration are necessary for discernment to become even more sensitive to the present moment. Thus, as the path spirals through its many feedback loops, it exercises discernment, making it stronger in the same way that muscles are strengthened with exercise. At the same time, the development of the path steadies the conditions that provide discernment with the solid basis it needs to become more and more precise, just as a solid foundation is necessary for sensitive measuring equipment. In this way discernment develops from a knowledge of what is skillful and unskillful, first gained through the advice and example of others, on through a more intuitive understanding of skillfulness gained through repeated action and reflection on one's actions, to a knowledge of the four noble truths and the duties appropriate to each, and finally to the knowledge that those duties have been fulfilled [§195]. The Wings thus put mundane discernment to use, and in so doing make it transcendent.

All of this explains why the Buddha said that of all the wings to self-Awakening, discernment is chief [§77]. In its more rudimentary forms it provides the conditions and feedback necessary for each step along the way; its transcendent form, at the culmination of the path, leads directly to Awakening.

The experience of Awakening, according to the texts, can take any one of four levels:

• *stream-entry,* i.e., entry into the stream leading to Unbinding—which cuts the fetters of self identity views, uncertainty, and grasping at precepts and practices—ensuring that one will be reborn no more than seven more times;

• *once-returning*—which further weakens passion, aversion, and delusion—ensuring that one will be reborn no more than once;

• *non-returning*—which cuts the fetters of sensual passion and irritation—ensuring that one will be reborn in the highest heavens, called the Pure Abodes, there to obtain Unbinding, never to return to this world; and

• *Arahantship*—which cuts the fetters of passion for form, passion for formlessness, conceit, restlessness, and ignorance—bringing total freedom from the cycle of rebirth.

In all four levels, the basic dynamic is the same: virtue, concentration, and discernment bring the mind skillfully to a state of "non-fashioning" *(atammayata)* [§179] where all present input into the cycle of kamma is suspended. This state of non-fashioning then opens the way for the experience of the Unfabricated. To put this in terms of the two knowledges that constitute Awakening, the skillful mastery of the processes of kamma to the point of non-fashioning corresponds to the knowledge of the regularity of the Dhamma, and the experience of the Unfabricated corresponds to the knowledge of Unbinding.

Although all four levels require mature levels of the path factors of virtue, concentration, and discernment to bring about the two knowledges that constitute Awakening, they differ in the relative maturity of the path factors that lead up to them. Stream-entry occurs at the full maturation of virtue; non-returning, at the full maturation of concentration; and Arahantship, at the full maturation of discernment [A.III.88; MFU, pp. 103]. Thus they also differ in the depth to which they penetrate the two knowledges of Awakening and in their ability to cut the fetters that perpetuate bondage to the cycle of kamma and rebirth. The texts report a few cases where meditators go straight through all four levels to the level of Arahantship, but in most cases the meditator will pass through the four levels step-by-step, sometimes over course of many years or even several lifetimes.

In this book, except where otherwise noted, discussions of the Awakening experience as described in the discourses focus on the level where virtue, concentration, and discernment are all fully mature, the Awakening total, and the resulting freedom absolutely unlimited. This is the point where all seven sets of the Wings to Awakening ultimately aim.

§ 18. Paharada, just as the ocean has these many treasures of various kinds—pearls, sapphires, lapis lazuli, shells, quartz, coral, silver, gold, rubies, & cat's eyes—in the same way, this doctrine & discipline has these many treasures of various kinds: the four frames of reference, the four right exertions, the four bases of power, the five faculties, the five strengths, the seven factors of awakening, the noble eightfold path. This is the seventh wonder & marvel...that the monks, having seen again & again in this doctrine & discipline, delight in.

A.VIII.19

§ 19. Then [after relinquishing the will to continue fabricating his life processes] the Blessed One went to the audience hall and on arrival sat down on the seat prepared for him. When he was seated, he addressed the monks: 'The qualities I have pointed out, having known them directly: You should grasp them thoroughly, cultivate them, develop them, & pursue them so that this holy life may long endure & remain steadfast for the benefit, welfare, & happiness of the multitude, out of sympathy for the world, for the benefit, welfare, & happiness of human & celestial beings. And what are those qualities? The four frames of reference, the four right exertions, the four bases of power, the five faculties, the five strengths, the seven factors of awakening, the noble eightfold path. These are the qualities I have pointed out, having known them directly, that you should grasp thoroughly, cultivate, develop, & pursue...for the benefit, welfare, & happiness of human & celestial beings.' Then the Blessed One addressed the monks, 'I exhort you, monks: All fabrications are subject to decay. Bring about completion by means of heedfulness. It will not be long before the Tathāgata's total Unbinding. He will attain total Unbinding in three month's time.'

That is what the Blessed One said. Then...he said further:

Young & old
wise & foolish
rich & poor:
  all end up dying.

As a potter's clay vessels
  large & small
  fired & unfired
all end up broken,
  so too life
  heads to death.

Then the Teacher said further:

Ripe my age, little the life
remaining to me.
Leaving you, I will go,
having made a refuge
for myself.

Be heedful, monks,
mindful, virtuous.
With your resolves well-concentrated,
look after your minds.

He who, in this
doctrine & discipline,
remains heedful,
leaving the round
of birth,
will make an end
of stress.

D.16

§ 20. Suppose a hen has eight, ten, or twelve eggs: If she doesn't cover them rightly, warm them rightly, or incubate them rightly, then even though this wish may occur to her—'O that my chicks might break through the egg shells with their spiked claws or beaks and hatch out safely!'—still it is not possible that the chicks will break through the egg shells with their spiked claws or beaks and hatch out safely. Why is that? Because the hen has not covered them rightly, warmed them rightly, or incubated them rightly. In the same way, even though this wish may occur to a monk who dwells without devoting himself to development—'O that my mind might be released from effluents through lack of clinging!'—still his mind is not released from the effluents through lack of clinging. Why is that? From lack of developing, it should be said. Lack of developing what? The four frames of reference, the four right exertions, the four bases of power, the five faculties, the five strengths, the seven factors of awakening, the noble eightfold path....

But suppose a hen has eight, ten, or twelve eggs that she covers rightly, warms rightly, & incubates rightly: Even though this wish may not occur to her—'O that my chicks might break through the egg shells with their spiked claws or beaks and hatch out safely!'—still it is possible that the chicks will break through the egg shells with their spiked claws or beaks and hatch out safely. Why is that? Because the hen has covered them, warmed them, & incubated them rightly. In the same way, even though this wish may not occur to a monk who dwells devoting himself to development—'O that my mind might be released from effluents through lack of clinging!'—still his mind is released from the effluents through lack of clinging. Why is that? From developing, it should be said. Developing what? The four frames of reference, the four right exertions, the four bases of power, the five faculties, the five strengths, the seven factors of awakening, the noble eightfold path.

Just as when a carpenter or carpenter's apprentice sees the marks of his fingers or thumb on the handle of his adze but does not know, 'Today my adze handle wore down this much, or yesterday it wore down that much, or the day before yesterday it wore down this much,' still he knows it is worn through when it is worn through. In the same way, when a monk dwells devoting himself to development, he does not know, 'Today my effluents wore down this much, or yesterday they wore down that much, or the day before yesterday they wore down this much,' still he knows they are worn through when they are worn through.

Just as when an ocean-going ship, rigged with masts & stays, after six months on the water, is left on shore for the winter: Its stays, weathered by the heat & wind, moistened by the clouds of the rainy season, easily wither & rot away. In the same way, when a monk dwells devoting himself to development, his fetters easily wither & rot away.

A.VII.68

§ 21. A certain monk went to his preceptor and on arrival said to him, 'My body, sir, now feels like it's drugged. I've lost my bearings. Things are unclear to me. Sloth & drowsiness surround my mind at all times. I am unhappy in leading the holy life. I have doubts about mental qualities (or: things—*dhammas*).'

Then the preceptor, taking his student, went to see the Buddha (and told him what his student had said. The Buddha replied:)

'That's the way it is for a person who does not guard the doors to his sense faculties, who does not know moderation in eating, who is not devoted to wakefulness, who does not clearly understand skillful qualities, and who is not devoted day after day to the development of the wings to awakening....Thus you should train yourself, monk: "I will guard my senses, will know moderation in eating, will devote myself to wakefulness, will clearly understand skillful qualities, and will devote myself day after day to the development of the wings to awakening." Thus you should train yourself.

Then the monk, having received this instruction from the Blessed One, got up from his seat, bowed down, circled the Blessed One, keeping him on his right, and then went away. Dwelling alone, secluded, heedful, ardent, & resolute, he in no long time reached & remained in the supreme goal of the holy life, for which clansmen rightly go forth from home into homelessness, knowing it & realizing it for himself in the here & now. He knew: 'Birth is ended, the holy life fulfilled, the task done. There is nothing further for the sake of this world.' And thus he became another one of the Arahants.

A.V.56

§ 22. Endowed with three qualities, a monk is one who follows the way that cannot be faulted and he has aroused the basis for ending the effluents. Which three? There is the case where a monk guards the doors to his sense faculties, knows moderation in eating, & is devoted to wakefulness.

And how does a monk guard the doors to his sense faculties? There is the case where a monk, on seeing a form with the eye, does not grasp at any theme or variations by which—if he were to dwell without restraint over the faculty of the eye—evil, unskillful qualities such as greed or distress might assail him. He practices with restraint. He guards the faculty of the eye. He achieves restraint with regard to the faculty of the eye. (Similarly with the ear, nose, tongue, body & intellect.) This is how a monk guards the doors to his sense faculties.

And how does a monk know moderation in eating? There is the case where a monk, considering it appropriately, takes his food not playfully, nor for intoxication, nor for putting on bulk, nor for beautification, but simply for the survival & continuance of this body, for ending its afflictions, for the support of the holy life, thinking, 'I will destroy old feelings [of hunger] & not create new feelings [from overeating]. Thus I will maintain myself, be blameless, & live in comfort.' This is how a monk knows moderation in eating.

And how is a monk devoted to wakefulness? There is the case where a monk during the day, sitting & pacing back & forth, cleanses his mind of any qualities that would hold the mind in check. During the first watch of the night [dusk to 10 p.m.], sitting & pacing back & forth, he cleanses his mind of any qualities that would hold the mind in check. During the second watch of the night [10 p.m. to 2 a.m.], reclining on his right side, he takes up the lion's posture, one foot placed on top of the other, mindful, alert, with his mind set on getting up [either as soon as he awakens or at a particular time]. During the last watch of the night [2 a.m. to dawn], sitting & pacing back & forth, he cleanses his mind of any qualities that would hold the mind in check. This is how a monk is devoted to wakefulness.

Endowed with these three qualities, a monk is one who follows the way that cannot be faulted and he has aroused the basis for ending the effluents.

A.III.16

§ 23. Monks, if wanderers who are members of other sects should ask you, 'What, friend, are the prerequisites for the development of the wings to self-awakening?'...you should answer, 'There is the case where a monk has admirable people as friends, companions, and colleagues. This is the first prerequisite for the development of the wings to self-awakening.

'Furthermore, the monk is virtuous. He dwells restrained in accordance with the Pāṭimokkha, consummate in his behavior & sphere of activity. He trains himself, having undertaken the training rules, seeing danger in the slightest faults. This is the second prerequisite for the development of the wings to self-awakening.

'Furthermore, he gets to hear at will, easily & without difficulty, talk that is truly sobering & conducive to the opening of awareness, i.e., talk on having few wants, on contentment, on seclusion, on non-entanglement, on arousing persistence, on virtue, on concentration, on discernment, on release, and on the knowledge & vision of release. This is the third prerequisite for the development of the wings to self-awakening.

'Furthermore, he keeps his persistence aroused for abandoning unskillful mental qualities and for taking on skillful mental qualities. He is steadfast, solid in his effort, not shirking his duties with regard to skillful mental qualities. This is the fourth prerequisite for the development of the wings to self-awakening.

'Furthermore, he is discerning, endowed with the discernment of arising & passing away—noble, penetrating, leading to the right ending of stress. This is the fifth prerequisite for the development of the wings to self-awakening.'

Monks, when a monk has admirable people as friends, companions, and colleagues, it is to be expected that he will be virtuous, will dwell restrained in accordance with the Pāṭimokkha, consummate in his behavior & sphere of activity, and will train himself, having undertaken the training rules, seeing danger in the slightest faults.

When a monk has admirable people as friends, companions, and colleagues, it is to be expected that he will get to hear at will, easily & without difficulty, talk that is truly sobering and conducive to the opening of awareness, i.e., talk on having few wants, on contentment, on seclusion, on non-entanglement, on activating persistence, on virtue, on concentration, on discernment, on release, and on the knowledge & vision of release...that he will keep his persistence aroused for abandoning unskillful mental qualities, and for taking on skillful mental qualities—steadfast, solid in his effort, not shirking his duties with regard to skillful qualities...that he will be discerning, endowed with discernment of arising & passing away—noble, penetrating, leading to the right ending of stress.

And furthermore, monks, when the monk is established in these five qualities, there are four additional qualities he should develop: He should develop [contemplation of] the unattractive so as to abandon lust. He should develop good will so as to abandon ill will. He should develop mindfulness of in-&-out breathing so as to cut off distractive thinking. He should develop the perception of inconstancy so as to uproot the conceit, 'I am.' For a monk perceiving inconstancy, the perception of not-self is made firm. One perceiving not-self attains the uprooting of the conceit, 'I am'—Unbinding in the here & now.

A.IX.1

§ 24. These three divine sounds sound forth among the devas on appropriate occasions. Which three? When a noble disciple, shaving off his hair & beard, clothing himself in the ochre robe, makes up his mind to go forth from the home life into homelessness, on that occasion the divine sound sounds forth among the devas: 'This noble disciple has made up his mind to do battle with Māra'....

When a noble disciple lives engaged in developing the seven [sets of] qualities that are wings to awakening, on that occasion the divine sound sounds forth among the devas: 'This noble disciple is doing battle with Māra'....

When a noble disciple, through the ending of effluents dwells in the release of awareness & release of discernment that are free from effluent, having known & made them manifest for himself in the here & now, on that occasion the divine sound sounds forth among the devas: 'This noble disciple has won the battle. Having been in the front lines of the battle, he now dwells victorious'....These are the three divine sounds that sound forth among the devas on appropriate occasions.

Iti.82

§ 25. A monk who has admirable virtue, admirable qualities, & admirable discernment is called, in this doctrine & discipline, one who is complete, fulfilled, supreme among men.

And how is a monk a person with admirable virtue? There is the case where a monk is virtuous. He dwells restrained in accordance with the Paṭimokkha, consummate in his behavior & sphere of activity. He trains himself, having undertaken the training rules, seeing danger in the slightest faults. In this way a monk is a person with admirable virtue. Thus he is of admirable virtue.

And how is a monk a person with admirable qualities? There is the case where a monk lives engaged in developing of the seven [sets of] qualities that are wings to awakening. In this way a monk is a person with admirable qualities. Thus he is of admirable virtue & admirable qualities.

And how is a monk a person with admirable discernment? There is the case where a monk, through the ending of effluents dwells in the release of awareness & release of discernment that are free from effluent, having known & made them manifest for himself in the here & now. In this way a monk is a person with admirable discernment. Thus he is of admirable virtue, admirable qualities, admirable discernment. In this doctrine & discipline he is called one who is complete, fulfilled, supreme among men.

One devoid of wrong-doing
in thought, word, or deed,
is called a person of admirable virtue:
the conscientious monk.

One well-developed in the qualities
that go to the attainment of self-awakening,
is called a person of admirable qualities:
the unassuming monk.

One discerning right here for himself
the ending of stress
is called a person of admirable discernment:
the monk without effluent.

One consummate in these things,
untroubled, with doubt cut away,
unattached in all the world,
is called one who has abandoned the All.

ITI.97

B. THE FOUR FRAMES OF REFERENCE

The four frames of reference *(satipatthana)* are a set of teachings that show where a meditator should focus attention and how. This dual role—the "where" and the "how"—is reflected in the fact that the term *satipatthana* can be explained etymologically in two ways. On the one hand, it can be regarded as a compound of *sati* (mindfulness, reference, the ability to keep something in mind) and *patthana* (foundation, condition, source), thus referring to the **object** that is kept in mind as a frame of reference for giving context to one's experience. Alternatively, *satipatthana* can be seen as a compound of *sati* and *upatthana* (establishing near, setting near), thus referring to the **approach** (the *how)* of keeping something closely in mind, of maintaining a solid frame of reference. Scholars are divided as to which interpretation is right, but for all practical purposes they both are. The Buddha was more a poet than a strict etymologist, and he may have deliberately chosen an ambiguous term that would have fruitful meanings on more than one level. In the practice of the frames of reference, both the proper object and the proper approach are crucial for getting the proper results. In fact, as we shall see, the taking of a proper object entails the beginning of the proper approach, and the approach ends by taking as its objects the qualities of mind developed in the course of pursuing the approach itself. In other words, as we mentioned in the Introduction concerning the Buddha's Awakening, the "what" merges with the "how" as the "how" of the investigation ultimately becomes what gets investigated.

The texts give two different pictures of the role that the frames of reference play in the practice. Some [§§33, 34, 36] state that developing the frames of reference is a precondition for jhana, which then forms a basis for transcendent discernment. Others [§§27, 43] make no mention of jhana, stating that one goes directly from the frames of reference to the transcendent. On the surface, this would seem to indicate that there are two alternate paths: one with and one without jhana. This reading, though, contradicts the many passages maintaining that jhana is necessary for the development of transcendent discernment [§§165, 166, 171, 173, 178; some of these passages simply say "concentration" instead of jhana, but there seems to be every reason to assume that concentration here means right concentration, which is nothing other than jhana]. Thus we must look for an alternative reading, and we find one suggested by passages indicating that the development of the frames of reference implicitly entails the full development of the seven factors of Awakening. Because these factors are closely associated with jhana, this would indicate that the proper development of the frames of reference necessarily incorporates, in and of itself, the practice of jhana.

This reading is confirmed by §29, which states that the way to develop the frames of reference is through the noble eightfold path, which includes jhana. It is also confirmed by §31, which describes how the frames of reference relate to the sixteen steps of breath meditation. As we shall see in III/E, these sixteen steps are also a description of how jhana is developed and then used as a vehicle for fostering discernment and ending the effluents of the mind. Thus, we can view the outline of frame-of-reference practice as a description of the stages in the mindful mastery of jhana and its application to the ending of the effluents.

The proper objects that act as frames of reference are four: the body in and of itself, feelings in and of themselves, the mind in and of itself, and mental qualities in and of themselves. The "in and of itself" here is important. To take the body as a frame of reference in this way, for instance, means that one views it not in terms of its function in the world—for then the world would be the frame of reference—but simply on its own terms, as it is directly experienced. In other words, one is not concerned with its relative worth or utility in terms of the values of the world—its beauty, strength, agility, etc.—but simply what it is when regarded in and of itself.

The four objects that act as frames of reference fall into two classes. The first class—the body, feelings, and the mind—act as the "given" objects of meditation practice: what experience presents, on its own, as an object for meditation. The meditator takes any one of these objects as a frame of reference, relating all of experience to his/her chosen frame. For example, although one will experience feelings and mind states in the course of taking the body as a frame of reference, one tries to relate them to the experience of the body as their primary frame. A feeling is viewed as it affects the body, or the body affects it. The same holds for a mind state. An analogy for this practice is holding an object in one's hand. When other objects come into contact with the hand, one is aware that they are making contact, but one does not let go of the object in one's hand in order to grasp after them.

The second class of object—mental qualities *(dhamma)*—denotes the qualities of mind that are developed and abandoned as one masters the meditation. The list of "dhammas" given in §30 would seem to belie the translation "mental qualities" here, as they include not only the five hindrances and seven factors of Awakening, which are obviously mental qualities, but also the five aggregates, the six sense media, and the four noble truths, which would seem to fit better with another meaning of the word *dhamma,* i.e., "phenomena." However, if we look more closely at each of these other classes, we will see that they actually deal with variant forms of abandoning the hindrances and developing the factors of Awakening. The section on the sense media focuses less on the media than on the abandoning of the fetters—passion and delight (S.XLI.1; MFU pp. 52-53)—associated with those media. The section on the aggregates describes a state of practice that is elsewhere [§149] identified as a developed form of concentration, in which the aggregates that comprise the state of jhana form the object of analysis [§173]. The section on the noble truths describes a state of practice that elsewhere [§169] is said to require the sort of mental stability and clarity found only in jhana. Thus all the approaches to "dhammas in and of themselves" would appear to be variations on the abandoning of the hindrances and the development of the factors of Awakening. Because the stated function of the frames of reference is to bring about the culmination of the factors of Awakening, and through them the development of clear knowing and release [§92], the translation of *dhamma* as "mental quality" seems an appropriate way to keep that function in mind and to avoid getting lost in the details of its different aspects.

There is historical support for this interpretation as well. The Vibhanga, an ancient Abhidhamma text, includes only the hindrances and the factors of Awakening in its discussion of this heading. The same holds true with the Sarvastivadin version of this discourse, preserved in Chinese translation. Scholars have questioned whether these two texts should be taken as evidence that the original discussion of *dhamma* here included only these two topics. The issue is impossible to decide from the texts available to us, but a case can be made for concluding that, regardless of what the original version may have been, the early tradition regarded the abandoning of the hindrances and the development of the factors of Awakening as encompassing all the factors that might be included under this heading.

Each of the four objects of mindfulness is said to be sufficient for bringing about Awakening [§44]. This point is easy to understand if we look at the approach taken to each of the objects, for then it becomes clear that the approach ultimately involves the development of mental qualities in and of themselves, regardless of what object is first taken up for meditation.

That approach falls into three stages. **The first stage**—here taking the body as an example—is simply called the frame of reference [§29]:

> There is the case where a monk remains focused on the body in & of itself—ardent, alert, & mindful—putting aside greed & distress with reference to the world.

Four terms in this passage are key. "Remaining focused" *(anupassin)* can also be translated as "keeping track." This denotes the element of concentration in the practice, as one tries to stay with one particular theme in the midst of the welter of experience. "Ardent" *(atapi)* denotes the factor of effort or exertion in the practice; the Commentary equates this with right exertion, which contains an element of discernment in its ability to distinguish skillful from unskillful mental qualities. "Alert" *(sampajano)* means being clearly aware of what is happening in the present. This, too, relates to discernment. "Mindful" *(satima)* literally means being able to remember or recollect. Here it means keeping one's task in mind. The task here is a dual one—remaining focused on one's frame of reference, and putting aside the distractions of greed and distress that would come from shifting one's frame of reference back to the world. In other words, one tries to stay with the phenomenology of immediate experience, without slipping back into the narratives and world views that make up one's sense of the world. In essence, this is a concentration practice, with the three qualities of ardency, alertness, and mindfulness devoted to attaining concentration. Mindfulness keeps the theme of the meditation in mind, alertness observes the theme as it is present to awareness, and also is aware of when the mind has slipped from its theme. Mindfulness then remembers where the mind should be focused, and ardency tries to return the mind to its proper theme as quickly and skillfully as possible. In this way, these three qualities help to seclude the mind from sensual preoccupations and unskillful mental qualities, thus bringing it to the first jhana.

Passage §33 confirms this reading by equating the successful performance of this first stage in the practice with the first jhana, whereas §§35-36 give advice on how to bring the mind to concentration if this method does not work: focus on the problem of the mind's not settling down, and bring the mind to an inspiring theme that will accomplish the desired end.

When the method does work, §33 describes the next step as a variation on the basic exercise:

> Remain focused on the body in & of itself, but do not think any thoughts connected with the body.

This, it says, takes the mind to the second jhana, where directed thought and evaluation are abandoned. From there the mind can go up to the third jhana and the fourth [§72].

These points may be illustrated with some meditation techniques that are currently popular in the West: In a "mental noting" practice, mindfulness is a matter of remembering to keep up the noting, alertness means seeing whatever phenomena arise to be noted, and ardency is a matter of sticking with the noting relentlessly and being ever more quick and precise in one's alertness. In terms of the factors constituting jhana practice, the mindfulness and alertness here would be related to directed thought, ardency to singleness of preoccupation, while alertness aimed at evaluating the results of the noting—and ardency in keeping the "pressure" of the noting just right—would be related to evaluation. If this practice is then conducted in line with the texts, it should reach a stage where the mind settles down into the singleness of the first jhana. Then the meditator would be encouraged to stop the noting, so that the mind could engage in subtler mindfulness and alertness, and thus enter the second jhana.

In a "scanning" or "body sweep" practice, mindfulness means remembering to stick with the process of scanning the body, while alertness would mean seeing the subtle sensations of the body being scanned. Ardency would mean sticking with the scanning process, and trying to be ever more sensitive to the subtlest sensations. As in the previous case, these activities are related to factors of jhana, and the process, if conducted in line with the texts, should culminate in a state of full-bodied singleness, at which time the motion of the scanning can be brought to stillness, and the mind can enter deeper concentration.

In "breath" practice, mindfulness means keeping the breath in mind as the theme of the meditation, alertness means being sensitive to the sensations of the breath. Ardency means sticking with the process relentlessly, as well as taking up the stages of "training" [§31; III/E], in which one tries to be aware of the entire body with each in and out breath, and to let the breath sensations grow calm. In terms of jhana factors, mindfulness would be related to directed thought, alertness to evaluation, and ardency to singleness of preoccupation. As awareness fills the body and the breath grows calm, one's alertness stays steadily with the breath, and the mind enters the singleness of jhana. At this point, one no longer needs consciously to direct the mind to the breath or to enlarge one's awareness any further. Thus the mind, as above, can develop subtler mindfulness and alertness, and so enter the second jhana.

According to §32, once concentration has been established on one's own body in this way, it may give rise to a similar "knowledge and vision" of the bodies of other people. Knowledge and vision, here, seems to denote intuitive knowledge through the psychic powers that some people develop through concentration. If used properly, this knowledge can help develop a sense of dispassion toward the processes of existence, as one sees that all bodies, even the most desirable, are subject to the same common shortcomings of being inconstant, stressful, and not-self.

Whether one pursues this meditation with one's own body or the bodies of others, it comes under the first stage of practice, as indicated by the following phrase:

> In this way he remains focused internally on the body in & of itself, or externally on the body in & of itself, or both internally & externally on the body in & of itself.

Once the first stage has produced a solid state of concentration, **the second stage**—the development of the frame of reference [§29]—can begin:

> One remains focused on the phenomenon of origination with regard to the body, on the phenomenon of passing away with regard to the body, or on the phenomenon of origination & passing away with regard to the body.

The "phenomena of origination and passing away" covers three sorts of events: conditioned occurrences in the object that forms one's frame of reference itself (in this case, the body); events in the other two "object" frames of reference (feelings and mind); or events in the "approach" frame of reference, i.e., the mental qualities that are developed (or interfere with) the process of taking a frame of reference to begin with. For instance, one may be focused on the body and may notice the arising and passing away of breath sensations in the body. Or one might notice the arising and passing away of feelings of pleasure or mental states of irritation while one remains anchored in the body. Or one might notice lapses of mindfulness in one's focus on the body.

In each of these cases, if the origination and passing away is of neutral events such as the aggregates, one is directed simply to be aware of them as events, and to let them follow their natural course unimpeded so as to see what factors accompany them and lead to their origination. As for events that are connected with the presence or absence of skillfulness, however, one is encouraged to manipulate and experiment with them so as to observe and further understand their causal interrelationships. This will enable one to become skillful in maximizing skillful mental qualities and minimizing unskillful ones. In other words, one develops insight into the process of origination and passing away by taking an active and sensitive role in the process, just as one learns about eggs by trying to cook with them, gathering experience from one's successes and failures in attempting increasingly difficult dishes.

The need for active participation in the practice explains why meditation must begin by mastering a particular technique, rather than passively watching whatever may arise in the present. The technique gives shape to one's present input into the present moment and makes one more sensitive to this aspect of this/that conditionality. It also provides an active context for appreciating mental qualities as they help or hinder one's success in the technique. Eventually, when one's sensitivity is sufficiently well developed, one can go beyond the technique to explore and master the process of causality as it functions in developing skillful qualities in the mind.

This process can be illustrated with the passage devoted to equanimity. In the first step, as one is still in the beginning stages of observing the mind in its attempts at meditation, one simply discerns the presence and absence of equanimity.

> There is the case where, there being equanimity as a factor of Awakening present within, he discerns that 'Equanimity as a factor of Awakening is present within me.' Or, there being no equanimity as a factor of Awakening present within, he discerns that 'Equanimity as a factor of Awakening is not present within me.'

In watching the course of this arising and passing away as one tries to bring the mind to the equanimity of jhana, one should begin to see patterns of cause and effect in what does and doesn't work. This enables one skillfully to give rise to equanimity even when it is not present of its own accord, and—once it is present—can strengthen it until it reaches the point of utmost development:

> He discerns how there is the arising of unarisen equanimity as a factor of Awakening. And he discerns how there is the culmination of the development of equanimity as a factor of Awakening once it has arisen.

A similar process is recommended for events in the "object" frames of reference. This is shown by the standard description of the sixteen steps of breath meditation [§31]. One trains oneself to breathe conscious of the entire body, or to breathe sensitive to feelings of rapture and pleasure, as this training fosters the factors of jhana. One trains oneself to satisfy, steady, and release the mind, as this training brings mastery over the stages of jhana. Passage §179 makes a similar point, directing the meditator to replace unskillful forms of distress, joy, and equanimity with more skillful versions of the same emotions, and then replacing skillful distress with skillful joy, and skillful joy with skillful equanimity.

As this process leads to stronger and more refined states of concentration, it refines one's sensitivity to the fact that the grosser one's participation in the process of origination and passing away in the mind, the grosser the level of stress that results. This leads one to let go of the grosser levels of one's participation as one is able to detect them. This can have one of two results. (1) It may lead to even more refined states of concentration, as one abandons the factors that obscure equanimity, or as one focuses one's equanimity on ever more refined objects. (2) Or, as one becomes able to focus on the activity involved even in refining equanimity, one comes to realize that it, too, is a process of input into the present, fabricated for the sake of non-becoming [§182]. Thus, as a sense of dispassion develops toward equanimity, one goes beyond it to a state called non-fashioning *(atammayata)* [§179], through **the third and final stage** of frame-of-reference practice:

> Or his mindfulness that 'There is a body (feeling, mind, mental quality)' is maintained [simply] to the extent of knowledge & recollection. And he remains independent, unsustained by (not clinging to) anything in the world.

This stage corresponds to a mode of perception that the Buddha in M.121 terms "entry into emptiness":

> Thus he regards it [this mode of perception] as empty of whatever is not there. Whatever remains, he discerns as present: "there is this."

This is the culminating equipoise where the path of the practice leads unmediated to state of non-fashioning and from there to the fruit of Awakening and release.

Some meditators, reading the two preceding passages, try to step immediately to the stage of non-fashioning without first having gained the inner sensitivity to cause and effect, action and non-action, that comes from developing concentration. In practice, though, this doesn't work. Only through that sensitivity can the basic causal relationships of dependent co-arising and this/that conditionality be discovered. This discovery is needed to give rise to a sense of dispassion, as one grows more and more disenchanted with the inconstant and artificial nature of all mental phenomena and develops a strong desire to gain release from them. It is also needed to uncover the precise point of non-fashioning between becoming and non-becoming where that release can be found.

As we shall see in later sections (in particular, III/E and III/H), the basic pattern of the three stages in frames-of-reference meditation—

- focusing on events in and of themselves in the present moment,
- understanding their causal relationships with other events by learning to manipulate them skillfully, and then
- arriving at a state of fully developed equipoise, transcending even one's skill, free from any present input into the causal network—

is basic to all aspects of Buddhist meditation practice. Among other things, it underlies the stages in breath meditation, the mastery of concentration, and the strategy of discernment leading to the transcendent. Thus it should be kept firmly in mind when reading passages not only in this section, but also throughout the entire book.

The texts contained in this section, for the most part, provide added details to the outline sketched here. For example, §§45-46 provide a variation on stage two by showing how mindfulness can be developed into equanimity by manipulating perceptions, viewing loathsome objects as unloathsome, and unloathsome objects as loathsome, etc.

Anyone attempting these perception games needs firm powers of concentration and sharp discernment so as not to become obsessed with perceptual distortions *(sañña vipallasa).* If handled properly, though, the process of manipulation gives important insights into the way the mind labels its objects, and can drive home lessons on the arbitrary nature of perception and the need not to be deceived by it.

The same point holds true for the contemplation of body parts mentioned in §30. This contemplation has been denounced in Western circles for promoting a negative self-image, but here it is necessary to distinguish between healthy and unhealthy negative images of one's own body. An unhealthy negative image is one that views the bodies of other people as attractive, and one's own as unattractive. This is unhealthy in that it creates feelings of inferiority concerning one's own body, compounded by lust and desire for the bodies of others. A healthy negative image sees that all bodies, no matter how attractive, young, or healthy they may seem at the skin level, are composed of the very same parts, all equally unattractive. The livers and intestines of even the most attractive people, if paraded down a walkway, would never capture a title in a beauty contest; if featured in an advertisement, they wouldn't sell. Thus there is no real reason to feel that one's body is inherently inferior to theirs. This perception of the equality of all bodies, if handled properly, is healthy in that it helps liberate one not only from feelings of inferiority but also from the disease of lust and desire, promoting a sense of dispassion toward lustful thoughts in general. As this theme of contemplation is developed through hands-on manipulation of one's perception of the body, it enables one to realize that, when reduced to their simple "bodyness," as bodies in and of themselves, all bodies are on a par, and that questions of attractiveness and unattractiveness derive ultimately from the context of one's frame of reference. One sees that the obstacles to equanimity and higher insights in the practice are not so much the objects of lust or hatred as they are the terms and contexts in which those objects are perceived. This insight can form the basis for perceptual skills that can act as a very liberating antidote to the mind's tendency to self-delusion.

One passage contained here that does not deal with the stages of frames-of-reference meditation is §47. This passage focuses on a charge that has been often leveled at Early Buddhism: that the practice it recommends is essentially selfish, in that one is striving simply for one's own welfare. The Buddha answers this charge by denying any radical distinction between one's own true welfare and that of others. To work for the true welfare of others is to work for one's own true welfare; to work for one's own is to work for theirs. The first point can be illustrated by a number of passages in this collection—showing, for example, how expressions of gratitude to one's parents can foster one's own true happiness [§§123, 124], how support for contemplatives enables one to hear the Dhamma [§128], how virtuous conduct toward other people and their possessions strengthens mindfulness [§27], and how attitudes of good will, compassion, appreciation, and equanimity foster concentration and release the mind from obstructive mental qualities [§98]. Thus, the quality of one's assistance to others cannot help but have an effect on the development of one's own mind.

As for the reverse dynamic—the way in which working for one's own welfare is to work for the welfare of others—the Buddha illustrates this point with an perceptive analogy for the interaction of living beings: two acrobats balancing on the end of a pole. If one acrobat loses balance, both will fall. To maintain balance, each must maintain his or her own balance. This analogy indicates that the act of developing good qualities in one's own mind is, in itself, an act of kindness to others. One protects them from the detrimental effects of one's uncontrolled anger, etc., and exposes them to the beneficial effects of one's own mindfulness, equanimity, and other skillful qualities. Thus it is not possible to practice the frames of reference properly without the rest of the world's benefiting to a greater or lesser degree. And in a world where no one can keep the balance of another person, the example of one's own skill in keeping balance is an instructive gift for those with the eyes to see and the intelligence to take one's example to heart.

Once one has attained full Awakening and needs to do nothing more for one's own welfare, one continues to act for the welfare of others within the framework of three frames of reference [§179], different from the four discussed in this section. The three are: the ability to remain (1) untroubled, mindful, and alert when others do not respond to one's teachings; (2) equanimous, mindful, and alert when some do and some do not respond to one's teachings; and (3) untroubled, mindful, and alert when others do respond to one's teachings. In other words, one's mental balance is so firm that other beings' success or failure in responding to one's help cannot disturb the mind. It is only in this context—the three frames of reference following full Awakening—that the Buddha allows for the possibility of helping others with no thought for one's own welfare, for at that point one's true welfare has no further needs. The Awakened person lives out the remainder of his/her life, insofar as his/her kamma allows, for "the welfare of the many, the happiness of the many, out of compassion for the world" [Mv.11.1].

§ 26. Imagine a tree devoid of branches & leaves: Its buds don't grow to maturity, its bark doesn't grow to maturity, its sapwood doesn't grow to maturity, its heartwood doesn't grow to maturity. In the same way, when—there being no mindfulness or alertness—a person is devoid of mindfulness or alertness, the prerequisite for a sense of conscience & concern [for the results of wrong-doing] becomes spoiled. There being no sense of conscience & concern...the prerequisite for restraint of the senses becomes spoiled. There being no restraint of the senses...the prerequisite for virtue becomes spoiled. There being no virtue...the prerequisite for right concentration becomes spoiled. There being no right concentration...the prerequisite for knowledge & vision of things as they actually are present becomes spoiled. There being no knowledge & vision of things as they actually are present, the prerequisite for disenchantment & dispassion becomes spoiled. There being no disenchantment & dispassion, the prerequisite for knowledge & vision of release becomes spoiled....

Now imagine a tree abundant in its branches & leaves: Its buds grow to maturity, its bark grows to maturity, its sapwood grows to maturity, its heartwood grows to maturity. In the same way, when—there being *mindfulness & alertness*—a person is abundant in mindfulness & alertness, the prerequisite for a sense of conscience & concern becomes abundant. There being a sense of conscience & concern... the prerequisite for restraint of the senses becomes abundant. There being restraint of the senses...the prerequisite for virtue becomes abundant. There being virtue...the prerequisite for right concentration becomes abundant. There being right concentration...the prerequisite for knowledge & vision of things as they actually are present becomes abundant. There being knowledge & vision of things as they are actually present, the prerequisite for disenchantment & dispassion becomes abundant. There being disenchantment & dispassion, the prerequisite for knowledge & vision of release becomes abundant.

A.VIII.81

§ 27. Uttiya: It would be good, Venerable Sir, if the Blessed One, would teach me the Dhamma in brief so that, having heard the Dhamma from the Blessed One, I might dwell alone, secluded, heedful, ardent, & resolute.

The Buddha: In that case, Uttiya, you should purify what is most basic with regard to skillful mental qualities. And what is the basis of skillful mental qualities? *Well-purified virtue & views made straight.* Then, when your virtue is well-purified and your views made straight, in dependence on virtue, established in virtue, you should develop the four frames of reference....Then, when in dependence on virtue, relying on virtue, you develop the four frames of reference, you will go beyond the realm of Death.

S.XLVII.16

§ 28. Mindful & Alert. Stay mindful, monks, and alert. This is our instruction to you all. And how is a monk mindful? There is the case where a monk remains focused on the body in & of itself—ardent, alert, & mindful—putting aside greed & distress with reference to the world. He remains focused on feelings...mind...mental qualities in & of themselves—ardent, alert, & mindful—putting aside greed & distress with reference to the world [§213]. This is how a monk is mindful.

And how is a monk alert? There is the case where feelings are known to the monk as they arise, known as they persist, known as they subside. Thoughts are known to him as they arise, known as they persist, known as they subside. Discernment *(vl:* perception) is known to him as it arises, known as it persists, known as it subsides. This is how a monk is alert. So stay mindful, monks, and alert. This is our instruction to you all.

S.XLVII.35

§ 29. Analysis. I will teach you the frames of reference, their development, and the path of practice leading to their development. Listen & pay close attention. I will speak.

Now, what are the frames of reference? There is the case where a monk remains focused on the body in & of itself—ardent, alert, & mindful—putting aside greed & distress with reference to the world. He remains focused on feelings...mind...mental qualities in & of themselves—ardent, alert, & mindful—putting aside greed & distress with reference to the world. This is called the frame of reference.

And what is the development of the frames of reference? There is the case where a monk remains focused on the phenomenon of origination with regard to the body, remains focused on the phenomenon of passing away with regard to the body, remains focused on the phenomenon of origination & passing away with regard to the body—ardent, alert, & mindful—putting aside greed & distress with reference to the world.

He remains focused on the phenomenon of origination with regard to feelings...with regard to the mind...with regard to mental qualities, remains focused on the phenomenon of passing away with regard to mental qualities, remains focused on the phenomenon of origination & passing away with regard to mental qualities—ardent, alert, & mindful—putting aside greed & distress with reference to the world. This is called the development of the frame of reference.

And what is the path of practice to the development of the frames of reference? Just this noble eightfold path: right view, right resolve, right speech, right action, right livelihood, right effort, right mindfulness, right concentration. This is called the path of practice to the development of the frame of reference.

S.XLVII.40

§ 30. In Detail. This is the direct path for the purification of beings, for the overcoming of sorrow & lamentation, for the disappearance of pain & distress, for the attainment of the right method, & for the realization of Unbinding—in other words, the four frames of reference. Which four?

There is the case where a monk remains focused on the body in & of itself—ardent, alert, & mindful—putting aside greed & distress with reference to the world [§213]. He remains focused on feelings... mind...mental qualities in & of themselves—ardent, alert, & mindful—putting aside greed & distress with reference to the world.

BODY

And how does the monk remain focused on the body in & of itself?

[a] There is the case where a monk—having gone to the wilderness, to the foot of a tree, or to an empty building—sits down folding his legs crosswise, holding his body erect and setting mindfulness to the fore *[parimukhaṁ:* in the Abhidhamma, this is translated literally as "around the mouth"; in the Vinaya, the same term is used to mean the front of the chest]. Always mindful, he breathes in; mindful he breathes out.

Breathing in long, he discerns that he is breathing in long; or breathing out long, he discerns that he is breathing out long. Or breathing in short, he discerns that he is breathing in short; or breathing out short, he discerns that he is breathing out short. He trains himself to breathe in sensitive to the entire body and to breathe out sensitive to the entire body. He trains himself to breathe in calming bodily fabrication [the breath] and to breathe out calming bodily fabrication. Just as a skilled turner or his apprentice, when making a long turn, discerns that he is making a long turn, or when making a short turn discerns that he is making a short turn; in the same way the monk, when breathing in long, discerns that he is breathing in long; or breathing out short, he discerns that he is breathing out short.... He trains himself to breathe in calming bodily fabrication, and to breathe out calming bodily fabrication.

In this way he remains focused internally on the body in & of itself, or externally on the body in & of itself, or both internally & externally on the body in & of itself. Or he remains focused on the phenomenon of origination with regard to the body, on the phenomenon of passing away with regard to the body, or on the phenomenon of origination & passing away with regard to the body. Or his mindfulness that 'There is a body' is maintained to the extent of knowledge & recollection. And he remains unsustained by (not clinging to) anything in the world. This is how a monk remains focused on the body in & of itself.

[b] Furthermore, when walking, the monk discerns that he is walking. When standing, he discerns that he is standing. When sitting, he discerns that he is sitting. When lying down, he discerns that he is lying down. Or however his body is disposed, that is how he discerns it.

In this way he remains focused internally on the body in & of itself, or focused externally...unsustained by anything in the world. This is how a monk remains focused on the body in & of itself.

[c] Furthermore, when going forward & returning, he makes himself fully alert; when looking toward & looking away...when bending & extending his limbs...when carrying his outer cloak, his upper robe & his bowl...when eating, drinking, chewing, & savoring...when urinating & defecating...when walking, standing, sitting, falling asleep, waking up, talking, & remaining silent, he makes himself fully alert.

In this way he remains focused internally on the body in & of itself, or focused externally...unsustained by anything in the world. This is how a monk remains focused on the body in & of itself.

[d] Furthermore...just as if a sack with openings at both ends were full of various kinds of grain—wheat, rice, mung beans, kidney beans, sesame seeds, husked rice—and a man with good eyesight, pouring it out, were to reflect, 'This is wheat. This is rice. These are mung beans. These are kidney beans. These are sesame seeds. This is husked rice,' in the same way, monks, a monk reflects on this very body from the soles of the feet on up, from the crown of the head on down, surrounded by skin and full of various kinds of unclean things: 'In this body there are head hairs, body hairs, nails, teeth, skin, flesh, tendons, bones, bone marrow, kidneys, heart, liver, pleura, spleen, lungs, large intestines, small intestines, gorge, feces, bile, phlegm, pus, blood, sweat, fat, tears, skin-oil, saliva, mucus, fluid in the joints, urine.' [§66]

In this way he remains focused internally on the body in & of itself, or focused externally...unsustained by anything in the world. This is how a monk remains focused on the body in & of itself.

[e] Furthermore...just as a skilled butcher or his apprentice, having killed a cow, would sit at a crossroads cutting it up into pieces, the monk contemplates this very body—however it stands, however it is disposed—in terms of properties: 'In this body there is the earth property, the liquid property, the fire property, & the wind property.'

In this way he remains focused internally on the body in & of itself, or focused externally...unsustained by anything in the world. This is how a monk remains focused on the body in & of itself.

[f] Furthermore, as if he were to see a corpse cast away in a charnel ground—one day, two days, three days dead—bloated, livid, & festering, he applies it to this very body, 'This body, too: Such is its nature, such is its future, such its unavoidable fate'...

Or again, as if he were to see a corpse cast away in a charnel ground, picked at by crows, vultures, & hawks, by dogs, hyenas, & various other creatures...a skeleton smeared with flesh & blood, connected with tendons...a fleshless skeleton smeared with blood, connected with tendons...a skeleton without flesh or blood, connected with tendons...bones detached from their tendons, scattered in all directions—here a hand bone, there a foot bone, here a shin bone, there a thigh bone, here a hip bone, there a back bone, here a rib, there a chest bone, here a shoulder bone, there a neck bone, here a jaw bone, there a tooth, here a skull...the bones whitened, somewhat like the color of shells...piled up, more than a year old...decomposed into a powder: He applies it to this very body, 'This body, too: Such is its nature, such is its future, such its unavoidable fate.'

In this way he remains focused internally on the body in & of itself, or externally on the body in & of itself, or both internally & externally on the body in & of itself. Or he remains focused on the phenomenon of origination with regard to the body, on the phenomenon of passing away with regard to the body, or on the phenomenon of origination & passing away with regard to the body. Or his mindfulness that 'There is a body' is maintained to the extent of knowledge & recollection. And he remains unsustained by (not clinging to) anything in the world. This is how a monk remains focused on the body in & of itself.

FEELINGS

And how does a monk remain focused on feelings in & of themselves? There is the case where a monk, when feeling a painful feeling, discerns that he is feeling a painful feeling. When feeling a pleasant feeling, he discerns that he is feeling a pleasant feeling. When feeling a neither-painful-nor-pleasant feeling, he discerns that he is feeling a neither-painful-nor-pleasant feeling.

When feeling a painful feeling of the flesh, he discerns that he is feeling a painful feeling of the flesh. When feeling a painful feeling not of the flesh, he discerns that he is feeling a painful feeling not of the flesh. When feeling a pleasant feeling of the flesh, he discerns that he is feeling a pleasant feeling of the flesh. When feeling a pleasant feeling not of the flesh, he discerns that he is feeling a pleasant feeling not of the flesh. When feeling a neither-painful-nor-pleasant feeling of the flesh, he discerns that he is feeling a neither-painful-nor-pleasant feeling of the flesh. When feeling a neither-painful-nor-pleasant feeling not of the flesh, he discerns that he is feeling a neither-painful-nor-pleasant feeling not of the flesh.

In this way he remains focused internally on feelings in & of themselves, or externally on feelings in & of themselves, or both internally & externally on feelings in & of themselves. Or he remains focused on the phenomenon of origination with regard to feelings, on the phenomenon of passing away with regard to feelings, or on the phenomenon of origination & passing away with regard to feelings. Or his mindfulness that 'There are feelings' is maintained to the extent of knowledge & recollection. And he remains unsustained by (not clinging to) anything in the world. This is how a monk remains focused on feelings in & of themselves.

MIND

And how does a monk remain focused on the mind in & of itself? There is the case where a monk, when the mind has passion, discerns that the mind has passion. When the mind is without passion, he discerns that the mind is without passion. When the mind has aversion, he discerns that the mind has aversion. When the mind is without aversion, he discerns that the mind is without aversion. When the mind has delusion, he discerns that the mind has delusion. When the mind is without delusion, he discerns that the mind is without delusion.

When the mind is restricted, he discerns that the mind is restricted. When the mind is scattered, he discerns that the mind is scattered. When the mind is enlarged, he discerns that the mind is enlarged. When the mind is not enlarged, he discerns that the mind is not enlarged. When the mind is surpassed, he discerns that the mind is surpassed. When the mind is unsurpassed, he discerns that the mind is unsurpassed. When the mind is concentrated, he discerns that the mind is concentrated. When the mind is not concentrated, he discerns that the mind is not concentrated. When the mind is released, he discerns that the mind is released. When the mind is not released, he discerns that the mind is not released.

In this way he remains focused internally on the mind in & of itself, or externally on the mind in & of itself, or both internally & externally on the mind in & of itself. Or he remains focused on the phenomenon of origination with regard to the mind, on the phenomenon of passing away with regard to the mind, or on the phenomenon of origination & passing away with regard to the mind. Or his mindfulness that 'There is a mind' is maintained to the extent of knowledge & recollection. And he remains unsustained by (not clinging to) anything in the world. This is how a monk remains focused on the mind in & of itself.

MENTAL QUALITIES

And how does a monk remain focused on mental qualities in & of themselves?

[a] There is the case where a monk remains focused on mental qualities in & of themselves with reference to *the five hindrances.* And how does a monk remain focused on mental qualities in & of themselves with reference to the five hindrances? There is the case where, there being sensual desire present within, a monk discerns that 'There is sensual desire present within me.' Or, there being no sensual desire present within, he discerns that 'There is no sensual desire present within me.' He discerns how there is the arising of unarisen sensual desire. And he discerns how there is the abandoning of sensual desire once it has arisen. And he discerns how there is no further arising in the future of sensual desire that has been abandoned. (The same formula is repeated for the remaining hindrances: ill will, sloth & drowsiness, restlessness & anxiety, and uncertainty.)

In this way he remains focused internally on mental qualities in & of themselves, or externally on mental qualities in & of themselves, or both internally & externally on mental qualities in & of themselves. Or he remains focused on the phenomenon of origination with regard to mental qualities, on the phenomenon of passing away with regard to mental qualities, or on the phenomenon of origination & passing away with regard to mental qualities. Or his mindfulness that 'There are mental qualities' is maintained to the extent of knowledge & recollection. And he remains unsustained by (not clinging to) anything in the world. This is how a monk remains focused on mental qualities in & of themselves with reference to the five hindrances. [§§131-147; 159]

[b] Furthermore, the monk remains focused on mental qualities in & of themselves with reference to *the five aggregates for sustenance/clinging.* And how does he remain focused on mental qualities in & of themselves with reference to the five aggregates for sustenance/clinging? There is the case where a monk [discerns]: 'Such is form, such its origination, such its disappearance. Such is feeling... Such is perception...Such are fabrications...Such is consciousness, such its origination, such its disappearance.'

In this way he remains focused internally on the mental qualities in & of themselves, or focused externally...unsustained by anything in the world. This is how a monk remains focused on mental qualities in & of themselves with reference to the five aggregates for sustenance/clinging. [§§149; 170; 173; 199-207]

[c] Furthermore, the monk remains focused on mental qualities in & of themselves with reference to *the sixfold internal & external sense media.* And how does he remain focused on mental qualities in & of themselves with reference to the sixfold internal & external sense media? There is the case where he discerns the eye, he discerns forms, he discerns the fetter that arises dependent on both. He discerns how there is the arising of an unarisen fetter. And he discerns how there is the abandoning of a fetter once it has arisen. And he discerns how there is no further appearance in the future of a fetter that has been abandoned. (Similarly with the ear, nose, tongue, body, & intellect.)

In this way he remains focused internally on the mental qualities in & of themselves, or focused externally...unsustained by anything in the world. This is how a monk remains focused on mental qualities in & of themselves with reference to the sixfold internal & external sense media.

[d] Furthermore, the monk remains focused on mental qualities in & of themselves with reference to *the seven factors of awakening.* And how does he remain focused on mental qualities in & of themselves with reference to the seven factors of awakening? There is the case where, there being mindfulness as a factor of awakening present within, he discerns that 'Mindfulness as a factor of awakening is present within me.' Or, there being no mindfulness as a factor of awakening present within, he discerns that 'Mindfulness as a factor of awakening is not present within me.' He discerns how there is the arising of unarisen mindfulness as a factor of awakening. And he discerns how there is the culmination of the development of mindfulness as a factor of awakening once it has arisen. (The same formula is repeated for the remaining factors of awakening: analysis of qualities, persistence, rapture, serenity, concentration, & equanimity.)

In this way he remains focused internally on mental qualities in & of themselves, or externally...unsustained by (not clinging to) anything in the world. This is how a monk remains focused on mental qualities in & of themselves with reference to the seven factors of awakening.

[e] Furthermore, the monk remains focused on mental qualities in & of themselves with reference to *the four noble truths.* And how does he remain focused on mental qualities in & of themselves with reference to the four noble truths? There is the case where he discerns, as it is actually present, that 'This is stress...This is the origination of

stress...This is the cessation of stress...This is the way leading to the cessation of stress."

In this way he remains focused internally on mental qualities in & of themselves, or externally on mental qualities in & of themselves, or both internally & externally on mental qualities in & of themselves. Or he remains focused on the phenomenon of origination with regard to mental qualities, on the phenomenon of passing away with regard to mental qualities, or on the phenomenon of origination & passing away with regard to mental qualities. Or his mindfulness that 'There are mental qualities' is maintained to the extent of knowledge & recollection. And he remains unsustained by (not clinging to) anything in the world. This is how a monk remains focused on mental qualities in & of themselves with reference to the four noble truths. [§§184-240]

Now, if anyone would develop these four frames of reference in this way for seven years, then one of two fruits can be expected for him: either gnosis [the knowledge of Awakening] right here & now, or—if there be any remnant of clinging/sustenance—non-return.

Let alone seven years. If anyone would develop these four frames of reference in this way for six years...five...four...three...two years...one year...seven months...six months...five...four...three...two months... one month...half a month, then one of two fruits can be expected for him: either gnosis right here & now, or—if there be any remnant of clinging/sustenance—non-return.

Let alone half a month. If anyone would develop these four frames of reference in this way for seven days,then one of two fruits can be expected for him: either gnosis right here & now, or—if there be any remnant of clinging/sustenance—non-return.

'This is the direct path for the purification of beings, for the overcoming of sorrow & lamentation, for the disappearance of pain & distress, for the attainment of the right method, & for the realization of Unbinding—in other words, the four frames of reference.' Thus was it said, and in reference to this was it said.

M.10

§ 31. In practice. Now, in what way does a monk develop & pursue mindfulness of in-&-out breathing so that the four frames of reference are brought to culmination?

On whatever occasion a monk breathing in long discerns that he is breathing in long; or breathing out long, discerns that he is breathing out long; or breathing in short, discerns that he is breathing in short; or breathing out short, discerns that he is breathing out short; trains himself to breathe in...&... out sensitive to the entire body; trains himself to breathe in...&...out calming bodily fabrication: On that occasion the monk remains focused on the *body* in & of itself—ardent, alert, & mindful—subduing greed & distress with reference to the world. I tell you, monks, that this—the in-&-out breath—is classed as a body among bodies, which is why the monk on that occasion remains focused on the body in & of itself—ardent, alert, & mindful—putting aside greed & distress with reference to the world.

On whatever occasion a monk trains himself to breathe in...&...out sensitive to rapture; trains himself to breathe in...&...out sensitive to pleasure; trains himself to breathe in...&...out sensitive to mental fabrication; trains himself to breathe in...&...out calming mental fabrication: On that occasion the monk remains focused on *feelings* in & of themselves—ardent, alert, & mindful—subduing greed & distress with reference to the world. I tell you, monks, that this—close attention to in-&-out breaths—is classed as a feeling among feelings, which is why the monk on that occasion remains focused on feelings in & of themselves—ardent, alert, & mindful—putting aside greed & distress with reference to the world.

On whatever occasion a monk trains himself to breathe in...&...out sensitive to the mind; trains himself to breathe in...&...out satisfying the mind; trains himself to breathe in...&...out steadying the mind; trains himself to breathe in...&...out releasing the mind: On that occasion the monk remains focused on the *mind* in & of itself—ardent, alert, & mindful—subduing greed & distress with reference to the world. I don't say that there is mindfulness of in-&-out breathing in one of confused mindfulness and no alertness, which is why the monk on that occasion remains focused on the mind in & of itself—ardent, alert, & mindful—putting aside greed & distress with reference to the world.

On whatever occasion a monk trains himself to breathe in...&...out focusing on inconstancy; trains himself to breathe in...&...out focusing on dispassion; trains himself to breathe in...&...out focusing on cessation; trains himself to breathe in...&...out focusing on relinquishment: On that occasion the monk remains focused on *mental qualities* in & of themselves—ardent, alert, & mindful—subduing greed & distress with reference to the world. He who sees clearly with discernment the abandoning of greed & distress is one who oversees with equanimity, which is why the monk on that occasion remains focused on mental qualities in & of themselves—ardent, alert, & mindful—putting aside greed & distress with reference to the world.

This is how developing & pursuing mindfulness of in-&-out breathing brings the four frames of reference to culmination.

M.118 {S.LIV.10}

§ 32. Internal & External. There is the case where a monk remains focused internally on the body in & of itself—ardent, alert, & mindful—putting aside greed & distress with reference to the world. As he remains focused internally on the body in & of itself, he becomes rightly concentrated there, and rightly clear. Rightly concentrated there and rightly clear, he gives rise to knowledge & vision externally of the bodies of others.

He remains focused internally on feelings in & of themselves—ardent, alert, & mindful—putting aside greed & distress with reference to the world. As he remains focused internally on feelings in & of themselves, he becomes rightly concentrated there, and rightly clear. Rightly concentrated there and rightly clear, he gives rise to knowledge & vision externally of the feelings of others.

He remains focused internally on the mind in & of itself—ardent, alert, & mindful—putting aside greed & distress with reference to the world. As he remains focused internally on the mind in & of itself, he becomes rightly concentrated there, and rightly clear. Rightly concentrated there and rightly clear, he gives rise to knowledge & vision externally of the minds of others.

He remains focused internally on mental qualities in & of themselves—ardent, alert, & mindful—putting aside greed & distress with reference to the world. As he remains focused internally on mental qualities in & of themselves, he becomes rightly concentrated there, and rightly clear. Rightly concentrated there and rightly clear, he gives rise to knowledge & vision externally of the mental qualities of others.

D.18

§ 33. Mindfulness & Concentration. Having abandoned the five hindrances—imperfections of awareness that weaken discernment—the monk remains focused on the body in & of itself—ardent, alert, & mindful—putting aside greed & distress with reference to the world. He remains focused on feelings...mind...mental qualities in & of themselves—ardent, alert, & mindful—putting aside greed & distress with reference to the world. Just as if an elephant trainer were to plant a large post in the ground and were to bind a forest elephant to it by the neck in order to break it of its forest habits, its forest memories & resolves, its distraction, fatigue, & fever over leaving the forest, to make it delight in the town and to inculcate in it habits congenial to human beings; in the same way, these four frames of reference are bindings for the awareness of the noble disciple, to break him of his household habits, his household memories & resolves, his distraction, fatigue, & fever over leaving the household life, for the attainment of the right method and the realization of Unbinding.

Then the Tathagata trains him further: 'Come, monk, remain focused on the body in & of itself, but do not think any thoughts connected with the body. Remain focused on feelings in & of themselves, but do not think any thoughts connected with feelings. Remain focused on the mind in & of itself, but do not think any thoughts connected with mind. Remain focused on mental qualities in & of themselves, but do not think any thoughts connected with mental qualities.' With the stilling of directed thought & evaluation, he enters the second jhana....

M.125

§ 34. Monks, those who are new, not long gone-forth, only recently come to this doctrine & discipline, should be roused, encouraged, & exhorted by you to develop the four frames of reference [in this way]:

'Come, friends, remain focused on the body in & of itself—being ardent, alert, with your minds unified, clear, concentrated, & single-minded for knowledge of the body as it actually is. Remain focused on feelings in & of themselves...focused on the mind in & of itself... focused on mental qualities in & of themselves—being ardent, alert, one-pointed, with your minds unified, clear, concentrated, & single-minded for knowledge of mental qualities as they actually are.'

Monks, even those who are learners [streamwinners to non-returners] —who have yet to attain their hearts' desire, who stay resolved on the unsurpassed security from bondage—even they remain focused on the body in & of itself—being ardent, alert, one-pointed, with their minds unified, clear, concentrated, & single-minded for complete comprehension of the body. They remain focused on feelings in & of themselves...focused on the mind in & of itself...focused on mental qualities in & of themselves—being ardent, alert, one-pointed, with their minds unified, clear, concentrated, & single-minded for complete comprehension of mental qualities.

Even those who are Arahants—whose mental effluents are ended, who have reached fulfillment, done the task, laid down the burden, attained the true goal, totally destroyed the fetter of becoming, and who are released through right gnosis—even they remain focused on the body in & of itself—being ardent, alert, one-pointed, with their minds unified, clear, concentrated, & single-minded, disjoined from the body.

They remain focused on feelings in & of themselves...focused on the mind in & of itself...focused on mental qualities in & of themselves—being ardent, alert, one-pointed, with their minds unified, clear, concentrated, & single-minded, disjoined from mental qualities.

So even those who are new, not long gone-forth, only recently come to this doctrine & discipline, should be roused, encouraged, & exhorted by you to develop the four frames of reference [in this way].

S.XLVII.4

§ 35. Taking Note. Suppose that there is a foolish, inexperienced, unskillful cook who has presented a king or a king's minister with various kinds of curry: mainly sour, mainly bitter, mainly peppery, mainly sweet, alkaline or non-alkaline, salty or non-salty. He does not take note of (lit: pick up on the theme of) his master, thinking, 'Today my master likes this curry, or he reaches out for that curry, or he takes a lot of this curry, or he praises that curry'....As a result, he is not rewarded with clothing or wages or gifts. Why is that? Because the foolish, inexperienced, unskillful cook does not pick up on the theme of his own master.

In the same way, there are cases where a foolish, inexperienced, unskillful monk remains focused on the body in & of itself—ardent, alert, & mindful—putting aside greed & distress with reference to the world. As he remains thus focused on the body in & of itself, his mind does not become concentrated, his defilements [Comm: the five Hindrances] are not abandoned. He does not take note of that fact (does not pick up on that theme). He remains focused on feelings in & of themselves...the mind in & of itself...mental qualities in & of themselves—ardent, alert, & mindful—putting aside greed & distress with reference to the world. As he remains thus focused on mental qualities in & of themselves, his mind does not become concentrated, his defilements are not abandoned. He does not take note of that fact. As a result, he is not rewarded with a pleasant abiding here & now, nor with mindfulness & alertness. Why is that? Because the foolish, inexperienced, unskillful monk does not take note of his own mind (does not pick up on the theme of his own mind).

Now suppose that there is a wise, experienced, skillful cook who has presented a king or a king's minister with various kinds of curry.... He takes note of his master, thinking, 'Today my master likes this curry, or he reaches out for that curry, or he takes a lot of this curry or he praises that curry'....As a result, he is rewarded with clothing, wages, & gifts. Why is that? Because the wise, experienced, skillful cook picks up on the theme of his own master.

In the same way, there are cases where a wise, experienced, skillful monk remains focused on the body in & of itself...feelings in & of themselves...the mind in & of itself...mental qualities in & of themselves—ardent, alert, & mindful—putting aside greed & distress with reference to the world. As he remains thus focused on mental qualities in & of themselves, his mind becomes concentrated, his defilements are abandoned. He takes note of that fact. As a result, he is rewarded with a pleasant abiding here & now, together with mindfulness & alertness. Why is that? Because the wise, experienced, skillful monk picks up on the theme of his own mind.

S.XLVII.8

§ 36. Directing & Not Directing the Mind. Ananda, if a monk or nun remains with mind well established in the four frames of reference, he/she may be expected to realize greater-than-ever distinction.

There is the case of a monk who remains focused on the body in & of itself—ardent, alert, & mindful—putting aside greed & distress with reference to the world. As he remains thus focused on the body in & of itself, a fever based on the body arises within his body, or there is sluggishness in his awareness, or his mind becomes scattered externally. He should then direct his mind to any inspiring theme [Comm: such as recollection of the Buddha]. As his mind is directed to any inspiring theme, delight arises within him. In one who feels delight, rapture arises. In one whose mind is enraptured, the body grows serene. His body serene, he feels pleasure. As he feels pleasure, his mind grows concentrated. He reflects, 'I have attained the aim to which my mind was directed. Let me withdraw [my mind from the inspiring theme]. He withdraws & engages neither in directed thought nor in evaluation. He discerns, 'I am not thinking or evaluating. I am inwardly mindful & at ease.'

Furthermore, he remains focused on feelings...mind...mental qualities in & of themselves—ardent, alert, & mindful—putting aside greed & distress with reference to the world. As he remains thus focused on mental qualities in & of themselves, a fever based on mental qualities arises within his body, or there is sluggishness in his awareness, or his mind becomes scattered externally. He should then direct his mind to any inspiring theme. As his mind is directed to any inspiring theme, delight arises within him. In one who feels delight, rapture arises. In one whose mind is enraptured, the body grows serene. His body serene, he is sensitive to pleasure. As he feels pleasure, his mind grows concentrated. He reflects, 'I have attained the aim to which my mind was directed. Let me withdraw. He withdraws & engages neither in directed thought nor in evaluation. He discerns, 'I am not thinking or evaluating. I am inwardly mindful & at ease.'

This, Ananda, is development based on directing. And what is development based on not directing? A monk, when not directing his mind to external things, discerns, 'My mind is not directed to external things. It is not attentive to what is in front or behind. It is released & undirected. And furthermore I remain focused on the body in & of itself. I am ardent, alert, mindful, & at ease.

When not directing his mind to external things, he discerns, 'My mind is not directed to external things. It is not attentive to what is in front or behind. It is released & undirected. And furthermore I remain focused on feelings... mind...mental qualities in & of themselves. I am ardent, alert, mindful, & at ease.

This, Ananda, is development based on not directing.

Now, Ananda, I have taught you development based on directing and development based on not directing. What a teacher should do out of compassion for his disciples, seeking their welfare, that I have done for you. Over there are [places to sit at] the foot of trees. Over there are empty dwellings. Practice jhana, Ānanda. Do not be heedless. Do not be remorseful in the future. That is our instruction to you all.

S.XLVII.10

§ 37. Proper Range 1. Once a hawk suddenly swooped down on a quail and seized it. Then the quail, as it was being carried off by the hawk, lamented, 'O, just my bad luck and lack of merit that I was wandering out of my proper range and into the territory of others! If only I had kept to my proper range today, to my own ancestral territory, this hawk would have been no match for me in battle.'

'But what is your proper range?' the hawk asked. 'What is your own ancestral territory?'

'A newly plowed field with clumps of earth all turned up.'

So the hawk, without bragging about its own strength, without mentioning its own strength, let go of the quail. 'Go, quail, but even when you have gone there you won't escape me.'

Then the quail, having gone to a newly plowed field with clumps of earth all turned up and climbing up on top of a large clump of earth, stood taunting the hawk, 'Now come and get me, you hawk! Now come and get me, you hawk!'

So the hawk, without bragging about its own strength, without mentioning its own strength, folded its two wings and suddenly swooped down toward the quail. When the quail knew, 'The hawk is coming at me full speed,' it slipped behind the clump of earth, and right there the hawk shattered its breast.

This is what happens to anyone who wanders into what is not his proper range and is the territory of others.

For this reason, you should not wander into what is not your proper range and is the territory of others. In one who wanders into what is not his proper range and is the territory of others, Māra gains an opening, Mara gains a foothold. And what, for a monk, is not his proper range and is the territory of others? The five strands of sensuality. Which five? Forms cognizable by the eye—agreeable, pleasing, charming, endearing, fostering desire, enticing. Sounds cognizable by the ear...Smells cognizable by the nose...Tastes cognizable by the tongue...Tactile sensations cognizable by the body—agreeable, pleasing, charming, endearing, fostering desire, enticing. These, for a monk, are not his proper range and are the territory of others.

Wander, monks, in what is your proper range, your own ancestral territory. In one who wanders in what is his proper range, his own ancestral territory, Mara gains no opening, Māra gains no foothold. And what, for a monk, is his proper range, his own ancestral territory? The four frames of reference....This, for a monk, is his proper range, his own ancestral territory.

S.XLVII.6

§ 38. Proper Range 2. There are in the Himalayas, the king of mountains, difficult, uneven areas where neither monkeys nor human beings wander. There are difficult, uneven areas where monkeys wander, but not human beings. There are level stretches of land, delightful, where both monkeys and human beings wander. In such spots hunters set a tar trap in the monkeys' tracks, in order to catch some monkeys. Those monkeys who are not foolish or careless by nature, when they see the tar trap, will keep their distance. But any monkey who is foolish & careless by nature comes up to the tar trap and grabs it with its paw, which then gets stuck there. Thinking, 'I'll free my paw,' he grabs it with his other paw. That too gets stuck. Thinking, 'I'll free both of my paws,' he grabs it with his foot. That too gets stuck. Thinking, 'I'll free both of my paws and my foot,' he grabs it with his other foot. That too gets stuck. Thinking, 'I'll free both of my paws and my feet as well,' he grabs it with his mouth. That too gets stuck. So the monkey, snared in five ways, lies there whimpering, having fallen on misfortune, fallen on ruin, a prey to whatever the hunter wants to do with him. Then the hunter, without releasing the monkey, skewers him right there, picks him up, and goes off as he likes.

This is what happens to anyone who wanders into what is not his proper range and is the territory of others. For this reason, you should not wander into what is not your proper range and is the territory of others....

S.XLVII.7

§ 39. Mindfulness of the Body. There is the case where a monk, seeing a form with the eye, is obsessed with pleasing forms, is repelled by unpleasing forms, and remains with body-mindfulness unestablished, with limited awareness. He does not discern, as it actually is present, the release of awareness, the release of discernment where any evil, unskillful mental qualities that have arisen utterly cease without remainder. (Similarly with ear, nose, tongue, body, & intellect.)

Just as if a person, catching six animals of different ranges, of different habitats, were to bind them with a strong rope. Catching a snake, he would bind it with a strong rope. Catching a crocodile...a bird... a dog...a hyena...a monkey, he would bind it with a strong rope. Binding them all with a strong rope, and tying a knot in the middle, he would set chase to them.

Then those six animals, of different ranges, of different habitats, would each pull toward its own range & habitat. The snake would pull, thinking, 'I'll go into the anthill.' The crocodile would pull, thinking, 'I'll go into the water.' The bird would pull, thinking, 'I'll fly up into the air.' The dog would pull, thinking, 'I'll go into the village.' The hyena would pull, thinking, 'I'll go into the charnel ground.' The monkey would pull, thinking, 'I'll go into the forest.' And when these six animals became internally exhausted, they would submit, they would surrender, they would come under the sway of whichever among them was the strongest. In the same way, when a monk whose mindfulness immersed in the body is undeveloped & unpursued, the eye pulls toward pleasing forms, while unpleasing forms are repellent. The ear pulls toward pleasing sounds...the nose pulls toward pleasing smells...the tongue pulls toward pleasing tastes...the body pulls toward pleasing tactile sensations...the mind pulls toward pleasing ideas, while unpleasing ideas are repellent. This, monks, is lack of restraint.

And what is restraint? There is the case where a monk, seeing a form with the eye, is not obsessed with pleasing forms, is not repelled by unpleasing forms, and remains with body-mindfulness established, with immeasurable awareness. He discerns, as it actually is present, the release of awareness, the release of discernment where all evil, unskillful mental qualities that have arisen utterly cease without remainder. (Similarly with ear, nose, tongue, body, & intellect.)

Just as if a person, catching six animals of different ranges, of different habitats, were to bind them with a strong rope...and tether them to a strong post or stake.

Then those six animals, of different ranges, of different habitats, would each pull toward its own range & habitat....And when these six animals became internally exhausted, they would stand, sit, or lie down right there next to the post or stake. In the same way, when a monk whose mindfulness immersed in the body is developed & pursued, the eye does not pull toward pleasing forms, and unpleasing forms are not repellent. The ear does not pull toward pleasing sounds...the nose does not pull toward pleasing smells...the tongue does not pull toward pleasing tastes...the body does not pull toward pleasing tactile sensations...the mind does not pull toward pleasing ideas, and unpleasing ideas are not repellent. This, monks, is restraint.

The strong post or stake is a term for mindfulness immersed in the body.

Thus you should train yourselves: 'We will develop mindfulness immersed in the body. We will pursue it, make it our vehicle, make it our home site. We will practice it, acquaint ourselves well with it, and set about it properly.' Thus you should train yourselves.

S.XXXV.206

§ 40. Suppose, monks, that a large crowd of people comes thronging together, saying, 'The beauty queen! The beauty queen!' And suppose that the beauty queen is highly accomplished at singing & dancing, so that an even greater crowd comes thronging, saying, 'The beauty queen is singing! The beauty queen is dancing!' Then a man comes along, desiring life & shrinking from death, desiring pleasure & abhorring pain. They say to him, 'Now look here, mister. You must take this bowl filled to the brim with oil and carry it on your head in between the great crowd & the beauty queen. A man with a raised sword will follow right behind you, and wherever you spill even a drop of oil, right there will he cut off your head.' Now what do you think, monks: Will that man, not paying attention to the bowl of oil, let himself get distracted outside?

No, lord.

I have given you this parable to convey a meaning. The meaning is this: The bowl filled to the brim with oil stands for mindfulness immersed in the body. Thus you should train yourselves: 'We will develop mindfulness immersed in the body. We will pursue it, make it our vehicle, make it our home site. We will practice it, acquaint ourselves well with it, and set about it properly.' Thus you should train yourselves.

S.XLVII.20

§ 41. With mindfulness immersed in the body
well established
Restrained with respect to the six
media of contact
Always concentrated, the monk
can know Unbinding for himself.

Ud.III.5

§ 42. Whoever pervades the great ocean with his awareness encompasses whatever rivulets flow down into the ocean. In the same way, whoever develops & pursues mindfulness immersed in the body encompasses whatever skillful qualities are on the side of clear knowing.

When one thing is practiced & pursued, the body is calmed, the mind is calmed, thinking & evaluating are stilled, and all qualities on the side of clear knowing go to the culmination of their development. Which one thing? Mindfulness immersed in the body.

When one thing is practiced & pursued, ignorance is abandoned, clear knowing arises, the conceit 'I am' is abandoned, latent tendencies are uprooted, fetters are abandoned. Which one thing? Mindfulness immersed in the body.

Those who do not taste mindfulness of the body do not taste the Deathless. Those who taste mindfulness of the body taste the Deathless.

Those who are heedless of mindfulness of the body are heedless of the Deathless.

Those who comprehend mindfulness of the body comprehend the Deathless.

A.I.225, 227, 230,
235, 239, 240

§ 43. **The Deathless.** There are these four frames of reference. Which four? There is the case where a monk remains focused on the body in & of itself—ardent, alert, & mindful—putting aside greed & distress with reference to the world. As he remains focused on the body in & of itself, he abandons desire with regard to the body. As he abandons desire with regard to the body, he realizes the Deathless.

He remains focused on feelings in & of themselves...mind in & of itself... mental qualities in & of themselves—putting aside greed & distress with reference to the world. As he remains focused on mental qualities in & of themselves, he abandons desire with regard to mental qualities. As he abandons desire with regard to mental qualities, he realizes the Deathless.

S.XLVII.37

§ 44. It is just as if there were a great pile of dust at a four-way intersection. If a cart or chariot came from the east, that pile of dust would be totally leveled. If a cart or chariot came from the west... from the north...from the south, that pile of dust would be totally leveled. In the same way, when a monk remains focused on the body in & of itself, then evil, unskillful qualities are totally leveled. If he remains focused on feelings...mind... mental qualities in & of themselves, then evil, unskillful qualities are totally leveled.

S.LIV.10

§ 45. Now when Ven. Anuruddha was meditating in solitude, this train of thought appeared in his awareness: 'Whoever neglects the four frames of reference neglects the noble path going to the right ending of stress. Whoever undertakes the four frames of reference undertakes the noble path going to the right ending of stress.'

Then Ven. Maha Moggallāna, as soon as he perceived with his awareness the train of thought in Ven. Anuruddha's awareness—as a strong man might stretch out his bent arm or bend his outstretched arm—appeared in front of Ven. Anuruddha and said to him, 'To what extent are the four frames of reference undertaken?'

Anuruddha: 'There is the case, my friend, of a monk who internally remains focused on the phenomenon of origination with regard to the body, remains focused on the phenomenon of passing away with regard to the body, remains focused on the phenomenon of origination & passing away with regard to the body—ardent, alert, & mindful—putting aside greed & distress with reference to the world.

'Externally he remains focused on the phenomenon of origination with regard to the body....

'Internally & externally he remains focused on the phenomenon of origination with regard to the body, remains focused on the phenomenon of passing away with regard to the body, remains focused on the phenomenon of origination & passing away with regard to the body—ardent, alert, & mindful—putting aside greed & distress with reference to the world.

'If he wants, he remains percipient of loathsomeness in the presence of what is not loathsome. If he wants, he remains percipient of unloathsomeness in the presence of what is loathsome. If he wants, he remains percipient of loathsomeness in the presence of what is not loathsome & what is. If he wants, he remains percipient of unloathsomeness in the presence of what is loathsome & what is not. If he wants—in the presence of what is loathsome & what is not—cutting himself off from both, he remains equanimous, alert, & mindful. [§§98; 181]

(Similarly with regard to feelings, mind & mental qualities.)

'It is to this extent, my friend, that the four frames of reference are undertaken....'

S.LII.1

§ 46. It is good for a monk if, at the appropriate times, he remains percipient of loathsomeness in the presence of what is not loathsome. It is good if, at the appropriate times, he remains percipient of unloathsomeness in the presence of what is loathsome....percipient of loathsomeness in the presence of what is not loathsome & what is...percipient of unloathsomeness in the presence of what is loathsome & what is not. It is good if, at the appropriate times—in the presence of what is loathsome & what is not—cutting himself off from both, he remains equanimous, alert, & mindful.

Now, with what purpose should a monk remain percipient of loathsomeness in the presence of what is not loathsome? 'Don't let passion arise within me in the presence of things that excite passion.' With this purpose should a monk remain percipient of loathsomeness in the presence of what is not loathsome.

And with what purpose should a monk remain percipient of unloathsomeness in the presence of what is loathsome? 'Don't let aversion arise within me in the presence of things that excite aversion'....

And with what purpose should a monk remain percipient of loathsomeness in the presence of what is not loathsome & what is? 'Don't let passion arise within me in the presence of things that excite passion. Don't let aversion arise within me in the presence of things that excite aversion'....

And with what purpose should a monk remain percipient of unloathsomeness in the presence of what is loathsome & what is not? 'Don't let aversion arise within me in the presence of things that excite aversion. Don't let passion arise within me in the presence of things that excite passion'....

And with what purpose should a monk—in the presence of what is loathsome & what is not—cutting himself off from both, remain equanimous, alert, & mindful? 'Don't let passion—in any object, in any place, in any amount—arise within me in the presence of things that excite passion. Don't let aversion—in any object, in any place, in any amount—arise within me in the presence of things that excite aversion. Don't let delusion—in any object, in any place, in any amount—arise within me in the presence of things that excite delusion.' With this purpose should a monk—in the presence of what is loathsome & what is not—cutting himself off from both, remain equanimous, alert, & mindful. [§§98; 181]

A.V.144

§ 47. Protecting Oneself & Others. Once upon a time, monks, a bamboo acrobat, having erected a bamboo pole, addressed his assistant, Frying Pan: 'Come, my dear Frying Pan. Climb up the bamboo pole and stand on my shoulders.'

'As you say, Master,' Frying Pan answered the bamboo acrobat and, climbing the bamboo pole, stood on his shoulders.

So then the bamboo acrobat said to his assistant, 'Now you watch after me, my dear Frying Pan, and I'll watch after you. Thus, protecting one another, watching after one another, we'll show off our skill, receive our reward, and come down safely from the bamboo pole.'

When he had said this, Frying Pan said to him, 'But that won't do at all, Master. You watch after yourself, and I'll watch after myself, and thus with each of us protecting ourselves, watching after ourselves, we'll show off our skill, receive our reward, and come down safely from the bamboo pole.'

What Frying Pan, the assistant, said to her Master was the right way in that case.

Monks, a frame of reference is to be practiced with the thought, 'I'll watch after myself.' A frame of reference is to be practiced with the thought, 'I'll watch after others.' When watching after oneself, one watches after others. When watching after others, one watches after oneself.

And how does one, when watching after oneself, watch after others? Through pursuing [the practice], through developing it, through devoting oneself to it. This is how one, when watching after oneself, watches after others.

And how does one, when watching after others, watch after oneself? Through endurance, through harmlessness, and through a mind of kindness & sympathy. This is how one, when watching after others, watches after oneself.

A frame of reference is to be practiced with the thought, 'I'll watch after myself.' A frame of reference is to be practiced with the thought, 'I'll watch after others.' When watching after oneself, one watches after others. When watching after others, one watches after oneself.

S.XLVII.19

§ 48. Then, when the Blessed One had entered the Rains Retreat, there arose a severe illness within him. Sharp & deadly were the pains, but he bore them mindfully, alert, & unperturbed. The thought occurred to him, 'It would not be proper for me to enter total Unbinding without addressing my attendants & without taking leave of the community of monks. Why don't I, suppressing this illness with persistence, remain resolved on the fabrication of life?' So he suppressed the illness with persistence & remained resolved on the fabrication of life. His illness abated.

Then he recovered from the illness. Soon after his recovery he came out of his dwelling & sat down in the shade of the building, on a seat prepared for him. Then Ven. Ānanda approached him and, on arrival, having bowed down to him, sat down to one side. As he was sitting there he said to the Blessed One, 'What a happy sight to see the Blessed One in comfort! What a happy sight to see the Blessed One at ease! Because of the Blessed One's sickness my own body felt as if it were drugged. I lost my bearings. Things were unclear to me. Yet I still took a measure of comfort in the thought that the Blessed One would not enter total Unbinding as long as he hadn't given at least some pronouncement concerning the community of monks.'

'What more does the community of monks want from me, Ānanda? I have taught the Dhamma without an inner or an outer version. The Tathagata has no closed fist with regard to teachings. Whoever has the thought, 'I will rule the community of monks,' or 'The community of monks is dedicated to me,' *he* should give some pronouncement concerning the community of monks. But the Tathagata has no such thoughts. So why should he give some pronouncement concerning the community of monks?

'I am old now, Ananda, & aged. My years have turned eighty. Just as an old cart is kept going with the help of bamboo strips, it seems to me as if the Tathagata's body is kept going with the help of bamboo strips. The only time the Tathagata's body feels at ease is when, not attending to any theme at all, and with the cessation of certain feelings, he enters & remains in the theme-less concentration of awareness. Therefore each of you should remain with your self as an island, your self as your refuge, without anything else as a refuge. Remain with the Dhamma as an island, the Dhamma as your refuge, without anything else as a refuge. And how does a monk remain with his self as an island, his self as his refuge, without anything else as a refuge? How does he remain with the Dhamma as an island, the Dhamma as his refuge, without anything else as a refuge? There is the case where a monk remains focused on the body in & of itself—ardent, alert, & mindful—putting aside greed & distress with reference to the world. He remains focused on feelings...mind... mental qualities in & of themselves—ardent, alert, & mindful—putting aside greed & distress with reference to the world. This is how a monk remains with his self as an island, his self as his refuge, without anything else as a refuge, with the Dhamma as an island, the Dhamma as his refuge, without anything else as a refuge. For those who—now or after I am gone—remain with their self as an island...the Dhamma as their refuge, without anything else as a refuge, they will be the highest of the monks who desire training.'

D.16

C. THE FOUR RIGHT EXERTIONS

The four activities included in this set show how effort can be applied to developing skillful qualities in the mind. The basic formula runs as follows:

> There is the case where a monk generates desire, endeavors, arouses persistence, upholds & exerts his intent:
>
> - for the sake of the non-arising of evil, unskillful qualities that have not yet arisen...
> - for the sake of the abandoning of evil, unskillful qualities that have arisen...
> - for the sake of the arising of skillful qualities that have not yet arisen...(and)
> - for the maintenance, non-confusion, increase, plenitude, development, & culmination of skillful qualities that have arisen.

These four aspects of effort are also termed guarding, abandoning, developing, and maintaining [§50]. All four play a necessary role in bringing the mind to Awakening, although in some cases they are simply four sides to a single process. The abandoning of unskillful mental qualities can frequently be accomplished simply by focusing on the development of skillful ones, such as mindfulness. The same principle can also act in reverse: in the skillful eradication of unskillful qualities, the skillfulness of the eradication is in and of itself the development of mindful discernment. As we will see when we deal with the seven factors of Awakening [II/G], the act of nourishing a factor of Awakening can in some cases simultaneously starve a hindrance, while the conscious starving of a hindrance can foster a factor of Awakening. Ultimately, though, right exertion requires more than simply abstaining from what is unskillful, for it must apply the basic factors of skillfulness—mindfulness and discernment—to gain an understanding of how even skillfulness can be transcended [§61].

Perhaps the most important point in developing right exertion is to realize that the effort to abandon unskillful qualities and to develop skillful qualities must be skillful itself. Unskillful efforts at eradicating unskillful states, even if well intended, can many times exacerbate problems instead of solving them. Treating hatred with hatred, for instance, is less effective than treating it with the kind of understanding developed in the second stage of frame-of-reference meditation [II/B], which sees into causes and effects, and learns how to manipulate causes properly so as to get the desired effects. For this reason, the basic formula for right exertion includes, both implicitly and explicitly, other factors of the path to ensure that the effort is skillfully applied. Three of the qualities that activate the mind in these exertions—desire, persistence, and intent—are also members of the bases of power [II/D], where they function as dominant factors in the attainment of concentration. The ability to discriminate between skillful and unskillful qualities, implicit in all of these exertions, requires a certain level of mindfulness and discernment. The skillful qualities that are mentioned most prominently as worthy of development are the seven factors of Awakening, which include mindfulness, analysis of mental qualities, and the factors of jhana, all of which must be reinvested in the process of right exertion to bring it to higher levels of finesse.

Passage §51 gives an idea of right exertion's range of application by listing seven ways in which unskillful qualities can be abandoned: seeing, restraining, using, tolerating, avoiding, destroying, and developing. The passage is deliberately vague as to which types of unskillful qualities respond to which type of treatment, for this is a point that each meditator must discover in practice for him or herself. This emphasis on personal exploration is crucial to the practice of right effort, for it encourages one to be sensitive to what can be discovered with one's own mindfulness and discernment. The same point applies to the question of how much effort must be applied to the practice. The Buddha notes that some meditators will have to undergo painful and slow practice, while others will find that their practice is painful and quick, pleasant and slow, or pleasant and quick [§§84-85]. Thus each has to adjust the effort applied to the practice accordingly. This need for differing levels of effort depends not only on the individual, but also on the situation. In some cases, simply watching an unskillful quality with equanimity will be enough to make it go away; in other cases, one has to exert a conscious effort to get rid of it [§§58-59]. Thus, through observation, one will realize that skillful effort has no room for doctrinaire approaches. The polar extremes of constant exertion to the point of exhaustion and its opposite, a knee-jerk fear of "efforting," are both misguided here, as is the seemingly "middle" way of moderation in all things. The true middle way means tuning one's efforts to one's abilities and to the task at hand [§86]. In some cases, this entails an all-out effort; in others, simple watchfulness. The ability to sense what kind and what level of effort is appropriate in any given situation is an important element in developing the basic requirements for skill—mindfulness and discernment—by putting them to use.

We have already noted that right exertion is equivalent to the factor of ardency in frame-of-reference meditation [II/B]. In the first stage of that practice, right exertion functions by keeping the mind with its frame of reference, and warding off unskillful mental qualities that would make it abandon that frame. In the second stage, the function of exertion becomes more refined: warding off the tendency to get involved with "what" is arising and passing away, and keeping the mind applied to its task of manipulating, observing, and mastering the **process** of origination and passing away as one steers the mind to the stillness of jhana. In the third stage, the function of exertion becomes finer yet, as it maintains a basic "empty" or radically phenomenological awareness of the frame of reference in order to bring the mind to the state of non-fashioning appropriate for the process of Awakening. The equipoise of this state—beyond the categories of effort or non-effort—explains the paradox expressed in §62, which states that the mind crosses the flood of rebirth by neither "pushing forward" nor "staying in place," an equipoise that embodies the ultimate skillfulness of right exertion in bringing the mind to a point beyond skill.

Implicit in this discussion of the effort involved in mastering skill to the point of its own transcendence is the fact that the goal of the practice is not an effort to return to a supposedly pure state of childlike awareness prior to social conditionings. Passage §61 makes this fact explicit. According to Buddhist analysis, the state of a child's mind is one, not of purity, but of ignorance filled with the potential for many unskilled qualities. These qualities show themselves in seemingly innocent ways simply because the infant's intellectual and physical powers are weak. Once those powers are strengthened, the mind's potentials become manifest. As one modern teacher has stated, the childlike mind is the source for the round of rebirth. If it were truly pure and fully aware, it would not be susceptible to unskillful social conditioning. Thus the way to purity lies, not in renouncing one's developed intellectual powers, but in developing those powers to higher levels of mastery and skill. This explains why right exertion is a necessary part of the practice.

§ 49. There are these four right exertions. Which four? There is the case where a monk generates desire, endeavors, arouses persistence, upholds & exerts his intent for the sake of the non-arising of evil, unskillful qualities that have not yet arisen...for the sake of the abandoning of evil, unskillful qualities that have arisen...for the sake of the arising of skillful qualities that have not yet arisen...(and) for the maintenance, non-confusion, increase, plenitude, development, & culmination of skillful qualities that have arisen. These are the four right exertions.

Just as the River Ganges flows to the east, slopes to the east, inclines to the east, in the same way when a monk develops & pursues the four right exertions, he flows to Unbinding, slopes to Unbinding, inclines to Unbinding.

S.XLIX.1

§ 50. There are these four exertions. Which four? The exertion to guard, the exertion to abandon, the exertion to develop, & the exertion to maintain.

And what is the exertion to guard? There is the case where a monk, on seeing a form with the eye, does not grasp at any theme or variations by which—if he were to dwell without restraint over the faculty of the eye—evil, unskillful qualities such as greed or distress might assail him. He practices with restraint. He guards the faculty of the eye. He achieves restraint with regard to the faculty of the eye. (Similarly with the ear, nose, tongue, body, & intellect.) This is called the exertion to guard.

And what is the exertion to abandon? There is the case where a monk does not acquiesce to a thought of sensuality that has arisen [in him]. He abandons it, destroys it, dispels it, wipes it out of existence. He does not acquiesce to a thought of ill will...a thought of harmfulness...any evil, unskillful qualities that have arisen [in him]. He abandons them, destroys them, dispels them, wipes them out of existence. This is called the exertion to abandon.

And what is the exertion to develop? There is the case where a monk develops the *mindfulness* factor of awakening dependent on seclusion...dispassion...cessation, resulting in letting go. He develops the *investigation of qualities* factor of awakening...the *persistence* factor of awakening...the *rapture* factor of awakening...the *serenity* factor of awakening...the *concentration* factor of awakening...the *equanimity* factor of awakening dependent on seclusion...dispassion...cessation, resulting in letting go. This is called the exertion to develop.

And what is the exertion to maintain? There is the case where a monk maintains a favorable theme of concentration—the skeleton perception, the worm-eaten perception, the livid perception, the festering perception, the falling-apart perception, the bloated perception. This is called the exertion to maintain. [§30]

These are the four exertions.

> Guarding & abandoning,
> developing & maintaining:
> these four exertions, taught
> by the Kinsman of the Sun
> [the Buddha].
>
> A monk who strives
> ardently at them
> reaches the ending
> of stress.

A.IV.14

§ 51. The ending of the effluents is for one who knows & sees, I tell you, not for one who does not know & does not see. For one who knows what & sees what? Appropriate attention & inappropriate attention. When a monk attends inappropriately, unarisen effluents arise, and arisen effluents increase. When a monk attends appropriately, unarisen effluents do not arise, and arisen effluents are abandoned. There are effluents that are to be abandoned by seeing, those that are to be abandoned by restraining, those that are to be abandoned by using, those that are to be abandoned by tolerating, those that are to be abandoned by avoiding, those that are to be abandoned by destroying, and those that are to be abandoned by developing.

And what are the effluents that are to be abandoned by seeing? There is the case where an uninstructed, run-of-the-mill person... does not discern what ideas are fit for attention, or what ideas are unfit for attention. This being so, he does not attend to ideas fit for attention, and attends [instead] to ideas unfit for attention. And what are the ideas unfit for attention that he attends to? Whatever ideas that, when a monk attends to them, the unarisen effluent of sensuality arises, and the arisen effluent of sensuality increases; the unarisen effluent of becoming...the unarisen effluent of ignorance arises, and the arisen effluent of ignorance increases....This is how he attends inappropriately: 'Was I in the past? Was I not in the past? What was I in the past? How was I in the past? Having been what, what was I in the past? Shall I be in the future? Shall I not be in the future? What shall I be in the future? How shall I be in the future? Having been what, what shall I be in the future?' Or else he is inwardly perplexed about the immediate present: 'Am I? Am I not? What am I? How am I? Where has this being come from? Where is it bound?'

As the monk attends inappropriately in this way, one of six kinds of view arises in him: The view *I have a self* arises in him as true & established, or the view *I have no self*...or the view *It is precisely by means of self that I perceive self*...or the view *It is precisely by means of self that I perceive not-self*...or the view *It is precisely by means of not-self that I perceive self* arises in him as true & established, or else he has a view like this: *This very self of mine—the knower that is sensitive here & there to the ripening of good & bad actions—is the self of mine that is constant, everlasting, eternal, not subject to change, and will endure as long as eternity.* This is called a thicket of views, a wilderness of views, a contortion of views, a writhing of views, a fetter of views. Bound by a fetter of views, the uninstructed run-of-the-mill person is not freed from birth, aging, & death, from sorrow, lamentation, pain, distress, & despair. He is not freed, I tell you, from stress. [§218]

The well-taught noble disciple...discerns what ideas are fit for attention, and what ideas are unfit for attention. This being so, he does not attend to ideas unfit for attention, and attends [instead] to ideas fit for attention....And what are the ideas fit for attention that he attends to? Whatever ideas that, when a monk attends to them, the unarisen effluent of sensuality does not arise, and the arisen effluent of sensuality is abandoned; the unarisen effluent of becoming...the unarisen effluent of ignorance does not arise, and the arisen effluent of ignorance is abandoned....He attends appropriately, *This is stress... This is the origination of stress...This is the cessation of stress...This is the way leading to the cessation of stress.* As he attends appropriately in this way, three fetters are abandoned in him: identity-view, doubt, and grasping at precepts & practices. These are called the effluents that are to be abandoned by seeing.

And what are the effluents that are to be abandoned by restraining? There is the case where a monk, reflecting appropriately, dwells restrained with the restraint of the eye-faculty. The effluents, vexation, or fever that would arise if he were to dwell unrestrained with the restraint of the eye-faculty do not arise for him when he dwells restrained with the restraint of the eye-faculty. (Similarly with the ear, nose, tongue, body, & intellect-faculties.) These are called the effluents that are to be abandoned by restraining.

And what are the effluents that are to be abandoned by using? There is the case where a monk, reflecting appropriately, uses the robe simply to counteract cold, to counteract heat, to counteract the touch of flies, mosquitoes, wind, sun, & reptiles; simply for the purpose of covering the parts of the body that cause shame.

Reflecting appropriately, he uses alms food, not playfully, nor for intoxication, nor for putting on bulk, nor for beautification; but simply for the survival & continuance of this body, for ending its afflictions, for the support of the holy life, thinking, 'Thus will I destroy old feelings [of hunger] and not create new feelings [from overeating]. I will maintain myself, be blameless, & live in comfort.

Reflecting appropriately, he uses lodging simply to counteract cold, to counteract heat, to counteract the touch of flies, mosquitoes, wind, sun, & reptiles; simply for protection from the inclemencies of weather and for the enjoyment of seclusion.

Reflecting appropriately, he uses medicinal requisites for curing the sick simply to counteract any pains of illness that have arisen and for maximum freedom from disease.

The effluents, vexation, or fever that would arise if he were not to use these things [in this way] do not arise for him when he uses them [in this way]. These are called the effluents that are to be abandoned by restraint.

And what are the effluents that are to be abandoned by tolerating? There is the case where a monk, reflecting appropriately, endures. He tolerates cold, heat, hunger, & thirst; the touch of flies, mosquitoes, wind, sun, & reptiles; ill-spoken, unwelcome words & bodily feelings that, when they arise, are painful, racking, sharp, piercing, disagreeable, displeasing, & menacing to life. The effluents, vexation, or fever that would arise if he were not to tolerate these things do not arise for him when he tolerates them. These are called the effluents that are to be abandoned by tolerating.

And what are the effluents that are to be abandoned by avoiding? There is the case where a monk, reflecting appropriately, avoids a wild elephant, a wild horse, a wild bull, a wild dog, a snake, a stump, a bramble patch, a chasm, a cliff, a cesspool, an open sewer. Reflecting appropriately, he avoids sitting in the sorts of unsuitable seats, wandering to the sorts of unsuitable habitats, and associating with the sorts of bad friends that would make his knowledgeable friends in the holy life suspect him of evil conduct. The effluents, vexation, or fever that would arise if he were not to avoid these things do not arise for him when he avoids them. These are called the effluents that are to be abandoned by avoiding.

And what are the effluents that are to be abandoned by destroying? There is the case where a monk, reflecting appropriately, does not tolerate an arisen thought of sensuality. He abandons it, destroys it, dispels it, & wipes it out of existence. (Similarly with thoughts of ill will, thoughts of cruelty, & evil, unskillful mental qualities.) The effluents, vexation, or fever that would arise if he were not to destroy these things do not arise for him when he destroys them. These are called the effluents that are to be abandoned by destroying.

And what are the effluents that are to be abandoned by developing? There is the case where a monk, reflecting appropriately, develops *mindfulness* as a factor of awakening dependent on seclusion... dispassion...cessation, resulting in letting go. He develops *analysis of qualities* as a factor of awakening...*persistence* as a factor of awakening... *rapture* as a factor of awakening...*serenity* as a factor of awakening... *concentration* as a factor of awakening...*equanimity* as a factor of awakening dependent on seclusion...dispassion...cessation, resulting in letting go. The effluents, vexation, or fever that would arise if he were not to develop these qualities do not arise for him when he develops them. These are called the effluents that are to be abandoned by developing.

When a monk's effluents that should be abandoned by seeing have been abandoned by seeing,

his effluents that should be abandoned by restraining have been abandoned by restraining,

his effluents that should be abandoned by using have been abandoned by using,

his effluents that should be abandoned by tolerating have been abandoned by tolerating,

his effluents that should be abandoned by avoiding have been abandoned by avoiding,

his effluents that should be abandoned by destroying have been abandoned by destroying,

his effluents that should be abandoned by developing have been abandoned by developing,

then he is called a monk who dwells restrained with the restraint of all the effluents. He has severed craving, thrown off the fetters, and—through the right penetration of conceit—has made an end of suffering & stress.

M.2

§ 52. These are the five factors for exertion. Which five?

[a] There is the case where a monk has conviction, is convinced of the Tathagata's Awakening: 'Indeed, the Blessed One is pure and

rightly self-awakened, consummate in knowledge & conduct, well-gone, an expert with regard to the world, unexcelled as a trainer for those people fit to be tamed, the Teacher of divine & human beings, awakened, blessed.' [§§71-72]

[b] The monk is free from illness & discomfort, endowed with good digestion—not too cold, not too hot, of moderate strength—fit for exertion.

[c] He is neither fraudulent nor deceitful. He declares himself to the Teacher or to his wise friends in the holy life in line with what he actually is.

[d] He keeps his persistence aroused for abandoning unskillful mental qualities and taking on skillful mental qualities. He is steadfast, solid in his effort, not shirking his duties with regard to skillful mental qualities.

[e] He is discerning, endowed with discernment leading to the arising of the goal—noble, penetrating, leading to the right ending of stress.

These are the five factors for exertion.

A.V.53

§ 53. With regard to internal factors, I do not envision any other single factor so helpful as appropriate attention for a monk who is a learner, who has not attained the goal but remains intent on the unexcelled security from bondage. A monk who attends appropriately abandons what is unskillful and develops what is skillful. [§96]

The quality of appropriate attention
in a learning monk:
Nothing else is so helpful
for attaining the supreme goal.
A monk, striving appropriately,
reaches the ending of stress.

Iti.16

§ 54. With regard to external factors, I do not envision any other single factor like friendship with admirable people in being so helpful for a monk who is a learner, who has not attained the goal but remains intent on the unexcelled security from bondage. A monk who is a friend with admirable people abandons what is unskillful and develops what is skillful. [§§115; 125]

A monk who is a friend
to admirable people,
—one reverential, respectful,
doing what his friends advise—

alert, mindful,
attains step by step
the ending of all fetters.

ITI.17

§ 55. A person without ardor, without concern, is incapable of self-awakening, incapable of Unbinding, incapable of attaining the unexcelled security from bondage. A person ardent & concerned is capable of self-awakening, capable of Unbinding, capable of attaining the unexcelled security from bondage.

Without ardor, without concern,
Lazy, with weak persistence,
Full of sloth & drowsiness,
Shameless, without respect:
This sort of monk is incapable
of touching the supreme self-awakening.

But whoever is mindful & wise,
absorbed in jhana,
ardent, concerned, & heedful,
cutting the fetter of birth & aging,
touches right here & how
the unexcelled self-awakening.

ITI.34

§ 56. Sariputta: It is said, friend, that a person without ardor, without concern, is incapable of self-awakening, incapable of Unbinding, incapable of attaining the unexcelled security from bondage. Now, how is a person without ardor, without concern, incapable of self-awakening, incapable of Unbinding, incapable of attaining the unexcelled security from bondage? And how is a person ardent & concerned capable of self-awakening, capable of Unbinding, capable of attaining the unexcelled security from bondage?

Maha Kassapa: There is the case where a monk thinks, 'The arising of unarisen evil, unskillful qualities would lead to what is unbeneficial,' yet he arouses no ardor. 'The non-abandoning of arisen evil, unskillful qualities would lead to what is unbeneficial,' yet he arouses no ardor. 'The non-arising of unarisen skillful qualities would lead to what is unbeneficial,' yet he arouses no ardor. 'The ceasing of arisen skillful qualities would lead to what is unbeneficial,' yet he arouses no ardor. This is what it means to be a person without ardor.

And how is one a person without concern? There is the case where a monk thinks, 'The arising of unarisen evil, unskillful qualities would lead to what is unbeneficial,' yet he feels no concern. 'The non-abandoning of arisen evil, unskillful qualities....The non-arising of unarisen skillful qualities....The ceasing of arisen skillful qualities would lead to what is unbeneficial,' yet he feels no concern. This is what it means to be a person without concern. This is how a person without ardor, without concern, is incapable of self-awakening, incapable of Unbinding, incapable of attaining the unexcelled security from bondage.

And how is a person ardent? There is the case where a monk thinks, 'The arising of unarisen evil, unskillful qualities would lead to what is unbeneficial,' and he arouses ardor. 'The non-abandoning of arisen evil, unskillful qualities...The non-arising of unarisen skillful qualities... The ceasing of arisen skillful qualities would lead to what is unbeneficial,' and he arouses ardor. This is what it means to be ardent.

And how is a person concerned? There is the case where a monk thinks, 'The arising of unarisen evil, unskillful qualities would lead to what is unbeneficial,' and he feels concern. 'The non-abandoning of arisen evil, unskillful qualities....The non-arising of unarisen skillful qualities....The ceasing of arisen skillful qualities would lead to what is unbeneficial,' and he feels concern. This is what it means to be concerned. This is how a person ardent & concerned is capable of self-awakening, capable of Unbinding, capable of attaining the unexcelled security from bondage.

S.XVI.2

§ 57. Sariputta: Imagine a bronze bowl brought back from a shop or a smith all covered with dust & dirt, that the owners would neither use nor clean, but would throw away in the dust. Wouldn't that bronze bowl eventually become even more dirty & defiled with time?

Maha Moggallana: Yes, my friend.

Sariputta: In the same way, when an individual with an internal blemish does not discern, as it actually is, that 'I have an internal blemish,' it can be expected of him that he will not generate desire, endeavor, or arouse persistence for the abandoning of that blemish. He will die with passion, aversion, delusion—blemished & with a mind defiled....

Now imagine a bronze bowl brought back from a shop or a smith all covered with dust & dirt, that the owners would both use & clean, and would not throw away in the dust. Wouldn't that bronze bowl eventually become clean & pure with time?

Maha Moggallana: Yes, my friend.

Sariputta: In the same way, when an individual with an internal blemish discerns, as it actually is, that 'I have an internal blemish,' it can be expected of him that he will generate desire, endeavor, & arouse persistence for the abandoning of that blemish. He will die without passion, aversion, delusion—unblemished & with a mind undefiled....

Now imagine a bronze bowl brought back from a shop or a smith all clean & pure, that the owners would neither use nor clean, but would throw away in the dust. Wouldn't that bronze bowl eventually become dirty & defiled with time?

Maha Moggallana: Yes, my friend.

Sariputta: In the same way, when an individual with no internal blemish does not discern, as it actually is, that 'I have no internal blemish,' it can be expected of him that he will attend to the theme of beauty. As he attends to the theme of beauty, passion will despoil his mind. He will die with passion, aversion, delusion—blemished & with a mind defiled....

Now imagine a bronze bowl brought back from a shop or a smith all clean & pure, that the owners would both use & clean, and would not throw away in the dust. Wouldn't that bronze bowl eventually become even more clean & pure with time?

Maha Moggallana: Yes, my friend.

Sariputta: In the same way, when an individual with no internal blemish discerns, as it actually is, that 'I have no internal blemish,' it can be expected of him that he will not attend to the theme of beauty. As he does not attend to the theme of beauty, passion will not despoil his mind. He will die without passion, aversion, delusion—unblemished & with a mind undefiled. This is the reason, this is the cause why, of the two individuals who are blemished, one [the first] is reckoned to be inferior, and the other superior...and why, of the two individuals who are unblemished, one [the first] is reckoned to be inferior, and the other superior.

Maha Moggallana: Now this word, 'blemish, blemish.' What is the meaning of blemish?

Sariputta: Consorting with evil, unskillful wishes—this is the meaning of 'blemish.'

M.5

§ 58. Even if a monk is not skilled in the ways of the minds of others (not skilled in reading the minds of others), he should train himself: 'I will be skilled in reading my own mind.'

And how is a monk skilled in reading his own mind? Imagine a young woman—or man—fond of adornment, examining the image of her own face in a bright, clean mirror or bowl of clear water: If she saw any dirt or blemish there, she would try to remove it. If she saw no dirt or blemish there, she would be pleased, her resolves fulfilled: 'How fortunate I am! How clean I am!' In the same way, a monk's self-examination is very productive in terms of skillful qualities [if he conducts it in this way]: Do I usually remain covetous or not? With thoughts of ill will or not? Overcome by sloth & drowsiness or not? Restless or not? Uncertain or gone beyond uncertainty? Angry or not? With soiled thoughts or unsoiled thoughts? With my body aroused or unaroused? Lazy or with persistence aroused? Unconcentrated or concentrated?'

If, on examination, a monk knows, 'I usually remain covetous, with thoughts of ill will, overcome by sloth & drowsiness, restless, uncertain, angry, with soiled thoughts, with my body aroused, lazy, or unconcentrated,' then he should put forth extra desire, effort, diligence, endeavor, undivided mindfulness, & alertness for the abandoning of those very same evil, unskillful qualities, just as when a person whose turban or head was on fire would put forth extra desire, effort, diligence, endeavor, undivided mindfulness, & alertness to put out the fire on his turban or head....

But if, on examination, a monk knows, 'I usually remain uncovetous, without thoughts of ill will...& concentrated,' then his duty is to make an effort in establishing ('tuning') those very same skillful qualities to a higher degree for the ending of the effluents.

A.X.51

§ 59. "And how is striving fruitful, how is exertion fruitful? There is the case where a monk, when not loaded down, does not load himself down with pain, nor does he reject pleasure that accords with the Dhamma, although he is not infatuated with that pleasure. He discerns that 'When I exert a [mental] fabrication against this cause of stress, then from the fabrication of *exertion* there is dispassion (fading away). When I look on with equanimity at that cause of stress, then from the development of *equanimity* there is dispassion. So he exerts a mental fabrication against the [first] cause of stress... and develops equanimity with regard to the [second] cause of stress.... Thus the stress [coming from any cause of the first sort] is abolished... & the stress [coming from any cause of the second sort] is abolished.

"Suppose that a man is in love with a woman, his mind ensnared with intense desire & passion. He sees her standing with another man, chatting, joking, & laughing. What do you think, monks: Would he...feel sorrow, lamentation, pain, distress, & despair?"

"Yes, lord...."

"Now suppose the thought were to occur to him, 'I am in love with this woman....When I see her standing with another man, chatting, joking, & laughing, I feel sorrow, lamentation, pain, distress, & despair. Why don't I abandon my desire & passion for that woman?' So he abandons his desire & passion for that woman, and afterwards sees her standing with another man, chatting, joking, & laughing. What do you think, monks: Would he...feel sorrow, lamentation, pain, distress, & despair?"

"No, lord...."

"In the same way, the monk, when not loaded down, does not load himself down with pain, nor does he reject pleasure that accords with the Dhamma, although he is not infatuated with that pleasure....He exerts a mental fabrication against the [first] cause of stress...and develops equanimity with regard to the [second] cause of stress.... Thus the stress [coming from any cause of the first sort] is abolished... & the stress [coming from any cause of the second sort] is abolished.

"Furthermore, the monk notices this: 'When I live according to my pleasure, unskillful mental qualities increase in me & skillful qualities decline. When I exert myself with stress & pain, though, unskillful qualities decline in me & skillful qualities increase. Why don't I exert myself with stress & pain?' So he exerts himself with stress & pain, and while he is exerting himself with stress & pain, unskillful qualities decline in him, & skillful qualities increase. Then at a later time he would no longer exert himself with stress & pain. Why is that? Because he has attained the goal for which he was exerting himself with stress & pain....

"Suppose that a fletcher were to heat & warm an arrow shaft between two flames, making it straight & pliable. Then at a later time he would no longer heat & warm the shaft between two flames, making it straight & pliable. Why is that? Because he has attained the goal for which he was heating & warming the shaft....In the same way, the monk...no longer exerts himself with stress & pain. Why is that? Because he has attained the goal for which he was exerting himself with stress & pain."

M.101

§ 60. Udayin, there are these four types of people to be found existing in the world. Which four? There is the case where a certain person is practicing for the abandoning & relinquishing of the paraphernalia of becoming. As he is practicing for the abandoning & relinquishing of the paraphernalia of becoming, memories & resolves associated with the paraphernalia of becoming assail him. He tolerates them. He does not abandon them, destroy them, dispel them, or wipe them out of existence. I tell you, Udāyin, that this sort of person is associated, not dissociated. Why is that? Because I have known the diversity of faculties with regard to this type of person.

Again, there is the case where a certain person practicing for the abandoning & relinquishing of the paraphernalia of becoming...is assailed by memories & resolves associated with the paraphernalia of becoming. He does not tolerate them. He abandons them, destroys them, dispels them, & wipes them out of existence. I tell you, Udāyin, that this sort of person is associated, not dissociated. Why is that? Because I have known the diversity of faculties with regard to this type of person.

Again, there is the case where a certain person is practicing for the abandoning & relinquishing of the paraphernalia of becoming.... Owing to lapses in mindfulness from time to time, he is assailed by memories & resolves associated with the paraphernalia of becoming. Slow is the arising of his mindfulness, but then he quickly abandons [those memories & resolves], destroys them, dispels them, & wipes them out of existence. Just as when two or three drops of water fall onto an iron pan heated all day: Slow is the falling of the drops of water, but they quickly vanish & disappear. In the same way...slow is the arising of his mindfulness, but then he quickly abandons [those memories & resolves], destroys them, dispels them, & wipes them out of existence. I tell you, Udāyin, that this sort of person is associated, not dissociated. Why is that? Because I have known the diversity of faculties with regard to this type of person. [§181]

Again, there is the case where a certain person, realizing that the paraphernalia of becoming are the root of suffering & stress, is without paraphernalia, released in the ending of paraphernalia. I tell you, Udāyin, that this sort of person is dissociated, not associated. Why is that? Because I have known the diversity of faculties with regard to this type of person.

M.66

§ 61. Pañcakaṅga the carpenter went to where Uggāhamāna, a follower of Muṇḍika the contemplative (or: the shaven contemplative—a Jain?), was staying and on arrival, after exchanging pleasantries, sat down to one side. As he was sitting there, Uggāhamāna said to him, "I describe an individual endowed with four qualities as being consummate in what is skillful, foremost in what is skillful, an invincible contemplative attained to the highest attainments. Which four? There is the case where he does no evil action with his body, speaks no evil speech, resolves on no evil resolve, and maintains himself with no evil means of livelihood. An individual endowed with these four qualities I designate as being consummate in what is skillful... an invincible contemplative attained to the highest attainments."

Then Pañcakaṅga the carpenter neither delighted in Uggahamana's words nor did he scorn them. Expressing neither delight nor scorn, he got up from his seat & left, thinking, 'I will learn the meaning of this statement in the presence of the Blessed One.'

Then the carpenter went to where the Blessed One was staying and on arrival, after bowing down to him, sat down to one side. As he was sitting there, he told the Blessed One the entire conversation he had had with Uggahamana.

When this was said, the Blessed One addressed Pañcakaṅga, saying, 'In that case, then according to Uggahamana's words a stupid baby boy, lying on its back, is consummate in what is skillful, foremost in what is skillful, an invincible contemplative attained to the highest attainments. For even the thought "body" does not occur to a stupid baby boy lying on its back, so from where would it do any evil action with its body, aside from a little kicking? Even the thought "speech" does not occur to it, so from where would it speak any evil speech, aside from a little crying? Even the thought "resolve" does not occur to it, so from where would it resolve on any evil resolve, aside from a little bad temper? Even the thought "livelihood" does not occur to it, so from where would it maintain itself with any evil means of livelihood, aside from its mother's milk? So according to Uggahamana's words a stupid baby boy, lying on its back, is...an invincible contemplative attained to the highest attainments.

'If an individual is endowed with these four qualities, I do not designate him as...an invincible contemplative attained to the highest attainments. Rather, he stands on the same level as a stupid baby boy lying on its back....

'I describe an individual endowed with ten qualities as being consummate in what is skillful, foremost in what is skillful, an invincible contemplative attained to the highest attainments. He should know from experience that "These are unskillful habits," I say. He should know from experience that "That is the cause of unskillful habits," I say. He should know from experience that "Here unskillful habits cease without remainder," I say. He should know from experience that "This sort of practice is the practice leading to the cessation of unskillful habits," I say.

'He should know from experience that "These are skillful habits"... "That is the cause of skillful habits"..."Here skillful habits cease without remainder"..."This sort of practice is the practice leading to the cessation of skillful habits," I say.

'He should know from experience that "These are unskillful resolves"... "That is the cause of unskillful resolves"..."Here unskillful resolves cease without remainder"..."This sort of practice is the practice leading to the cessation of unskillful resolves" I say.

'He should know from experience that "These are skillful resolves"... "That is the cause of skillful resolves"..."Here skillful resolves cease without remainder"..."This sort of practice is the practice leading to the cessation of skillful resolves," I say.

'Now what are unskillful habits? Unskillful bodily actions, unskillful verbal actions, evil means of livelihood....What is the cause of unskillful habits?...The mind....Which mind?—for the mind has many modes & permutations...Any mind with passion, aversion or delusion: That is the cause of unskillful habits. Now where do unskillful habits cease without remainder?...There is the case where a monk abandons wrong bodily conduct & develops right bodily conduct, abandons wrong verbal conduct & develops right verbal conduct, abandons wrong livelihood & maintains his life with right livelihood. This is where unskillful habits cease without remainder. And what sort of practice is the practice leading to the cessation of unskillful habits? There is the case where a monk generates desire, endeavors, arouses persistence, upholds & exerts his intent for the sake of the non-arising of evil, unskillful qualities that have not yet arisen...for the sake of the abandoning of evil, unskillful qualities that have arisen...for the sake of the arising of skillful qualities that have not yet arisen...(and) for the maintenance, non-confusion, increase, plenitude, development & culmination of skillful qualities that have arisen. This sort of practice is the practice leading to the cessation of unskillful habits.

'And what are skillful habits? Skillful bodily actions, skillful verbal actions, purity of livelihood....What is the cause of skillful habits?... The mind.... Which mind?—for the mind has many modes & permutations....Any mind without passion, without aversion, without delusion: That is the cause of skillful habits. Now where do skillful habits cease without remainder? ...There is the case where a monk is virtuous, but is not entirely defined by his virtue. He discerns, as it actually is, the release of awareness & release of discernment where his skillful habits cease without remainder. And what sort of practice is the practice leading to the cessation of skillful habits? There is the case where a monk generates desire...for the sake of the non-arising of evil, unskillful qualities that have not yet arisen...for the sake of the abandoning of evil, unskillful qualities that have arisen...for the sake of the arising of skillful qualities that have not yet arisen...(and) for the...development & culmination of skillful qualities that have arisen. This sort of practice is the practice leading to the cessation of skillful habits.

'And what are unskillful resolves? Being resolved on sensuality, on ill will, on harmfulness....What is the cause of unskillful resolves?... Perception....Which perception?—for perception has many modes & permutations....Any sensuality-perception, ill will-perception or harmfulness-perception: That is the cause of unskillful resolves. Now where do unskillful resolves cease without remainder?...There is the case where a monk, quite withdrawn from sensuality, withdrawn from unskillful mental qualities, enters & remains in the first jhana: rapture & pleasure born from withdrawal, accompanied by directed thought & evaluation. This is where unskillful resolves cease without remainder. And what sort of practice is the practice leading to the cessation of unskillful resolves? There is the case where a monk generates desire...for the sake of the non-arising of evil, unskillful qualities that have not yet arisen...for the sake of the abandoning of evil, unskillful qualities that have arisen...for the sake of the arising of skillful qualities that have not yet arisen...(and) for the...development & culmination of skillful qualities that have arisen. This sort of practice is the practice leading to the cessation of unskillful resolves.

'And what are skillful resolves? Being resolved on renunciation (freedom from sensuality), on non-ill will, on harmlessness....What is the cause of skillful resolves?...Perception....Which perception?—for perception has many modes & permutations....Any renunciation-perception, non-ill will-perception or harmlessness-perception: That is the cause of skillful resolves. Now where do skillful resolves cease without remainder?...There is the case where a monk, with the stilling of directed thought & evaluation, enters & remains in the second jhana: rapture & pleasure born of composure, unification of awareness free from directed thought & evaluation—internal assurance. This is where skillful resolves cease without remainder. And what sort of practice is the practice leading to the cessation of skillful resolves? There is the case where a monk generates desire...for the sake of the non-arising of evil, unskillful qualities that have not yet arisen...for the sake of the abandoning of evil, unskillful qualities that have arisen...for the sake of the arising of skillful qualities that have not yet arisen...(and) for the... development & culmination of skillful qualities that have arisen. This sort of practice is the practice leading to the cessation of skillful resolves.

'Now, an individual endowed with which ten qualities is one whom I describe as being consummate in what is skillful, foremost in what is skillful, an invincible contemplative attained to the highest attainments. He is endowed with the right view of one beyond training, the right resolve of one beyond training, the right speech...the right action...the right livelihood...the right effort...the right mindfulness... the right concentration... the right knowledge...the right release of one beyond training. [§106] An individual endowed with these ten qualities I designate as being consummate in what is skillful, foremost in what is skillful, an invincible contemplative attained to the highest attainments.'

That is what the Blessed One said. Glad at heart, Pañcakaṅga the carpenter delighted in the Blessed One's words.

M.78

§ 62. A deva: Tell me, dear sir, how you crossed over the flood.

The Buddha: I crossed over the flood without pushing forward, without staying in place.

The deva: But how did you cross over the flood without pushing forward, without staying in place?

The Buddha: When I pushed forward, I was whirled about. When I stayed in place, I sank. And so I crossed over the flood without pushing forward, without staying in place.

The deva:

At long last I see,
an honorable one, totally unbound,
who without pushing forward,
without staying in place,
has crossed over
the entanglements of the world.

S.I.1

D. THE FOUR BASES OF POWER

Iddhi, the Pali word translated here as "power," has so many meanings that no one English equivalent can do them all justice. Other equivalents that have been suggested include success, accomplishment, and prowess. In the context of the bases for power, however, the word specifically means the supranormal powers that can be developed through concentration, such as levitation, walking on water, clairaudience, clairvoyance, remembrance of past lives, the ability to read the minds of others, and the ending of mental effluents. In the Buddhist analysis, only the last of these powers is transcendent. It is the only one absolutely necessary on the path to Awakening. The others are optional and not always desirable, for an unawakened person might find that the attainment of any one of them can cause supranormal greed, aversion, or delusion to arise in the mind. The texts record cases where even Arahants, not fully sensitive to the effect that their actions might have on others, display their powers in inappropriate contexts. This was why the Buddha forbade his monastic disciples from displaying their powers before the laity. None of the displayable powers, he said, is any match for the wonder of a teaching that, like his, gave the promised results when put into practice [D.11].

Still, there is no denying that some people acquire these powers in the course of their meditation, and they need guidance in how to use them properly so that their powers can actually help, rather than hinder, their practice. This is the role that the standard formulae for the bases of power play in the teaching. They show how the mastery of any of the first five powers can be fit into the outline of frame-of-reference meditation [II/B] so that the process of mastery can lead to the sixth and most important power, the ending of the effluents, thus resulting in release.

The texts explain the bases of power in two standard formulae: brief and extended. The brief formula runs as follows:

> There is the case where a monk develops the base of power endowed with concentration founded on *desire* & the fabrications of exertion. He develops the base of power endowed with concentration founded on *persistence*...concentration founded on *intent*...concentration founded on *discrimination* & the fabrications of exertion.

One of the texts [§64] states that these formulae define the process whereby the bases of power are developed; another [§63] states that they are the bases of power themselves. The contradiction here can be resolved by noting that the first text defines the bases of power as "whatever practice leads to the attainment of power, the winning of power." Because these processes definitely lead to the attainment of power, they would count as at least part of the bases of power. The first text is probably alluding to the fact that there is more to the process, which is included in the extended formula, discussed below.

Each of these four bases has three component parts: the "fabrications of exertion" (which the texts equate with the four right exertions), concentration, and the mental quality—desire, persistence, intent, or discrimination—on which the concentration is based. According to §172, desire, persistence, and intent are present in all states of jhana. Thus the phrase "concentration based on desire" refers to a concentration in which all three qualities are present, but with desire dominant. We should note here that *desire* in this case means desire directed toward the goal of the practice. This desire does not count as craving, which as a cause of stress is directed at further states of becoming in the round of rebirth. Although the desire for Awakening, when it is not yet realized, can be a cause for frustration, that frustration is counted as a skillful emotion, as it leads to further efforts along the path [§179]. It is to be transcended, not by abandoning the desire, but by acting on it properly, as explained below, until gaining the desired results.

Discrimination, the fourth mental quality, is not always inherent in jhana, although when functioning as evaluation it plays a role in the first jhana, and is definitely present in the fifth factor of noble right concentration [§150], which leads to Awakening. Furthermore, the extended formula for the bases of power shows that discrimination is necessary for the thorough mastery of concentration based on desire, persistence, intent, or discrimination itself so that—in the course of gaining mastery—one develops mindful discernment into the causal patterns of the mind and so can reach Awakening.

We have already shown that the development of concentration involves the three qualities called for in the first stage of frames-of-reference meditation [II/B]: ardency (right exertion), alertness, and mindfulness. Thus the brief formula for the bases of power, as a description of concentration practice, can be equated with the first stage of frame-of-reference meditation.

Many popular Western writings criticize the four qualities listed in the bases of power—desire, persistence (effort), intent (will), and discrimination (the discriminating mind)—as enemies of proper meditation, both in that they interfere with the calming of the mind and are antithetical to the goal of the Unfabricated, which lies beyond desire, effort, and the categories of discrimination. The first part of the extended formula deals with the first of these criticisms.

> There is the case where a monk develops the base of power endowed with concentration founded on desire & the fabrications of exertion, thinking, 'This desire of mine will be neither overly sluggish nor overly active, neither inwardly restricted nor outwardly scattered.' (Similarly with concentration founded on persistence, intent, and discrimination.)

This passage shows that the problem lies, not in the desire, effort, intent, or discrimination, but in the fact that these qualities are unskillfully applied or improperly tuned to their task. If they were absent, the practice—if it could be called a practice—would stagnate from loss of direction or motivation. If they ran wild, they would interfere with mindful concentration. So the trick is not to deny them, but to tune them skillfully so that they will help focus the mind on the present moment. Thus, for instance, in the practice of meditation, as with any skill, it is important not to focus desire too strongly on the results one hopes to get, for that would interfere with the mind's ability to focus on giving rise to the causes leading to those results. If, instead, one focuses desire on putting the causes in proper order in the present moment, desire becomes an indispensable part of the process of mastery.

Passage §67 deals with the second criticism—that desire, etc., are antithetical to the goal—by showing that these qualities are necessary for anyone who pursues a path, but are automatically abandoned on reaching the goal at the path's end. The image of the path is important here, for it carries important implications. First, the path is not the goal; it is simply the way there, just as the road to the Grand Canyon should not be confused with the Grand Canyon itself. Even though many stretches of the road bear no resemblance to the Grand Canyon, that does not mean that the road does not lead there. Secondly, the path of practice does not cause the goal, it simply leads there, just as neither the road to the Grand Canyon nor the act of walking to the Grand Canyon can cause the Grand Canyon to be. The goal at the end of the Buddhist path is unfabricated, and therefore no amount of desire or effort can bring it into being. Nevertheless, the path to the goal is a fabricated process [§105], and in that process desire, effort, intent, and discrimination all have an important role to play, just as the effort of walking plays a role in arriving at the Grand Canyon.

The final section of the extended formula hints at how these qualities may be directed toward Awakening.

> He keeps perceiving what is in front & behind so that what is in front is the same as what is behind, what is behind is the same as what is in front. What is below is the same as what is above, what is above is the same as what is below. [He dwells] by

night as by day, and by day as by night. By means of an awareness thus open & unhampered, he develops a brightened mind.

This passage refers to the total mastery of concentration. As one frees the mind from such distinctions as front/behind, above/below, and day/night, one creates an awareness that is open and bright, unhampered by the normal limitations that come with a conscious sense of being located in time and space. This is the type of awareness needed for the attainment of the supranormal powers. Many meditators tend to stop here, satisfied with their new-found powers, but the Buddha urges them to go further. As §161 shows, the full perfection of this type of awareness requires that one be extremely sensitive to the presence of mental defilements that might place subtle limitations on it. This process of sensitivity is nothing other than the second stage of frames-of-reference meditation [II/B], in which one focuses on the phenomenon of origination and passing away of mind states that are limited and unlimited, concentrated and unconcentrated, taking the brightness of one's awareness—the mind in-and-of itself—as one's frame of reference.

The next stage of practice is outlined in a passage that builds on §161. This passage [§167], shows that full mastery of power requires that one abandon even the notion that "I am" the master of the power, or that "my mind" is concentrated. The proper attitude, in the face of the power, is to "incline the mind to the Deathless." Such an attitude, according to M.102 [MFU, pp. 81-82], involves simply noting what is present as present, without fashioning anything further out of it. This is the third stage of frames-of-reference meditation [II/B], the entry into emptiness that simply notes, "There is this...." When this level of skilled discrimination is reached, the power has been fully mastered at the same time that the mind stands on the verge of non-fashioning and Awakening.

Because of their association with supranormal powers, the bases of power have generally been slighted in Western writings on Buddhism. If we count the five strengths as identical with the five faculties, the bases of power are the only set in the Wings of Awakening that has not yet been the subject of a book in the English language. The situation in Asia, however, is very different. There, the bases of power have been extrapolated from their specific context and are frequently cited as guides to success in general. In whatever task one may undertake—directed toward worldly ends or toward the Dhamma—one must bring to bear the qualities of desire, persistence, intent, and discrimination, skillfully balanced with concentration and right exertion, if one wants to succeed at one's task.

§ 63. Monks, whoever neglects these four bases of power neglects the noble path going to the right ending of stress. Whoever undertakes these four bases of power undertakes the noble path going to the right ending of stress. Which four?

There is the case where a monk develops the base of power endowed with concentration founded on desire & the fabrications of exertion. He develops the base of power endowed with concentration founded on persistence... concentration founded on intent...concentration founded on discrimination & the fabrications of exertion.

Whoever neglects these four bases of power neglects the noble path going to the right ending of stress. Whoever undertakes these four bases of power undertakes the noble path going to the right ending of stress.

S.LI.2

§ 64. Ananda: What, venerable sir, is power? What is the base of power? What is the development of the base of power? And what is the path of practice leading to the development of the base of power?

The Buddha: There is the case, Ānanda, where a monk [1] wields manifold supranormal powers. Having been one he becomes many; having been many he becomes one. He appears. He vanishes. He goes unimpeded through walls, ramparts, & mountains as if through space. He dives in & out of the earth as if it were water. He walks on water without sinking as if it were dry land. Sitting cross-legged he flies through the air like a winged bird. With his hand he touches & strokes even the sun & moon, so mighty & powerful. He exercises influence with his body even as far as the Brahma worlds. {Just as a skilled potter or his assistant could craft from well-prepared clay whatever kind of pottery vessel he likes, or as a skilled ivory-carver or his assistant could craft from well-prepared ivory any kind of ivory-work he likes, or as a skilled goldsmith or his assistant could craft from well-prepared gold any kind of gold article he likes; in the same way, the monk wields manifold supranormal powers....}

[2] He hears—by means of the divine ear-element, purified & surpassing the human—both kinds of sounds: divine & human, whether near or far. {Just as if a man traveling along a highway were to hear the sounds of kettledrums, small drums, conchs, cymbals, & tom-toms. He would know, 'That is the sound of kettledrums, that is the sound of small drums, that is the sound of conchs, that is the sound of cymbals, & that is the sound of tom-toms.' In the same way...the monk hears...both kinds of sounds: divine & human....}

[3] He knows the awareness of other beings, other individuals, having encompassed it with his own awareness. He discerns a mind

with passion as a mind with passion, and a mind without passion as a mind without passion. He discerns a mind with aversion as a mind with aversion, and a mind without aversion as a mind without aversion. He discerns a mind with delusion as a mind with delusion, and a mind without delusion as a mind without delusion. He discerns a restricted mind as a restricted mind, and a scattered mind as a scattered mind. He discerns an enlarged mind as an enlarged mind, and an unenlarged mind as an unenlarged mind. He discerns an excelled mind [one that is not an the most excellent level] as an excelled mind, and an unexcelled mind as an unexcelled mind. He discerns a concentrated mind as a concentrated mind, and an unconcentrated mind as an unconcentrated mind. He discerns a released mind as a released mind, and an unreleased mind as an unreleased mind. {Just as if a young woman—or man—fond of ornaments, examining the reflection of her own face in a bright mirror or a bowl of clear water would know 'blemished' if it were blemished, or 'unblemished' if it were not. In the same way...the monk knows the awareness of other beings....}

[4] He recollects his manifold past lives (lit: previous homes), i.e., one birth, two births, three births, four, five, ten, twenty, thirty, forty, fifty, one hundred, one thousand, one hundred thousand, many aeons of cosmic contraction, many aeons of cosmic expansion, many aeons of cosmic contraction & expansion, [recollecting], 'There I had such a name, belonged to such a clan, had such an appearance. Such was my food, such my experience of pleasure & pain, such the end of my life. Passing away from that state, I re-arose there. There too I had such a name, belonged to such a clan, had such an appearance. Such was my food, such my experience of pleasure & pain, such the end of my life. Passing away from that state, I re-arose here.' Thus he remembers his manifold past lives in their modes & details. {Just as if a man were to go from his home village to another village, and then from that village to yet another village, and then from that village back to his home village. The thought would occur to him, 'I went from my home village to that village over there. There I stood in such a way, sat in such a way, talked in such a way, & remained silent in such a way. From that village I went to that village over there, and there I stood in such a way, sat in such a way, talked in such a way, & remained silent in such a way. From that village I came back home.' In the same way...the monk recollects his manifold past lives....}

[5] He sees—by means of the divine eye, purified & surpassing the human—beings passing away and re-appearing, and he discerns how they are inferior & superior, beautiful & ugly, fortunate & unfortunate in accordance with their kamma: 'These beings—who were endowed with bad conduct of body, speech, & mind, who reviled the noble ones, held wrong views and undertook actions

under the influence of wrong views—with the break-up of the body, after death, have re-appeared in the plane of deprivation, the bad destination, the lower realms, in hell. But these beings—who were endowed with good conduct of body, speech, & mind, who did not revile the noble ones, who held right views and undertook actions under the influence of right views—with the break-up of the body, after death, have re-appeared in the good destinations, in the heavenly world.' Thus—by means of the divine eye, purified & surpassing the human—he sees beings passing away and re-appearing, and he discerns how they are inferior & superior, beautiful & ugly, fortunate & unfortunate in accordance with their kamma. {Just as if there were a tall building in the central square [of a town], and a man with good eyesight standing on top of it were to see people entering a house, leaving it, walking along the street, & sitting in the central square. The thought would occur to him, 'These people are entering a house, leaving it, walking along the streets, & sitting in the central square.' In the same way...the monk sees—by means of the divine eye, purified & surpassing the human—beings passing away and re-appearing....}

[6] Through the ending of the mental effluents, he remains in the effluent-free release of awareness & release of discernment, having known & made them manifest for himself right in the here & now. {Just as if there were a pool of water in a mountain glen—clear, limpid, & unsullied—where a man with good eyesight standing on the bank could see shells, gravel, & pebbles, and also shoals of fish swimming about & resting, and it would occur to him, 'This pool of water is clear, limpid, & unsullied. Here are these shells, gravel, & pebbles, and also these shoals of fish swimming about & resting.' In the same way, the monk discerns, as it is actually present, that 'This is stress...This is the origination of stress...This is the cessation of stress...This is the way leading to the cessation of stress...These are effluents...This is the origination of effluents...This is the cessation of effluents...This is the way leading to the cessation of effluents.' His heart, thus knowing, thus seeing, is released from the effluent of sensuality, released from the effluent of becoming, released from the effluent of ignorance. With release, there is the knowledge, 'Released.' He discerns that 'Birth is ended, the holy life fulfilled, the task done. There is nothing further for this world.'}

This is called power.

And what is the base of power? Whatever path, whatever practice, leads to the attainment of power, the winning of power: That is called the base of power.

And what is the development of the base of power? There is the case where a monk develops the base of power endowed with concentration founded on desire & the fabrications of exertion. He develops the base of power endowed with concentration founded on persistence... concentration founded on intent... concentration founded on discrimination & the fabrications of exertion. This is called the development of the base of power.

And what is the path of practice leading to the development of the base of power? Just this noble eightfold path: right view, right resolve, right speech, right action, right livelihood, right effort, right mindfulness, right concentration. This is called the path of practice leading to the development of the base of power.

S.LI.26 {+ D.2}

§ 65. If a monk attains concentration, attains singleness of mind founded on desire, that is called concentration founded on desire. He generates desire, endeavors, arouses persistence, upholds & exerts his intent for the sake of the non-arising of evil, unskillful qualities that have not yet arisen...for the sake of the abandoning of evil, unskillful qualities that have arisen...for the sake of the arising of skillful qualities that have not yet arisen...(and) for the maintenance, non-confusion, increase, plenitude, development, & culmination of skillful qualities that have arisen. These are called the fabrications of exertion. This is desire, this is concentration founded on desire, these are the fabrications of exertion. This is called the base of power endowed with concentration founded on desire & the fabrications of exertion.

If a monk attains concentration, attains singleness of mind founded on persistence, that is called concentration founded on persistence...

If a monk attains concentration, attains singleness of mind founded on intent, that is called concentration founded on intent...

If a monk attains concentration, attains singleness of mind founded on discrimination, that is called concentration founded on discrimination. He generates desire, endeavors, arouses persistence, upholds & exerts his intent for the sake of the non-arising of evil, unskillful qualities that have not yet arisen... for the sake of the abandoning of evil, unskillful qualities that have arisen...for the sake of the arising of skillful qualities that have not yet arisen...(and) for the maintenance, non-confusion, increase, plenitude, development & culmination of skillful qualities that have arisen. These are called the fabrications of exertion. This is discrimination, this is concentration founded on discrimination, these are the fabrications of exertion. This is called the base of power endowed with concentration founded on discrimination & the fabrications of exertion.

S.LI.13

§ 66. Analysis. These four bases of power, when developed & pursued, are of great fruit & great benefit. And how are the four bases of power developed & pursued so as to be of great fruit & great benefit?

There is the case where a monk develops the base of power endowed with concentration founded on desire & the fabrications of exertion, thinking, 'This desire of mine will be neither overly sluggish nor overly active, neither inwardly restricted nor outwardly scattered.' He keeps perceiving what is in front & behind so that what is in front is the same as what is behind, what is behind is the same as what is in front. What is below is the same as what is above, what is above is the same as what is below. Night is the same as day, day is the same as night. By means of an awareness thus open & unhampered, he develops a brightened mind.

He develops the base of power endowed with concentration founded on persistence...concentration founded on intent...concentration founded on discrimination & the fabrications of exertion, thinking, 'This discrimination of mine will be neither overly sluggish nor overly active, neither inwardly restricted nor outwardly scattered.' He keeps perceiving what is in front & behind so that what is in front is the same as what is behind, what is behind is the same as what is in front. What is below is the same as what is above, what is above is the same as what is below. [He dwells] by night as by day, and by day as by night. By means of an awareness thus open & unhampered, he develops a brightened mind.

And how is desire overly sluggish? Whatever desire is accompanied by laziness, conjoined with laziness, that is called overly sluggish desire.

And how is desire overly active? Whatever desire is accompanied by restlessness, conjoined with restlessness, that is called overly active desire.

And how is desire inwardly restricted? Whatever desire is accompanied by sloth & drowsiness, conjoined with sloth & drowsiness, that is called inwardly restricted desire.

And how is desire outwardly scattered? Whatever desire is stirred up by the five strands of sensuality, outwardly dispersed & dissipated, that is called outwardly scattered desire.

And how does a monk dwell perceiving what is in front & behind so that what is in front is the same as what is behind, and what is behind is the same as what is in front? There is the case where a monk's perception of what is in front & behind is well in hand, well-attended to, well-considered, well-tuned ('penetrated') by means of discernment. This is how a monk keeps perceiving what is in front and behind so that what is in front is the same as what is behind, and what is behind is the same as what is in front.

And how does a monk dwell so that what is below is the same as what is above, and what is above is the same as what is below? There is the case where a monk reflects on this very body, from the soles of the feet on up, from the crown of the head on down, surrounded by skin, & full of various kinds of unclean things: 'In this body there are head hairs, body hairs, nails, teeth, skin, flesh, tendons, bones, bone marrow, kidneys, heart, liver, pleura, spleen, lungs, large intestines, small intestines, gorge, feces, bile, phlegm, pus, blood, sweat, fat, tears, skin-oil, saliva, mucus, fluid in the joints, urine.' This is how a monk dwells so that what is below is the same as what is above, and what is above is the same as what is below. [§30]

And how does a monk dwell by night as by day, and by day as by night? There is the case where a monk at night develops the base of power endowed with concentration founded on desire & the fabrications of exertion by means of the same modes (permutations) & signs & themes that he uses by day, and by day he develops the base of power endowed with concentration founded on desire & the fabrications of exertion by means of the same modes & signs & themes that he uses by night. This is how a monk dwells by night as by day, and by day as by night.

And how does a monk—by means of an awareness open & unhampered—develop a brightened mind? There is the case where a monk has the perception of light, the perception of daytime [at any hour of the day] well in hand & well-established. This is how a monk—by means of an awareness open & unhampered—develops a brightened mind. [§147]

(The above discussion is then repeated for persistence, intent, & discrimination.)

When a monk has thus developed & pursued the four bases of power, he experiences manifold supranormal powers....He hears—by means of the divine ear-element, purified & surpassing the human—both kinds of sounds: divine & human, whether near or far....He knows the awareness of other beings, other individuals, having encompassed it with his own awareness....He recollects his manifold past lives....He sees—by means of the divine eye, purified & surpassing the human—beings passing away and re-appearing.... Through the ending of the mental effluents—remains in the effluent-free release of awareness & release of discernment, having known & made them manifest for himself right in the present.

This is how these four bases of power, when developed & pursued, are of great fruit & great benefit.

S.LI.20

§ 67. I have heard that on one occasion Ven. Ananda was staying in Kosambı, at Ghosita's Park. Then the Brahman Uṇṇabha went to where Ven. Ananda was staying and on arrival greeted him courteously. After an exchange of friendly greetings & courtesies, he sat down to one side. As he was sitting there, he said to Ven. Ananda: What is the aim of this holy life lived under the contemplative Gotama?

Ananda: The holy life is lived under the Blessed One with the aim of abandoning desire.

Uṇṇabha: Is there a path, is there a practice, for the abandoning of that desire?

Ananda: Yes, there is....

Uṇṇabha: What is the path, the practice, for the abandoning of that desire?

Ananda: There is the case where a monk develops the base of power endowed with concentration founded on desire & the fabrications of exertion. He develops the base of power endowed with concentration founded on persistence...concentration founded on intent...concentration founded on discrimination & the fabrications of exertion. This, Brahman, is the path, this is the practice for the abandoning of that desire.

Uṇṇabha: If that's so, then it's an endless path, and not one with an end, for it's impossible that one could abandon desire by means of desire.

Ananda: Well then, Brahman, let me question you on this matter. Answer as you see fit....Didn't you first have desire, thinking, 'I'll go to the park,' and then when you reached the park, wasn't that particular desire allayed?

Uṇṇabha: Yes, sir.

Ananda: Didn't you first have persistence, thinking, 'I'll go to the park,' and then when you reached the park, wasn't that particular persistence allayed?

Uṇṇabha: Yes, sir.

Ananda: Didn't you first have the intent, thinking, 'I'll go to the park,' and then when you reached the park, wasn't that particular intent allayed?

Uṇṇabha: Yes, sir.

Ananda: Didn't you first have [an act of] discrimination, thinking, 'I'll go to the park,' and then when you reached the park, wasn't that particular act of discrimination allayed?

Uṇṇabha: Yes, sir.

Ananda: So it is with an Arahant whose mental effluents are ended, who has reached fulfillment, done the task, laid down the burden, attained the true goal, totally destroyed the fetter of becoming, and who is released through right gnosis. Whatever desire he first had for the attainment of Arahantship, on attaining Arahantship that particular desire is allayed. Whatever persistence he first had for the attainment of Arahantship, on attaining Arahantship that particular persistence is allayed. Whatever intent he first had for the attainment of Arahantship, on attaining Arahantship that particular intent is allayed. Whatever discrimination he first had for the attainment of Arahantship, on attaining Arahantship that particular discrimination is allayed. So what do you think, Brahman? Is this an endless path, or one with an end?

Uṇṇabha: You're right, sir. This is a path with an end, and not an endless one....

S.LI.15

§ 68. Ananda: Venerable sir, does the Blessed One have direct experience of going to the Brahma world by means of supranormal power with a mind-made body?

The Buddha: Yes, Ananda....

Ananda: But does the Blessed One also have direct experience of going to the Brahma world by means of supranormal power with this very physical body, composed of the four great elements?

The Buddha: Yes....

Ananda: It's awesome & marvelous that the Blessed One should have direct experience of going to the Brahma world by means of supranormal power with a mind-made body, and of going to the Brahma world by means of supranormal power with this very physical body, composed of the four great elements.

The Buddha: Tathagatas are both awesome, Ananda, and endowed with awesome qualities. They are both marvelous and endowed with marvelous qualities. Whenever the Tathagata merges his body with his mind and his mind with his body, and remains having alighted on the perception of ease and buoyancy with regard to the body, then his body becomes lighter, more pliant, more malleable, & more radiant.

Just as when an iron ball heated all day becomes lighter, more pliant, more malleable, & more radiant; in the same way, whenever the Tathagata merges his body with his mind and his mind with his body, and remains having alighted on the perception of ease and buoyancy with regard to the body, then his body becomes lighter, more pliant, more malleable, & more radiant.

Now, whenever the Tathagata merges his body with his mind and his mind with his body, and remains having alighted on the perception of ease and buoyancy with regard to the body, then his body rises effortlessly from the earth up into the sky. He then experiences manifold supranormal powers. Having been one he becomes many; having been many he becomes one. He appears. He vanishes. He goes unimpeded through walls, ramparts, & mountains as if through space. He dives in & out of the earth as if it were water. He walks on water without sinking as if it were dry land. Sitting cross-legged he flies through the air like a winged bird. With his hand he touches & strokes even the sun & moon, so mighty & powerful. He exercises influence with his body even as far as the Brahma worlds.

Just as a tuft of cotton seed or a ball of thistle down, lightly wafted by the wind, rises effortlessly from the earth up into the sky, in the same way, whenever the Tathāgata concentrates his body in his mind & his mind in his body, and remains having alighted on the perception of ease and buoyancy, then his body rises effortlessly from the earth up into the sky. He then experiences manifold supranormal powers...even as far as the Brahma worlds.

S.LI.22

E. THE FIVE FACULTIES

Indriya—the Pali word translated here as "faculty"—is connected with the name of the dominant Vedic god, Indra. Thus it carries connotations of *dominance* or *control.* Buddhist texts contain several lists of faculties, both physical and mental, but here the word denotes a list of five mental factors that must reach a state of dominance in the mind for Awakening to take place. This set is one of the most comprehensive in the Wings to Awakening, as it covers all of the factors explicitly mentioned in the sets we have covered so far, and in addition lists conviction, which the other sets imply but never specifically mention. This is why this set forms the framework for Part III of this book, in which all of the main factors of the Wings to Awakening will be discussed in detail.

As we noted in II/A, the faculties in this set form a loop in the causal progression of the mind along the path, as opposed to the "holographic" formulae of the sets we have discussed so far. Two of the faculties—the frames of reference and right exertion—we have covered in detail already. The other three—conviction, concentration, and discernment—we will discuss in detail in Part III. Here we will limit ourselves to some general observations about the set as a whole.

In the causal loop depicted by five faculties, the emphasis is on how the elements of the "concentration aggregate" in the noble eightfold path—right effort, right mindfulness, and right concentration—can lead the mind from a state of conviction to one of discernment. To borrow terminology from §106, this is the process by which the mind goes from the preliminary level to the noble or transcendent level of right view. This set can also be regarded as a description of how conviction, when put into action, inherently leads through the concentration aggregate to transcendent discernment.

Passage §69 defines the faculty of conviction as the four factors of stream-entry. Other passages define these four factors in two separate ways: one [§70] listing the factors leading to stream-entry, another [§71] giving the factors that characterize the person who has already entered the stream. Both lists are relevant here, as the person working toward stream-entry must act on conviction, while a person who has entered the stream is endowed with the unwavering conviction that comes with the first glimpse of the Deathless.

In both cases, the factor of conviction has several dimensions: trust in the ability of wise people to know the ideal path of practice, belief in their teachings, and a willingness to put those teachings into practice. Western analyses of faith tend to separate these aspects of conviction, and some writers have tried to decide which aspect is dominant in the Buddhist tradition. In practice, however, all three must work together, for in Buddhism the object of conviction inherently involves all three at once. The primary focus of conviction is the Awakening of the Buddha, and this in turn ultimately comes down to a conviction in the primacy of the mind in creating kamma, a conviction in the efficacy of kamma in shaping experience in the round of rebirth, and a belief that the Buddha made use of mental qualities accessible to all in using the laws of kamma to bring about an end to kamma and thus escape from the round. Kamma and the use of kamma to transcend kamma constitute both the truth that the Buddha taught and the explanation of how he discovered it. Thus, trust in the Buddha and belief in his teaching are two sides of the same coin. At the same time, these truths concerning kamma are also the situation in which the listener is currently placed: the causal nexus that determines both the dynamic of continued life in the cycle of rebirth and the way out of that cycle. So, by definition, conviction in the Buddha's Awakening is something that must be acted on. If one is convinced that one is entangled in a kammic web that can nevertheless be unraveled, one will naturally try to learn from the example of the Buddha or his disciples, developing the same mental qualities they did and attaining release oneself. Thus, unlike a religion where trust involves the belief that the deity will provide for one's salvation—either through grace or as a reward for unquestioning obedience—trust in the Buddha and belief in his teachings means that one's salvation is ultimately one's own responsibility. In this way, trust, belief, and a willingness to act are inseparably combined.

This is why conviction, the first member of the set of five faculties, leads naturally to persistence, the second. Persistence here is equal to right exertion, which develops mindfulness as the most essential skillful quality in the mind. As we saw under the frames of reference, the proper development of mindfulness leads to concentration, or the four jhanas, while the jhanas provide the foundation for the arising of discernment, the fifth and final member of this set. When discernment is strengthened to the point of transcendence, leading to the attainment of stream-entry, it then confirms the truths that were previously taken as a matter of conviction and faith [§74]. This confirmation feeds back into the causal loop, strengthening conviction, which provides the basis for developing the faculties still further until Arahantship is attained. At that point there is no need to be convinced that the practice leads to release into the Deathless, for one has fully realized that release through direct experience [§89].

The underlying element throughout the development of this causal loop is the mental quality of heedfulness [§78]. The texts explain heedfulness as a combination of right effort and relentless mindfulness, but as a quality of mind it goes deeper than that. Heedfulness realizes the dangers inherent in the round of rebirth and redeath, and the fact that those dangers are inherent in each careless act of the mind. It thus fosters conviction in the possibility of a release from those dangers and a sense of urgency and precision in the practice. This combination of urgency and precision provides the impetus for the full and thorough development of the faculties as one seriously pursues the possibility of release through the skillful development of the mind. This pattern of heedfulness developing the five faculties in the quest of the security of Deathlessness mirrors Prince Siddhattha's own quest, which began with his conviction that there was no need to resign himself to the tyranny of aging, illness, and death, and ended with the discernment that brought about his actual escape from that tyranny. This pattern also calls to mind the famous verse from the Dhammapada, that heedfulness is the path to the Deathless [§80]. The five faculties can be taken as an elaboration of that verse.

Because the five faculties are means to Deathlessness—rather than ends in themselves—they must not only be developed skillfully but also used skillfully as they are developed. The texts emphasizing this point focus on two of the faculties: persistence and discernment.

The passage dealing with persistence [§86] is probably the Canon's most explicit analogy between the performance of music and the practice of meditation [I/A]. One should tune one's effort so that it is neither too intense nor too slack, just as the main string of a musical instrument should be neither too sharp nor too flat. (We have already encountered this issue of balance in the proper development of the four bases of power, and we will encounter it again in the factors of Awakening.) One then tunes the remaining faculties to the pitch of one's effort, just as one would tune the notes of one's scale to the tonic. Only then can one take up the theme of one's meditation—the four frames of reference [§148]—just as one would take up and develop the basic theme of one's musical piece.

As for discernment, passage §88 brings out the point that one's mastery of the faculties is not complete until one discerns the "escape" from them. Normally the texts make this comment only about deceptively attractive objects or unskillful qualities in the mind, but here they use it in connection with skillful qualities. What this means is that there comes a point in the practice where one must go beyond even such skillful qualities as concentration and discernment. They are skillful precisely because their full development allows one to go beyond them. This point is made explicit in §187, which shows exactly why the right view constituting discernment is right: it is the only view that opens the way going beyond attachment to views. D.1 [MFU, p. 111] adds that an awakened person—through regarding views not in terms of their content, but in terms of the effect they have on the mind—comes to discern what lies beyond views, and yet does not hold even to that act of discernment. As a result of knowing but not holding, the mind experiences Unbinding in the here and now. This "knowing but not holding" is yet another reference to the perceptual mode of emptiness verging on non-fashioning: the culminating point for each set in the Wings to Awakening.

§ 69. Monks, there are these five faculties. Which five? The faculty of conviction, the faculty of persistence, the faculty of mindfulness, the faculty of concentration, and the faculty of discernment.

Now where is the faculty of conviction to be seen? In the four factors of stream-entry....

And where is the faculty of persistence to be seen? In the four right exertions....

And where is the faculty of mindfulness to be seen? In the four frames of reference....

And where is the faculty of concentration to be seen? In the four jhanas....

And where is the faculty of discernment to be seen? In the four noble truths....

S.XLVIII.8

§ 70. Factors of Stream-entry. Association with good people is a factor of stream-entry [§115]. Listening to the true Dhamma is a factor of stream-entry. Appropriate attention is a factor of stream-entry [§51]. Practice in accordance with the Dhamma is a factor of stream-entry.

S.LV.5

§ 71. Now with what four factors of stream-entry is the noble disciple endowed? There is the case where the noble disciple is endowed with unwavering faith in the Awakened One: 'Indeed, the Blessed One is pure and rightly self-awakened, consummate in knowledge & conduct, well-gone, an expert with regard to the world, unexcelled as a trainer for those people fit to be tamed, the Teacher of divine & human beings, awakened, blessed.'

He is endowed with unwavering faith in the Dhamma: 'The Dhamma is well-expounded by the Blessed One, to be seen here & now, timeless, inviting verification, pertinent, to be realized by the wise for themselves.'

He is endowed with unwavering faith in the Saṅgha: 'The Saṅgha of the Blessed One's disciples who have practiced well...who have practiced straight-forwardly...who have practiced methodically... who have practiced masterfully—in other words, the four types of noble disciples when taken as pairs, the eight when taken as individual types—they are the Saṅgha of the Blessed One's disciples: worthy of gifts, worthy of hospitality, worthy of offerings, worthy of respect, the incomparable field of merit for the world.'

He is endowed with virtues that are appealing to the noble ones: untorn, unbroken, unspotted, unsplattered, liberating, praised by the wise, untarnished, leading to concentration.

A.X.92

§ 72. Analysis. Now what, monks, is the faculty of conviction? There is the case where a monk, a noble disciple, has conviction, is convinced of the Tathagata's Awakening: 'Indeed, the Blessed One is pure and rightly self-awakened, consummate in knowledge & conduct, well-gone, an expert with regard to the world, unexcelled as a trainer for those people fit to be tamed, the Teacher of divine & human beings, awakened, blessed.' This, monks, is called the faculty of conviction.

And what is the faculty of persistence? There is the case where a monk, a noble disciple, keeps his persistence aroused for abandoning unskillful mental qualities and taking on skillful mental qualities. He is steadfast, solid in his effort, not shirking his duties with regard to skillful mental qualities. He generates desire, endeavors, arouses persistence, upholds & exerts his intent for the sake of the non-arising of evil, unskillful qualities that have not yet arisen...for the sake of the abandoning of evil, unskillful qualities that have arisen...for the sake of the arising of skillful qualities that have not yet arisen...(and) for the maintenance, non-confusion, increase, plenitude, development, & culmination of skillful qualities that have arisen. This is called the faculty of persistence. [§§49-50]

And what is the faculty of mindfulness? There is the case where a monk, a noble disciple, is mindful, highly meticulous, remembering & able to call to mind even things that were done & said long ago. He remains focused on the body in & of itself—ardent, alert, & mindful—putting aside greed & distress with reference to the world. He remains focused on feelings in & of themselves...the mind in & of itself...mental qualities in & of themselves—ardent, alert, & mindful—putting aside greed & distress with reference to the world. This is called the faculty of mindfulness. [§§29-30]

And what is the faculty of concentration? There is the case where a monk, a noble disciple, making it his object to let go, attains concentration, attains singleness of mind. Quite withdrawn from sensuality, withdrawn from unskillful mental qualities, he enters & remains in the first jhana: rapture & pleasure born from withdrawal, accompanied by directed thought & evaluation. With the stilling of directed thought & evaluation, he enters & remains in the second jhana: rapture & pleasure born of composure, unification of awareness free from directed thought & evaluation—internal assurance. With the fading of rapture he remains in equanimity, mindful & alert, and physically sensitive of pleasure. He enters & remains in the third jhana, and of him the Noble Ones declare, 'Equanimous & mindful, he has a pleasurable abiding.' With the abandoning of pleasure & pain—as with the earlier disappearance of elation & distress—he enters & remains in the fourth jhana: purity of equanimity & mindfulness, neither pleasure nor pain. This is called the faculty of concentration. [§150]

And what is the faculty of discernment? There is the case where a monk, a noble disciple, is discerning, endowed with discernment of arising & passing away—noble, penetrating, leading to the right ending of stress. He discerns, as it is actually present: 'This is stress... This is the origination of stress...This is the cessation of stress...This is the path of practice leading to the cessation of stress.' This is called the faculty of discernment. [§§184-240]

S.XLVIII.10

§ 73. Just as a royal frontier fortress has a foundation post—deeply rooted, well embedded, immovable, & unshakable—for the protection of those within and to ward off those without; in the same way a noble disciple has conviction, is convinced of the Tathagata's Awakening: 'Indeed, the Blessed One is pure and rightly self-awakened, consummate in knowledge & conduct, well-gone, an expert with regard to the world, unexcelled as a trainer for those people fit to be tamed, the Teacher of divine & human beings, awakened, blessed.' With conviction as his foundation post, the noble disciple abandons what is unskillful & develops what is skillful, abandons what is blameworthy & develops what is blameless, and looks after himself with purity....

Just as a royal frontier fortress has a large army stationed within—elephant soldiers, cavalry, charioteers, bowmen, standard-bearers, billeting officers, soldiers of the supply corps, noted princes, commando heroes, infantry, & slaves—for the protection of those within and to ward off those without; in the same way a noble disciple keeps his persistence aroused for abandoning unskillful mental qualities and taking on skillful mental qualities, is steadfast, solid in his effort, not shirking his duties with regard to skillful mental qualities. With persistence as his army, the noble disciple abandons what is unskillful & develops what is skillful, abandons what is blameworthy & develops what is blameless, and looks after himself with purity....

Just as a royal frontier fortress has a wise, experienced, intelligent gate-keeper to keep out those he doesn't know and to let in those he does, for the protection of those within and to ward off those without; in the same way a noble disciple is mindful, highly meticulous, remembering & able to call to mind even things that were done & said long ago. With mindfulness as his gate-keeper, the noble disciple abandons what is unskillful & develops what is skillful, abandons what is blameworthy & develops what is blameless, and looks after himself with purity....

Just as a royal frontier fortress has ramparts that are high & thick & completely covered with plaster, for the protection of those within and to ward off those without; in the same way a noble disciple is discerning, endowed with discernment leading to the arising of the goal—noble, penetrating, leading to the right ending of stress. With discernment as his covering of plaster, the noble disciple abandons what is unskillful & develops what is skillful, abandons what is blameworthy & develops what is blameless, and looks after himself with purity....

Just as a royal frontier fortress has large stores of grass, timber & water for the delight, convenience, & comfort of those within, and to ward off those without; in the same way the noble disciple...enters &

remains in the first jhana...for his own delight, convenience, & comfort, and to alight on Unbinding....

Just as a royal frontier fortress has large stores of rice & barley for the delight, convenience, & comfort of those within, and to ward off those without; in the same way the noble disciple...enters & remains in the second jhana...for his own delight, convenience, & comfort, and to alight on Unbinding....

Just as a royal frontier fortress has large stores of sesame, green gram, & other beans for the delight, convenience, & comfort of those within, and to ward off those without; in the same way the noble disciple...enters & remains in the third jhana...for his own delight, convenience, & comfort, and to alight on Unbinding....

Just as a royal frontier fortress has large stores of tonics—ghee, fresh butter, oil, honey, molasses, & salt—for the delight, convenience, & comfort of those within, and to ward off those without; in the same way the noble disciple...enters & remains in the fourth jhana...for his own delight, convenience, & comfort, and to alight on Unbinding....

A.VII.63

§ 74. The Buddha: Tell me, Sariputta: A noble disciple who is thoroughly inspired by the Tathagata, who has gone solely to the Tathagata [for refuge], could he have any doubt or uncertainty concerning the Tathagata or the Tathagata's teachings?

Sariputta: No, venerable sir....With a noble disciple who has conviction, it may be expected that he will keep his persistence aroused for abandoning unskillful mental qualities and taking on skillful mental qualities, that he will be steadfast, solid in his effort, not shirking his duties with regard to skillful mental qualities. Whatever persistence he has, is his faculty of persistence.

With a noble disciple who has conviction, who is resolute & persistent, it may be expected that he will be mindful, highly meticulous, remembering and able to call to mind even things that were done & said long ago. Whatever mindfulness he has, is his faculty of mindfulness.

With a noble disciple who has conviction, who is resolute & persistent, and whose mindfulness is established ('tuned'), it may be expected that—making it his object to let—he will attain concentration & singleness of mind. Whatever concentration he has, is his faculty of concentration.

With a noble disciple who has conviction, who is resolute & persistent, whose mindfulness is established, and whose mind is rightly concentrated, it may be expected that he will discern: 'From an inconceivable beginning comes transmigration. A beginning point is not evident, though beings hindered by ignorance and fettered by craving are transmigrating & wandering on. The total fading & cessation of ignorance, of this mass of darkness, is this peaceful, exquisite state: the resolution of all fabrications; the relinquishment of all the paraphernalia of becoming; the ending of craving; dispassion; cessation; Unbinding.' Whatever discernment he has, is his faculty of discernment.

And so this convinced noble disciple, thus striving again & again, recollecting again & again, concentrating his mind again & again, discerning again & again, becomes thoroughly convinced: 'Those phenomena that once I had only heard about, I here & now dwell touching them with my body and, through discernment, I see them clear through.' Whatever conviction he has, is his faculty of conviction.

S.XLVIII.50

§ 75. Just as, in a house with a ridged roof, the rafters are not stable or firm as long as the ridge beam is not in place, but are stable & firm when it is; in the same way, four faculties are not stable or firm as long as noble knowledge has not arisen in a noble disciple, but are stable & firm when it has. Which four? The faculty of conviction, the faculty of persistence, the faculty of mindfulness & the faculty of concentration.

When a noble disciple is discerning, the conviction that follows from that stands solid. The persistence that follows from that stands solid. The mindfulness that follows from that stands solid. The concentration that follows from that stands solid.

S.XLVIII.52

§ 76. It is through the development & pursuit of two faculties that a monk whose effluents are ended declares gnosis: 'Birth is ended, the holy life fulfilled, the task done. There is nothing further for the sake of this world.' Through which two? Through noble discernment & noble release. Whatever is his noble discernment is his faculty of discernment. Whatever is his noble release is his faculty of concentration.

S.XLVIII.46

§ 77. Just as, of all scented woods, red sandalwood is reckoned the chief, even so of all the mental qualities that are wings to self-awakening, the faculty of discernment is reckoned the chief in terms of leading to awakening. And what are the mental qualities that are wings to self-awakening? The faculty of conviction is a mental quality that is a wing to self-awakening leading to awakening. The faculty of persistence...mindfulness...concentration... discernment is a mental quality that is a wing to self-awakening leading to Awakening.

S.XLVIII.55

§ 78. When one quality is established in a monk, the five faculties are developed & developed well. Which one quality? Heedfulness.

And what is heedfulness? There is the case where a monk guards his mind in the midst of mental effluents & their concomitants. When his mind is guarded in the midst of mental effluents & their concomitants, the faculty of conviction goes to the culmination of its development. The faculty of persistence...mindfulness...concentration... discernment goes to the culmination of its development.

This is how when one quality is established in a monk, the five faculties are developed & developed well.

S.XLVIII.56

§ 79. Just as the footprints of all legged animals are encompassed by the footprint of the elephant, and the elephant's footprint is reckoned their chief in terms of size; in the same way, all skillful qualities are rooted in heedfulness, lie gathered in heedfulness, and heedfulness is reckoned their chief....

Just as all the light of the constellations does not equal one sixteenth of the light of the moon, and the light of the moon is reckoned their chief; in the same way, all skillful qualities are rooted in heedfulness, lie gathered in heedfulness, and heedfulness is reckoned their chief.

A.X.15

§ 80. Heedfulness: the path to the Deathless;
Heedlessness: the path to death.
The heedful do not die;
The heedless are as if
already dead.

DHP.21

§ 81. He would not relive after the past,
nor place expectations on the future.
What is past
is left behind.
The future
is as yet unreached.
Whatever quality is present
he clearly sees right there,

right there.
Unvanquished, unshaken,
that's how he develops the mind.
Ardently doing his duty today,
for—who knows?—tomorrow
death may come.
There is no bargaining
with Death & his mighty horde.

Whoever lives thus ardently,
relentlessly
both day & night,
has truly had an auspicious day:
So says the Peaceful Sage.

M.131

§ 82. The Buddha: 'Mindfulness of death, when developed & pursued, is of great fruit & great benefit. It plunges into the Deathless, has the Deathless as its final end. Therefore you should develop mindfulness of death.'

When this was said, a certain monk addressed the Blessed One, 'I already develop mindfulness of death.'

'And how do you develop mindfulness of death?'

'I think, "O, that I might live for a day & night, that I might attend to the Blessed One's instructions. I would have accomplished a great deal." This is how I develop mindfulness of death.'

Then another monk addressed the Blessed One, 'I, too, already develop mindfulness of death.'

'And how do you develop mindfulness of death?'

'I think, "O, that I might live for a day, that I might attend to the Blessed One's instructions. I would have accomplished a great deal." This is how I develop mindfulness of death.'

Then another monk addressed the Blessed One, 'I, too, develop mindfulness of death....'I think, "O, that I might live for the interval that it takes to eat a meal, that I might attend to the Blessed One's instructions. I would have accomplished a great deal"....

Then another monk addressed the Blessed One, 'I, too, develop mindfulness of death....'I think, "O, that I might live for the interval that it takes to swallow having chewed up four morsels of food, that I might attend to the Blessed One's instructions. I would have accomplished a great deal"....

Then another monk addressed the Blessed One, 'I, too, develop mindfulness of death....'I think, "O, that I might live for the interval that it takes to swallow having chewed up one morsel of food, that I might attend to the Blessed One's instructions. I would have accomplished a great deal"....

Then another monk addressed the Blessed One, 'I, too, develop mindfulness of death....'I think, "O, that I might live for the interval that it takes to breathe out after breathing in, or to breathe in after breathing out, that I might attend to the Blessed One's instructions. I would have accomplished a great deal." This is how I develop mindfulness of death.'

When this was said, the Blessed One addressed the monks. 'Whoever develops mindfulness of death, thinking, "O, that I might live for a day & night...for a day...for the interval that it takes to eat a meal...for the interval that it takes to swallow having chewed up four morsels of food, that I might attend to the Blessed One's instructions. I would have accomplished a great deal"—they are said to dwell heedlessly. They develop mindfulness of death slowly for the sake of ending the effluents.

'But whoever develops mindfulness of death, thinking, "O, that I might live for the interval that it takes to swallow having chewed up one morsel of food...for the interval that it takes to breathe out after breathing in, or to breathe in after breathing out, that I might attend to the Blessed One's instructions. I would have accomplished a great deal"—they are said to dwell heedfully. They develop mindfulness of death acutely for the sake of ending the effluents.

'Therefore you should train yourselves: "We will dwell heedfully. We will develop mindfulness of death acutely for the sake of ending the effluents." That is how you should train yourselves.'

A.VI.19

§ 83. Then the Blessed One addressed the monks, *'I exhort you, monks: All fabrications are subject to decay. Attain consummation through heedfulness.'* Those were the Tathāgata's last words.

D.16

§ 84. These are the four modes of practice. Which four? Painful practice with slow intuition, painful practice with quick intuition, pleasant practice with slow intuition, & pleasant practice with quick intuition.

And what is painful practice with slow intuition? There is the case where a certain individual is normally of an intensely passionate nature. He perpetually experiences pain & distress born of passion.

Or he is normally of an intensely aversive nature. He perpetually experiences pain & distress born of aversion. Or he is normally of an intensely deluded nature. He perpetually experiences pain & distress born of delusion. His five faculties—the faculty of conviction... persistence...mindfulness... concentration...discernment—are present in a weak form. Because of their weakness, he attains only slowly the immediacy [Comm: the concentration forming the Path] that leads to the ending of the effluents. This is called painful practice with slow intuition.

And what is painful practice with quick intuition? There is the case where a certain individual is normally of an intensely passionate... aversive...deluded nature. He perpetually experiences pain & distress born of delusion. His five faculties...are present in an acute form. Because of their acuity, he attains quickly the immediacy that leads to the ending of the effluents. This is called painful practice with quick intuition.

And what is pleasant practice with slow intuition? There is the case where a certain individual is normally not of an intensely passionate nature. He does not perpetually experience pain & distress born of passion. Or he is normally not of an intensely aversive nature... normally not of an intensely deluded nature. He does not perpetually experience pain & distress born of delusion. His five faculties...are present in a weak form. Because of their weakness, he attains only slowly the immediacy that leads to the ending of the effluents. This is called pleasant practice with slow intuition.

And what is pleasant practice with quick intuition? There is the case where a certain individual is normally not of an intensely passionate nature...normally not of an intensely aversive nature...normally not of an intensely deluded nature. He does not perpetually experience pain & distress born of delusion. His five faculties...are present in an acute form. Because of their acuity, he attains quickly the immediacy that leads to the ending of the effluents. This is called pleasant practice with quick intuition.

A.IV.162

§ 85. These are the four modes of practice. Which four? Painful practice with slow intuition, painful practice with quick intuition, pleasant practice with slow intuition, & pleasant practice with quick intuition.

And what is painful practice with slow intuition? There is the case where a monk remains focused on unattractiveness with regard to the body. Percipient of loathsomeness with regard to food & non-delight with regard to the entire world, he remains focused on impermanence with regard to all fabrications. The perception of death is well established within him. He dwells in dependence on the five strengths of a learner—strength of conviction, strength of conscience, strength of concern, strength of persistence, & strength of discernment—but his five faculties...are present in a weak form. Because of their weakness, he attains only slowly the immediacy that leads to the ending of the effluents. This is called painful practice with slow intuition.

And what is painful practice with quick intuition? There is the case where a monk remains focused on unattractiveness with regard to the body...focused on impermanence with regard to all fabrications. The perception of death is well established within him. He dwells in dependence on the five strengths of a learner...and his five faculties.. .are present in an acute form. Because of their acuity, he attains quickly the immediacy that leads to the ending of the effluents. This is called painful practice with quick intuition.

And what is pleasant practice with slow intuition? There is the case where a monk...enters & remains in the first jhāna...second jhāna... third jhāna...fourth jhāna. He dwells in dependence on the five strengths of a learner...but his five faculties...are present in a weak form. Because of their weakness, he attains only slowly the immediacy that leads to the ending of the effluents. This is called pleasant practice with slow intuition.

And what is pleasant practice with quick intuition? There is the case where a monk...enters & remains in the first jhāna...second jhāna... third jhāna...fourth jhāna. He dwells in dependence on the five strengths of a learner...and his five faculties...are present in an acute form. Because of their acuity, he attains quickly the immediacy that leads to the ending of the effluents. This is called pleasant practice with quick intuition.

These are the four modes of practice.

A.IV.163

§ 86. As Ven. Soṇa was meditating in seclusion [after doing walking meditation until the skin of his soles was split & bleeding], this train of thought arose in his awareness: 'Of the Blessed One's disciples who have aroused their persistence, I am one, but my mind is not released from the effluents through lack of clinging/sustenance. Now, my family has enough wealth that it would be possible to enjoy wealth & make merit. What if I were to disavow the training, return to the lower life, and to enjoy wealth & make merit?'

Then the Blessed One, as soon as he perceived with his awareness the train of thought in Ven. Soṇa's awareness—as a strong man might stretch out his bent arm or bend his outstretched arm—disappeared from Mount Vulture Peak, appeared in the Cool Wood right in front of Ven. Soṇa, and sat down on a prepared seat. Ven. Soṇa, after bowing down to the Blessed One, sat down to one side. As he was sitting there, the Blessed One said to him, 'Just now, as you were meditating in seclusion, didn't this train of thought appear to your awareness: "Of the Blessed One's disciples who have aroused their persistence, I am one, but my mind is not released from the effluents....What if I were to disavow the training, return to the lower life, and to enjoy wealth & make merit?"'

'Yes, lord.'

'Now what do you think, Soṇa. Before, when you were a house-dweller, were you skilled at playing the vina?'

'Yes, lord.'

'...And when the strings of your vina were too taut, was your vina in tune & playable?'

'No, lord.'

'...And when the strings of your vina were too loose, was your vina in tune & playable?'

'No, lord.'

'...And when the strings of your vina were neither too taut nor too loose, but tuned (lit: "established") to be right on pitch, was your vina in tune & playable?'

'Yes, lord.'

'In the same way, Soṇa, over-aroused persistence leads to restlessness, overly slack persistence leads to laziness. Thus you should determine the right pitch for your persistence, attune ('penetrate, 'ferret out') the pitch of the [five] faculties [to that], and there pick up your theme.'

'Yes, lord,' Ven. Soṇa answered the Blessed One. Then, having given this exhortation to Ven. Soṇa, the Blessed One—as a strong man might stretch out his bent arm or bend his outstretched arm—disappeared from the Cool Wood and appeared on Mount Vulture Peak.

So after that, Ven. Soṇa determined the right pitch for his persistence, attuned the pitch of the [five] faculties [to that], and there picked up his theme. Dwelling alone, secluded, heedful, ardent, & resolute, he in no long time reached & remained in the supreme goal of the holy life for which clansmen rightly go forth from home into homelessness, knowing & realizing it for himself in the here & now. He knew: 'Birth is ended, the holy life fulfilled, the task done. There is nothing further for the sake of this world.' And thus Ven. Soṇa became another one of the Arahants.

A.VI.55

§ 87. There is a manner of reckoning whereby a monk who is a learner, standing at the level of a learner, can discern that 'I am a learner,' and whereby a monk who is an adept (Arahant), standing at the level of an adept, can discern that 'I am an adept.'

...There is the case where a monk is a learner. He discerns, as it actually is, that 'This is stress...This is the origination of stress...This is the cessation of stress...This is the path of practice leading to the cessation of stress.' This is a manner of reckoning whereby a monk who is a learner, standing at the level of a learner, can discern that 'I am a learner.'

Furthermore, the monk who is a learner reflects, 'Is there outside of this [doctrine & discipline] any priest or contemplative who teaches the true, genuine, & accurate Dhamma like the Blessed One?' And he discerns, 'No, there is no priest or contemplative outside of this doctrine & discipline who teaches the true, genuine, & accurate Dhamma like the Blessed One.' This too is a manner of reckoning whereby a monk who is a learner, standing at the level of a learner, can discern that 'I am a learner.'

Furthermore, the monk who is a learner discerns the five faculties: the faculty of conviction...persistence...mindfulness...concentration... discernment. He sees clear through with discernment their destiny, excellence, rewards, & consummation, but he does not touch them with his body. This too is a manner of reckoning whereby a monk who is a learner, standing at the level of a learner, can discern that 'I am a learner.'

And what is the manner of reckoning whereby a monk who is an adept, standing at the level of an adept, can discern that 'I am an adept'? There is the case where a monk who is an adept discerns the five faculties: the faculty of conviction...persistence...mindfulness.. .concentration...discernment. He touches with his body and sees clear through with discernment what their destiny, excellence, rewards, & consummation are. This is a manner of reckoning whereby a monk who is an adept, standing at the level of an adept, can discern that 'I am an adept.'

Furthermore, the monk who is an adept discerns the six sense faculties: the faculty of the eye...ear...nose...tongue...body...intellect. He discerns, 'These six sense faculties will disband entirely, everywhere, & in every way without remainder, and no other set of six sense faculties will arise anywhere or in any way.' This too is a manner of reckoning whereby a monk who is an adept, standing at the level of an adept, can discern that 'I am an adept.'

S.XLVIII.53

§ 88. When a Noble Disciple discerns, as they actually are present, the origination, the disappearance, the allure, the drawbacks—and the emancipation from—these five faculties, he is called a Noble Disciple, one who has attained the stream, not subject to perdition, certain, destined for self-awakening...When, having discerned as they actually are present, the origination, the disappearance, the allure, the drawbacks—and the emancipation from—these five faculties, he is released from lack of clinging/sustenance, he is called an Arahant....

S.XLVIII.3, 5

§ 89. The Buddha: Sariputta, do you take it on conviction that the faculty of conviction, when developed & pursued, plunges into the Deathless, has the Deathless as its goal & consummation? Do you take it on conviction that the faculty of persistence...mindfulness...concentration...discernment, when developed & pursued, plunges into the Deathless, has the Deathless as its goal & consummation?

Sariputta: It's not that I take it on conviction in the Blessed One that the faculty of conviction...persistence...mindfulness...concentration... discernment, when developed & pursued, plunges into the Deathless, has the Deathless as its goal & consummation. Those who have not known, seen, penetrated, realized, or attained it by means of discernment would have to take it on conviction in others that the faculty of conviction...discernment... has the Deathless as its goal & consummation; whereas those who have known, seen, penetrated, realized, & attained it by means of discernment would have no doubt or uncertainty that the faculty of conviction...discernment.. has the Deathless as its goal & consummation. And as for me, I have known, seen, penetrated, realized, & attained it by means of discernment. I have no doubt or uncertainty that the faculty of conviction... discernment...has the Deathless as its goal & consummation.

S.XLVIII.44

F. THE FIVE STRENGTHS

§ 90. There are these five strengths. Which five? Strength of conviction, strength of persistence, strength of mindfulness, strength of concentration, & strength of discernment. These are the five strengths.

Just as the River Ganges flows to the east, slopes to the east, inclines to the east, in the same way when a monk develops & pursues the five strengths, he flows to Unbinding, slopes to Unbinding, inclines to Unbinding.

And how is it that when a monk develops & pursues the five strengths, he flows...slopes...inclines to Unbinding?

There is the case where the monk develops strength of conviction dependent on seclusion, dependent on dispassion, dependent on cessation, resulting in letting go. He develops strength of persistence... mindfulness... concentration...discernment dependent on seclusion... dispassion...cessation, resulting in letting go.

This is how a monk, when developing & pursuing the five strengths, flows...slopes...inclines to Unbinding.

S.L.1

§ 91. There is a manner of reckoning whereby the five faculties are the same as the five strengths, and the five strengths the same as the five faculties. And what is that method?

Whatever is the faculty of conviction, that is the strength of conviction. Whatever is the strength of conviction, that is the faculty of conviction. Whatever is the faculty of persistence, that is the strength of persistence. Whatever is the strength of persistence, that is the faculty of persistence. Whatever is the faculty of mindfulness, that is the strength of mindfulness. Whatever is the strength of mindfulness, that is the faculty of mindfulness. Whatever is the faculty of concentration, that is the strength of concentration. Whatever is the strength of concentration, that is the faculty of concentration. Whatever is the faculty of discernment, that is the strength of discernment. Whatever is the strength of discernment, that is the faculty of discernment.

Imagine a river—flowing, sloping, inclining toward the east—in whose midst is an island. There is a manner of reckoning whereby the river is classified as one current, and another manner of reckoning whereby it is classified as two.

And what is the first manner of reckoning? Whatever water lies to the east of the island, and whatever water lies to the west. This is the manner of reckoning whereby the river is classified as one current.

And what is the second manner of reckoning? Whatever water lies to the north of the island, and whatever water lies to the south. This is the manner of reckoning whereby the river is classified as two.

In the same way, whatever is the faculty of conviction, that is the strength of conviction. Whatever is the strength of conviction, that is the faculty of conviction....Whatever is the faculty of discernment, that is the strength of discernment. Whatever is the strength of discernment, that is the faculty of discernment.

S.XLVIII.43

G. THE SEVEN FACTORS OF AWAKENING

The seven factors of Awakening *(bojjhanga)* are closely related to the practice of the four frames of reference. The texts use two patterns to describe this relationship. **The first pattern** is a spiral, showing how the seven factors of Awakening build on the four frames of reference [§92]. This point is reflected in the position of mindfulness—defined as the practice of any one of the four frames of reference—as the first factor in the list. Discernment, in the role of the analysis of mental qualities into skillful and unskillful, builds on right mindfulness and leads to persistence, which in the form of right effort/exertion maximizes the skillful qualities and minimizes the unskillful ones. This in turn leads to four factors associated with jhana: rapture, serenity, concentration, and equanimity. Equanimity, here, is not a neutral feeling, but rather a balancing or moderation—an evenness of mind—with regard to any feeling or object that arises. It is identical with the equanimity in the fourth jhana [§149] and with the inherent equanimity in the fifth factor of five-factored noble concentration [§150], which can develop out of any of the four jhanas. As such it can either lead to greater mastery of meditation—as the purity of mindfulness that accompanies the fourth jhana provides the basis for even more precise analysis of qualities, thus allowing the causal loop to spiral to a higher level—or else develop into the state of non-fashioning that opens to Awakening.

Abhidhamma texts seem to contradict the point that equanimity feeds back into mindfulness in this way, for they maintain that the factors of Awakening are transcendent—in other words, that they come into play only as one reaches the point of Awakening, where no temporal feedback would take place. The discourses, however, show that the factors of Awakening can function in the development of mundane concentration as well. Passage §96 shows how the "feeding" of the factors of Awakening is needed to "starve" the hindrances, mental qualities that have to be suppressed before mundane concentration can be attained. Passage §98 shows how the factors function in developing the four attitudes that lead to "release of awareness"—a mundane form of release—and indicates the highest state to which those attitudes can lead for one who has penetrated no higher, i.e., who has attained none of the transcendent levels. These passages demonstrate that the factors of Awakening can function on the level of mundane jhana in addition to the level at the verge of Awakening. Thus, equanimity as a factor of

Awakening on the mundane plane can feed back into the process of meditation, providing a steady basis for more continuous mindfulness and clearer analysis of mental qualities, until all the factors of the list ripen to transcendence.

The second pattern for describing the relationship between the factors of Awakening and the four frames of reference is more holographic. As we have already noted [II/B], all the factors in the list are all implicit in the "approach" stage of frames-of-reference meditation, and the texts themselves make this point by saying that the development of any one of the frames of reference involves bringing the factors of Awakening to the culmination of their development [§92].

The differences between these two patterns—a spiraling sequence building on the four frames of reference, and a holographic formula implicit in the frames of reference—is largely one of emphasis. As the dual nature of this/that conditionality indicates—with mental factors building on one another over time and strengthening one another in the present—both aspects act together in actual practice.

Viewed as a spiraling sequence, the factors of Awakening offer some interesting contrasts to the five faculties. Both sets depict one of the causal loops in the skillful development of the mind, but here the emphasis is not on how mindfulness and concentration help to develop discernment, but on how mindfulness and discernment help to develop concentration. This different dynamic is reflected in the mental qualities that act as underlying agents in the development of each set. As we have seen [II/E], heedfulness underlies the development of the faculties; it grows from a sense of conviction in the principle of kamma into members of the "concentration aggregate"—right effort and right mindfulness—in the noble eightfold path. In the case of the factors of Awakening, appropriate attention is what underlies the development of every element in the set [§95]; it grows from a component factor of conviction [§70] into a member of the "discernment aggregate": right view. Thus, in each set, the agent underlying its development reflects the intermediate members of the set in their role of fostering the final member.

A closer look at the topic of ***appropriate attention*** will show how the processes of discernment can foster concentration to the point where both issue in Awakening. Because this topic is so central to the practice, we will have to treat it in detail.

The term "appropriate attention" *(yoniso manasikara)* can also be rendered as "wise reflection," "the proper approach," or "systematic attention." It is essentially the basic insight that enables one to see which issues are worth paying attention to, and which ones should be ignored. Passage §51 gives what is probably the best depiction of this process. One ignores questions that lead to the proliferation of mental effluents, and pays attention to questions that help weaken them. As we noted in I/B, the knowledge that puts an end to the effluents deals with experience in the phenomenological mode. Thus, the best questions for weakening the effluents are ones that lead the mind into that mode. Now, not all questions are helpful in this way. Some deal in terms that focus the mind on narrative or cosmological issues in ways that actually obstruct a phenomenological viewpoint. For this reason, the Buddha found it necessary to divide questions into four classes: those meriting a categorical answer, those meriting an analytical answer, those deserving a counter-question, and those deserving to be put aside [A.IV.43]. The first class includes questions that are already well-phrased and can yield straight answers useful in weakening one's mental effluents. The second class includes those that are poorly phrased but are close enough to becoming useful that they can be clarified by a redefinition of terms. The third class covers instances where the real issue is not the question as phrased, but the confused line of thinking or hidden agendas behind the asking of the question. Once these underlying elements are exposed and corrected by the proper counter-question, fruitful questions can then be framed. The final class of questions covers instances where both the question and the act of asking it are so misguided that any attempt to get involved in the issue would lead only to the proliferation of mental effluents, and so the whole issue should be put aside.

Of these four classes of questions, the class that merits categorical answers is of most interest here, for it's the class that can act as a focal point for appropriate attention. The vast majority of the questions that the Buddha asks and answers categorically in the texts fall into three general sorts: (a) those that seek to identify terms and categories useful for the task of ending of stress and suffering; (b) those that seek to place particular events in their proper category; and (c) those that seek to understand the causal role of events assigned to the various categories: how they condition, and are conditioned by, one another. A sub-set of (c) consists of questions concerning the effect that one's questions and one's approach to the practice in general have on the mind. All of these three sorts of question are closely related to the three stages of frames-of-reference meditation: sorts (a) and (b) relate to the first stage, and sort (c) to the second, whereas the sub-set of (c) dealing with the questioning approach itself leads directly to the third. This last sub-set also forms the overall principle for delineating all four classes of questions mentioned above: the effect that the process of asking and answering has on the mind. In simple terms, this principle means viewing experience in terms of cause and effect, viewing questions in terms of cause and effect, classifying them according to the results that come from trying to answer them, and treating them only in ways that will help lead to the ending of suffering and stress. This is the proper function of appropriate attention in its most mature form.

To arrive at this mature level, however, appropriate attention must be developed step by step. These steps can be shown by taking the passages given in this section and viewing them in the context of the practice of the fourth frame of reference: focusing on the mental qualities of the hindrances and the factors of Awakening in and of themselves in the course of developing concentration.

The first step is simply to identify the hindrances and factors of Awakening as they are experienced, noting their presence and absence in the mind—a movement toward what the Buddha called "entering into emptiness" [II/B]. As III/D makes clear, there are several preliminary steps in concentration practice leading up to the ability to do this. When these are mastered, one can focus on, say, the hindrance of ill-will not in terms of the object of the ill-will, but on the quality of ill-will as a mere event in the mind. The question here is not, "What am I angry about?" or "What did that person do wrong?" but simply "What is happening in my mind? How can it be classed?" Given the well-known Buddhist teaching on not-self, some people have wondered why the questions of appropriate attention at this step would use such concepts as "me" and "my," but these concepts are essential at this stage—where the mind is still more at home in the narrative mode of "self" and "others"—in pointing out that the focus of the inquiry should be directed within, rather than without. This helps to bring one's frame of reference to the experience of mental qualities as phenomena in and of themselves, and away from the narratives that provoked the anger to begin with. Only when this shift in reference is secure can the concepts of "me" and "my" be dispensed with, in the third step below.

The second step in appropriate attention—corresponding to the second stage of frames-of-reference practice—is to inquire into the causal functioning of the hindrances and factors of Awakening, to see how they arise and cease in the course of one's concentration practice. The aim here is to gain insight into the workings of the hindrances and factors of Awakening as one tries to eliminate the former and bring the latter to full development. The passages in this section dealing with this step treat the issue in terms of two metaphors—balance on the one hand, feeding and starving on the other—and list the desired results of the meditation as a standard of measurement for gauging the success of one's practice.

We have met with the role of **balance** already in the four bases of power and the five faculties. What is special here is that, instead of finding a balance within each factor of Awakening, the meditator is to use different factors to balance out specific hindrances. The more active members—analysis of qualities, persistence, and rapture—can be used to offset sluggish mind states; the more passive members—serenity, concentration, and equanimity—counteract restless mind states. Mindfulness is the only member of the set that is inherently skillful at all times [§97], for it is the one that keeps the need for balance in mind. To combine the portrayals of balance under this set and under the bases of power, we can say that the more active factors of Awakening should be used to prevent specific bases of power—such as desire—from being too sluggish or restricted, whereas the more passive factors of Awakening should be used to prevent desire, etc., from being too active or scattered [§66]. It is interesting also to note that, although analysis of qualities is a potential cause for restlessness, it is also the factor needed to judge when its own activity is going overboard and needs to be calmed with concentration.

Under the metaphor of **feeding and starving,** the skill of appropriate attention is said to feed all the factors of Awakening, just as inappropriate attention starves them and feeds the hindrances in their place. As §96 points out, the role of appropriate attention at this level is to inquire into the property that acts as a foothold for each hindrance or factor of Awakening. The feeding process is especially direct with analysis of qualities as a factor of Awakening—a near equivalent of appropriate attention—and the hindrance of uncertainty. These two form a pair, in that the feeding of analysis of qualities as a factor of Awakening in and of itself starves the hindrance of uncertainty, and vice versa. Appropriate attention to the effects of skillful and unskillful qualities in the mind—in other words, focusing on questions that identify such qualities as the hindrances and the factors of Awakening, and inquire into their causes and effects—not only feeds this factor of Awakening but also enables one to develop its fellow factors. Inappropriate attention to issues that excite uncertainty—asking questions that can lead only to doubt and perplexity—not only feeds the hindrance of uncertainty, but leads to a sense of confusion that prevents all the factors of Awakening from developing.

With some of the other factors of Awakening—such as mindfulness, rapture, and equanimity—the texts are vague as to exactly which properties form their potential footholds. A few of these properties can be inferred from other texts, so they are cross-referenced in the relevant passages. The remaining instances can serve as challenges for each meditator to explore through practice. Challenges of this sort are valuable in forcing one to become self-reliant at observing cause and effect and asking the right questions: two skills that are basic to the development of appropriate attention and the path of practice as a whole.

As one becomes more successful in identifying these properties and attending to them in the appropriate way, one's skill at concentration practice improves. Concentration and equanimity then feed back into the loop by purifying mindfulness in the practice of jhana [§72], providing a steady basis for discernment in terms of more precise analysis of qualities and more subtlety in one's attention. This can lead either to improved abilities at concentration or to a more self-referential mode away from the "object" of the practice and turning toward the "approach" [II/B], where these activities of discernment become sensitive to themselves as events in the causal network. In particular, they can begin to ask questions about their own acts of questioning, to see what latent assumptions are still causing them uncertainty and getting in the way of their further development. In this way, they come to *the third step* in their development.

According to the texts, the most insidious issues that can excite uncertainty are questions that center on the concept of "I": "Do I exist?" "Do I not exist?" In the cosmological or metaphysical mode, this concept leads to such questions as: "Does the self exist?" "Does it not exist?" In the psychological or personal narrative mode, it leads to a sense of self-identity, attachment to the object with which one identifies, and all the suffering that inherently results. In either mode, this concept leads to uncertainty about the past and future: "Did I exist in the past?" "Will I exist in the future?" "What will I be?" All of these questions obviously pull the mind out of the phenomenological mode; passage §51 shows that the Buddha regarded them as leading to mental effluents and thus unworthy of attention. The one time he was asked point-blank as to whether or not there is a self [S.XLIV.10; MFU, pp. 85-86], he refused to answer, thus showing that the question deserves to be put aside.

What then of the well-known Buddhist teachings on not-self? From a few of the ways in which these teachings are expressed in the texts, it might be inferred that the Buddha held to the principle that there is no self. Here, though, it is important to remember the Buddha's own comment on how his teachings are to be interpreted [A.II.25]. With some of them, he said, it is proper to draw inferences, whereas with others it is not. Unfortunately, he did not illustrate this principle with specific examples. However, it seems safe to assume that if one tries to draw inferences from his statements to give either a categorical answer (No, there is no self; or Yes, there is) or an analytical answer (It depends on how you define "self") to a question that the Buddha showed by example should not be asked or answered, one is drawing inferences where they should not be drawn.

A more fruitful line of inquiry is to view experience, not in terms of the existence or non-existence of the self, but in terms of the categories of the four noble truths, which §51 identifies as the truly proper subject of appropriate attention. If we look at the way the Buddha phrases questions about not-self [S.XXII.59, MFU, pp. 79-80] in the context of the duties appropriate to the four noble truths [§195], we see that they function as tools for comprehending stress and abandoning the attachment and clinging that function as its cause. Thus they help bring about the ending of the mental effluents. Rather than asking, "Do I exist?", one should ask, "Is this mine? Is this me? If these things are regarded as me or mine, will there be suffering?" These questions, when properly answered (No, No, and Yes), can lead directly to the phenomenological mode and on to release from attachment and from suffering and stress. Thus they are worth asking.

When applied to the hindrances and factors of Awakening, this line of inquiry can bring the mind to the third stage of frames-of-reference meditation by calling into question the "me" and "my" assumed in the first step of questioning. This undermines any sense of self-identification, first with the hindrances—such as "I'm drowsy"—and then with the factors of Awakening—such as "My mind is serene" [§167]. All that then remains is the radically phenomenological mode that enters fully into the emptiness on the verge of non-fashioning [II/B], where there are no longer any questions, but simply awareness that "There are mental qualities"..."There is this." This is the threshold to Awakening.

Throughout the process of developing appropriate attention in the course of the second and third stages of frames-of-reference meditation, the spiraling loop of the factors of Awakening continually feeds back on itself, as the factor of equanimity allows the factors of mindfulness and analysis of qualities to gauge the success of the practice and call for adjustments where needed. The **standard of measurement** to be used in this evaluation is given in the formula that frequently accompanies the definition of the factors of Awakening in the texts: each factor ideally should depend on "seclusion...dispassion...cessation, resulting in letting go." The terms in this list occur both in mundane [§98] and in transcendent [§92] contexts, which indicates that they have both mundane and transcendent levels of meaning. On the mundane level, they play a role in the practice of jhana [for the role of letting go in concentration see §71]. As they develop and reach transcendence, they bring the mind to the state of non-fashioning. By basing one's practice on the seclusion, dispassion, and cessation found in the jhana that takes letting go as its object [§72], and by feeding it through the constant evaluation provided by appropriate attention and analysis of qualities to the point of ever more refined levels of letting go, one brings together the mental qualities of attention and intention in a mutually reinforcing way that heads in the direction of Awakening. At the highest level of letting go—the "knowing but not holding" that we equated with the perceptual mode of emptiness on the verge of non-fashioning in section II/E—appropriate attention gives way to transcendent clear knowing, and the intention underlying the practice of jhana gives way to the stillness of the resulting transcendent freedom. This is how the factors of Awakening, in the words of the texts [§92], "when developed & pursued, lead to the culmination of clear knowing & release."

§ 92. Once the Blessed One was staying at Sāketa, in the Añjana Forest Game Refuge. Then Kuṇḍaliya the Wanderer came to where the Blessed One was staying and on arrival greeted him courteously and, after engaging in pleasant conversation, sat to one side. As he was sitting there he said to the Blessed One, 'Ven. Gotama, I like to frequent gatherings in parks. It is my habit at midday, after my morning meal, to go from park to park, from garden to garden. There I encounter various priests & contemplatives discoursing on the rewards of defending their own tenets in debate, and the rewards of condemning those of others. Now in the experience of what reward does Ven. Gotama dwell?'

'The Tathāgata dwells experiencing the reward of the fruits of clear knowing & release.'

'But what are the qualities that, developed & pursued, lead to the culmination of clear knowing & release?'

'The seven factors of Awakening....'

'And what are the qualities that...lead to the culmination of the seven factors of Awakening?'

'The four frames of reference....'

'And what are the qualities that...lead to the culmination of the four frames of reference?'

'The three courses of right conduct....'

'And what are the qualities that...lead to the culmination of the three courses of right conduct?'

'Restraint of the senses....And how does restraint of the senses, when developed & pursued, lead to the culmination of the three courses of right conduct? There is the case where a monk, on seeing a pleasant form with the eye, does not hanker after it, does not delight in it, does not give rise to passion for it. Unmoved in body & unmoved in mind, he is inwardly well composed & well released. On seeing an unpleasant form with the eye, he is not upset, his mind is not unsettled, his feelings are not wounded, his mind does not become resentful. Unmoved in body & unmoved in mind, he is inwardly well-composed & well-released.

On hearing a pleasant...unpleasant sound with the ear...On smelling a pleasant...unpleasant smell with the nose...On tasting a pleasant... unpleasant taste with the tongue...On feeling a pleasant...unpleasant tactile sensation with the body...

On cognizing a pleasant idea with the intellect, he does not hanker after it, does not delight in it, does not give rise to passion for it. Unmoved in body & unmoved in mind, he is inwardly well-composed & well-released. On cognizing an unpleasant idea with the intellect, he is not upset, his mind is not unsettled, his feelings are not wounded, his mind does not become resentful. Unmoved in body & unmoved in mind, he is inwardly well-composed & well-released. This is how, Kuṇḍaliya, restraint of the senses, when developed & pursued, leads to the culmination of the three courses of right conduct.

And how are the three courses of right conduct developed & pursued so as to lead to the culmination of the four frames of reference? There is the case where a monk abandons wrong conduct in terms of his deeds and develops right conduct in terms of his deeds; abandons wrong conduct in terms of his speech and develops right conduct in terms of his speech; abandons wrong conduct in terms of his thoughts and develops right conduct in terms of his thoughts. This is how, Kuṇḍaliya, the three courses of right conduct, when developed & pursued, lead to the culmination of the four frames of reference.

And how are the four frames of reference developed & pursued so that the seven factors of Awakening come to completion?

{[1] On whatever occasion the monk remains focused on the *body* in & of itself—ardent, alert, & mindful—putting aside greed & distress with reference to the world, on that occasion his mindfulness is steady & without lapse. When his mindfulness is steady & without lapse, then *mindfulness* as a factor of Awakening becomes aroused. He develops it, and for him it goes to the culmination of its development.

[2] Remaining mindful in this way, he examines, analyzes, & comes to a comprehension of that quality with discernment. When he remains mindful in this way, examining, analyzing, & coming to a comprehension of that quality with discernment, then *analysis of qualities* as a factor of Awakening becomes aroused. He develops it, and for him it goes to the culmination of its development.

[3] In one who examines, analyzes, & comes to a comprehension of that quality with discernment, unflagging persistence is aroused. When unflagging persistence is aroused in one who examines, analyzes, & comes to a comprehension of that quality with discernment, then *persistence* as a factor of Awakening becomes aroused. He develops it, and for him it goes to the culmination of its development.

[4] In one whose persistence is aroused, a rapture not-of-the-flesh arises. When a rapture not-of-the-flesh arises in one whose persistence is aroused, then *rapture* as a factor of Awakening becomes aroused. He develops it, and for him it goes to the culmination of its development.

[5] For one who is enraptured, the body grows calm and the mind grows calm. When the body & mind of an enraptured monk grow calm, then *serenity* as a factor of Awakening becomes aroused. He develops it, and for him it goes to the culmination of its development.

[6] For one who is at ease—his body calmed—the mind becomes concentrated. When the mind of one who is at ease—his body calmed—becomes concentrated, then *concentration* as a factor of Awakening becomes aroused. He develops it, and for him it goes to the culmination of its development.

[7] He oversees the mind thus concentrated with equanimity. When he oversees the mind thus concentrated with equanimity, *equanimity* as a factor of Awakening becomes aroused. He develops it, and for him it goes to the culmination of its development.

(Similarly with the other three frames of reference: feelings, mind, & mental qualities.)}

This is how, Kuṇḍaliya, the four frames of reference, when developed & pursued, lead to the culmination of the seven factors of Awakening.

And how are the seven factors of Awakening developed & pursued so as to lead to the culmination of clear knowing & release? There is the case where a monk develops *mindfulness* as a factor of Awakening dependent on seclusion...dispassion...cessation, resulting in letting go. He develops *analysis of qualities* as a factor of Awakening...*persistence* as a factor of Awakening...*rapture* as a factor of Awakening... *serenity* as a factor of Awakening...*concentration* as a factor of Awakening... *equanimity* as a factor of Awakening dependent on seclusion... dispassion...cessation, resulting in letting go. This is how, Kuṇḍaliya, the seven factors of Awakening, when developed & pursued, lead to the culmination of clear knowing & release.'

When this had been said, Kuṇḍaliya the Wanderer said to the Blessed One: 'Magnificent, Ven. Gotama, magnificent. In many ways has Ven. Gotama made the Dhamma clear—just as if one were to place upright what has been overturned, to reveal what has been hidden, to point out the way to one who is lost, or to set out a lamp in the darkness so that those with eyes might see forms. I go to Ven. Gotama for refuge, to the Dhamma, & to the community of monks. May Ven. Gotama regard me as a lay follower gone for refuge from this day forth as long as life shall last.'

S.XLVI.6 { + M.118}

§ 93. Now in what way does a monk develop & pursue mindfulness of in-&-out breathing so that it bears great fruit & great benefits?

There is the case where a monk develops *mindfulness* as a factor of Awakening accompanied by mindfulness of in-&-out breathing—dependent on seclusion...dispassion...cessation, resulting in letting go. He develops *analysis of qualities* as a factor of Awakening...*persistence* as a factor of Awakening...*rapture* as a factor of Awakening...*serenity* as a factor of Awakening...*concentration* as a factor of Awakening...*equanimity* as a factor of Awakening dependent on seclusion...dispassion...cessation, resulting in letting go. This is how mindfulness of in-&-out breathing is developed & pursued so that it bears great fruit & great benefits.

S.LIV.2

§ 94. Now what is the manner of reckoning by which the seven factors of Awakening are fourteen?

[1] Any mindfulness with regard to internal qualities is mindfulness as a factor of Awakening. And any mindfulness with regard to external qualities is also mindfulness as a factor of Awakening. Thus this forms the definition of 'mindfulness as a factor of Awakening,' and it is in this manner that it is two.

[2] Any time one examines, investigates, & scrutinizes internal qualities with discernment, that is analysis of qualities as a factor of Awakening. And any time one examines, investigates, & scrutinizes external qualities with discernment, that too is analysis of qualities as a factor of Awakening. Thus this forms the definition of 'analysis of qualities as a factor of Awakening,' and it is in this manner that it is two.

[3] Any bodily persistence is persistence as a factor of Awakening. And any mental persistence is also persistence as a factor of Awakening. Thus this forms the definition of 'persistence as a factor of Awakening,' and it is in this manner that it is two.

[4] Any rapture accompanied by directed thought & evaluation is rapture as a factor of Awakening. And any rapture unaccompanied by directed thought & evaluation is also rapture as a factor of Awakening. Thus this forms the definition of 'rapture as a factor of Awakening,' and it is in this manner that it is two.

[5] Any bodily serenity is serenity as a factor of Awakening. And any mental serenity is also serenity as a factor of Awakening. Thus this forms the definition of 'serenity as a factor of Awakening,' and it is in this manner that it is two.

[6] Any concentration accompanied by directed thought & evaluation is concentration as a factor of Awakening. And any concentration unaccompanied by directed thought & evaluation is also concentration

as a factor of Awakening. Thus this forms the definition of 'concentration as a factor of Awakening,' and it is in this manner that it is two.

[7] Any equanimity with regard to internal qualities is equanimity as a factor of Awakening. And any equanimity with regard to external qualities is also equanimity as a factor of Awakening. Thus this forms the definition of 'equanimity as a factor of Awakening,' and it is in this manner that it is two.

This is the manner of reckoning by which the seven factors of Awakening are fourteen.

S.XLVI.52

§ 95. I do not envision any one quality by which unarisen factors of Awakening do not arise, and arisen factors of Awakening do not go to the culmination of their development, like inappropriate attention. When a person's attention is inappropriate, unarisen factors of Awakening do not arise, and arisen factors of Awakening do not go to the culmination of their development.

I do not envision any one quality by which unarisen factors of Awakening arise, and arisen factors of Awakening go to the culmination of their development, like appropriate attention. When a person's attention is appropriate, unarisen factors of Awakening arise, and arisen factors of Awakening go to the culmination of their development. [§§51; 53]

A.I.75-76

§ 96. Monks, I will teach you the feeding & starving of the five hindrances & of the seven factors of Awakening. Listen & pay close attention. I will speak....

Feeding the Hindrances. And what is the food for the arising of unarisen *sensual desire,* or for the growth & increase of sensual desire once it has arisen? There is the theme of beauty. To foster inappropriate attention to it: This is the food for the arising of unarisen sensual desire, or for the growth & increase of sensual desire once it has arisen.

And what is the food for the arising of unarisen *ill will,* or for the growth & increase of ill will once it has arisen? There is the theme of irritation. To foster inappropriate attention to it: This is the food for the arising of unarisen ill will, or for the growth & increase of ill will once it has arisen.

And what is the food for the arising of unarisen *sloth & drowsiness,* or for the growth & increase of sloth & drowsiness once it has arisen? There are boredom, weariness, yawning, drowsiness after a meal, &

sluggishness of awareness. To foster inappropriate attention to them: This is the food for the arising of unarisen sloth & drowsiness, or for the growth & increase of sloth & drowsiness once it has arisen.

And what is the food for the arising of unarisen *restlessness & anxiety,* or for the growth & increase of restlessness & anxiety once it has arisen? There is non-stillness of awareness. To foster inappropriate attention to that: This is the food for the arising of unarisen restlessness & anxiety, or for the growth & increase of restlessness & anxiety once it has arisen.

And what is the food for the arising of unarisen *uncertainty,* or for the growth & increase of uncertainty once it has arisen? There are phenomena that act as a foothold for uncertainty. To foster inappropriate attention to them: This is the food for the arising of unarisen uncertainty, or for the growth & increase of uncertainty once it has arisen.

Feeding the Factors of Awakening. Now, what is the food for the arising of unarisen *mindfulness* as a factor of Awakening, or for the growth & increase of mindfulness...once it has arisen? There are mental qualities that act as a foothold for mindfulness as a factor of Awakening [well-purified virtue & views made straight; see §27]. To foster appropriate attention to them: This is the food for the arising of unarisen mindfulness as a factor of Awakening, or for the growth & increase of mindfulness...once it has arisen.

And what is the food for the arising of unarisen *analysis of qualities* as a factor of Awakening, or for the growth & increase of analysis of qualities... once it has arisen? There are mental qualities that are skillful & unskillful, blameworthy & blameless, gross & refined, siding with darkness & with light [§§2-3]. To foster appropriate attention to them: This is the food for the arising of unarisen analysis of qualities as a factor of Awakening, or for the growth & increase of analysis of qualities...once it has arisen.

And what is the food for the arising of unarisen *persistence* as a factor of Awakening, or for the growth & increase of persistence...once it has arisen? There is the potential for effort, the potential for exertion, the potential for striving. To foster appropriate attention to them: This is the food for the arising of unarisen persistence as a factor of Awakening, or for the growth & increase of persistence...once it has arisen.

And what is the food for the arising of unarisen *rapture* as a factor of Awakening, or for the growth & increase of rapture...once it has arisen? There are mental qualities that act as a foothold for rapture as a factor of Awakening. To foster appropriate attention to them: This is the food for the arising of unarisen rapture as a factor of Awakening, or for the growth & increase of rapture...once it has arisen.

And what is the food for the arising of unarisen *serenity* as a factor of Awakening, or for the growth & increase of serenity...once it has arisen? There is physical serenity & there is mental serenity. To foster appropriate attention to them: This is the food for the arising of unarisen serenity as a factor of Awakening, or for the growth & increase of serenity...once it has arisen.

And what is the food for the arising of unarisen *concentration* as a factor of Awakening, or for the growth & increase of concentration... once it has arisen? There are themes for calm, themes for non-distraction [these are the four frames of reference; see §148]. To foster appropriate attention to them: This is the food for the arising of unarisen concentration as a factor of Awakening, or for the growth & increase of concentration...once it has arisen.

And what is the food for the arising of unarisen *equanimity* as a factor of Awakening, or for the growth & increase of equanimity.. once it has arisen? There are mental qualities that act as a foothold for equanimity as a factor of Awakening. To foster appropriate attention to them: This is the food for the arising of unarisen equanimity as a factor of Awakening, or for the growth & increase of equanimity... once it has arisen.

Starving the Hindrances. Now, what is lack of food for the arising of unarisen *sensual desire,* or for the growth & increase of sensual desire once it has arisen? There is the theme of unattractiveness. To foster appropriate attention to it: This is lack of food for the arising of unarisen sensual desire, or for the growth & increase of sensual desire once it has arisen.

And what is lack of food for the arising of unarisen *ill will,* or for the growth & increase of ill will once it has arisen? There is the release of the mind [through good will, compassion, appreciation, or equanimity]. To foster appropriate attention to that: This is lack of food for the arising of unarisen ill will, or for the growth & increase of ill will once it has arisen.

And what is lack of food for the arising of unarisen *sloth & drowsiness,* or for the growth & increase of sloth & drowsiness once it has arisen? There is the potential for effort, the potential for exertion, the potential for striving. To foster appropriate attention to them: This is lack of food for the arising of unarisen sloth & drowsiness, or for the growth & increase of sloth & drowsiness once it has arisen.

And what is lack of food for the arising of unarisen *restlessness & anxiety,* or for the growth & increase of restlessness & anxiety once it has arisen? There is stillness of awareness. To foster appropriate attention to that: This is lack of food for the arising of unarisen restlessness & anxiety, or for the growth & increase of restlessness & anxiety once it has arisen.

And what is lack of food for the arising of unarisen *uncertainty,* or for the growth & increase of uncertainty once it has arisen? There are mental qualities that are skillful & unskillful, blameworthy & blameless, gross & refined, siding with darkness & with light. To foster appropriate attention to them: This is lack of food for the arising of unarisen uncertainty, or for the growth & increase of uncertainty once it has arisen.

Starving the Factors of Awakening. Now, what is lack of food for the arising of unarisen *mindfulness* as a factor of Awakening, or for the growth & increase of mindfulness...once it has arisen? There are mental qualities that act as a foothold for mindfulness as a factor of Awakening. Not fostering attention to them: This is lack of food for the arising of unarisen mindfulness as a factor of Awakening, or for the growth & increase of mindfulness...once it has arisen.

And what is lack of food for the arising of unarisen *analysis of qualities* as a factor of Awakening, or for the growth & increase of analysis of qualities... once it has arisen? There are mental qualities that are skillful & unskillful, blameworthy & blameless, gross & refined, siding with darkness & with light. Not fostering attention to them: This is lack of food for the arising of unarisen analysis of qualities as a factor of Awakening, or for the growth & increase of analysis of qualities...once it has arisen.

And what is lack of food for the arising of unarisen *persistence* as a factor of Awakening, or for the growth & increase of persistence... once it has arisen? There is the potential for effort, the potential for exertion, the potential for striving. Not fostering attention to them: This is lack of food for the arising of unarisen persistence as a factor of Awakening, or for the growth & increase of persistence...once it has arisen.

And what is lack of food for the arising of unarisen *rapture* as a factor of Awakening, or for the growth & increase of rapture...once it has arisen? There are mental qualities that act as a foothold for rapture as a factor of Awakening. Not fostering attention to them: This is lack of food for the arising of unarisen rapture as a factor of Awakening, or for the growth & increase of rapture...once it has arisen.

And what is lack of food for the arising of unarisen *serenity* as a factor of Awakening, or for the growth & increase of serenity...once it has arisen? There is physical serenity & there is mental serenity. Not fostering attention to them: This is lack of food for the arising of unarisen serenity as a factor of Awakening, or for the growth & increase of serenity...once it has arisen.

And what is lack of food for the arising of unarisen *concentration* as a factor of Awakening, or for the growth & increase of concentration... once it has arisen? There are the themes for concentration, themes for non-confusion. Not fostering attention to them: This is lack of food for the arising of unarisen concentration as a factor of Awakening, or for the growth & increase of concentration...once it has arisen.

And what is lack of food for the arising of unarisen *equanimity* as a factor of Awakening, or for the growth & increase of equanimity... once it has arisen? There are mental qualities that act as a foothold for equanimity as a factor of Awakening. Not fostering attention to them: This is lack of food for the arising of unarisen equanimity as a factor of Awakening, or for the growth & increase of equanimity...once it has arisen.

S.XLVI.51

§ 97. Fire. Monks, on occasions when the mind is sluggish, that is the wrong time to develop serenity as a factor of Awakening, concentration as a factor of Awakening, equanimity as a factor of Awakening. Why is that? The sluggish mind is hard to raise up by those mental qualities. Just as if a man, wanting to make a small fire blaze up, were to place wet grass in it, wet cow dung, & wet sticks; were to give it a spray of water and smother it with dust. Is it possible that he would make the small fire blaze up?

No, lord.

In the same way, when the mind is sluggish, that is the wrong time to develop serenity as a factor of Awakening, concentration as a factor of Awakening, equanimity as a factor of Awakening. Why is that? The sluggish mind is hard to raise up by those mental qualities.

Now, on occasions when the mind is sluggish, that is the right time to develop analysis of qualities as a factor of Awakening, persistence as a factor of Awakening, rapture as a factor of Awakening. Why is that? The sluggish mind is easy to raise up by those mental qualities. Just as if a man, wanting to make a small fire blaze up, were to place dry grass in it, dry cow dung, & dry sticks; were to blow on it with his mouth and not smother it with dust. Is it possible that he would make the small fire blaze up?

Yes, lord.

In the same way, when the mind is sluggish, that is the right time to develop analysis of qualities as a factor of Awakening, persistence as a factor of Awakening, rapture as a factor of Awakening....

Now, on occasions when the mind is restless, that is the wrong time to develop analysis of qualities as a factor of Awakening, persistence as a factor of Awakening, rapture as a factor of Awakening. Why is that? The restless mind is hard to calm down with those mental qualities. Just as if a man, wanting to put out a large fire, were to place dry grass in it, dry cow dung, & dry sticks; were to blow on it with his mouth and not smother it with dust. Is it possible that he would put it out?

No, lord.

In the same way, when the mind is restless, that is the wrong time to develop analysis of qualities as a factor of Awakening, persistence as a factor of Awakening, rapture as a factor of Awakening....

Now, on occasions when the mind is restless, that is the right time to develop serenity as a factor of Awakening, concentration as a factor of Awakening, equanimity as a factor of Awakening. Why is that? The restless mind is easy to calm down with those mental qualities. Just as if a man, wanting to put out a large fire, were to place wet grass in it, wet cow dung, & wet sticks; were to give it a spray of water and smother it with dust. Is it possible that he would put it out?

Yes, lord.

In the same way, when the mind is restless, that is the right time to develop serenity as a factor of Awakening, concentration as a factor of Awakening, equanimity as a factor of Awakening. Why is that? The restless mind is easy to calm down with those mental qualities.

As for mindfulness, I tell you, that is beneficial everywhere.

S.XLVI.53

§ 98. Release of Awareness. And how is the release of awareness through good will developed, what is its destiny, what is its excellence, its reward, & its consummation?

There is the case where a monk develops *mindfulness* as a factor of Awakening accompanied by good will, dependent on seclusion... dispassion... cessation, resulting in letting go. He develops *analysis of qualities* as a factor of Awakening...*persistence* as a factor of Awakening...*rapture* as a factor of Awakening...*serenity* as a factor of Awakening...*concentration* as a factor of Awakening...*equanimity* as a factor of Awakening accompanied by good will, dependent on seclusion...dispassion...cessation, resulting in letting go. If he wants, he remains percipient of loathsomeness in the presence of what is not loathsome. If he wants, he remains percipient of unloathsomeness in the presence of what is loathsome. If he wants, he remains percipient of loathsomeness in the presence of what is not loathsome & what is.

If he wants, he remains percipient of unloathsomeness in the presence of what is loathsome & what is not. If he wants—in the presence of what is loathsome & what is not—cutting himself off from both, he remains equanimous, alert, & mindful [§§46; 181]. Or he may enter & remain in the beautiful liberation. I tell you, monks, the release of awareness through good will has the beautiful as its excellence—in the case of one who has penetrated to no higher release.

And how is the release of awareness through compassion developed, what is its destiny, what is its excellence, its reward, & its consummation?

There is the case where a monk develops mindfulness as a factor of Awakening accompanied by compassion...etc....If he wants—in the presence of what is loathsome & what is not—cutting himself off from both, he remains equanimous, alert, & mindful. Or, with the complete transcending of perceptions of [physical] form, with the disappearance of perceptions of resistance, and not heeding perceptions of diversity, thinking, 'Infinite space,' he enters & remains in the sphere of the infinitude of space. I tell you, monks, the release of awareness through compassion has the sphere of the infinitude of space as its excellence—in the case of one who has penetrated to no higher release.

And how is the release of awareness through appreciation developed, what is its destiny, what is its excellence, its reward, & its consummation?

There is the case where a monk develops mindfulness as a factor of Awakening accompanied by appreciation...etc....If he wants—in the presence of what is loathsome & what is not—cutting himself off from both, he remains equanimous, alert, & mindful. Or, with the complete transcending of the sphere of infinitude of space, thinking 'Infinite consciousness,' he enters & remains in the sphere of the infinitude of consciousness. I tell you, monks, the release of awareness through appreciation has the sphere of the infinitude of consciousness as its excellence—in the case of one who has penetrated to no higher release.

And how is the release of awareness through equanimity developed, what is its destiny, what is its excellence, its reward, & its consummation?

There is the case where a monk develops mindfulness as a factor of Awakening accompanied by equanimity...etc....If he wants—in the presence of what is loathsome & what is not—cutting himself off from both, he remains equanimous, alert, & mindful. Or, with the complete transcending of the sphere of infinitude of consciousness, thinking 'There is nothing,' he enters & remains in the sphere of nothingness. I tell you, monks, the release of awareness through equanimity has the sphere of nothingness as its excellence—in the case of one who has penetrated to no higher release.

S.XLVI.54

§ 99. Imagine, Uttiya, a royal frontier fortress, with strong foundations, strong walls & towers, and a single gate. There at the gate is a wise gate-keeper, experienced & intelligent, who keeps out strangers and lets in only those he knows. As he patrols along the road around the fortress he would not see any joints or openings in the wall large enough for even a cat to slip through. And although he wouldn't know exactly how many living beings entered or left the fortress, he would know that whatever living beings of any size entered or left the fortress, they would all leave or enter through the gate.

In the same way, the Tathāgata is not concerned that the whole world or half of it or one third of it will escape by means of [the Dhamma]. What he does know is this: 'All of those who have escaped from the world or are escaping or will escape, have done so by abandoning the five hindrances—those defilements of awareness that weaken discernment—their minds well-established in (well-tuned to) the four frames of reference, developing as they actually are the seven factors of Awakening. That is how they escaped from the world or are escaping or will escape.

A.X.95

§ 100. Whose minds are well-developed
in the factors of self-awakening,
who delight in non-clinging,
relinquishing grasping:
　　Resplendent,
　　their effluents ended,
　　they, in the world,
　　are Unbound.

Dhp.89

H. THE NOBLE EIGHTFOLD PATH

The noble eightfold path is the most standard description of the Buddhist way of practice. The Buddha taught it to his first disciples and to his last [§240], as well as to the majority of those in between. It is called noble because when all of its factors come together in a fully developed form, they stand on the threshold to stream-entry, the first of the noble or transcendent attainments.

The image of "path" used for the factors of this set has two major implications, which we have already encountered in II/D. First, the image implies that these factors are means to an end, not an end in themselves; second, they lead to, rather than cause, the goal. In the context of this set, this image has two levels of meaning: On the beginning level, the path is a series of qualities that one must consciously develop, step by step, in order to bring oneself nearer to the goal. On the ultimate or "noble" level, it is a convergence of those qualities, fully developed, within the mind at the point of non-fashioning, leading inexorably to the Deathless. On the beginning level, one must work at following the path, but on the noble level the path becomes a vehicle that delivers one to the goal.

The eight factors of the noble eightfold path fall under the "aggregates" of discernment, virtue, and concentration *(pañña-khandha, sila-khandha, samadhi-khandha):* right view and right resolve fall under the discernment aggregate; right speech, right action, and right livelihood under the virtue aggregate; and right effort, right mindfulness, and right concentration under the concentration aggregate. Passage §105 states that although the factors of the noble path fall under the three aggregates, the three aggregates do not fall under the factors of the noble path. What this means is that not every instance of discernment, virtue, or concentration within the mind would count as a factor of the noble path. To begin with, there are such things as wrong virtue, wrong concentration, and wrong discernment [see, for example, §152]. Secondly, even right virtue, concentration, and discernment count as noble only when they are brought to a point of advanced development. This point is reflected in §106, which distinguishes mundane and noble levels for each factor of the path. Even though the mundane factors counteract blatant cases of wrong view, wrong resolve, etc., they still are conjoined with subtle levels of mental effluents and can lead to further becoming. Nevertheless, one must first nurture the mundane levels of the eight factors before they can develop into their noble counterparts.

On the mundane level, the first five factors of the path correspond to the faculty of conviction. Right view on this level means believing the principle of kamma and trusting that those who have practiced properly truly understand the workings of kamma in this life and the next. In the Buddha's words, this level of right view holds that "There is what is given, what is offered, what is sacrificed. There are fruits & results of good & bad actions. There is this world & the next world. There is mother & father. There are spontaneously reborn beings; there are priests & contemplatives who, faring rightly & practicing rightly, proclaim this world & the next after having directly known & realized it for themselves." What this passage means is that there is merit in generosity; the moral qualities of good and bad are inherent parts of the cosmos, and not simply social conventions; there is life after death; one has a true moral debt to one's parents; and there are people who have lived the renunciate's life properly in such a way that they have gained true and direct knowledge of these matters. These beliefs are the minimum prerequisites for following the path to skillfulness, as they necessarily underlie any solid conviction in the principle of kamma. Mundane levels of right resolve then build on right view, as one resolves to act in ways that will not create bad kamma; mundane right speech, right action, and right livelihood result naturally as one follows through with one's resolve. Right effort, right mindfulness, and right concentration, on this level, correspond to the faculties of persistence, mindfulness, and concentration. Jhana, in turn, provides a basis for insight into the four noble truths, which counts both as the faculty of discernment and the noble level of right view.

Once right view reaches the noble level, it brings the remaining factors of the path up to the noble level as well. One of the striking features of this level of the path is that it consists primarily of discernment and concentration [see the "qualities that are to be developed" in §111], with the boundaries between the two increasingly blurred. The noble level of right resolve, part of the discernment aggregate, consists of directed thought, evaluation, and mental singleness, all of which are factors of jhana. The noble level of right speech, right action, and right livelihood differ from the mundane levels of those factors in that the emphasis here is on the state of mind of the person abstaining from wrong speech, action, and livelihood. Although §106 does not define the noble levels of right effort, mindfulness, and concentration, it seems safe to assume that they are equivalent to the fifth factor of noble right concentration [§150], to be discussed under III/E and III/F, in which all three of these factors converge with right view and right resolve in a state of full development. In fact, their mutual reinforcement is what makes these factors all "right." This point is confirmed by §111, which states that when the noble eightfold path goes to the culmination of its development, tranquility and insight act in concert. This point also explains the statement at the beginning of §106 to the effect that the path consists primarily of right concentration, with the remaining factors as its supports and requisite conditions: These supports and conditions not only lead to right concentration, but when they all become noble, all eight factors coalesce in the mind in a state of solid oneness. Whereas on the mundane level the path factors, though interconnected, were separate, on the noble level they form a single, unified path.

When the noble eightfold path is attained, the mind reaches the level of stream-entry, the first of the four levels of Awakening [§107]. Thus the noble eightfold path represents the culmination of all seven sets in the Wings to Awakening [§111]. To attain each of the next two levels of Awakening—once-returning and non-returning—the eight noble path factors must converge again in the mind. However, to attain the highest level—Arahantship—the eight noble factors must converge together with two more: right knowledge and right release. Right knowledge is nowhere defined *per se* in the Canon, but §195 would seem to indicate the following relationship between it and right view: Right view is realization of the four noble truths and the duties appropriate to each, while right knowledge is the realization that the duties have been brought to fulfillment. The conjunction of right knowledge and right release reflects, on a higher level, the conjunction of discernment and concentration on the noble level of the eightfold path. Passage §76 indicates that release here can be considered as analogous to concentration, albeit totally unshakable. Right knowledge would include awareness of the unshakability of the release [§195], while the release would remain unshaken even in the face of that knowledge.

At this point, even the path can be abandoned, for one has reached the goal [§113]. Abandoning, here, does not mean that one reverts to wrongs views, wrong action, etc.; rather, one no longer needs to use right view, etc., as a means to a further attainment. As M.107 and S.XXII.122 state, the Awakened one continues practicing meditation and exercising right view as pleasant dwellings for the mind, conducive to mindfulness and alertness, and leads a moral life both for its inherent pleasure and for the sake of the example it offers to those still on the path.

The noble eightfold path, like the seven factors of Awakening, is explicitly explained both as a causal loop and as a holographic formula. We have already described the causal loop above, in showing how the development of the mundane and noble path factors follows the pattern of the five faculties [see also §101]. Passage §106 presents a holographic pattern, in which the development of each factor needs three main supporting factors: right view, which acts as the leader so as to know what the right and wrong versions of the factors are; right effort, which makes the effort to abandon the wrong version and develop the right; and right mindfulness, which keeps the task of right effort in mind. Thus three factors that we have identified as essential to the development of skillfulness—discernment, mindfulness, and effort [I/A]—are involved at each step along the path. As a result of that involvement, they grow stronger to the point where they can help turn mundane right concentration—the fourth factor essential to the development of skillfulness—into noble right concentration. In this sense, they play a role analogous to that of heedfulness in the five faculties and appropriate attention in the seven factors of Awakening. In fact, they seem to be a complete working out of the elements implicit in those two qualities.

A quick review of the seven sets will show that *all* of them develop both in a linear and in a holographic way. Even the "holographic" sets—the frames of reference, right exertion, and the bases of power—contain implicit versions of causal loops, in that all three must follow the three stages of frames-of-reference meditation. Even the linear causal-loop sets—the five faculties and strengths, the seven factors of Awakening, and the noble eightfold path—contain implicit holographic formulae, in that the dynamic of their development is inherent in specific qualities or clusters of qualities: heedfulness in the case of the faculties and strengths, appropriate attention in the case of the factors of Awakening, and the cluster of right view, right mindfulness, and right effort in the case of the noble eightfold path. This combination of linear and holographic patterns grows more complex as we remember that each of the first two stages of frames-of-reference meditation can form linear causal loops within themselves [II/B], while two of the factors in the three-part cluster that develops the eightfold path—right mindfulness and right effort—are equivalent to the holographic sets of the frames of reference and the right exertions.

This formal convergence of two causal patterns in the development of the path reflects not only the dual principle of this/that conditionality, but also a very practical point in the task of developing the skills of the mind. The holographic pattern reflects the fact that all the skillful qualities needed for the path are already there in the mind and continually interact along the path. All that is needed is for them to be ferreted out and nourished, their coordination fine-tuned, and they can deliver the mind to the goal. The causal loop pattern reflects the fact that the process must take place over time, as specific qualities are stressed at specific junctures and strengthened by being put to use, and as different skillful qualities need to alternate in helping one another, step by step, along the way. An analogy can be made with learning how to walk: A child who can't yet walk already has all the muscles needed to walk, but she must locate them and exercise them in a coordinated way, so that the right and left leg can help and receive help from each other, in order to move from the first tentative step to the point where walking seems natural and can be done with grace.

§ 101. Monks, ignorance is the leader in the attainment of unskillful qualities, followed by lack of conscience & lack of concern. In a unknowledgeable person, immersed in ignorance, wrong view arises. In one of wrong view, wrong resolve arises. In one of wrong resolve, wrong speech....In one of wrong speech, wrong action....In one of wrong action, wrong livelihood....In one of wrong livelihood, wrong effort....In one of wrong effort, wrong mindfulness....In one of wrong mindfulness, wrong concentration arises.

Clear knowing is the leader in the attainment of skillful qualities, followed by conscience & concern. In a knowledgeable person, immersed in clear knowing, right view arises. In one of right view, right resolve arises. In one of right resolve, right speech....In one of right speech, right action.... In one of right action, right livelihood.... In one of right livelihood, right effort....In one of right effort, right mindfulness....In one of right mindfulness, right concentration arises.

S.XLV.1

§ 102. Analysis of the Path. Monks, what is the noble eightfold path? Right view, right resolve, right speech, right action, right livelihood, right effort, right mindfulness, right concentration.

And what is right view? Knowledge with regard to stress, knowledge with regard to the origination of stress, knowledge with regard to the cessation of stress, knowledge with regard to the way of practice leading to the cessation of stress: This is called right view. [§§184-240]

And what is right resolve? Being resolved on renunciation, on freedom from ill will, on harmlessness: This is called right resolve.

And what is right speech? Abstaining from lying, from divisive speech, from abusive speech, & from idle chatter: This is called right speech.

And what is right action? Abstaining from taking life, from stealing, & from sexual intercourse. This is called right action.

And what is right livelihood? There is the case where a noble disciple, having abandoned dishonest livelihood, keeps his life going with right livelihood: This is called right livelihood.

And what is right effort? There is the case where a monk generates desire, endeavors, arouses persistence, upholds & exerts his intent for the sake of the non-arising of evil, unskillful qualities that have not yet arisen...for the sake of the abandoning of evil, unskillful qualities that have arisen...for the sake of the arising of skillful qualities that have not yet arisen...(and) for the maintenance, non-confusion, increase, plenitude, development, & culmination of skillful qualities that have arisen: This is called right effort. [§49]

And what is right mindfulness? There is the case where a monk remains focused on the body in & of itself—ardent, alert, & mindful—putting aside greed & distress with reference to the world. He remains focused on feelings in & of themselves...the mind in & of itself...mental qualities in & of themselves—ardent, alert, & mindful—putting aside greed & distress with reference to the world. This is called right mindfulness. [§30]

And what is right concentration? There is the case where a monk—quite withdrawn from sensuality, withdrawn from unskillful [mental] qualities—enters & remains in the first jhāna: rapture & pleasure born from withdrawal, accompanied by directed thought & evaluation. With the stilling of directed thought & evaluation, he enters & remains in the second jhāna: rapture & pleasure born of composure, unification of awareness free from directed thought & evaluation—internal assurance. With the fading of rapture he remains in equanimity, mindful & alert, and physically sensitive of pleasure. He enters & remains in the third jhāna, and of him the Noble Ones declare, 'Equanimous & mindful, he has a pleasurable abiding.' With the abandoning of pleasure & pain—as with the earlier disappearance of elation & distress—he enters & remains in the fourth jhāna: purity of equanimity & mindfulness, neither pleasure nor pain. This is called right concentration. [§150]

S.XLV.8

§ 103. More on Right Action & Right Speech. Having thus gone forth, following the training & way of life of the monks, abandoning the taking of life, he abstains from the taking of life. He dwells with his rod laid down, his knife laid down, scrupulous, merciful, compassionate for the welfare of all living beings. Abandoning the taking of what is not given, he abstains from taking what is not given. He takes only what is given, accepts only what is given, lives not by stealth but by means of a self that has become pure. Abandoning uncelibacy, he lives a celibate life, aloof, refraining from the sexual act that is the villager's way.

Abandoning false speech, he abstains from false speech. He speaks the truth, holds to the truth, is firm, reliable, no deceiver of the world. Abandoning divisive speech he abstains from divisive speech. What he has heard here he does not tell there to break those people apart from these people here. What he has heard there he does not tell here to break these people apart from those people there. Thus reconciling those who have broken apart or cementing those who are united, he loves concord, delights in concord, enjoys concord, speaks things that create concord. Abandoning abusive speech, he abstains from abusive speech. He speaks words that are soothing to the ear, that are affectionate, that go to the heart, that are polite, appealing & pleasing to people at large. Abandoning idle chatter, he abstains from idle chatter. He speaks in season, speaks what is factual, what is in accordance with the goal, the Dhamma, & the Vinaya. He speaks words worth treasuring, seasonable, reasonable, circumscribed, connected with the goal.

A.X .99

§ 104. More on Right Action & Right Speech for Lay People. Abandoning sensual misconduct, he abstains from sensual misconduct. He does not get sexually involved with those who are protected by their mothers, their fathers, their brothers, their sisters, their relatives, or their Dhamma; those with husbands, those who entail punishments, or even those crowned with flowers by another man.

Abandoning false speech, he abstains from false speech. When he has been called to a town meeting, a group meeting, a gathering of his relatives, his guild, or of the royalty [i.e., a royal court proceeding], if he is asked as a witness, 'Come & tell, good man, what you know': If he doesn't know, he says, 'I don't know.' If he does know, he says, 'I know.' If he hasn't seen, he says, 'I haven't seen.' If he has seen, he says, 'I have seen.' Thus he doesn't consciously tell a lie for his own sake, for the sake of another, or for the sake of any reward. *[This paragraph is missing in the PTS translation.]*

A.X.176

§ 105. Visakha: Is the noble eightfold path compounded or uncompounded?

Sister Dhammadinna: The noble eightfold path is compounded.

Visakha: And are the three aggregates [of virtue, concentration, & discernment] included under the noble eightfold path, or is the noble eightfold path included under the three aggregates?

Sister Dhammadinna: The three aggregates are not included under the noble eightfold path, but the noble eightfold path is included under the three aggregates. Right speech, right action, & right livelihood come under the aggregate of virtue. Right effort, right mindfulness, & right concentration come under the aggregate of concentration. Right view & right resolve come under the aggregate of discernment.

M.44

§ 106. And what, monks, is noble right concentration with its supports & requisite conditions? Any singleness of mind equipped with these seven factors—right view, right resolve, right speech, right action, right livelihood, right effort, & right mindfulness—is called noble right concentration with its supports & requisite conditions.

[1] Of those, right view is the forerunner. And how is right view the forerunner? One discerns wrong view as wrong view, and right view as right view. This is one's right view. And what is wrong view? 'There is nothing given, nothing offered, nothing sacrificed. There is no fruit or result of good or bad actions. There is no this world, no next world, no mother, no father, no spontaneously reborn beings; no priests or contemplatives who, faring rightly & practicing rightly, proclaim this world & the next after having directly known & realized it for themselves.' This is wrong view.

And what is right view? Right view, I tell you, is of two sorts: There is right view with effluents, siding with merit, resulting in the paraphernalia [of becoming]; and there is noble right view, without effluents, transcendent, a factor of the path.

And what is the right view that has effluents, sides with merit, & results in paraphernalia? 'There is what is given, what is offered, what is sacrificed. There are fruits & results of good & bad actions. There is this world & the next world. There is mother & father. There are spontaneously reborn beings; there are priests & contemplatives who, faring rightly & practicing rightly, proclaim this world & the next after having directly known & realized it for themselves.' This is the right view that has effluents, sides with merit, & results in paraphernalia.

And what is the right view that is without effluents, transcendent, a factor of the path? The discernment, the faculty of discernment, the strength of discernment, analysis of qualities as a factor of Awakening, the path factor of right view in one developing the noble path whose mind is noble, whose mind is free from effluents, who is fully possessed of the noble path. This is the right view that is without effluents, transcendent, a factor of the path.

One tries to abandon wrong view & to enter into right view: This is one's right effort. One is mindful to abandon wrong view & to enter & remain in right view: This is one's right mindfulness. Thus these three qualities—right view, right effort, & right mindfulness—run & circle around right view.

[2] Of those, right view is the forerunner. And how is right view the forerunner? One discerns wrong resolve as wrong resolve, and right resolve as right resolve. And what is wrong resolve? Being resolved on sensuality, on ill will, on harmfulness. This is wrong resolve.

And what is right resolve? Right resolve, I tell you, is of two sorts: There is right resolve with effluents, siding with merit, resulting in the paraphernalia [of becoming]; and there is noble right resolve, without effluents, transcendent, a factor of the path.

And what is the right resolve that has effluents, sides with merit, & results in paraphernalia? Being resolved on renunciation, on freedom from ill will, on harmlessness. This is the right resolve that has effluents, sides with merit, & results in paraphernalia.

And what is the right resolve that is without effluents, transcendent, a factor of the path? The thinking, directed thinking, resolve, mental absorption, mental fixity, focused awareness, & verbal fabrications in one developing the noble path whose mind is noble, whose mind is without effluents, who is fully possessed of the noble path. This is the right resolve that is without effluents, transcendent, a factor of the path.

One tries to abandon wrong resolve & to enter into right resolve: This is one's right effort. One is mindful to abandon wrong resolve & to enter & remain in right resolve: This is one's right mindfulness. Thus these three qualities—right view, right effort, & right mindfulness—run & circle around right resolve.

[3] Of those, right view is the forerunner. And how is right view the forerunner? One discerns wrong speech as wrong speech, and right speech as right speech. And what is wrong speech? Lying, divisive tale-bearing, abusive speech, & idle chatter. This is wrong speech.

And what is right speech? Right speech, I tell you, is of two sorts: There is right speech with effluents, siding with merit, resulting in the paraphernalia [of becoming]; and there is noble right speech, without effluents, transcendent, a factor of the path.

And what is the right speech that has effluents, sides with merit, & results in paraphernalia? Abstaining from lying, from divisive tale-bearing, from abusive speech, & from idle chatter. This is the right speech that has effluents, sides with merit, & results in paraphernalia.

And what is the right speech that is without effluents, transcendent, a factor of the path? The abstaining, desisting, abstinence, avoidance of the four forms of verbal misconduct in one developing the noble path whose mind is noble, whose mind is without effluents, who is fully possessed of the noble path. This is the right speech that is without effluents, transcendent, a factor of the path.

One tries to abandon wrong speech & to enter into right speech: This is one's right effort. One is mindful to abandon wrong speech & to enter & remain in right speech: This is one's right mindfulness. Thus these three qualities—right view, right effort, & right mindfulness—run & circle around right speech.

[4] Of those, right view is the forerunner. And how is right view the forerunner? One discerns wrong action as wrong action, and right action as right action. And what is wrong action? Killing, taking what is not given, illicit sex. This is wrong action.

And what is right action? Right action, I tell you, is of two sorts: There is right action with effluents, siding with merit, resulting in the paraphernalia [of becoming]; and there is noble right action, without effluents, transcendent, a factor of the path.

And what is the right action that has effluents, sides with merit, & results in paraphernalia? Abstaining from killing, from taking what is not given, & from illicit sex. This is the right action that has effluents, sides with merit, & results in paraphernalia.

And what is the right action that is without effluents, transcendent, a factor of the path? The abstaining, desisting, abstinence, avoidance of the three forms of bodily misconduct in one developing the noble path whose mind is noble, whose mind is without effluents, who is fully possessed of the noble path. This is the right action that is without effluents, transcendent, a factor of the path.

One tries to abandon wrong action & to enter into right action: This is one's right effort. One is mindful to abandon wrong action & to enter & remain in right action: This is one's right mindfulness. Thus these three qualities—right view, right effort, & right mindfulness—run & circle around right action.

[5] Of those, right view is the forerunner. And how is right view the forerunner? One discerns wrong livelihood as wrong livelihood, and right livelihood as right livelihood. And what is wrong livelihood? Scheming, persuading, hinting, belittling, & pursuing gain with gain. This is wrong livelihood.

And what is right livelihood? Right livelihood, I tell you, is of two sorts: There is right livelihood with effluents, siding with merit, resulting in the paraphernalia [of becoming]; and there is noble right livelihood, without effluents, transcendent, a factor of the path.

And what is the right livelihood that has effluents, sides with merit, & results in paraphernalia? There is the case where a noble disciple abandons wrong livelihood and maintains his life with right livelihood. This is the right livelihood that has effluents, sides with merit, & results in paraphernalia.

And what is the right livelihood that is without effluents, transcendent, a factor of the path? The abstaining, desisting, abstinence, avoidance of wrong livelihood in one developing the noble path whose mind is noble, whose mind is without effluents, who is fully possessed of the noble path. This is the right livelihood that is without effluents, transcendent, a factor of the path.

One tries to abandon wrong livelihood & to enter into right livelihood: This is one's right effort. One is mindful to abandon wrong livelihood & to enter & remain in right livelihood: This is one's right mindfulness. Thus these three qualities—right view, right effort, & right mindfulness—run & circle around right livelihood.

Of those, right view is the forerunner. And how is right view the forerunner? In one of right view, right resolve comes into being. In one of right resolve, right speech comes into being. In one of right speech, right action....In one of right action, right livelihood....In one of right livelihood, right effort....In one of right effort, right mindfulness....In one of right mindfulness, right concentration....In one of right concentration, right knowledge....In one of right knowledge, right release comes into being. Thus the learner is endowed with eight factors, and the Arahant with ten.

Of those, right view is the forerunner. And how is right view the forerunner? In one of right view, wrong view is abolished. The many evil, unskillful qualities that come into play with wrong view as their condition are also abolished, while the many skillful qualities that have right view as their condition go to the culmination of their development. (Similarly with the remaining factors up through:) In one of right release, wrong release is abolished. The many evil, unskillful qualities that come into play with wrong release as their condition are also abolished, while the many skillful qualities that have right release as their condition go to the culmination of their development.

M.117

§ 107. The Buddha: 'The stream, the stream,' it is said. Now what is the stream?

Sariputta: Just this noble eightfold path is the stream: right view, right resolve, right speech, right action, right livelihood, right effort, right mindfulness, right concentration.

The Buddha: Well said, Sāriputta, well said. Just this noble eightfold path is the stream....'Streamwinner, streamwinner,' it is said. Now what is a streamwinner?

Sariputta: Whoever is endowed with this noble eightfold path is called a 'streamwinner.'

The Buddha: Well said, Sāriputta, well said. Whoever is endowed with this noble eightfold path is called a 'streamwinner.'

S.LV.5

§ 108. Monks, just as a pot without a stand is easy to tip over, and a pot with a stand is hard to tip over, so too the mind without a stand is easy to tip over, and a mind with a stand is hard to tip over. And what is the mind's stand? Just this noble eightfold path.

S.XLV.27

§ 109. It is possible that a well-aimed spike of bearded wheat or bearded barley, if pressed by a hand or foot, will cut into the hand or foot and draw blood. Why is that? Because the spike is well-aimed. In the same way, it is possible that if one's views are well-aimed, one's development of the path is well aimed, they will cut into ignorance, give rise to clear knowing, and lead to the realization of Unbinding. Why is that? Because one's views are well-aimed.

And how do well-aimed views and a well-aimed development of the path cut into ignorance, give rise to clear knowing and lead to the realization of Unbinding? There is the case where a monk develops right view dependent on seclusion, dependent on dispassion, dependent on cessation, resulting in letting go. He develops right resolve...right speech...right action... right livelihood...right effort... right mindfulness...right concentration dependent on seclusion... dispassion...cessation, resulting in letting go. This is how well-aimed views and a well-aimed development of the path cut into ignorance, give rise to clear knowing, and lead to the realization of Unbinding.

S.XLV.154

§ 110. Just as many kinds of wind blow in the air—east winds, west winds, north winds, south winds, dusty winds, dustless winds, cold winds, warm winds, gentle winds, & strong winds—in the same way, when a monk develops the noble eightfold path, pursues the noble eightfold path, the four frames of reference go to the culmination of their development, the four right exertions...the four bases of power...the five faculties...the five strengths...the seven factors of Awakening go to the culmination of their development.

S.XLV.155

§ 111. Knowing & seeing the eye as it actually is present, knowing & seeing forms...eye-consciousness...eye-contact as they actually are present, knowing & seeing whatever arises conditioned through eye-contact—experienced as pleasure, pain, or neither-pleasure-nor-pain—as it actually is present, one is not infatuated with the eye...forms...eye-consciousness...eye-contact...whatever arises conditioned by eye-contact and is experienced as pleasure, pain, or neither-pleasure-nor-pain....

Knowing & seeing the ear....Knowing & seeing the nose.... Knowing & seeing the tongue....Knowing & seeing the body....

Knowing & seeing the intellect as it actually is present, knowing & seeing ideas...intellect-consciousness...intellect-contact as they actually are present, knowing & seeing whatever arises conditioned through intellect-contact—experienced as pleasure, pain, or neither-pleasure-nor-pain—as it actually is present, one is not infatuated with the intellect...ideas...intellect-consciousness...intellect-contact... whatever arises conditioned by intellect-contact and is experienced as pleasure, pain, or neither-pleasure-nor-pain.

For him—uninfatuated, unattached, unconfused, remaining focused on their drawbacks—the five aggregates for sustenance head toward future diminution. The craving that makes for further becoming—accompanied by passion & delight, relishing now this & now that—is abandoned by him. His bodily disturbances & mental disturbances are abandoned. His bodily torments & mental torments are abandoned. His bodily distresses & mental distresses are abandoned. He is sensitive both to ease of body & ease of awareness.

Whatever view is his, is his as right view. Whatever resolve, as right resolve. Whatever effort, as right effort. Whatever mindfulness, as right mindfulness. Whatever concentration, as right concentration: just as earlier his actions, speech, & livelihood were already well-purified. Thus for him, having thus developed the noble eightfold path, the four frames of reference go to the culmination of their development...the four right exertions...the four bases of power...the five faculties...the five strengths...the seven factors of Awakening go to the culmination of their development. [And] for him these two qualities occur in concert: tranquility & insight.

He comprehends through direct knowledge whatever qualities are to be comprehended through direct knowledge, abandons through direct knowledge whatever qualities are to be abandoned through direct knowledge, realizes through direct knowledge whatever qualities are to be realized through direct knowledge, and develops through direct knowledge whatever qualities are to be developed through direct knowledge.

And what qualities are to be comprehended through direct knowledge? 'The five aggregates of clinging/sustenance,' should be the reply. Which five? Form as an aggregate of clinging/sustenance...

.feeling...perception...fabrications...consciousness as an aggregate of clinging/sustenance....

And what qualities are to be abandoned through direct knowledge? 'Ignorance & craving for becoming'....

And what qualities are to be realized through direct knowledge? 'Clear knowing & release'....

And what qualities are to be developed through direct knowledge? 'Tranquility & insight'....

M.149

§ 112. Just as when there is a guest house where people come from the east to take up residence, from the west...the north...the south to take up residence: Noble warriors come there to take up residence, brahmins... commoners...vassals come there to take up residence. In the same way, when a monk develops the noble eightfold path, pursues the noble eightfold path, he comprehends through direct knowledge whatever qualities are to be comprehended through direct knowledge, abandons through direct knowledge whatever qualities are to be abandoned through direct knowledge, realizes through direct knowledge whatever qualities are to be realized through direct knowledge, and develops through direct knowledge whatever qualities are to be developed through direct knowledge.

S.XLV.159

§ 113. 'Suppose that a man, in the course of traveling along a path, were to come to a great expanse of water, with the near shore dubious & risky, the further shore secure & free from risk, but with neither a ferryboat nor a bridge going from this shore to the other. The thought would occur to him, "Here is this great expanse of water, with the near shore dubious & risky, the further shore secure & free from risk, but with neither a ferryboat nor a bridge going from this shore to the other. What if I were to gather grass, twigs, branches, & leaves and, having bound them together to make a raft, were to cross over to safety on the other shore in dependence on the raft, making an effort with my hands & feet?" Then the man, having gathered grass, twigs, branches, & leaves, having bound them together to make a raft, would cross over to safety on the other shore in dependence on the raft, making an effort with his hands & feet. Having crossed over to the further shore, he might think, "How useful this raft has been to me! For it was in dependence on this raft that, making an effort with my hands & feet, I have crossed over to safety on the further shore. Why don't I, having hoisted it on my head or carrying on my back, go wherever I like?" What do you think, monks: would the man, in doing that, be doing what should be done with the raft?'

'No, lord.'

'And what should the man do in order to be doing what should be done with the raft? There is the case where the man, having crossed over, would think, "How useful this raft has been to me! For it was in dependence on this raft that, making an effort with my hands & feet, I have crossed over to safety on the further shore. Why don't I, having dragged it on dry land or sinking it in the water, go wherever I like?" In doing this, he would be doing what should be done with the raft. Even so monks, I have taught you the Dhamma like a raft, for the purpose of crossing over, not for the purpose of holding onto. Knowing the Dhamma to be like a raft, you should let go even of [skillful] qualities, to say nothing of those that are not.'

M.22

§ 114. The great expanse of water stands for the fourfold flood: the flood of sensuality, the flood of becoming, the flood of views, & the flood of ignorance.

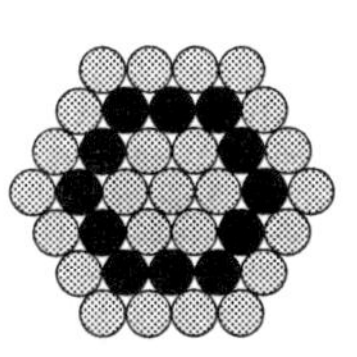

The near shore, dubious & risky, stands for self-identity. The further shore, secure and free from risk, stands for Unbinding. The raft stands for just this noble eightfold path: right view...right concentration. Making an effort with hands & feet stands for the arousing of persistence.

S.XXXV.197

III: The Basic Factors

A. CONVICTION

As we noted in the Introduction, all of the 37 factors listed in the Wings to Awakening can be subsumed under the five faculties. Whereas Part II focused on the interrelationships among these various factors, this part of the book is devoted to using the five faculties as a framework for discussing the individual factors in and of themselves.

Of the five faculties, the faculty of conviction covers the most ground, as it includes the total context for the practice of the Buddha's teachings. The many issues related to the attitudes and ethics needed to lead a Buddhist life, whether as a lay person or a monastic, fall under this category.

Passage §69 defines the faculty of conviction as the four factors of stream-entry [II/A], so to understand the nature of conviction, it is necessary to know what these four factors are. Passages §70 and §71 give different definitions for the four. The first list gives prerequisites for stream-entry: association with good people, listening to the true Dhamma, appropriate attention, and practice in accordance with the Dhamma. The second list gives qualities that characterize a person who has entered the stream: unwavering conviction in the Buddha, Dhamma, and Sangha; and virtues that are appealing to the noble ones. Both lists are relevant here, for conviction is a quality that leads to stream-entry, whereas the attainment of stream-entry is the point where conviction becomes unshakable. Only on the attainment of Arahantship does knowledge become so total that conviction is no longer needed [§89].

The two lists of the factors of stream-entry are similar in that they both cover all three aspects of conviction: social (whom to trust), intellectual (what to believe), and practical (how to act as a result). Because conviction is focused not on a descriptive proposition but on a course of action—the skillful mastery of the processes of kamma in a social context—these aspects are inextricably intertwined. The social aspect comes from the need to associate with people who have already mastered these processes, learning from their words and emulating their actions. The intellectual aspect—belief in the principle of kamma—is necessary because the development of skillfulness within the mind requires that one understand the nature of kamma, take responsibility for one's actions, and have conviction in one's ability to benefit from developing one's skills. The practical aspect is necessary, for if one does not follow through in developing skill, it shows that one's conviction in the development of skillfulness is not genuine, and that one is not fully benefiting from one's beliefs.

The relationship of these factors to the development of skillfulness is shown in several passages. For instance, §53 and §54 cite association with good people and appropriate attention—both of which are members of the first list above—as the primary external and internal prerequisites for the development of what is skillful. At the same time, the intellectual and practical aspects of conviction help to counteract the grosser levels of the roots of unskillfulness [§3]: belief in the principle of kamma helps to undercut delusion, while the practice of virtue helps to weaken the force of greed and aversion in the mind.

To understand the detailed interaction of the social, intellectual, and practical aspects of conviction, we first have to examine them separately. Because having admirable people as friends is the whole of the holy life [§115], we will begin with the **social aspect** first.

The passages in this section that focus on the social aspect of conviction touch on two major issues: how to recognize good people, and why one should associate with them.

Passages §119 lists three basic teachings of good people. These can be taken as criteria for judging whether a person qualifies as good. If one meets people who criticize the practice of generosity, the practice of going forth into the renunciate life, or the practice of giving service to one's parents, one would do well to avoid associating with them, for their wisdom and motives cannot be trusted. If one must associate with them, one should not regard them as people to learn from or to emulate. Thus the social and intellectual aspects of conviction interact in that one way of knowing whether to associate with a person is by listening to what that person teaches; at the same time, the teachings of good people enable one to know what is good. Passage §117 carries this point further, listing positive qualities to look for in a good person: conviction in the principle of kamma, generosity, virtue, and discernment. People who teach these qualities and embody them in their lives qualify as good. The important point here, of course, is that good people are ultimately recognized by what they habitually do, rather than simply by what they say. These habits can be known only through long association over time. This is why, in the Buddhist monkhood, a student does not take a lifetime vow of obedience to a teacher. If he feels that the teacher does not have his best interests at heart—i.e., if he sees that the teacher does not really embody the above qualities—he is free to leave the teacher in search of another.

A person who has attained stream-entry finds it easier to recognize good people, for he/she is now a member of the noble Sangha and can recognize the qualities of that attainment in others as well. "Good people" for a member of the Sangha means the Buddha and the rest of the noble Sangha. Of course the Buddha has long since passed into total Unbinding, but he left his Dhamma and Vinaya as a teacher in his stead [D.16], and so on that level one may still associate with him.

The reason why a person embarking on the path to practice would need to associate with good people, rather than trying to be totally self-dependent, is that the roots of skillfulness within the mind lie mixed with the roots of unskillfulness, and the roots of unskillfulness make it difficult to tell which is which. Thus one needs the advice and example of others more experienced on the path to help identify one's own skillful qualities and to give encouragement in the task of developing them [§9]. Even if one is not yet committed to following the path, one would be wise to associate with good people who embody conviction, generosity, virtue, and discernment, for they are unlikely to treat one in an unfair or harmful manner. If they truly embody conviction and virtue, one can trust that their sense of conscience and concern will prevent them from acting on unskillful intentions. If they truly embody generosity and discernment, they have wisdom worth acquiring and will be willing to share it. This sharing of wisdom forms the basis for further benefits—as listed in §125 & §126—setting in motion a causal chain leading all the way to the experience of Awakening. This causal chain requires that one listen to the teachings of good people so as to understand the implications of the principle of kamma. It also requires that one take such people as examples to emulate in one's own life. In this way, one can become a better person oneself, and can enjoy the benefits that come with one's own improved mastery over the principle of kamma.

The wide availability of books on Buddhism tends to obscure the fact that the truths of the Buddha's teachings are not simply words or propositions, but are qualities of the heart and mind: the skillful mastery of thoughts, words, and deeds. These qualities are best learned not from books but from people who are actually skilled. This is like learning a sport. One can pick up important principles from books written about the sport, but there is much more on a non-verbal level that can be learned only by associating with people who have actually mastered the sport. This might include a sense of how much practice is enough, a sense of one's own strengths and weaknesses, a sense of timing, a sense of one's teammates and opponents, and so forth. A.VII.64 gives a similar list of the principles that characterize a good person, many of which cannot be verbalized in simple rules: knowledge of the Dhamma, knowledge of the meaning of statements, a sense of one's own strengths and weaknesses, a sense of moderation in the use of the requisites of life, a sense of the proper time and season for doing things, a sense of different levels of societies, and a sense of how to judge people. Although the first two types of knowledge in this list are verbal and can be passed on in words, the others are more subliminal and can be picked up only by associating with good people and watching them in action.

With the issue of verbal knowledge we move from the social aspect of conviction to its **intellectual aspect.** The content of the verbal knowledge that can be picked up from good people begins with what §106 defines as mundane right view:

> There is what is given, what is offered, what is sacrificed. There are fruits & results of good & bad actions. There is this world & the next world. There is mother & father. There are spontaneously reborn beings; there are priests & contemplatives who, faring rightly & practicing rightly, proclaim this world & the next after having directly known & realized it for themselves.

As noted in II/H, this passage means that there is merit in generosity; that the moral qualities of good and bad are inherent in the universe, and not simply social conventions; that there is life after death; that one has a true moral debt to one's parents; and that there are people who have lived the renunciate's life properly in such a way that they have gained true and direct knowledge of these matters. These beliefs form the minimum prerequisite for following the path to skillfulness. If one doubts them, one will find it difficult to muster the energy or commitment needed to develop skillful qualities in the mind. One would be more likely to revert to the selfish gratification of immediate desires, with little thought for right or wrong. The willingness to accept these beliefs on faith thus counts as the first step from the stage of mere acquaintance with the Buddha's teachings to the stage of commitment.

These beliefs form the basis for the three points mentioned above as the teachings of good people: generosity, going forth, and service to one's parents [§119]. Appreciating the value of these principles, and following them to the extent of one's abilities, enables one to develop the proper character needed for comprehending the higher levels of the Buddha's teachings, culminating in the four noble truths. As the first list of factors of stream-entry points out, simply listening to the Dhamma is not enough. One has to develop appropriate attention as well, which as we have already seen [II/G] involves knowing how to focus on the right questions. In this context, one begins by learning how to ask productive questions of one's teacher and then moves on to using the categories of the four noble truths to ask questions of one's experience in general. In this sense, the act of listening and paying appropriate attention covers the first two levels in the development of discernment—understanding based on listening and on reasoning—and gets one started on the third: understanding based on the development of skillful qualities in the mind [D.33].

Although listening to the Dhamma is a prerequisite for appropriate attention, appropriate attention does not follow automatically from listening to the Dhamma. It has to be consciously cultivated; otherwise, the causal process will not lead to clear knowledge and release. This point is expressed in a famous stanza from the Dhammapada (64-65):

> Even if for a lifetime
> the fool stays with the wise,
> he knows nothing of the Dhamma—
> like the ladle,
> the taste of the soup.
>
> Even if for a moment,
> the perceptive person stays with the wise,
> he immediately knows the Dhamma—
> like the tongue,
> the taste of the soup.

The purpose of meditation, in which one consciously develops mindfulness and discernment so as to master and understand the skillful use of the mind, is to turn one into the perceptive person who can fully understand the Dhamma.

With the attainment of stream-entry on one's first taste of the Deathless, the intellectual aspect of conviction is expressed in terms of unshakable conviction in the Awakening of the Buddha [§72], which branches out into unshakable conviction in the Triple Gem: the Buddha, the Dhamma, and the Sangha [§71]. One's own taste of Awakening confirms the reality of the Buddha's Awakening and that of the noble Sangha; one's understanding of how the Awakening came about through the practice of the Dhamma confirms that the noble eightfold path is the ideal synopsis of that practice, with nothing lacking or in excess. From this comes the standard expression of conviction in the Triple Gem: The Buddha is rightly self-awakened; the Dhamma, well taught; and the noble Sangha, worthy of honor [§71]. What this means in practical terms is that one is now convinced beyond a doubt that the human ability to develop skillfulness can lead all the way to the Deathless, and that the Deathless is the highest excellence.

Several passages [§87] emphasize that the experience of stream-entry reinforces one's conviction that the true Dhamma is fully expressed only in the Buddha's teachings. This point will come as a surprise to many people who are aware of Buddhism's long history of tolerance toward other religions, and who assume that the enlightened attitude toward alternative teachings is to endorse the statement that many roads lead to the top of the mountain. This assumption, though, is based on a confusion between "tolerance" and "endorsement." As we have already noted, from the streamwinner's point of view the noble eightfold path is the ideal expression of the way to Awakening. To endorse any other path to the same goal would be to concede that the noble eightfold path either lacks something essential or contains something superfluous. The Buddha is quoted as saying that any other supposed path to Awakening would by definition be wrong: wrong view, wrong resolve, wrong speech, etc. To try to get results from such a path, he says, would be like trying to squeeze sesame oil out of gravel or to churn butter out of water [M.126]. He did not deny that other teachings, advocating virtue and concentration, can lead one to states of great peace or to rebirth in the higher heavens, but if one views those attainments as equivalent to Unbinding, one is suffering from wrong view. To hold to that wrong view puts the total release to be found with Unbinding beyond reach.

This unwillingness to endorse other paths, however, does not necessarily lead to intolerance. Buddhism's basic premise is the principle of kamma, that happiness and suffering are the results of one's own past and present actions. The noble eightfold path grows out of this principle as the most skillful mode of acting by which one can escape from the cycle of kammic retribution and attain the Deathless. Other paths are either incomplete expressions of the noble eightfold path or are based on other principles. For example, they may state that there is a being who can sidestep the law of kamma and provide for one's happiness without one's having to master the skills of the noble eightfold path, or that certain ritual actions or words can provide a similar shortcut to happiness. People who follow either of these two latter beliefs could well feel threatened by outsiders who do not share their beliefs, for the outsiders are in effect denying the existence of a shortcut on which the insiders are placing their hopes. This explains why such people have often been intolerant of outside views.

But because the principle of kamma is a teaching of full personal responsibility, no one who believes in kamma will feel threatened by people who teach shortcuts around kamma. Buddhists who have yet to attain stream-entry may waver in their conviction—as the path can seem long and arduous, and the results slow in coming—and this is one reason why they are encouraged not to associate with anyone who rejects the principle of kamma. But those who have had their first taste of Awakening can in no way be persuaded to doubt the principle, for they have seen that the Deathless can be touched only through a process that requires the utmost skill in mindfulness and discernment applied to the processes of one's own mind. Their attitude toward other teachings is that of a skilled artisan toward those with lesser skills, or of a woman who has learned how to extract sesame oil from sesame seeds toward those who are still trying to extract it from gravel: She will want to teach them the right way if they are willing to listen, but if they are unwilling, she will tolerate their ignorance and hope that someday they will be ready to learn.

To attain this level of unshakable conviction requires that one put the Dhamma into practice. This shows the intimate relationship between the intellectual and practical aspects of conviction: one must have a certain level of intellectual understanding of the doctrinal Dhamma before one can practice it, and one must practice it to the point of touching the Dhamma of Deathlessness as an attainment before one's conviction in the teaching of the Dhamma can become unshakably firm. The commentaries bring out this relationship by applying the term Dhamma to all three of these levels: doctrine, practice, and attainment, or in other words, Dhamma as an object of awareness (on the intellectual level), as a means of releasing awareness from bondage to its objects (on the practical level), and as the awareness released (at the point of Awakening).

The **practical aspect** of conviction, prior to stream-entry, is covered by the factor of stream-entry called "practicing in accordance with the Dhamma." What this factor means is that one must be willing to put the Dhamma ahead of one's preferences, so that one is not practicing simply in line with one's likes and dislikes. This is the true test of one's conviction. It is all too easy to pick and choose from the teachings on the basis of other standards—here in the West it is common to judge the Dhamma against Western psychology or other social sciences, and to pick and choose accordingly—but one must ask oneself the same question that Prince Siddhattha posed for himself: Which is a more worthwhile use of one's time, the pursuit of objects and ideals subject to change and death, or the pursuit of the Deathless? Although there is a long-standing recognition in the Buddhist tradition that people benefit even if they follow only part of the teaching, the Dhamma can give its full results only if one commits oneself fully to developing the skill of release in one's thoughts, words, and deeds. This training is similar to following a doctor's regimen: One will benefit even from following the regimen only occasionally, but a full cure requires sticking to the regimen consistently and putting the goal of recovery ahead of one's other preferences. The skill of release requires that one order one's priorities, taking the teachings and example of those who have attained that skill as one's primary guide, and regarding everything else as secondary.

With the attainment of stream-entry, one's conviction in the principle of kamma and its skillful mastery becomes so firm that one would not intentionally break any of the basic precepts that comprise right speech, right action, or right livelihood. This is the import of the factor of stream-entry called "virtues that are appealing to the noble ones." In addition to virtue, streamwinners have also begun to develop the other two aggregates in the noble path—concentration and discernment—but those two aggregates are not yet fully matured [II/A; MFU, pp. 103-04]. As §74 & §75 make clear, conviction cannot become firm until the remaining four faculties, including concentration and discernment, have been strengthened to at least some extent. Once conviction does becomes firm, it can then function to strengthen those faculties even further. The streamwinner realizes, from the experience of stream-entry, not only that he/she attained that experience through mastery of the processes of kamma, but also that his/her Awakening is not yet complete because there are gaps in that mastery. This realization is what gives impetus for the further development of all five faculties until they issue in the full realization of the Deathless.

§ 115. As he was seated to one side, Ven. Ananda said to the Blessed One, 'This is half of the holy life, lord: having admirable people as friends, companions, & colleagues.'

'Don't say that, Ananda. Don't say that. Having admirable people as friends, companions, & colleagues is actually the whole of the holy life. When a monk has admirable people as friends, companions, & colleagues, he can be expected to develop & pursue the noble eightfold path.

'And how does a monk who has admirable people as friends, companions, & colleagues, develop & pursue the noble eightfold path? There is the case where a monk develops right view dependent on seclusion, dependent on dispassion, dependent on cessation, resulting in letting go. He develops right resolve...right speech...right action... right livelihood...right effort...right mindfulness...right concentration dependent on seclusion... dispassion...cessation, resulting in letting go. This is how a monk who has admirable people as friends, companions, & colleagues, develops & pursues the noble eightfold path.

'And through this line of reasoning one may know how having admirable people as friends, companions, & colleagues is actually the whole of the holy life: It is in dependence on me as an admirable friend that beings subject to birth have gained release from birth, that beings subject to aging have gained release from aging, that beings subject to death have gained release from death, that beings subject to sorrow, lamentation, pain, distress, & despair have gained release from sorrow, lamentation, pain, distress, & despair.'

S.XLV.2

§ 116. Mahanama, to the Buddha: There may be the case where a Dhamma disagreement arises, with the Blessed One on one side and the community of monks on the other. I would be on the same side as the Blessed One. May the Blessed One remember this as my confidence in him.

There may be the case where a Dhamma disagreement arises, with the Blessed One on one side and the community of monks & the community of nuns on the other. I would be on the same side as the Blessed One. May the Blessed One remember this as my confidence in him....

There may be the case where a Dhamma disagreement arises, with the Blessed One on one side and the community of monks & the community of nuns & the male lay followers & the female lay followers & the world with its devas, māras, brahmas, its generations with their priests & contemplatives, their royalty & common folk on the other. I would be on the same side as the Blessed One. May the Blessed One remember this as my confidence in him.

The Buddha [turning to Mahānāma's companion, Godha]: Now Godha, what do you have to say about Mahānāma when he speaks in such a way?

Godha: I have nothing to say about Mahānāma when he speaks in such a way, except that he is admirable & skillful.

S.LV.23

§ 117. **Advice to a lay person.** Now what, TigerPaw (Byagghapajja), is meant by having admirable people as friends? There is the case where a lay person, in whatever town or village he may dwell, spends time with householders or householders' sons, young or old, who are advanced in virtue. He talks with them, engages them in discussions. He emulates consummate conviction in those who are consummate in conviction, consummate virtue in those who are consummate in virtue, consummate generosity in those who are consummate in generosity, & consummate discernment in those who are consummate in discernment. This is called friendship with admirable people.

A.VIII.54

§ 118. A friend endowed with these three qualities is worth associating with. Which three? He gives what is hard to give, he does what is hard to do, he endures what is hard to endure. A friend endowed with these three qualities is worth associating with.

A.III.133

§ 119. These three things have been promulgated by wise people, by people who are truly good. Which three? Generosity...going-forth [from the home life]...& service to one's mother & father. These three things have been promulgated by wise people, by people who are truly good.

A.III.45

§ 120. And what, monks, is the treasure of generosity? There is the case of a noble disciple, his awareness cleansed of the stain of stinginess, living at home, freely generous, openhanded, delighting in being magnanimous, responsive to requests, delighting in the distribution of alms. This is called the treasure of generosity.

A.VII.6

§ 121. If beings knew, as I know, the results of giving & sharing, they would not eat without have given, nor would the stain of miserliness overcome their minds. Even if it were their last bite, their last mouthful, they would not eat without having shared, if there were someone to receive their gift. But because beings do not know, as I know, the results of giving & sharing, they eat without have given. The stain of miserliness overcomes their minds.

Iti.26

§ 122. Monks, brahmins & householders are very helpful to you, as they provide you with the requisites of robes, alms food, lodgings, & medical requisites for the sick. And you, monks, are very helpful to brahmins & householders, as you teach them the Dhamma admirable in the beginning, admirable in the middle, & admirable in the end, as you expound the holy life both in its particulars & in its essence, entirely complete, surpassingly pure. In this way the holy life is lived in mutual dependence, for the purpose of crossing over the flood, for making a right end to stress.

Householders & the homeless
in dependence on one another
both accomplish the true Dhamma—
the unsurpassed security from bondage.

From householders, the homeless
receive requisites—robes, lodgings,
protection from inclemencies.
While in dependence on those well-gone,
home-loving householders
have conviction in Arahants

of noble discernment,
absorbed in jhāna.

Here practicing the Dhamma,
the path leading to good destinations,
those wishing for pleasure rejoice
in delight in the heavenly world.

Iti.107

§ 123. Now what is the level of a person who is not truly good? A person who is not truly good is ungrateful, does not acknowledge the help given to him. This ingratitude, this lack of acknowledgment is second nature among rude people. It is entirely on the level of people who are not truly good. A person who is truly good is grateful & acknowledges the help given to him. This gratitude, this acknowledgment is second nature among fine people. It is entirely on the level of people who are truly good.

I tell you, monks, there are two people who are not easy to repay. Which two? Your mother & father. Even if you were to carry your mother on one shoulder & your father on the other shoulder for 100 years, and were to look after them by anointing, massaging, bathing, & rubbing their limbs, and they were to defecate & urinate right there [on your shoulders], you would not in that way pay or repay your parents. If you were to establish your mother & father in absolute sovereignty over this great earth, abounding in the seven treasures, you would not in that way pay or repay your parents. Why is that? Mother & father do much for their children. They care for them, they nourish them, they introduce them to this world. But anyone who rouses his unbelieving mother & father, settles & establishes them in conviction; rouses his unvirtuous mother & father, settles & establishes them in virtue; rouses his stingy mother & father, settles & establishes them in generosity; rouses his foolish mother & father, settles & establishes them in discernment: To this extent one pays & repays one's mother & father.

A.II 31-32

§ 124. Living with Brahma are those families where, in the home, mother & father are revered by the children. Living with the first devas are those families where, in the home, mother & father are revered by the children. Living with the first teachers are those families where, in the home, mother & father are revered by the children. Living with those worthy of gifts are those families where, in the home, mother & father are revered by the children. 'Brahma' is a designation for mother & father. 'The first devas'...'the first teachers'... 'those worthy of gifts' is a designation for mother & father. Why is that? Mother & father do much for their children. They care for them, they nourish them, they introduce them to this world.

Mother & father
compassionate to their family
are called
Brahma,
the first teachers
those worthy of gifts from their children.

So the sage should pay them
homage
honor
with food & drink
clothing & bedding
anointing & bathing
& washing their feet.

Performing these services to their parents, the wise
are praised here & now
and after death
rejoice in heaven.

Iti.106

§ 125. A beginning point for ignorance—[such that one might say], 'Before, this, ignorance did not exist; then it came into play'—cannot be discerned. This has been said. Nevertheless, it can be discerned, 'Ignorance comes from this condition.' And I tell you, ignorance has its nutriment. It is not without nutriment. And what is the nutriment for ignorance? The five hindrances.... And what is the nutriment for the five hindrances? The three forms of misconduct....And what is the nutriment for the three forms of misconduct? Lack of restraint of the senses....And what is the nutriment for lack of restraint of the senses? Lack of mindfulness & alertness....And what is the nutriment for lack of mindfulness & alertness? Inappropriate attention....And what is the nutriment for inappropriate attention? Lack of conviction.... And what is the nutriment for lack of conviction? Not hearing the true Dhamma....And what is the nutriment for not hearing the true Dhamma? Associating with people who are not truly good, (or: not associating with people who are truly good)....

Just as when the gods pour rain in heavy drops & crash thunder on the upper mountains: The water, flowing down along the slopes, fills the mountain clefts & rifts & gullies. When the mountain clefts & rifts & gullies are full, they fill the little ponds. When the little ponds are full, they fill the big lakes...the little rivers...the big rivers. When the big rivers are full, they fill the great ocean, and thus is the great ocean fed, thus is it filled. In the same way, when not associating with truly good people is brought to fulfillment, it fulfills [the conditions for] not hearing the true Dhamma...lack of conviction... inappropriate attention...lack of mindfulness & alertness...lack of restraint of the senses...the three forms of misconduct...the five hindrances. When the five hindrances are brought to fulfillment, they fulfill [the conditions for] ignorance. Thus is ignorance fed, thus is it brought to fulfillment.

Now, I tell you, clear knowing & release have their nutriment. They are not without nutriment. And what is their nutriment? The seven factors of awakening....And what is the nutriment for the seven factors of awakening? The four frames of reference....And what is the nutriment for the four frames of reference? The three forms of right conduct....And what is the nutriment for the three forms of right conduct? Restraint of the senses....And what is the nutriment for restraint of the senses? Mindfulness & alertness....And what is the nutriment for mindfulness & alertness? Appropriate attention.... And what is the nutriment for appropriate attention? Conviction.... And what is the nutriment for conviction? Hearing the true Dhamma....And what is the nutriment for hearing the true Dhamma? Associating with people who are truly good....

Just as when the gods pour rain in heavy drops & crash thunder on the upper mountains: The water, flowing down along the slopes, fills the mountain clefts & rifts & gullies...the little ponds...the big lakes...the little rivers...the big rivers. When the big rivers are full, they fill the great ocean, and thus is the great ocean fed, thus is it filled. In the same way, when associating with truly good people is brought to fulfillment, it fulfills [the conditions for] hearing the true Dhamma...conviction...appropriate attention...mindfulness & alertness...restraint of the senses...the three forms of right conduct... the four frames of reference...the seven factors of awakening. When the seven factors of awakening are brought to fulfillment, they fulfill [the conditions for] clear knowing & release. Thus is clear knowing & release fed, thus is it brought to fulfillment.

A.X.61

§ 126. These are eight causes, eight conditions, for the attainment of discernment basic to the holy life when it has not yet been attained, and for its growth, its increase, & for the culmination of its development when it has. Which eight?

There is the case where a monk dwells in dependence on the Master, or another fellow in the holy life worthy of being a teacher, under whom he becomes firmly established in a strong sense of conscience & concern, love & respect. This is the first cause, the first condition....

{And what is the treasure of conscience? There is the case where a noble disciple feels shame at [the thought of engaging in] bodily misconduct, verbal misconduct, mental misconduct. This is called the treasure of conscience.

And what is the treasure of concern? There is the case where a noble disciple feels concern for [the suffering that results from] bodily misconduct, verbal misconduct, mental misconduct. This is called the treasure of concern.}

As he so lives, he periodically approaches his teacher to ask & inquire of him, 'How, venerable sir, does this happen? What is the meaning of this?' To him the teacher reveals what is hidden, clarifies what is obscure, and dispels any doubt he may have in the various things that give him reason to doubt. This is the second cause, the second condition....

When he has heard the Dhamma, he accomplishes twofold seclusion: seclusion of body & seclusion of mind. This is the third cause, the third condition....

He is virtuous & lives restrained by the Paṭimokkha, consummate in his behavior & range of activity. Seeing danger in the slightest fault, he undertakes & trains himself in the training rules. This is the fourth cause, the fourth condition....

He is erudite, a keeper & storehouse of learning. He is erudite in the teachings—admirable in their beginning, admirable in their middle, admirable in their end—that affirm the holy life, entirely perfect & pure in its letter & meaning; he has resolved on them, has made them familiar to his speech, has pondered them over in his mind, and has penetrated them (attuned himself to them) in terms of his views. This is the fifth cause, the fifth condition....

He keeps his persistence aroused for abandoning unskillful mental qualities and taking on skillful mental qualities. He is steadfast, solid in his effort, not shirking his duties with regard to skillful mental qualities. This is the sixth cause, the sixth condition....

When he joins the Community he is not talkative, nor does he discuss low topics. He either speaks Dhamma himself or asks someone else to, and he does not despise noble silence [the second jhana]. This is the seventh cause, the seventh condition....

Finally, he remains focused on the arising & passing away of the five aggregates of clinging/sustenance: 'Such is form, such its origination, such its disappearance. Such is feeling...Such is perception...Such are fabrications...Such is consciousness, such its origination, such its disappearance.' This is the eighth cause, the eighth condition for the attainment of discernment basic to the holy life when it has not yet been attained, and for its growth, its increase, & for the culmination of its development when it has.

A.VIII.2 { + A.VII.6}

§ 127. Regard him as one who
points out
treasure,
the wise man who
seeing your faults
reproves you.

Associate with this sort of sage.
For one associating
with one of this sort,
things get better,

not worse.

DHP.76

§ 128. These are the five rewards of conviction in a lay person. Which five?

When the truly good people in the world show compassion, they will first show compassion to people of conviction, and not to people without conviction. When visiting, they first visit people of conviction, and not people without conviction. When accepting gifts, they will first accept those from people with conviction, and not from people without conviction. When teaching the Dhamma, they will first teach those with conviction, and not those without conviction. A person of conviction, on the break-up of the body, after death, will arise in a good destination, the heavenly world. These are the five rewards of conviction in a lay person.

Just as a large banyan tree, on level ground where four roads meet, is a haven for the birds all around, even so a lay person of conviction is a haven for many people: monks, nuns, male lay followers, & female lay followers.

A massive tree whose branches carry fruits & leaves,
with trunks & roots & an abundance of fruits:

There the birds find rest.

In that delightful sphere they make their home,
Those seeking shade come to the shade,
those seeking fruit find fruit to eat.

So with the person consummate
in virtue & conviction,
humble, sensitive, gentle, delightful, & mild:
To him come those without effluent,
free from passion
free from aversion
free from delusion:
The field of merit for the world.
They teach him the Dhamma
that dispels all stress.
And when he understands,
he is freed from effluents,
totally unbound.

A.V.38

§ 129. A female noble disciple who grows in terms of these five types of growth grows in the noble growth, grasps hold of what is essential, what is excellent in the body. Which five? She grows in terms of conviction, in terms of virtue, in terms of learning, in terms of generosity, in terms of discernment. Growing in terms of these five types of growth, the female noble disciple grows in the noble growth, grasps hold of what is essential, what is excellent in the body.

Growing in conviction & virtue
discernment, generosity, & learning,
a virtuous female lay disciple
such as this
takes hold of the essence within herself.

S.XXXVII.34

§ 130. For a disciple who has conviction in the Teacher's message & lives to penetrate it, it is a principle that, 'The Blessed One is the Teacher, I am a disciple. He is the one who knows, not I.' For a disciple who has conviction in the Teacher's message & lives to penetrate it, the Teacher's message is healing & nourishing. For a disciple who has conviction in the Teacher's message & lives to penetrate it, it is a principle that, 'Gladly would I let the flesh & blood in my body dry up, leaving just the skin, tendons, & bones, but if I have not attained what can be reached through human firmness, human persistence, human striving, there will be no relaxing my persistence.' For a disciple who has conviction in the Teacher's message & lives to penetrate it, one of two fruits can be expected: either gnosis here & now, or—if there be any remnant of clinging/sustenance—non-return.

M.70

B. PERSISTENCE

See the Four Right Exertions [II/C].

C. MINDFULNESS

See the Four Frames of Reference [II/B].

D. CONCENTRATION: ABANDONING THE HINDRANCES

Several discourses in the Canon [such as D.2] state that the first step in concentration practice is to abandon the five hindrances, which we have already discussed in conjunction with the seven factors of Awakening [II/G]. They are: sensual desire, ill will, sloth & torpor, restlessness & anxiety, and uncertainty. These hindrances need to be abandoned because they function as intermediate levels of the three roots of unskillfulness [§3]. Sensual desire is a form of greed; ill will, a form of aversion; and the remaining three hindrances, forms of delusion. All five, in their various ways, block concentration and weaken discernment by making it difficult to realize what is beneficial for oneself, for others, or for both. This last point makes them particularly tricky to deal with, for one needs to have a sense that they are unbeneficial states of mind before one can work at abandoning them, yet while one is overcome with them, they impair one's ability to see that they are in fact unbeneficial [§133]. For instance, when one feels sensual desire for another person, it is hard to focus on the unattractive side of that person or on the drawbacks of the desire itself. Similarly, when one feels anger, it is hard not to feel that the anger is justified; when one feels sleepy, it is hard not to feel that one should get some sleep; when one is worried, it is hard not to believe that one needs to worry, and so forth.

Although the hindrances cannot be totally relinquished prior to the various stages of Awakening, they can be lessened on a preliminary level to the point where the mind can settle down in jhana. This preliminary level is the focus of the passages in this section. Passage §189 lists five methods for dealing with unskillful thoughts in the course of meditation. The passages included here focus almost exclusively on using the first two of those methods—replacing the unskillful thoughts with skillful ones, and contemplating the drawbacks of the unskillful thoughts until one feel repulsed by them—so as to escape from the power of any hindrances that have overcome the mind. Examples of the first method include focusing on the unattractive side of any sensual object to which one may be attracted [§§30, 140, 142]; focusing on the good qualities of a person who has aroused thoughts of ill will [§144]; focusing on the foolishness of expecting all people to act in line with one's wants [§145]; and changing one's object of concentration when finding that the current object is inducing sleepiness [§147]. Examples of the second method include realizing that the hindrance is placing the mind in a state of bondage and limitation [§§134, 137-138], and that one can find freedom only by releasing oneself from its power. In practice, these are not the only ways of applying these two general approaches. The examples in the texts can act as inspiration for any similar techniques that a meditator might devise to obtain the desired effect.

To escape the double bind mentioned above—the fact that the hindrances blind one to one's own true best interests, and yet one needs to see those true interests if one is to overcome the hindrances—one must depend on all five faculties as one has been able to develop them. Conviction is needed so that one will listen to the advice of those who point out the drawbacks of the hindrances. A certain momentum of persistence, as right exertion, is needed so that one will make the effort to abandon the hindrance as soon as one is aware that it has arisen and before it grows into anything stronger. Mindfulness, based on the frames of reference, is needed so that one can be alert to the arising of the hindrances and can remember why they should be abandoned in the first place. This mindfulness can be strengthened by remembering the teachings of others who have pointed out the drawbacks of the hindrances—the many similes for the hindrances given in passages §§131-134 and §138 serve the purpose of keeping those memories vivid. It can also be strengthened by remembering the drawbacks of the hindrances as encountered in one's own personal experience: the damage that has come when another person has given in to them, and the things that one regrets having done oneself when under their influence.

Because preliminary levels of concentration and discernment are present in right exertion and the practice of the frames of reference, these faculties play a role in abandoning the hindrances as well. As they develop strength, they make one more and more skilled in cutting off the hindrances as effectively as possible. The seven factors of Awakening, which are developed in concentration, act as direct antidotes to the hindrances [§76], while discernment—combined with concentrated mindfulness—helps in mastering what is probably the most effective tool for not being fooled by the hindrances: the ability to separate the hindrance, as an act of the mind, from its object. For instance, discernment makes one able to see the feeling of sensual desire as one thing, and the object of the desire as something separate. This ability is crucial in a number of ways. To begin with, it helps separate the positive qualities of the object from the act of desiring the object, so that one does not confuse the two. The tendency to confuse the two is what makes it hard to see the drawbacks of the desire when it is present in the mind, and at the same time, serves to harden the mind in general against the Buddha's admonishments against sensuality.

There is a widespread feeling that Buddhism gives an unfair valuation of sensuality and is blind to the positive beauties of sensual objects, but this is simply not true. The Buddha admitted that sensual objects have their beauty and can give a measure of satisfaction [M.13]. He pointed out, however, that the beauty of an object is not the whole story, for all beautiful objects must decay. If one's happiness is based on them, that happiness is in for a fall. More importantly, though, the Buddha defined sensuality not as the objects of the senses, but as the passion and delight that one feels for such objects [A.VI.63; MFU, p. 53]. Although the objects of the senses are neither good nor evil *per se,* the act of passion and delight forms a bond on the mind, disturbing its immediate peace and ensuring its continued entrapment in the round of rebirth and redeath. Only by separating the desire from its object can one directly perceive the truth of these teachings.

This point applies to the other hindrances as well. For instance, when one can separate the object of one's anger from the anger itself as a mental event, one can see the obvious drawbacks of allowing anger to take over the mind.

In addition, the ability to separate the act from its object enables one to become sensitive to the act before it becomes overpowering, at the same time allowing one to regard it simply as a mental quality in and of itself. One can then engage in the practice outlined in §30—that of observing the coming and going of the hindrances as one tries to bring the mind to concentration. In this way, one eventually becomes so familiar with the patterns underlying their occurrence that one can undercut them and eliminate them from the mind for good. Passage §137 gives an example of one of the patterns that one will see when sensual desire arises: sexual attraction for another person begins with a sense of attraction for one's own sexuality. Passage §96, in a more abstract fashion, lists other patterns of mind that feed the hindrances. By perceiving such patterns, one can take one's analysis of the roots of unskillfulness in the mind to ever more subtle levels. In this way, the skill of being able to abandon the hindrances will go beyond simply the preliminary level of concentration practice, exercising all five of the faculties to the point where they issue in Awakening.

§ 131. These are the five hindrances & obstructions that overcome awareness & weaken discernment. Which five? Sensual desire is a hindrance & obstruction that overcomes awareness & weakens discernment. Ill will... Sloth & drowsiness...Restlessness & anxiety... Uncertainty is a hindrance & obstruction that overcomes awareness & weakens discernment....

Suppose there were a river, flowing down from the mountains, going far, its current swift, carrying everything with it: If a man were to open watercourses leading off from both sides, the current in the middle of the river would be interrupted, diverted, & dispersed. The river would not go far, its current would not be swift, and it would not carry everything with it. In the same way, if a monk has not rid himself of these five hindrances...there is no possibility that he can know what is for his own benefit, or the benefit of others, or both; or that he should come to realize a superior human attainment, a truly noble knowledge & vision....

But suppose there were a river, flowing down from the mountains, going far, its current swift, carrying everything with it: If a man were to close off the watercourses leading off from both sides, the current in the middle of the river would not be interrupted, diverted, or dispersed. The river would go far, its current swift, carrying everything with it. In the same way, if a monk has rid himself of these five hindrances...there is the possibility that he can know what is for his own benefit, or the benefit of others, or both, and that he should come to realize a superior human attainment, a truly noble knowledge & vision.

A.V.51

§ 132. When gold is debased by these five impurities, it is not pliant, malleable, or luminous. It is brittle and not ready to be worked. Which five? Iron, copper, tin, lead, & silver....But when gold is not debased by these five impurities, it is pliant, malleable, & luminous. It is not brittle and is ready to be worked. Then whatever sort of ornament one has in mind—whether a belt, an earring, a necklace, or a gold chain—it would serve one's purpose.

In the same way, when the mind is debased by these five impurities, it is not pliant, malleable, or luminous. It is brittle and not rightly concentrated for the ending of the effluents. Which five? Sensual desire, ill will, sloth & drowsiness, restlessness & anxiety, and uncertainty....But when the mind is not debased by these five impurities, it is pliant, malleable, & luminous. It is not brittle and is rightly concentrated for the ending of the effluents. Then whichever of the six higher knowledges [§64] one turns one's mind to know & realize, one can witness them for oneself whenever there is an opening....

A.V.23

§ 133. Similes for the Hindrances. Imagine a bowl of water mixed with lac, yellow orpiment, indigo, or crimson, such that a man with good eyesight examining the reflection of his face in it would not be able to know or see his face as it actually is. In the same way, when one remains with awareness possessed by *sensual passion,* overcome with sensual passion, and neither knows nor sees the escape, as it is actually present, from sensual passion once it has arisen, then one neither knows nor sees what is for one's own benefit, or for the benefit of others, or for the benefit of both....

Now imagine a bowl of water heated on a fire, boiling & bubbling over, such that a man with good eyesight examining the reflection of his face in it would not be able to know or see his face as it actually is. In the same way, when one remains with awareness possessed by *ill will,* overcome with ill will, and neither knows nor sees the escape, as it is actually present, from ill will once it has arisen, then one neither knows nor sees what is for one's own benefit, or for the benefit of others, or for the benefit of both....

Now imagine a bowl of water covered with algae & slime, such that a man with good eyesight examining the reflection of his face in it would not be able to know or see his face as it actually is. In the same way, when one remains with awareness possessed by *sloth & drowsiness,* overcome with sloth & drowsiness, and neither knows nor sees the escape, as it is actually present, from sloth & drowsiness once it has arisen, then one neither knows nor sees what is for one's own benefit, or for the benefit of others, or for the benefit of both....

Now imagine a bowl of water ruffled by the wind, disturbed, & covered with waves, such that a man with good eyesight examining the reflection of his face in it would not be able to know or see his face as it actually is. In the same way, when one remains with awareness possessed by *restlessness & anxiety,* overcome with restlessness & anxiety, and neither knows nor sees the escape, as it is actually present, from restlessness & anxiety once it has arisen, then one neither knows nor sees what is for one's own benefit, or for the benefit of others, or for the benefit of both....

Now imagine a bowl of water stirred up, turbid, muddied, & left in the dark, such that a man with good eyesight examining the reflection of his face in it would not be able to know or see his face as it actually is. In the same way, when one remains with awareness possessed by *uncertainty,* overcome with uncertainty, and neither knows nor sees the escape, as it is actually present, from uncertainty once it has arisen, then one neither knows nor sees what is for one's own benefit, or for the benefit of others, or for the benefit of both....

S.XLVI.55

§ 134. Suppose that a man, taking a loan, invests it in his business affairs. His business affairs succeed. He repays his old debts and there is extra left over for maintaining his wife. The thought would occur to him, 'Before, taking a loan, I invested it in my business affairs. Now my business affairs have succeeded. I have repaid my old debts and there is extra left over for maintaining my wife.' Because of that he would experience joy & happiness.

Now suppose that a man falls sick—in pain & seriously ill. He does not enjoy his meals, and there is no strength in his body. As time passes, he eventually recovers from that sickness. He enjoys his meals and there is strength in his body. The thought would occur to him, 'Before, I was sick....Now I am recovered from that sickness. I enjoy my meals and there is strength in my body.' Because of that he would experience joy & happiness.

Now suppose that a man is bound in prison. As time passes, he eventually is released from that bondage, safe & sound, with no loss of property. The thought would occur to him, 'Before, I was bound in prison. Now I am released from that bondage, safe & sound, with no loss of my property.' Because of that he would experience joy & happiness.

Now suppose that a man is a slave, subject to others, not subject to himself, unable to go where he likes. As time passes, he eventually is released from that slavery, subject to himself, not subject to others, freed, able to go where he likes. The thought would occur to him, 'Before, I was a slave....Now I am released from that slavery, subject to myself, not subject to others, freed, able to go where I like.' Because of that he would experience joy & happiness.

Now suppose that a man, carrying money & goods, is traveling by a road through desolate country. As time passes, he eventually emerges from that desolate country, safe & sound, with no loss of property. The thought would occur to him, 'Before, carrying money & goods, I was traveling by a road through desolate country. Now I have emerged from that desolate country, safe & sound, with no loss of my property.' Because of that he would experience joy & happiness.

In the same way, when these five hindrances are not abandoned in himself, the monk regards it as a debt, a sickness, a prison, slavery, a road through desolate country. But when these five hindrances are abandoned in himself, he regards it as unindebtedness, good health, release from prison, freedom, a place of security.

M.39

§ 135. Sensual desire. I have heard that on one occasion the Blessed One was staying near Savatthı in Jeta's Grove, Anathapiṇḍika's Park. Now on that occasion the Blessed One was sitting out in the open in the pitch black of the night, while oil lamps were burning. Many flying insects were meeting their downfall & misfortune in those oil lamps. Seeing this...the Blessed One exclaimed,

> Rushing headlong, missing what is worthwhile,
> Bringing on one new bond after another,
> Like insects falling into the flame,
> Some are intent only on what is seen & heard.

Ud.VI.9

> § 136. Clinging to sense pleasures, to sensual ties,
> Seeing no blame in the fetter,
> Never will those tied up in the fetter
> Cross over the flood so great & wide.

Ud.VII.3

§ 137. I will teach you a Dhamma discourse on bondage & lack of bondage....A woman attends inwardly to her feminine faculties, her feminine gestures, her feminine manners, feminine poise, feminine desires, feminine voice, feminine charms. She is excited by that, delighted by that. Being excited & delighted by that, she attends outwardly to masculine faculties, masculine gestures, masculine manners, masculine poise, masculine desires, masculine voices, masculine charms. She is excited by that, delighted by that...wants to be bonded to what is outside her, wants whatever pleasure & happiness that arise based on that bond. Delighting, caught up in her femininity, a woman goes into bondage with reference to men. This is how a woman does not transcend her femininity.

A man attends inwardly to his masculine faculties, masculine gestures, masculine manners, masculine poise, masculine desires, masculine voice, masculine charms. He is excited by that, delighted by that. Being excited & delighted by that, he attends outwardly to feminine faculties, feminine gestures, feminine manners, feminine poise, feminine desires, feminine voices, feminine charms. He is excited by that, delighted by that...wants to be bonded to what is outside him, wants whatever pleasure & happiness that arise based on that bond. Delighting, caught up in his masculinity, a man goes into bondage with reference to women. This is how a man does not transcend his masculinity.

And how is there lack of bondage? A woman does not attend inwardly to her feminine faculties...feminine charms. She is not excited by that, not delighted by that...does not attend outwardly to masculine faculties...masculine charms. She is not excited by that, not delighted by that...does not want to be bonded to what is outside her, does not want whatever pleasure & happiness that arise based on that bond. Not delighting, not caught up in her femininity, a woman does not go into bondage with reference to men. This is how a woman transcends her femininity.

A man does not attend inwardly to his masculine faculties...masculine charms. He is not excited by that, not delighted by that...does not attend outwardly to feminine faculties...feminine charms. He is not excited by that, not delighted by that...does not want to be bonded to what is outside him, does not want whatever pleasure & happiness that arise based on that bond. Not delighting, not caught up in his masculinity, a man does not go into bondage with reference to women. This is how a man transcends his masculinity.

This is how there is lack of bondage. And this is the Dhamma discourse on bondage & lack of bondage.

A.VII.48

§ 138. 'Suppose a dog, overcome with weakness & hunger, were to come across a slaughterhouse, and there a skilled butcher or butcher's apprentice were to fling him a chain of bones—thoroughly scraped, without any flesh, smeared with blood. What do you think: Would the dog, gnawing on that chain of bones—thoroughly scraped, without any flesh, smeared with blood—appease his weakness & hunger?'

'No, lord. And why is that? Because the chain of bones is thoroughly scraped, without any flesh, & smeared with blood. The dog would get nothing but weariness & vexation.'

'In the same way, householder, a noble disciple considers this point: "The Blessed One has compared sensuality to a chain of bones, of much stress, much despair, & greater drawbacks." Seeing this with right discernment, as it actually is, then avoiding the equanimity coming from multiplicity, dependent on multiplicity, he develops the equanimity coming from singleness, dependent on singleness [III/G], where sustenance/clinging for the baits of the world ceases entirely.

'Now suppose a vulture, a kite, or a hawk were to take off, having seized a lump of flesh, and other vultures, kites, or hawks—following right after it—were to tear at it & pull at it. What do you think: If that vulture, kite, or hawk were not quickly to drop that lump of flesh, would it meet with death from that cause, or with death-like pain?'

'Yes, lord.'

'In the same way, householder, a noble disciple considers this point: "The Blessed One has compared sensuality to a lump of flesh, of much stress, much despair, & greater drawbacks"....He develops the equanimity coming from singleness, dependent on singleness, where sustenance/clinging for the baits of the world ceases entirely.

'Now suppose a man were to come against the wind, carrying a burning grass torch. What do you think: If he were not quickly to drop that grass torch, would he burn his hand or his arm or some other part of his body, so that he would meet with death from that cause, or with death-like pain?'

'Yes, lord.'

'In the same way, householder, a noble disciple considers this point: "The Blessed One has compared sensuality to a grass torch, of much stress, much despair, & greater drawbacks"....He develops the equanimity coming from singleness, dependent on singleness, where sustenance/clinging for the baits of the world ceases entirely.

'Now suppose there were a pit of glowing embers, deeper than a man's height, full of embers that were neither flaming nor smoking, and a man were to come along—loving life, hating death, loving pleasure, abhorring pain—and two strong men, having grabbed him with their arms, were to drag him to the pit of embers. What do you think: Wouldn't the man twist his body this way & that?'

'Yes, lord. And why is that? Because he would realize, "If I fall into this pit of glowing embers, I will meet with death from that cause, or with death-like pain."'

'In the same way, householder, a noble disciple considers this point: "The Blessed One has compared sensuality to a pit of glowing embers, of much stress, much despair, & greater drawbacks"....He develops the equanimity coming from singleness, dependent on singleness, where sustenance/clinging for the baits of the world ceases entirely.

'Now suppose a man, when dreaming, were to see delightful parks, delightful forests, delightful stretches of land, & delightful lakes, and on awakening were to see nothing. In the same way, householder, a noble disciple considers this point: "The Blessed One has compared sensuality to a dream, of much stress, much despair, & greater drawbacks"....He develops the equanimity coming from singleness, dependent on singleness, where sustenance/clinging for the baits of the world ceases entirely.

'Now suppose a man having borrowed some goods—a manly carriage, fine jewels, & ear ornaments—were to go into the market preceded & surrounded by his borrowed goods, and people seeing him would say, "How wealthy is this man, for this is how the wealthy enjoy their possessions," but the actual owners, wherever they might see him, would strip him then & there of what is theirs. What do you think: Should the man rightly be surprised?'

'No, lord. And why is that? The owners are stripping him of what is theirs.'

'In the same way, householder, a noble disciple considers this point: "The Blessed One has compared sensuality borrowed goods, of much stress, much despair, & greater drawbacks"....He develops the equanimity coming from singleness, dependent on singleness, where sustenance/clinging for the baits of the world ceases entirely.

'Now suppose that, not far from a village or town, there were a dense forest grove, and there in the grove was a tree with delicious fruit, abundant fruit, but with no fruit fallen to the ground. A man would come along, desiring fruit, looking for fruit, searching for fruit. Plunging into the forest grove, he would see the tree...and the thought would occur to him, "This is a tree with delicious fruit, abundant fruit, and there is no fruit fallen to the ground, but I know how to climb a tree. Why don't I climb the tree, eat what I like, and fill my clothes with the fruit?" So, having climbed the tree, he would eat what he liked and fill his clothes with the fruit. Then a second man would come along, desiring fruit...searching for fruit and carrying a sharp ax. Plunging into the forest grove, he would see the tree...and the thought would occur to him, "...I don't know how to climb a tree. Why don't I chop down this tree at the root, eat what I like, and fill my clothes with the fruit?" So he would chop the tree at the root. What do you think: If the first man who climbed the tree didn't quickly come down, wouldn't the falling tree crush his hand or foot or some other part of his body, so that he would meet with death from that cause, or with death-like pain?'

'Yes, lord.'

'In the same way, householder, a noble disciple considers this point: "The Blessed One has compared sensuality to the fruits of a tree, of much stress, much despair, & greater drawbacks." Seeing this with right discernment, as it actually is present, then avoiding the equanimity coming from multiplicity, dependent on multiplicity, he develops the equanimity coming from singleness, dependent on singleness, where sustenance/clinging for the baits of the world ceases entirely.

M.54

§ 139. The Buddha: Magandiya, suppose that there was a leper covered with sores and infections, devoured by worms, picking the scabs off the openings of his wounds with his nails, cauterizing his body over a pit of glowing embers. Then suppose his friends, companions, & relatives brought a doctor to treat him. The doctor would concoct medicine, and by means of that medicine he would be cured of his leprosy: well & happy, free, master of himself, going wherever he liked. Then suppose two strong men, having seized hold of him with their arms, were to drag him to a pit of glowing embers. What do you think? Wouldn't he twist his body this way and that?

Magandiya: Yes, lord. Why is that? The fire is painful to the touch, very hot & scorching.

The Buddha: Now what do you think? Is the fire painful to the touch, very hot & scorching, only now, or was it also that way before?

Magandiya: Both now & before is it painful to the touch, very hot & scorching. It's just that when the man was a leper...his faculties were impaired, which was why, even though the fire was actually painful to the touch, he had the distorted perception of 'pleasant.'

The Buddha: In the same way, sensual pleasures in the past were painful to the touch, very hot & scorching; sensual pleasures in the future will be painful to the touch, very hot & scorching; sensual pleasures at present are painful to the touch, very hot & scorching; but when beings are not free from passion for sensual pleasures—devoured by sensual craving, burning with sensual fever—their faculties are impaired, which is why, even though sensual pleasures are actually painful to the touch, they have the distorted perception of 'pleasant.'

Now suppose that there was a leper covered with sores & infections, devoured by worms, picking the scabs off the openings of his wounds with his nails, cauterizing his body over a pit of glowing embers. The more he cauterized his body over the pit of glowing embers, the more disgusting, foul-smelling, & putrid the openings of his wounds would become, and yet he would feel a modicum of enjoyment & satisfaction because of the itchiness of his wounds. In the same way, beings not free from passion for sensual pleasures—devoured by sensual craving, burning with sensual fever—indulge in sensual pleasures. The more they indulge in sensual pleasures, the more their sensual craving increases and the more they burn with sensual fever, and yet they feel a modicum of enjoyment & satisfaction dependent on the five strands of sensuality.

Now what do you think? Have you ever seen or heard of a king or king's minister—enjoying himself, provided & endowed with the five strands of sensual pleasure, without abandoning sensual craving, without removing sensual fever—who has dwelt or will dwell or is dwelling free from thirst, his mind inwardly at peace?

Magandiya: No, Master Gotama.

The Buddha: Very good, Māgandiya. Neither have I....But whatever priests or contemplatives who have dwelt or will dwell or are dwelling free from thirst, their minds inwardly at peace, all have done so having realized—as it actually is present—the origination & disappearance, the allure, the danger, & the escape from sensual pleasures, having abandoned sensual craving and removed sensual fever.

M.75

§ 140. Look at the beautified image,
a heap of festering wounds, shored up:
ill, but the object
of many resolves,
where there is nothing
lasting or sure.

A city made of bones,
plastered over with blood & flesh,
whose hidden treasures are:

pride & deceit,
aging & death.

Dhp.147, 150

§ 141. Not even if it rained gold coins
would we have our fill
of sensual pleasures.
'They give little enjoyment,
much stress'—
knowing this, the wise one finds no delight
even in celestial sensual pleasures.
His delight is in the ending of craving—
the disciple of the Rightly Self-Awakened One.

Dhp.186-87

§ 142. As Subha the nun was going through Jīvaka's delightful mango grove, a libertine [a goldsmith's son] blocked her path, so she said to him:

"What wrong have I done you
that you stand in my way?
It's not proper, my friend,
that a man should touch
a woman gone forth.
I respect the Master's message,
the training pointed out by the one well-gone.
I am pure, without blemish:
Why do you stand in my way?

You—your mind agitated, impassioned;
I—unagitated, unimpassioned,
without blemish,
with a mind entirely freed:
Why do you stand in my way?"

"You are young & not bad-looking,
what need do you have for going forth?
Throw off your ochre robe—
Come, let's delight in the flowering grove.
A sweetness they exude everywhere,
the towering trees with their pollen.
The beginning of spring is a pleasant season—
Come, let's delight in the flowering grove.
The trees with their blossoming tips
moan, as it were, in the breeze:
What delight will you have
if you plunge into the grove alone?
Frequented by herds of wild beasts,
disturbed by elephants rutting & aroused:
you want to go
unaccompanied
into the great, lonely, frightening grove?

Like a doll made of gold, you will go about,
like a goddess in the gardens of heaven.
With delicate, smooth Kasi fabrics,
you will shine, O beauty without compare.
I would gladly do your every bidding
if we were to dwell in the glade.
For there is no creature dearer to me
than you,
O nymph with the languid regard.
If you do as I ask, happy, come live in my house.
Dwelling in the calm of a palace,
have women wait on you,
wear delicate Kāsi fabrics,
adorn yourself with garlands & creams.
I will make you many & varied ornaments
of gold, jewels, & pearls.
Climb onto a costly bed,
scented with sandalwood carvings,
with a well-washed coverlet, beautiful,
spread with a woolen quilt, brand new.
Like a blue lotus rising from the water,
where there dwell non-human spirits,

(*or:* where no human beings dwell)
you will go to old age with your limbs unseen,
if you stay as you are in the holy life."

"What do you assume of any essence,
here in this cemetery grower, filled with corpses,
this body destined to break up?
What do you see when you look at me,
you who are out of your mind?"

"Your eyes are like those of a fawn,
like those of a sprite in the mountains.
Seeing your eyes, my sensual delight
grows all the more.
Like tips they are, of blue lotuses,
in your golden face
—spotless:
Seeing your eyes, my sensual delight
grows all the more.
Even if you should go far away,
I will think only of your pure,
long-lashed gaze,
for there is nothing dearer to me
than your eyes,
O nymph with the languid regard."

"You want to stray from the road,
you want the moon as a plaything,
you want to jump over Mount Sineru,
you who have designs on one born of the Buddha.
For there is nothing anywhere at all
in the world with its gods,
that would be an object of passion for me.
I don't even know what that passion would be,
for it's been killed, root & all, by the path.
Like embers from a pit—scattered,
like a bowl of poison—evaporated,
I don't even see what that passion would be,
for it's been killed, root & all, by the path.
Try to seduce one who hasn't reflected on this,
or who has not followed the Master's teaching.
But try it with this one who knows
and you suffer.

For in the midst of praise & blame,
pleasure & pain,
my mindfulness stands firm.

Knowing the unattractiveness
 of things compounded,
my heart adheres to nothing at all.
I am a follower of the one well-gone,
riding the vehicle of the eightfold way:
My arrow removed, effluent-free,
I delight, having gone to an empty dwelling.

For I have seen well-painted puppets,
hitched up with sticks & strings,
made to dance in various ways.
When the sticks & strings are removed,
thrown away, scattered, shredded,
smashed into pieces, not to be found,
 in what will the mind there make its home?
This body of mine, which is just like that,
when devoid of dhammas doesn't function.
When, devoid of dhammas, it doesn't function,
 in what will the mind there make its home?
Like a mural you've seen, painted on a wall,
smeared with yellow orpiment,
there your vision has been distorted,
meaningless your perception of a human being.
Like an evaporated mirage,
like a tree of gold in a dream,
like a magic show in the midst of a crowd—
 you run blind after what is unreal.

Resembling a ball of sealing wax,
set in a hollow,
with a bubble in the middle
& bathed with tears,
eye secretions are born there too:
The parts of the eye
are rolled all together
in various ways."

Plucking out her lovely eye,
with mind unattached
she felt no regret.

"Here, take this eye. It's yours."

Straightaway she gave it to him.
Straightaway his passion faded right there,
and he begged her forgiveness.

"Be well, follower of the holy life.
This sort of thing
won't happen again.
Harming a person like you
is like embracing a blazing fire,
It is as if I have seized a poisonous snake.
So may you be well. Forgive me."

And released from there, the nun
went to the excellent Buddha's presence.
When she saw the mark of his excellent merit,
her eye became
as it was before.

THIG.XIV

§ **143. Ill will.** These are five ways of subduing hatred by which, when hatred arises in a monk, he should wipe it out completely. Which five?

When one gives birth to hatred for an individual, one should develop good will for that individual. Thus the hatred for that individual should be subdued.

When one gives birth to hatred for an individual, one should develop compassion for that individual...equanimity toward that individual...one should pay him no mind & pay him no attention.... When one gives birth to hatred for an individual, one should direct one's thoughts to the fact of his being the product of his kamma: 'This venerable one is the doer of his kamma, heir of his kamma, born of his kamma, related by his kamma, and is dependent on his kamma. Whatever kamma he does, for good or for evil, to that will he fall heir.' Thus the hatred for that individual should be subdued.

These are five ways of subduing hatred by which, when hatred arises in a monk, he should wipe it out completely.

A.V.161

§ 144. Sariputta: There are some people who are impure in their bodily behavior but pure in their verbal behavior. Hatred for a person of this sort should be subdued.

There are some people who are impure in their verbal behavior but pure in their bodily behavior. Hatred for a person of this sort should also be subdued.

There are some people who are impure in their bodily behavior & verbal behavior, but who periodically experience mental clarity & calm. Hatred for a person of this sort should also be subdued.

There are some people who are impure in their bodily behavior & verbal behavior, and who do not periodically experience mental clarity & calm. Hatred for a person of this sort should also be subdued.

There are some people who are pure in their bodily behavior & their verbal behavior, and who periodically experience mental clarity & calm. Hatred for a person of this sort should also be subdued.

Now as for a person who is impure in his bodily behavior but pure in his verbal behavior, how should one subdue hatred for him? Just as when a monk who makes use of things that are thrown away sees a rag in the road: Taking hold of it with his left foot and spreading it out with his right, he would tear off the sound part and go off with it. In the same way, when the individual is impure in his bodily behavior but pure in his verbal behavior, one should at that time pay no attention to the impurity of his bodily behavior, and instead pay attention to the purity of his verbal behavior. Thus the hatred for him should be subdued.

And as for a person who is impure in his verbal behavior, but pure in his bodily behavior, how should one subdue hatred for him? Just as when there is a pool overgrown with slime & water plants, and a person comes along, burning with heat, covered with sweat, exhausted, trembling, & thirsty. He would jump into the pool, part the slime & water plants with both hands, and then, cupping his hands, drink the water and go on his way. In the same way, when the individual is impure in his verbal behavior but pure in his bodily behavior, one should at that time pay no attention to the impurity of his verbal behavior, and instead pay attention to the purity of his bodily behavior. Thus the hatred for him should be subdued.

And as for a person who is impure in his bodily behavior & verbal behavior, but who periodically experiences mental clarity & calm, how should one subdue hatred for him? Just as when there is a little puddle in a cow's footprint, and a person comes along, burning with heat, covered with sweat, exhausted, trembling, & thirsty. The thought would occur to him, 'Here is this little puddle in a cow's footprint. If I tried to drink the water using my hand or cup, I would disturb it, stir it up, & make it unfit to drink. What if I were to get down on all fours and slurp it up like a cow, and then go on my way?' So he would get down on all fours, slurp up the water like a cow, and then go on his way. In the same way, when an individual is impure in his bodily behavior & verbal behavior, but periodically experiences mental clarity & calm, one should at that time pay no attention to the impurity of his bodily behavior...the impurity of his verbal behavior, and instead pay attention to the fact that he periodically experiences mental clarity & calm. Thus the hatred for him should be subdued.

And as for a person who is impure in his bodily behavior & verbal behavior, and who does not periodically experience mental clarity & calm, how should one subdue hatred for him? Just as when there is a sick man—in pain, seriously ill—traveling along a road, far from the next village & far from the last, unable to get the food he needs, unable to get the medicine he needs, unable to get a suitable assistant, unable to get anyone to take him to human habitation. Now suppose another person were to see him coming along the road. He would do what he could out of compassion, pity, & sympathy for the man, thinking, 'O that this man should get the food he needs, the medicine he needs, a suitable assistant, someone to take him to human habitation. Why is that? So that he won't fall into ruin right here.' In the same way, when a person is impure in his bodily behavior & verbal behavior, and who does not periodically experience mental clarity & calm, one should do what one can out of compassion, pity, & sympathy for him, thinking, 'O that this man should abandon wrong bodily conduct and develop right bodily conduct, abandon wrong verbal conduct and develop right verbal conduct, abandon wrong mental conduct and develop right mental conduct. Why is that? So that, on the break-up of the body, after death, he won't fall into the plane of deprivation, the bad destination, the lower realms, purgatory.' Thus the hatred for him should be subdued.

And as for a person who is pure in his bodily behavior & verbal behavior, and who periodically experiences mental clarity & calm, how should one subdue hatred for him? Just as when there is a pool of clear water—sweet, cool, & limpid, with gently sloping banks, & shaded on all sides by trees of many kinds—and a person comes along, burning with heat, covered with sweat, exhausted, trembling, & thirsty. Having plunged into the pool, having bathed & drunk & come back out, he would sit down or lie down right there in the shade of the trees. In the same way, when an individual is pure in his bodily behavior & verbal behavior, and periodically experiences mental clarity & calm, one should at that time pay attention to the purity of his bodily behavior...the purity of his verbal behavior, and to the fact that he periodically experiences mental clarity & calm. Thus the hatred for him should be subdued. An entirely inspiring individual can make the mind grow serene.

These are five ways of subduing hatred by which, when hatred arises in a monk, he should wipe it out completely.

A.V.162

§ 145. There are these ten ways of subduing hatred. Which ten? 1) Thinking, 'He has done me harm. But what should I expect?' one subdues hatred. 2) Thinking, 'He is doing me harm. But what should I expect?... 3) He is going to do me harm. But what should I expect?...

4) He has done harm to people who are dear & pleasing to me. But what should I expect?... 5) He is doing harm to people who are dear & pleasing to me. But what should I expect?... 6) He is going to do harm to people who are dear & pleasing to me. But what should I expect?... 7) He has aided people who are not dear or pleasing to me. But what should I expect?... 8) He is aiding people who are not dear or pleasing to me. But what should I expect?... 9) He is going to aid people who are not dear or pleasing to me. But what should I expect?' one subdues hatred. 10) One does not get worked up over impossibilities. These are ten ways of subduing hatred.

A.X.80

§ 146. 'He reviled me, hit me, beat me, robbed me'—
Those who gird themselves this way,
Their enmity is not quelled.

'He reviled me, hit me, beat me, robbed me'—
Those who don't gird themselves this way,
Their enmity is quelled.

Enmity is not quelled by enmity,
whatever may be happening here.
Enmity is quelled by non-enmity:
This is an unending truth.

Dhp.3-5

§ 147. Sloth & drowsiness. Once the Blessed One was living among the Bhaggus in the Deer Park at Bhesakalā Grove, near Crocodile Hill. At that time Ven. Mahā Moggallāna [prior to his Awakening] sat nodding near the village of Kallavalaputta, in Magadha. The Blessed One saw this with his purified divine eye, surpassing the human, and as soon as he saw this—just as a strong man might stretch out his bent arm or bend his outstretched arm—disappeared from the Deer Park...appeared right in front of Ven. Mahā Moggallāna, and sat down on a prepared seat. As he was sitting there, the Blessed One said to Ven. Mahā Moggallāna, 'Are you nodding, Moggallāna? Are you nodding?'

'Yes, lord.'

'Well then, Moggallāna, whatever perception you have in mind when drowsiness descends on you, don't attend to that perception, don't pursue it. It's possible that by doing this you will shake off your drowsiness.

'But if by doing this you don't shake off your drowsiness, then recall to your awareness the Dhamma as you have heard & memorized it, re-examine it & ponder it over in your mind. It's possible that by doing this you will shake off your drowsiness.

'But if by doing this you don't shake off your drowsiness, then repeat aloud in detail the Dhamma as you have heard & memorized it. It's possible that by doing this you will shake off your drowsiness.

'But if by doing this you don't shake off your drowsiness, then pull both you earlobes and rub your limbs with your hands. It's possible that by doing this you will shake off your drowsiness.

'But if by doing this you don't shake off your drowsiness, then get up from your seat and, after washing your eyes out with water, look around in all directions and upward to the major stars & constellations. It's possible that by doing this you will shake off your drowsiness.

'But if by doing this you don't shake off your drowsiness, then attend to the perception of light, resolve on the perception of daytime, [dwelling] by night as by day, and by day as by night. By means of an awareness thus open & unhampered, develop a brightened mind [§66]. It's possible that by doing this you will shake off your drowsiness.

'But if by doing this you don't shake off your drowsiness, then—percipient of what lies in front & behind—set a distance to meditate walking back & forth, your senses inwardly immersed, your mind not straying outwards. It's possible that by doing this you will shake off your drowsiness.

'But if by doing this you don't shake off your drowsiness, then—reclining on your right side—take up the lion's posture, one foot placed on top of the other, mindful, alert, with your mind set on getting up. As soon as you wake up, get up quickly, with the thought, "I won't stay indulging in the pleasure of lying down, the pleasure of reclining, the pleasure of drowsiness."

'Thus, Moggallana, should you train yourself....'

A.VII.58

E. RIGHT CONCENTRATION

The passages in this section deal with right concentration in terms of three questions that deserve appropriate attention:

- What is right concentration?
- How is it mastered?
- How can it be put to use?

To answer **the first question:** Passage §148 defines concentration as singleness of mind, but not every instance of mental singleness counts as right concentration. Passage §102 identifies right concentration with the four levels of jhana—meditative absorption—and §152 makes the point that jhana can be considered right concentration only if it is devoid of unskillful qualities like the hindrances. Absorption in sensual passion, for instance, even though it may be very single-minded, does not count as part of the path. Thus the definition for the first level of jhana specifies that counts as a path factor only when the mind is secluded from sensuality and unskillful mental qualities.

The singleness of jhana means not only that awareness is focused on a single object, but also that the object is reduced to a single quality that fills the entirety of one's awareness, at the same time that one's awareness broadens to suffuse the entire object. This mutual pervasion of awareness and object in a state of expansion is what is meant by *absorption.* The similes used to illustrate the various levels of jhana repeatedly make mention of "expansion," "suffusing," "stretching," and "filling" [§150; also M.121; MFU, pp. 82-85], culminating in the fourth jhana where one's body is filled with a bright sense of awareness. This sense of expansion and making-single is also indicated in passages that teach specific meditation techniques. The directions for keeping the breath in mind, for instance, state that one should be sensitive to the entire body while breathing in and out. This accounts for the term *"mahaggata"*—enlarged or expanded—used to describe the mind in the state of jhana.

There are two basic types of jhana, which the commentaries term "form jhana" *(rupa jhana)* and "formless jhana" *(arupa jhana).* Each type has several levels. In the case of form jhana, different passages in the Canon list the levels in different ways. The differences revolve around two different senses of the word "form." In one sense, "form" denotes the body, and form jhana is a state of mental absorption in the form of one's own physical body, as sensed from within. Jhana focused on this type of form comes in four levels, identical with the four levels mentioned in the definition of the faculty of concentration [§72] and of right concentration under the noble eightfold path [§102]. In another sense, "form" can also denote the visible forms and light that some meditators can see in the mind's eye in the course of their meditation. This type of form jhana is analyzed into two patterns, one with two levels [§164], the other with three [§163]. Both patterns end with the perception of the "beautiful," which in terms of its function is equivalent to the sense of radiance filling the body on the fourth level of "body form" jhana.

For a person practicing form jhana in either sense of the term, the equanimity experienced with the sense of beautiful radiance can then act as the basis for the formless levels of jhana, which the Canon terms the four "formlessnesses beyond form." These are invariably defined as progressive absorption in the perceptions of "infinite space," "infinite consciousness," and "there is nothing," leading to a fourth state of neither perception nor non-perception.

As for **the second question,** on how to master right concentration: Passage §154 notes that the ability to attain the first level of jhana—however one experiences the "form" acting as its focus—depends on the abandoning of the hindrances, because the feeling of freedom that comes with their abandoning provides the sense of joy and pleasure that lets the mind settle skillfully in the present moment. How to master this process is best shown by following the Buddha's most detailed set of meditation instructions—the sixteen steps in the practice of keeping the breath in mind [§151]—and comparing them with the standard description of the four stages of jhana [§§149-150]. Before we analyze these maps of the practice, however, we must make a few comments on how to use them skillfully.

To begin with, internal obstacles to the practice of jhana do not end with the preliminary ground-clearing of the hindrances discussed in the preceding section. More refined levels of unskillful mental states can get in the way [§§160-61]. Lapses in mindfulness and alertness can leave openings for the hindrances to return. Thus, although the maps of the various stages of concentration proceed in a smooth, seemingly inevitable progression, the actual experience of the practice does not. For this reason, the Buddha gives specific instructions on how to deal with these obstacles as they arise in the course of the practice. Passage §159 lists five basic approaches, the first two of which we have already covered in the preceding section. The remaining three are: 1) One ignores the obstacles. This works on the principle that paying attention to the distraction feeds the distraction, just as paying attention to a crazy person—even if one is simply trying to drive him away—encourages him to stay. 2) One notices that the act of thinking a distracting thought actually takes more energy than not thinking the thought, and one consciously relaxes whatever tension or energy happens to accompany it. This approach works best when one is sensitive enough to bodily sensations to see the pattern of physical tension that appears in conjunction with the thought, and can intentionally relax it. 3) The approach of last resort is simply to exert force on the mind to drive out the distracting thought. This is a temporary stopgap measure that works only as long as mindfulness is firm and determination strong. It is useful in cases where discernment is not yet sharp enough to make the other approaches work, but once discernment is up to the task, the other approaches are more effective in the long run.

Another point to keep in mind in understanding the maps of the practice is that they list the steps of meditation, not in the order in which they will be experienced, but in the order in which they can be mastered. There are cases, for instance, where one will feel rapture in the course of the practice (step 5 in the practice of breath meditation) before one is able to breath in and out sensitive to the entire body (step 3). In such cases, it is important not to jump to any conclusions as to one's level of attainment, or to feel that one has bypassed the need to master an earlier step. Instead—when several different experiences arise together in a jumble, as they often do—one should use the maps to tell which experience to focus on first for the sake of developing one's meditation as a skill.

One qualification here is that it is not necessary to master all the levels of concentration in order to gain Awakening. The relationship of concentration to discernment is a controversial issue, which we will cover in the following section, but here we may simply note that many texts [§§173-74] point out that the experience of the first jhana can be a sufficient basis for the discernment leading to Awakening. The same holds true for the first four steps in breath mediation, which constitute one of the alternative ways of developing the body in and of itself as a frame of reference [§30]. In this case, one's practice of breath meditation would jump from a mastery of step 4 straight to step 13, skipping the intervening steps. In fact, beginning with step 4, it is possible to jump directly to 13 from any of the steps, and from there to progress all the way to Awakening.

The fact that the higher stages are unnecessary in some cases, however, does not mean that they are superfluous. Many people, as they develop the skill of their meditation, will find that their minds naturally go to deeper levels of stillness with no liberating insight arising. For them, the maps are valuable aids for a number of reasons. To begin with, the maps can help indicate what does and does not count as Awakening. When one arrives at a new, more refined level of awareness in one's practice, it is easy to assume that one has attained the goal. Comparing one's experience to the maps, however, can show that the experience is simply a higher level of concentration. Furthermore, awareness of the distinct levels can help one review them after attaining them, so that in the course of trying to master them, moving from one level to another, one can begin to gain insight into the element of will and fabrication that goes into them. This insight can then provide an understanding into the pattern of cause and effect in the mind and, as passage §182 shows, can lead to a sense of dispassion and ultimately to Awakening.

However, the maps should not be used to plan one's practice in advance. This is the message of §162, which makes the point that one should not try to use one's knowledge of the various levels of the practice to force one's way through them. In other words, one should not try to concoct a particular state of jhana based on ideas picked up from the maps. On reaching a particular level, one should not be in a hurry to go to the next. Instead, one should familiarize oneself with that level of mind, perfecting one's mastery; eventually that state of concentration will ripen naturally into the next level. To continue the image of the passage, one will find that there is no need to jump to another pasture to taste different grass and water, for the new grass and water will develop right in one's own pasture.

Finally, although the maps to the various stages of concentration seem exhaustive and complete, bear in mind that they list only the stages of *right* concentration, and not the varieties of wrong. In addition to the types of wrong concentration mentioned in §152, there are states of mind that may be very quiet but lack the mindfulness that would make them right. One of these stages is a blurred state—essentially a concentration of delusion—half-way between waking and sleep, in which one's object becomes hazy and ill-defined. On leaving it, one is hard put to say where the mind was focused, or whether it was awake or asleep. Another type of wrong concentration is one that a modern practice tradition calls a state of non-perception *(asaññi).* In this state, which is essentially a concentration of subtle aversion—the result of a strongly focused determination not to stay with any one object—everything seems to cease: the mind blanks out, with no perception of sights or sounds, or of one's own body or thoughts. There is just barely enough mindfulness to know that one hasn't fainted or fallen asleep. One can stay there for long periods of time, and yet the experience will seem momentary. One can even determine beforehand when one will leave the state; but on emerging from it, one will feel somewhat dazed or drugged, a reaction caused by the intense aversive force of the concentration that induced the state to begin with. There are other forms of wrong concentration, but a general test is that right concentration is a mindful, fully alert state. Any state of stillness without clear mindfulness and alertness is wrong.

With these points in mind we can now turn to the maps to see their answer to the question of how breath meditation leads to the mastery of jhana. As noted above, the practice of keeping the breath in mind is the meditation method that the Canon teaches in most detail. There are two possible reasons for this, one historical and the other more theoretical. From the historical point of view, the breath was the focal point that the Buddha himself used on the night of his own Awakening. From the theoretical perspective, a state of concentration focused on the breath is the meeting place of all the elements of the factor of "fabrication" *(sankhara)* in the formula for dependent co-arising [§§218, 223]. This factor, as experienced in the present, consists of bodily fabrication (the breath itself), verbal fabrication (the factors of directed thought and evaluation applied to the breath in the first jhana), and mental fabrication (feeling and perception, in this case the feelings of pleasure and equanimity experienced in the four jhanas, plus the mental label of "breath" or "form" that act as the basis for the state of jhana). Because transcendent discernment must deal directly with these three types of fabrication if it is to eliminate the ignorance that underlies them, the practice of jhana based on the breath is an ideal point to focus on all three at once.

The first two steps of breath meditation [§151] involve simple tasks of directed thought and evaluation: directing one's thoughts and attention to the breath in and of itself, in the present, at the same time evaluating it as one begins to discern variations in the length of the breath. Some modern teachers maintain that the factor of evaluation here also includes taking one's observations of short and long breathing as a basis for adjusting the rhythm of the breath to make it as comfortable as possible. Because the first level of jhana must be based on a sense of pleasure [§238], this advice is very practical.

The remaining steps are willed or determined: One "trains oneself," first by manipulating one's sense of conscious awareness, making it sensitive to the body as a whole. Then one can begin manipulating the bodily sensations of which one is aware, reducing them to a single sensation of calm by letting "bodily fabrication"—the breath—grow calm so as to create an easeful sense of rapture and pleasure. A comparison between the stages of breath meditation and the graphic analogies for jhana [§150] indicates that the fifth and sixth steps—being sensitive to rapture and pleasure—involve making these feelings "single" as well, by letting them suffuse the entire body, just as the bathman kneads the moisture throughout his ball of bath powder. With bodily fabrications stilled, mental fabrications—feelings and perceptions—become clearly apparent as they occur, just as when a radio is precisely tuned to a certain frequency, static is eliminated and the message sent by the radio station broadcasting at that frequency becomes clear. These mental fabrications, too, are calmed, a step symbolized in the analogies for jhana by the still waters in the simile for the third level, in contrast to the spring waters welling up in the second. What remains is simply a sense of the mind itself, corresponding to the level of fourth jhana, in which the body is filled from head to toe with a single sense of bright, radiant awareness. This completes the first level of frames-of-reference practice [II/B].

Once this stage is reached, steps 10-12 indicate that one can now turn one's attention to consolidating one's mastery of concentration. One does this by reviewing the various levels of jhana, focusing not so much on the breath as on the mind as it relates to the breath. This allows a perception of the different ways in which the mind can be satisfied and steadied, and the different factors from which it can be released by taking it through the different levels of jhana—for example, releasing it from rapture by taking it from the second level to the third, and so forth [§175]. One comes to see that, although the breath feels different on the different levels of jhana, the cause is not so much the breath as it is the way the mind relates to the breath, shedding the various mental activities surrounding its single preoccupation. As one ascends through the various levels, directed thought and evaluation are stilled, rapture fades, and pleasure is abandoned. Another way of consolidating one's skills in the course of these steps is to examine the subtle defilements that interfere with full mastery of concentration. The fact that one's focus is now on the mind makes it possible to see these defilements clearly, and then to steady the mind even further by releasing it from them. Passage §161, although aimed specifically at the problems faced by those who have visions in their meditation, gives a useful checklist of subtle mental defilements that can hamper the concentration of any meditator. The image of grasping the quail neither too loosely nor too tight has become a standard one in Buddhist meditation manuals.

The mastery of concentration developed in steps 9-12 provides an excellent chance to develop discernment into the pattern of cause and effect in the process of concentrating the mind, in that one must master the causal factors before one can gain the desired results in terms of satisfaction, steadiness, and release. Here we see at work the basic pattern of skillfulness mentioned in several earlier sections: that discernment is sharpened and strengthened by employing it in developing the skills of concentration. This would correspond to the second level of frames-of-reference meditation—focusing on the phenomenon of origination and passing away—mentioned in II/B.

Another development that can happen during these steps—although this takes one outside of the practice of breath meditation *per se*—is the discovery of how the equanimity developed in the fourth jhana can be applied to other refined objects of the mind. These are the four formless jhanas: the sphere of the infinitude of space, the sphere of the infinitude of consciousness, the sphere of nothingness, and the sphere of neither perception nor non-perception. These states may sound impossibly abstract, but in actual practice they grow directly from the way the mind relates to the still sense of the body in the fourth jhana. The first stage comes when the mind consciously ignores its perception (mental label) of the form of the body, attending instead to the remaining sense of space that surrounds and pervades that form; the second stage comes when the mind sheds its perception of "space," leaving a limitless sense of awareness; the third, when it lets go of its perception or mental label of "awareness," leaving a perception of inactivity; and the fourth, when it sheds the perception of that lack of activity. What is left is a state where perception is so refined that it can hardly be called perception at all, even though it is still there. As one masters these steps, one sees that whereas the first four levels of jhana differ in the type of activity the mind focuses on its one object, the four formless jhanas differ in their objects, as one level of mental labeling falls away to be replaced by a more subtle one.

Passages §162 and §164 list one more meditative attainment beyond the sphere of neither perception nor non-perception—the cessation of feeling and perception—but this is qualitatively different from the others, in that a meditator cannot attain it without at the same time awakening to the level of at least non-returning. The reason behind this is related, once more, to the factor of "fabrication" *(sankhara)* in dependent co-arising [§218]. In the course of mastering the levels of jhana, verbal fabrication grows still as one enters the second jhana; bodily fabrication, as one enters the fourth; and mental fabrication, as one enters this last stage. For all three types of fabrication to stop, however, ignorance—the condition for fabrication—must stop as well, and this can happen only with the insight that leads to Awakening.

We have come to the end of the list of the stages of mastery in meditative attainment, but four steps in breath meditation remain unexplained. This is because, aside from the ninth level of attainment, the stages of mastery can all be attained without developing the discernment that constitutes Awakening, while the last four steps in breath meditation deal specifically with giving rise to that discernment. This brings us to **the third question** that was broached at the beginning of this introduction: how right concentration can be put to use.

Passage §149 lists four possible uses for concentration:

- a pleasant abiding in the here and now,
- the attainment of knowledge and vision,
- mindfulness and alertness, and
- the ending of the effluents.

The first use is the simple enjoyment of the experience of jhana; the second relates to the first five supranormal powers [II/D]. The third relates to the development of the frames of reference [II/B]; and the fourth, to the discernment that constitutes Awakening. We have already discussed the second and third uses of concentration in the passages just cited in brackets. This leaves us with the first and fourth.

The Canon [M.138; MFU, pp. 114-15] notes that meditators can become "chained and fettered" to the attractions of the pleasure to be found in jhana. As a result, many meditators are afraid to let their minds settle into blissfully still states, for fear of becoming stuck. The Canon, however, never once states that stream-entry can be attained without at least some experience in jhana; and it states explicitly [A.III.88; MFU, p. 103] that the attainment of non-returning requires a mastery of concentration. M.36 relates that the turning point in the Buddha's own practice—when he abandoned the path of self-affliction and turned to the middle way—hinged on his realization that there is nothing blameworthy in the pleasure to be found in jhana. Thus, there is nothing to fear.

This pleasure plays an important function in the practice. To begin with, it enables the mind to stay comfortably in the present moment, helping it attain the stability it needs for gaining insight. This can be compared to a scientific experiment, in which the measuring equipment needs to be absolutely steady in order to give reliable readings. Secondly, because a great deal of sensitivity is required to "tune" the mind to the refined pleasure of jhana, the practice serves to increase one's sensitivity, making one more acutely aware of even the most refined levels of stress as well. Thirdly, because the pleasure and equanimity of jhana are more exquisite than sensory pleasures, and because they exist independently of the five senses, they can enable the mind to become less involved in sensory pleasures and less inclined to search for emotional satisfaction from them. In this sense, the skillful pleasures of jhana can act as a fulcrum for prying loose one's attachments to the less skillful pleasures of sensuality. The fact that fully mature mastery of jhana brings about the attainment of non-returning, the preliminary level of Awakening where sensual passion is abandoned, shows the necessary role that jhana plays in letting go of this particular defilement. Finally, the pleasure of jhana provides a place of rest and rehabilitation along the path when the mind's powers of discernment become dulled or it must be coaxed into the proper mood to accept some of the harsher lessons that it needs to learn in order to abandon its cravings. Just as a person who is well-fed and rested is more open to receiving criticism than when he is tired and hungry, the mind is often more willing to admit its own foolishness and lack of skill when it is nourished by the pleasure of jhana than when it is not.

Thus, although the pleasure of jhana can become an obstacle if treated as an end in itself, there are phases of the practice where the pursuit of this form of pleasure is a useful strategy toward the fourth use of concentration: the ending of the mental effluents. This fourth use is the topic of the next section, but here we can simply note that it is related to the fifth factor of noble right concentration mentioned in §150. As the simile illustrating it suggests—with the standing person reflecting on the person sitting down—this factor is a pulling back or a lifting of the mind above the object of its absorption, without at the same time disturbing the absorption. This factor corresponds to steps 9 through 12 in the guide to breath meditation, in that one is able to focus on the way the mind relates to its object at the same time that the mind is actually in a state of concentration. Passage §172 shows that this factor can be applied to any level of jhana except for the states of neither perception nor non-perception and the cessation of perception and feeling. As for those two states, one can reflect on their component factors only after leaving them. With the other states, one stays with the object, but one's prime focus is on the mind. One sees the various mental events that go into maintaining that state of concentration, and as one contemplates these events, one becomes struck by how inconstant they are, how fabricated and willed. This provides insight into how the present aspect of kamma—one's present intentions—shape one's present experience. It also gives insight into the general pattern of cause and effect in the mind.

Realizing the inconstancy and unreliability of the factors in this pattern gives rise to the realization that they are also stressful and not-self, i.e., not to be identified as "me" or "mine." When this realization goes straight to the heart, there occurs a sense of dispassion for these factors and an experience of their fading away and cessation. Finally, one relinquishes attachment not only to these events, but also to the discernment that sees through to their true nature. This completes steps 13 through 16 in the guide to breath meditation, at the same time bringing the seven factors of Awakening to completion in a state "dependent on seclusion...dispassion...cessation, resulting in letting go [§193]," where "letting go" would appear to be equivalent to the "relinquishment" in step 16. When one is able simply to experience the act of relinquishment, without feeling that one is "doing" the relinquishing, one passes through the third stage of frames-of-reference meditation to the state of non-fashioning [§§179, 183], which forms the threshold to release.

Even after attaining release, the Arahant continues to practice meditation, although now that the effluents are ended, the concentration is not needed to put them to an end. M.107 mentions that Arahants practice concentration both for the sake of a pleasant abiding in the here and now, and for mindfulness and alertness. A number of passages in the Canon mention the Buddha and his Arahant disciples exercising their supranormal powers, which shows that they were practicing concentration for the sake of attaining knowledge and vision as well, to use in instructing those around them. The description of the Buddha's passing away tells that he entered total Unbinding after exercising his mastery in the full range of jhanic attainments. Thus the practice of concentration is useful all the way to the point where one gains total release from the round of death and rebirth.

§ 148. Visakha: Now what is concentration, what qualities are its themes, what qualities are its requisites, and what is its development?

Sister Dhammadinna: Singleness of mind is concentration; the four frames of reference are its themes; the four right exertions are its requisites; and any cultivation, development, & pursuit of these qualities is its development.

M.44

§ 149. These are the four developments of concentration. Which four? There is the development of concentration that, when developed & pursued, leads to a pleasant abiding in the here & now. There is the development of concentration that...leads to the attainment of knowledge & vision. There is the development of concentration that...leads to mindfulness & alertness. There is the development of concentration that, when developed & pursued, leads to the ending of the effluents.

And what is the development of concentration that, when developed & pursued, leads to a pleasant abiding in the here & now? There is the case where a monk—quite withdrawn from sensuality, withdrawn from unskillful qualities—enters & remains in the first jhana: rapture & pleasure born from withdrawal, accompanied by directed thought & evaluation. With the stilling of directed thought & evaluation, he enters & remains in the second jhana: rapture & pleasure born of composure, unification of awareness free from directed thought & evaluation—internal assurance. With the fading of rapture he remains in equanimity, mindful & alert, and physically sensitive to pleasure. He enters & remains in the third jhana, and of him the Noble Ones declare, 'Equanimous & mindful, he has a pleasurable abiding.' With the abandoning of pleasure & pain—as with the earlier disappearance of elation & distress—he enters & remains in the fourth jhana: purity of equanimity & mindfulness, neither pleasure nor pain. This is the development of concentration that... leads to a pleasant abiding in the here & now.

And what is the development of concentration that...leads to the attainment of knowledge & vision? There is the case where a monk attends to the perception of light and is resolved on the perception of daytime [at any hour of the day]. Day [for him] is the same as night, night is the same as day. By means of an awareness open & unhampered, he develops a brightened mind. This is the development of concentration that...leads to the attainment of knowledge & vision. [§§64; 66]

And what is the development of concentration that...leads to mindfulness & alertness? There is the case where feelings are known to the monk as they arise, known as they persist, known as they subside. Perceptions are known to him as they arise, known as they persist, known as they subside. Thoughts are known to him as they arise, known as they persist, known as they subside. This is the development of concentration that...leads to mindfulness & alertness. [§30]

And what is the development of concentration that...leads to the ending of the effluents? There is the case where a monk remains focused on arising & falling away with reference to the five aggregates for sustenance/clinging: 'Such is form, such its origination, such its disappearance. Such is feeling... Such is perception...Such are fabrications...Such is consciousness, such its origination, such its disappearance.' This is the development of concentration that...leads to the ending of the effluents. [§173]

These are the four developments of concentration.

A.IV.41

§ 150. Noble right concentration. Now what, monks, is five-factored noble right concentration? There is the case where a monk— quite withdrawn from sensuality, withdrawn from unskillful qualities— enters & remains in the first jhāna: rapture & pleasure born from withdrawal, accompanied by directed thought & evaluation. He permeates & pervades, suffuses & fills this very body with the rapture & pleasure born from withdrawal. There is nothing of his entire body unpervaded by rapture & pleasure born from withdrawal.

Just as if a skilled bathman or bathman's apprentice would pour bath powder into a brass basin and knead it together, sprinkling it again & again with water, so that his ball of bath powder—saturated, moisture-laden, permeated within & without—would nevertheless not drip; even so, the monk permeates...this very body with the rapture & pleasure born of withdrawal. There is nothing of his entire body unpervaded by rapture & pleasure born from withdrawal. This is the first development of the five-factored noble right concentration.

Furthermore, with the stilling of directed thought & evaluation, he enters & remains in the second jhāna: rapture & pleasure born of composure, unification of awareness free from directed thought & evaluation—internal assurance. He permeates & pervades, suffuses & fills this very body with the rapture & pleasure born of composure. There is nothing of his entire body unpervaded by rapture & pleasure born of composure.

Just like a lake with spring-water welling up from within, having no inflow from east, west, north, or south, and with the skies periodically supplying abundant showers, so that the cool fount of water welling up from within the lake would permeate & pervade, suffuse & fill it with cool waters, there being no part of the lake unpervaded by the cool waters; even so, the monk permeates...this very body with the rapture & pleasure born of composure. There is nothing of his entire body unpervaded by rapture & pleasure born of composure. This is the second development of the five-factored noble right concentration.

And furthermore, with the fading of rapture, he remains in equanimity, mindful & alert, and physically sensitive to pleasure. He enters & remains in the third jhana, and of him the Noble Ones declare, 'Equanimous & mindful, he has a pleasurable abiding.' He permeates & pervades, suffuses & fills this very body with the pleasure divested of rapture, so that there is nothing of his entire body unpervaded with pleasure divested of rapture.

Just as in a blue-, white-, or red-lotus pond, there may be some of the blue, white, or red lotuses which, born & growing in the water, stay immersed in the water and flourish without standing up out of the water, so that they are permeated & pervaded, suffused & filled with cool water from their roots to their tips, and nothing of those blue, white, or red lotuses would be unpervaded with cool water; even so, the monk permeates...this very body with the pleasure divested of rapture. There is nothing of his entire body unpervaded with pleasure divested of rapture. This is the third development of the five-factored noble right concentration.

And furthermore, with the abandoning of pleasure & stress—as with the earlier disappearance of elation & distress—he enters & remains in the fourth jhana: purity of equanimity & mindfulness, neither-pleasure-nor-pain. He sits, permeating the body with a pure, bright awareness, so that there is nothing of his entire body unpervaded by pure, bright awareness.

Just as if a man were sitting wrapped from head to foot with a white cloth so that there would be no part of his body to which the white cloth did not extend; even so, the monk sits, permeating his body with a pure, bright awareness. There is nothing of his entire body unpervaded by pure, bright awareness. This is the fourth development of the five-factored noble right concentration.

And furthermore, the monk has his theme of reflection well in hand, well attended to, well-considered, well-tuned (well-penetrated) by means of discernment.

Just as if one person were to reflect on another, or a standing person were to reflect on a sitting person, or a sitting person were to reflect on a person lying down; even so, monks, the monk has his theme of reflection well in hand, well attended to, well-pondered, well-tuned (well-penetrated) by means of discernment. This is the fifth development of the five-factored noble right concentration.

When a monk has developed & pursued the five-factored noble right concentration in this way, then whichever of the six higher knowledges he turns his mind to know & realize, he can witness them for himself whenever there is an opening. [§64]

Suppose that there were a water jar, set on a stand, brimful of water so that a crow could drink from it. If a strong man were to tip it in any way at all, would water spill out?

Yes, lord.

In the same way, when a monk has developed & pursued the five-factored noble right concentration in this way, then whichever of the six higher knowledges he turns his mind to know & realize, he can witness them for himself whenever there is an opening.

Suppose there were a rectangular water tank—set on level ground, bounded by dikes—brimful of water so that a crow could drink from it. If a strong man were to loosen the dikes anywhere at all, would water spill out?

Yes, lord....

Suppose there were a chariot on level ground at four crossroads, harnessed to thoroughbreds, waiting with whips lying ready, so that a skilled driver, a trainer of tamable horses, might mount and—taking the reins with his left hand and the whip with his right—drive out & back, to whatever place and by whichever road he liked; in the same way, when a monk has developed & pursued the five-factored noble right concentration in this way, then whichever of the six higher knowledges he turns his mind to know & realize, he can witness them for himself whenever there is an opening.

A.V.28

§ 151. Breath Meditation. Now in what way does a monk develop & pursue mindfulness of in-&-out breathing so that it bears great fruit & great benefits?

There is the case where a monk, having gone to the wilderness, to the shade of a tree, or to an empty building, sits down folding his legs crosswise, holding his body erect, and setting mindfulness to the fore. Always mindful, he breathes in; mindful he breathes out.

[1] Breathing in long, he discerns that he is breathing in long; or breathing out long, he discerns that he is breathing out long.
[2] Or breathing in short, he discerns that he is breathing in short; or breathing out short, he discerns that he is breathing out short.
[3] He trains himself to breathe in sensitive to the entire body, and to breathe out sensitive to the entire body. [4] He trains himself to breathe in calming bodily fabrication, and to breathe out calming bodily fabrication.

[5] He trains himself to breathe in sensitive to rapture, and to breathe out sensitive to rapture. [6] He trains himself to breathe in sensitive to pleasure, and to breathe out sensitive to pleasure. [7] He trains himself to breathe in sensitive to mental fabrication, and to breathe out sensitive to mental fabrication. [8] He trains himself to breathe in calming mental fabrication, and to breathe out calming mental fabrication.

[9] He trains himself to breathe in sensitive to the mind, and to breathe out sensitive to the mind. [10] He trains himself to breathe in satisfying the mind, and to breathe out satisfying the mind. [11] He trains himself to breathe in steadying the mind, and to breathe out steadying the mind. [12] He trains himself to breathe in releasing the mind, and to breathe out releasing the mind.

[13] He trains himself to breathe in focusing on inconstancy, and to breathe out focusing on inconstancy. [14] He trains himself to breathe in focusing on dispassion *(literally,* fading), and to breathe out focusing on dispassion. [15] He trains himself to breathe in focusing on cessation, and to breathe out focusing on cessation. [16] He trains himself to breathe in focusing on relinquishment, and to breathe out focusing on relinquishment.

This is how mindfulness of in-&-out breathing is developed & pursued so that it bears great fruit & great benefits.

M.118

§ 152. Vassakara: Once, Ven. Ananda, Ven. Gotama was living at Vesali in the Hall with the peaked roof in the Great Forest. I went to where he was staying in the Great Forest...and there he spoke in a variety of ways on jhana. Ven. Gotama was both endowed with jhana and made jhana his habit. In fact, he praised all sorts of jhana.

Ananda: It was not the case that the Blessed One praised all sorts of jhana, nor did he criticize all sorts of jhana. And what sort of jhana did he not praise? There is the case where a certain person dwells with his awareness overcome by sensual passion, obsessed with sensual passion. He does not discern the escape, as it actually is present, from sensual passion once it has arisen. Making that sensual passion the focal point, he absorbs himself with it, besorbs, resorbs, & supersorbs himself with it.

He dwells with his awareness overcome by ill will...sloth & drowsiness... restlessness & anxiety...uncertainty, obsessed with uncertainty. He does not discern the escape, as it actually is present, from uncertainty once it has arisen. Making that uncertainty the focal point, he absorbs himself with it, besorbs, resorbs, & supersorbs himself with it. This is the sort of jhana that the Blessed One did not praise.

And what sort of jhana did he praise? There is the case where a monk—quite withdrawn from sensuality, withdrawn from unskillful qualities—enters & remains in the first jhana...the second jhana...the third jhana...the fourth jhana: purity of equanimity & mindfulness, neither pleasure nor pain. This is the sort of jhana that the Blessed One praised.

Vassakara: It would seem, Ven. Ananda, that the Ven. Gotama criticized the jhana that deserves criticism, and praised that which deserves praise.

M.108

§ 153. A monk endowed with these five qualities is incapable of entering & remaining in right concentration. Which five? He cannot withstand [the impact of] sights, he cannot withstand sounds... aromas...tastes...tactile sensations. A monk endowed with these five qualities is not capable of entering & remaining in right concentration.

A monk endowed with these five qualities is capable of entering & remaining in right concentration. Which five? He can withstand [the impact of] sights...sounds...aromas...tastes...tactile sensations. A monk endowed with these five qualities is capable of entering & remaining in right concentration.

A.V.113

§ 154. A monk who has not abandoned these six qualities is incapable of entering & remaining in the first jhana. Which six? Sensual desire, ill will, sloth & drowsiness, restlessness & anxiety, uncertainty, and not seeing well with right discernment, as they actually are present, the drawbacks of sensual pleasures....

A monk who has not abandoned these six qualities is incapable of entering & remaining in the first jhana. Which six? Thoughts of sensuality, thoughts of ill will, thoughts of harmfulness, perceptions of sensuality, perceptions of ill will, perceptions of harmfulness.

A.VI.73-74

§ 155. A monk endowed with these six qualities is capable of mastering strength in concentration. Which six?

There is the case where a monk is skilled in the attaining of concentration, in the maintenance of concentration, & in the exit from concentration. He is deliberate in doing it, persevering in doing it, and amenable to doing it.

A monk endowed with these six qualities is capable of mastering strength in concentration.

A.VI.72

§ 156. A monk endowed with these six qualities could break through the Himalayas, king of mountains, to say nothing of miserable ignorance. Which six?

There is the case where a monk is skilled in the attaining of concentration, in the maintenance of concentration, in the exit from concentration, in the [mind's] preparedness for concentration, in the range of concentration, & in the application of concentration.

A monk endowed with these six qualities could break through the Himalayas, king of mountains, to say nothing of miserable ignorance.

A.VI.24

§ 157. Imagine a great pool of water to which there comes a great bull elephant, seven or seven and a half cubits tall. The thought occurs to him, 'What if I were to plunge into this pool of water, to amuse myself by squirting water into my ears and along my back, and then to bathe & drink & come back out & go off as I please.' So he plunges into the pool of water, amuses himself by squirting water into his ears and along his back, and then bathes & drinks & comes back out & goes off as he pleases. Why is that? Because his large body finds a footing in the depth.

Now suppose a rabbit or a cat were to come along & think, 'What's the difference between me & a bull elephant? What if I were to plunge into this pool of water, to amuse myself by squirting water into my ears and along my back, and then to bathe & drink & come back out & go off as I please.' So he plunges rashly into the pool of water without reflecting, and of him it can be expected that he will either sink to the bottom or float away on the surface. Why is that? Because his small body doesn't find a footing in the depth.

In the same way, whoever says, 'Without having attained concentration, I will go live in solitude, in isolated wilderness places,' of him it can be expected that he will either sink to the bottom or float away on the surface.

A.X.99

§ 158. These are the five rewards for one who practices walking meditation. Which five? He can endure traveling by foot; he can endure exertion; he becomes free from disease; whatever he has eaten & drunk, chewed & savored, becomes well-digested; the concentration he wins while doing walking meditation lasts for a long time.

A.V.29

§ 159. Distracting Thoughts. When a monk is intent on the heightened mind, there are five themes he should attend to at the appropriate times. Which five?

There is the case where evil, unskillful thoughts—connected with desire, aversion, or delusion—arise in a monk while he is referring to & attending to a particular theme. He should attend to another theme, apart from that one, connected with what is skillful. When he is attending to this other theme...those evil, unskillful thoughts...are abandoned & subside. With their abandoning, he steadies his mind right within, settles it, unifies it, & concentrates it. Just as a skilled carpenter or his apprentice would use a small peg to knock out, drive out, & pull out a large one; in the same way...he steadies his mind right within, settles it, unifies it, & concentrates it.

If evil, unskillful thoughts—connected with desire, aversion, or delusion—still arise in the monk while he is attending to this other theme, connected with what is skillful, he should scrutinize the drawbacks of those thoughts: 'Truly, these thoughts of mine are unskillful...blameworthy...these thoughts of mine result in stress.' As he is scrutinizing their drawbacks...those evil, unskillful thoughts... are abandoned & subside. With their abandoning, he steadies his mind right within, settles it, unifies it, & concentrates it. Just as a young woman—or man—fond of adornment, would be horrified, humiliated, & disgusted if the carcass of a snake or a dog or a human being were hung from her neck; in the same way...the monk steadies his mind right within, settles it, unifies, it & concentrates it.

If evil, unskillful thoughts—connected with desire, aversion or delusion—still arise in the monk while he is scrutinizing the drawbacks of those thoughts, he should pay no mind & pay no attention to those thoughts. As he is paying no mind & paying no attention to them...those evil, unskillful thoughts are abandoned & subside. With their abandoning, he steadies his mind right within, settles it, unifies it, & concentrates it. Just as a man with good eyes, not wanting to see forms that had come into range, would close his eyes or look away; in the same way...the monk steadies his mind right within, settles it, unifies it, & concentrates it.

If evil, unskillful thoughts—connected with desire, aversion or delusion—still arise in the monk while he is paying no mind & paying no attention to those thoughts, he should attend to the relaxing of thought-fabrication with regard to those thoughts. As he is attending to the relaxing of thought-fabrication with regard to those thoughts... those evil, unskillful thoughts are abandoned & subside. With their abandoning, he steadies his mind right within, settles it, unifies it, & concentrates it. Just as the thought would occur to a man walking quickly, 'Why am I walking quickly? Why don't I walk slowly?' So he walks slowly. The thought occurs to him, 'Why am I walking slowly? Why don't I stand?' So he stands. The thought occurs to him, 'Why am I standing? Why don't I sit down?' So he sits down. The thought occurs to him, 'Why am I sitting? Why don't I lie down?' So he lies down. In this way, giving up the grosser posture, he takes up the more refined one. In the same way...the monk steadies his mind right within, settles it, unifies it, & concentrates it.

If evil, unskillful thoughts—connected with desire, aversion or delusion—still arise in the monk while he is attending to the relaxing of thought-fabrication with regard to those thoughts, then—with his teeth clenched & his tongue pressed against the roof of his mouth—he should beat down, constrain, & crush his mind with his awareness. As—with his teeth clenched & his tongue pressed against the roof of his mouth—he is beating down, constraining, & crushing his mind with his awareness...those evil, unskillful thoughts are abandoned & subside. With their abandoning, he steadies his mind right within, settles it, unifies it, & concentrates it. Just as a strong man, seizing a weaker man by the head or the throat or the shoulders, would beat him down, constrain, & crush him; in the same way...the monk steadies his mind right within, settles it, unifies it, & concentrates it.

Now when a monk...attending to another theme...scrutinizing the drawbacks of those thoughts...paying no mind & paying no attention to those thoughts...attending to the relaxing of thought-fabrication with regard to those thoughts...beating down, constraining & crushing his mind with his awareness... steadies his mind right within, settles it, unifies it & concentrates it: He is then called a monk with mastery over the ways of thought sequences. He thinks whatever thought he wants to, and doesn't think whatever thought he doesn't. He has severed craving, thrown off the fetters, and—through the right penetration of conceit—has made an end of suffering & stress.

M.20

§ 160. There are these gross impurities in gold: dirty sand, gravel, & grit. The dirt-washer or his apprentice, having placed [the gold] in a vat, washes it again & again until he has washed them away.

When he is rid of them, there remain the moderate impurities in the gold: coarse sand & fine grit. He washes the gold again & again until he has washed them away.

When he is rid of them, there remain the fine impurities in the gold: fine sand & black dust. The dirt-washer or his apprentice washes the gold again & again until he has washed them away.

When he is rid of them, there remains just the gold dust. The goldsmith or his apprentice, having placed it in a crucible, blows on it again & again to blow away the dross. The gold, as long as it has not been blown on again & again to the point where the impurities are blown away, as long as it is not refined & free from dross, is not pliant, malleable, or luminous. It is brittle and not ready to be worked. But there comes a time when the goldsmith or his apprentice has blown on the gold again & again until the dross is blown away. The gold...is then refined, free from dross, plaint, malleable, & luminous. It is not brittle, and is ready to be worked. Then whatever sort of ornament he has in mind—whether a belt, an earring, a necklace, or a gold chain—the gold would serve his purpose.

In the same way, there are these gross impurities in a monk intent on heightened mind: misconduct in body, speech, & mind. These the monk—aware & able by nature—abandons, destroys, dispels, wipes out of existence. When he is rid of them, there remain in him the moderate impurities: thoughts of sensuality, ill will, & harmfulness. These he...wipes out of existence. When he is rid of them there remain in him the fine impurities: thoughts of his caste, thoughts of his home district, thoughts related to not wanting to be despised. These he...wipes out of existence.

When he is rid of them, there remain only thoughts of the Dhamma. His concentration is neither calm nor refined, it has not yet attained serenity or unity, and is kept in place by the fabrication of forceful restraint. But there comes a time when his mind grows steady inwardly, settles down, grows unified & concentrated. His concentration is calm & refined, has attained serenity & unity, and is no longer kept in place by the fabrication of forceful restraint. Then whichever of the six higher knowledges he turns his mind to know & realize, he can witness them for himself whenever there is an opening.... [§64; 182]

A.III.100

§ 161. Ven. Anuruddha: It has happened that, as we were remaining heedful, ardent, & resolute, we perceived light & the vision of forms. But soon after that the light disappeared, together with the vision of forms, and we can't become attuned to that theme.

The Buddha: You should become attuned to that theme. Before my Awakening, while I was still only an unawakened Bodhisatta, I too perceived light & the vision of forms, and soon after that the light disappeared, together with the vision of forms. The thought occurred to me, 'What is the cause, what is the reason, why the light disappeared, together with the vision of forms?' Then it occurred to me, 'Uncertainty arose in me, and because of the uncertainty my concentration fell away; when my concentration fell away, the light disappeared together with the vision of forms. I will act in such a way that uncertainty will not arise in me again.'

As I was remaining heedful, ardent, & resolute, I perceived light & the vision of forms. But soon after that the light disappeared, together with the vision of forms. The thought occurred to me, 'What is the cause, what is the reason, why the light disappeared, together with the vision of forms?' Then it occurred to me, 'Inattention...sloth & drowsiness...fear...elation...inertia arose in me, and because of the inattention...inertia my concentration fell away; when my concentration fell away, the light disappeared together with the vision of forms. I will act in such a way that uncertainty, inattention, sloth & drowsiness, fear, elation, & inertia will not arise in me again.'

As I was remaining heedful, ardent, & resolute...it occurred to me, 'Excessive persistence [§ 66] arose in me, and because of the excessive persistence my concentration fell away; when my concentration fell away, the light disappeared together with the vision of forms. Just as if a man might hold a quail tightly with both hands; it would die then & there. In the same way, excessive persistence arose in me.... I will act in such a way that uncertainty...& excessive persistence will not arise in me again.'

As I was remaining heedful, ardent, & resolute...it occurred to me, 'Sluggish persistence [§66] arose in me, and because of the sluggish persistence my concentration fell away; when my concentration fell away, the light disappeared together with the vision of forms. Just as if a man might hold a quail loosely; it would fly out of his hand. In the same way, sluggish persistence arose in me....I will act in such a way that uncertainty...excessive & sluggish persistence will not arise in me again.'

As I was remaining heedful, ardent, & resolute...it occurred to me, 'Longing...the perception of multiplicity...excessive absorption in forms arose in me, and because of the excessive absorption in forms my concentration fell away; when my concentration fell away, the light disappeared together with the vision of forms....I will act in such a way that uncertainty...longing, the perception of multiplicity, excessive absorption in forms will not arise in me again.'

When I knew, 'Uncertainty is a defilement of the mind,' I abandoned the uncertainty that was a defilement of the mind. (Similarly with inattention, sloth & drowsiness, fear, elation, inertia, excessive persistence, sluggish persistence, longing, the perception of multiplicity, & excessive absorption in forms.)

As I was remaining heedful, ardent, & resolute, I perceived light without seeing forms, or saw forms without perceiving light for a whole day, a whole night, a whole day & night. The thought occurred to me, 'What is the cause, what is the reason...?' Then it occurred to me, 'When I attend to the theme of light without attending to the theme of forms, I perceive light without seeing forms.

When I attend to the theme of forms without attending to the theme of light, I see forms without seeing light for a whole day, a whole night, a whole day & night.'

As I was remaining heedful, ardent, & resolute, I perceived limited light & saw limited forms; I perceived unlimited light & saw unlimited forms for a whole day, a whole night, a whole day & night. The thought occurred to me, 'What is the cause, what is the reason...?' Then it occurred to me, 'When my concentration is limited, my sense of [inner] vision is limited. When my concentration is unlimited, my sense of [inner] vision is unlimited. With an unlimited sense of vision I perceive unlimited light & see unlimited forms for a whole day, a whole night, a whole day & night'....

'I have abandoned those defilements of the mind. Let me develop concentration in three ways.' So [1] I developed concentration with directed thought & evaluation. I developed concentration without directed thought but with a modicum of evaluation. I developed concentration without directed thought or evaluation. [2] I developed concentration with rapture... without rapture.... [3] I developed concentration accompanied by enjoyment...accompanied by equanimity.

When my concentration with directed thought & evaluation was developed, when my concentration without directed thought but with a modicum of evaluation...without directed thought or evaluation...with rapture...without rapture...accompanied by enjoyment... accompanied by equanimity was developed, then the knowledge & vision arose in me: 'My release is unprovoked. This is my last birth. There is no further becoming.'

That was what the Blessed One said. Satisfied, Ven. Anuruddha delighted in the Blessed One's words.

M.128

§ 162. Skill in concentration. Suppose there was a mountain cow—foolish, inexperienced, unfamiliar with her pasture, unskilled in roaming on rugged mountains—and she were to think, 'What if I were to go in a direction I have never gone before, to eat grass I have never eaten before, to drink water I have never drunk before!' She would lift her hind hoof without having placed her front hoof firmly and [as a result] would not get to go in a direction she had never gone before, to eat grass she had never eaten before, or to drink water she had never drunk before. And as for the place where she was standing when the thought occurred to her, 'What if I were to go where I have never been before...to drink water I have never drunk before,' she would not return there safely. Why is that? Because she is a foolish, inexperienced mountain cow, unfamiliar with her pasture, unskilled in roaming on rugged mountains.

In the same way, there are cases where a monk—foolish, inexperienced, unfamiliar with his pasture, unskilled in...entering & remaining in the first jhana: rapture & pleasure born from withdrawal, accompanied by directed thought & evaluation—doesn't stick with that theme, doesn't develop it, pursue it, or establish himself firmly in it. The thought occurs to him, 'What if I, with the stilling of directed thought & evaluation, were to enter & remain in the second jhāna: rapture & pleasure born of composure, unification of awareness free from directed thought & evaluation—internal assurance.' He is not able...to enter & remain in the second jhāna....The thought occurs to him, 'What if I...were to enter & remain in the first jhāna....He is not able...to enter & remain in the first jhāna. This is called a monk who has slipped & fallen from both sides, like the mountain cow, foolish, inexperienced, unfamiliar with her pasture, unskilled in roaming on rugged mountains.

But suppose there was a mountain cow—wise, experienced, familiar with her pasture, skilled in roaming on rugged mountains—and she were to think, 'What if I were to go in a direction I have never gone before, to eat grass I have never eaten before, to drink water I have never drunk before!' She would lift her hind hoof only after having placed her front hoof firmly and [as a result] would get to go in a direction she had never gone before...to drink water she had never drunk before. And as for the place where she was standing when the thought occurred to her, 'What if I were to go in a direction I have never gone before...to drink water I have never drunk before,' she would return there safely. Why is that? Because she is a wise, experienced mountain cow, familiar with her pasture, skilled in roaming on rugged mountains.

In the same way, there are some cases where a monk—wise, experienced, familiar with his pasture, skilled in...entering & remaining in the first jhāna...sticks with that theme, develops it, pursues it, & establishes himself firmly in it. The thought occurs to him, 'What if I...were to enter & remain in the second jhāna....' Without jumping at the second jhāna, he—with the stilling of directed thought & evaluation—enters & remains in the second jhāna. He sticks with that theme, develops it, pursues it, & establishes himself firmly in it. The thought occurs to him, 'What if I...were to enter & remain in the third jhāna'.... Without jumping at the third jhāna, he...enters & remains in the third jhana. He sticks with that theme, develops it, pursues it, & establishes himself firmly in it. The thought occurs to him, 'What if I...were to enter & remain in the fourth jhāna'....Without jumping at the fourth jhana, he...enters & remains in the fourth jhāna. He sticks with that theme, develops it, pursues it, & establishes himself firmly in it.

The thought occurs to him, 'What if I, with the complete transcending of perceptions of [physical] form, with the disappearance of perceptions of resistance, and not heeding perceptions of diversity, thinking, "Infinite space," were to enter & remain in the sphere of the infinitude of space.' Without jumping at the sphere of the infinitude of space, he...enters & remains in sphere of the infinitude of space. He sticks with that theme, develops it, pursues it, & establishes himself firmly in it.

The thought occurs to him, 'What if I, with the complete transcending of the sphere of the infinitude of space, thinking, "Infinite consciousness," were to enter & remain in the sphere of the infinitude of consciousness.' Without jumping at the sphere of the infinitude of consciousness, he...enters & remains in sphere of the infinitude of consciousness. He sticks with that theme, develops it, pursues it, & establishes himself firmly in it.

The thought occurs to him, 'What if I, with the complete transcending of the sphere of the infinitude of consciousness, thinking, "There is nothing," were to enter & remain in the sphere of the nothingness.' Without jumping at the sphere of nothingness, he...enters & remains in sphere of nothingness. He sticks with that theme, develops it, pursues, it & establishes himself firmly in it.

The thought occurs to him, 'What if I, with the complete transcending of the sphere of nothingness, were to enter & remain in the sphere of neither perception nor non-perception.' Without jumping at the sphere of neither perception nor non-perception, he...enters & remains in the sphere of neither perception nor non-perception. He sticks with that theme, develops it, pursues it, & establishes himself firmly in it.

The thought occurs to him, 'What if I, with the complete transcending of the sphere of neither perception nor non-perception, were to enter & remain in the cessation of perception & feeling.' Without jumping at the cessation of perception & feeling, he...enters & remains in the cessation of perception & feeling.

When a monk enters & emerges from that very attainment, his mind is pliant & malleable. With his pliant, malleable mind, limitless concentration is well developed. With his well-developed, limitless concentration, then whichever of the six higher knowledges he turns his mind to know & realize, he can witness them for himself whenever there is an opening.

A.IX.35

§ 163. Guided by the elephant trainer, the elephant to be tamed goes only in one direction: east, west, north, or south....Guided by the Tathagata...the person to be tamed goes in eight directions.

Possessed of form, he sees forms. This is the first direction. Not percipient of form internally, he sees forms externally. This is the second direction. He is intent only on the beautiful. This is the third direction. With the complete transcending of perceptions of [physical] form, with the disappearance of perceptions of resistance, and not heeding perceptions of diversity, thinking, 'Infinite space,' he enters & remains in the sphere of the infinitude of space. This is the fourth direction. With the complete transcending of the sphere of the infinitude of space, thinking, 'Infinite consciousness,' he enters & remains in the sphere of the infinitude of consciousness. This is the fifth direction. He...enters & remains in the sphere of nothingness. This is the sixth direction. He...enters & remains in the sphere of neither perception nor non-perception. This is the seventh direction. With the complete transcending of the sphere of neither perception nor non-perception, he enters & remains in the cessation of perception & feeling. This is the eighth direction.

M.137

§ 164. 'There are these seven properties. Which seven? The property of light, the property of beauty, the property of the sphere of the infinitude of space, the property of the sphere of the infinitude of consciousness, the property of the sphere of nothingness, the property of the sphere of neither perception nor non-perception, the property of the sphere of the cessation of feeling & perception. These are the seven properties.'

When this was said, a certain monk addressed the Blessed One: '...In dependence on what are these properties discerned?'

'The property of light is discerned in dependence on darkness. The property of beauty is discerned in dependence on the unattractive. The property of the sphere of the infinitude of space is discerned in dependence on form. The property of the sphere of the infinitude of consciousness is discerned in dependence on the sphere of the infinitude of space. The property of the sphere of nothingness is discerned in dependence on the sphere of the infinitude of consciousness. The property of the sphere of neither perception nor non-perception is discerned in dependence on the sphere of nothingness. The property of the sphere of the cessation of feeling & perception is discerned in dependence on cessation.'

'...And how, lord, is the attainment of these properties to be reached?'

'The property of light, the property of beauty, the property of the sphere of the infinitude of space, the property of the sphere of the infinitude of consciousness, the property of the sphere of nothingness: These properties are to be reached as perception attainments.

The property of the sphere of neither perception nor non-perception is to be reached as a what-remains-of fabrications attainment. The property of the sphere of the cessation of feeling & perception is to be reached as a cessation attainment.'

S.XIII.11

F. CONCENTRATION & DISCERNMENT

We noted in II/A that some of the sets in the Wings to Awakening list jhana as a condition for discernment, while others list discernment as a condition for jhana. Place both of these patterns into the context of this/that conditionality, and they convey the point that jhana and discernment in practice are mutually supporting. Passage §171 states this point explicitly, while §165 and §166 show that the difference between the two causal patterns relates to differences in meditators: some develop strong powers of concentration before developing strong discernment, whereas others gain a sound theoretical understanding of the Dhamma before developing strong concentration. In either case, both strong concentration and sound discernment are needed to bring about Awakening. Passage §111 makes the point that when the practice reaches the culmination of its development, concentration and discernment act in concert. The passages in this section deal with this topic in more detail.

The role of jhana as a condition for transcendent discernment is one of the most controversial issues in the Theravada tradition. Three basic positions have been advanced in modern writings. One, following the commentarial tradition, asserts that jhana is not necessary for any of the four levels of Awakening and that there is a class of individuals—called "dry insight" meditators—who are "released through discernment" based on a level of concentration lower than that of jhana. A second position, citing a passage in the Canon [A.III.88; MFU, pp. 103] stating that concentration is mastered only on the level of non-returning, holds that jhana is necessary for the attainment of non-returning and Arahantship, but not for the lower levels of Awakening. The third position states that the attainment of at least the first level of jhana is essential for all four levels of Awakening.

Evidence from the Canon supports the third position, but not the other two. As §106 points out, the attainment of stream-entry has eight factors, one of which is right concentration, defined as jhana. In fact, according to this particular discourse, jhana is the heart of the streamwinner's path. Secondly, there is no passage in the Canon describing the development of transcendent discernment without at least some skill in jhana. The statement that concentration is mastered only on the level of non-returning must be interpreted in the light of the distinction between mastery and attainment. A streamwinner may have attained jhana without mastering it; the discernment developed in the process of gaining full mastery over the practice of jhana will then lead him/her to the level of non-returning. As for the term "released through discernment," passage §168 shows that it denotes people who have become Arahants without experiencing the four formless jhanas. It does not indicate a person who has not experienced jhana.

Part of the controversy over this question may be explained by the fact that the commentarial literature defines jhana in terms that bear little resemblance to the canonical description. *The Path of Purification*—the cornerstone of the commentarial system—takes as its paradigm for meditation practice a method called *kasina,* in which one stares at an external object until the image of the object is imprinted in one's mind. This image then gives rise to a countersign that is said to indicate the attainment of jhana. The text then tries to fit all other meditation methods into the mold of kasina practice, and admits that breath meditation does not fit very well. As a result, it states that only Buddhas can use the breath as a focal point for attaining jhana.

None of these assertions have any support in the Canon. Although a practice called kasina is mentioned tangentially in some of the discourses, the only point where it is described in any detail [M.121; MFU, pp. 82-85] makes no mention of staring at an object or gaining a countersign. If breath meditation were useful only to Buddhas, there seems little reason for the Buddha to have taught it so frequently and to such a wide variety of people. If the arising of a countersign were essential to the attainment of jhana, one would expect it to be included in the steps of breath meditation and in the graphic analogies used to describe jhana, but it isn't. Some Theravadins insist that questioning the commentaries is a sign of disrespect for the tradition, but it seems to be a sign of greater disrespect for the Buddha—or the compilers of the Canon—to assume that he or they would have left out something absolutely essential to the practice.

All of these points seem to indicate is that what jhana means in the commentaries is something quite different from what it means in the Canon. Because of this difference we can say that the commentaries are right in viewing their type of jhana as unnecessary for Awakening, but Awakening cannot occur without the attainment of jhana in the canonical sense.

We have already given a sketch in the preceding section of how jhana in its canonical sense can act as the basis for transcendent discernment. To recapitulate: On attaining any of the first seven levels of jhana, one may step back slightly from the object of jhana—entering the fifth factor of noble right concentration [§150]—to perceive how the mind relates to the object. In doing this, one sees the process of causation as it plays a role in bringing the mind to jhana, together with the various mental acts of fabrication that go into keeping it there [§182]. Passage §172 lists these acts in considerable detail. The fact that the passage emphasizes the amazing abilities of Sariputta, the Buddha's foremost disciple in terms of discernment, implies that there is no need for every meditator to perceive all these acts in such a detailed fashion. What is essential is that one develop a sense of dispassion for the state of jhana, seeing that even the relatively steady sense of refined pleasure and equanimity it provides is artificial and willed, inconstant and stressful [§182], a state fabricated from many different events, and thus not worth identifying with. Jhana thus becomes an ideal test case for understanding the workings of kamma and dependent co-arising in the mind. Its stability gives discernment a firm basis for seeing clearly; its refined sense of pleasure and equanimity allow the mind to realize that even the most refined mundane states involve the inconstancy and stress common to all willed phenomena. Passage §167 lists a number of verbal mental acts surrounding the exercise of supranormal powers that can be regarded in a similar light, as topics to be analyzed so as to give rise to a sense of dispassion. The dispassion that results in either case enables one to experience the fading away and cessation of the last remaining activities in the mind, even the activity of discernment itself. When this process fully matures, it leads on to total relinquishment, resulting in the clear knowing and release of Arahantship.

In contrast to the issue of the role of jhana as a condition for discernment, the role of discernment as a condition for jhana is uncontroversial. Discernment aids jhana on two levels: mundane and transcendent. On the mundane level, it enables one to perceive the various factors that go into one's state of jhana so that one can master them and shed the factors that prevent one from attaining a higher level of jhana. This again involves the reflection that constitutes the fifth factor of noble right concentration, but in this case the results stay on the mundane level. For instance, as one masters the first level of jhana and can reflect on the elements of stress it contains, one may perceive that directed thought and evaluation should be abandoned because they have become unnecessary in maintaining one's concentration, just as the forms used in pouring a cement wall become unnecessary when the cement has hardened. In dropping these factors, one then goes on to the second level of jhana. Passage §175 gives a list of the factors that, in succession, are dropped in this way as one attains higher and higher levels of concentration.

On the transcendent level, the discernment that precipitates Awakening results in a supramundane level of jhana called the fruit of gnosis, which is described in §§176-77—a type of jhana independent of all perceptions (mental labels) and intentional processes, beyond all limitations of cosmos, time, and the present: the Arahant's foretaste, in this lifetime, of the absolutely total Unbinding experienced by the awakened mind at death.

§ 165. These four types of individuals are to be found existing in world. Which four?

There is the case of the individual who has attained internal tranquility of awareness, but not insight into phenomena through heightened discernment. There is...the individual who has attained insight into phenomena through heightened discernment, but not internal tranquility of awareness. There is...the individual who has attained neither internal tranquility of awareness nor insight into phenomena through heightened discernment. And there is...the individual who has attained both internal tranquility of awareness & insight into phenomena through heightened discernment.

The individual who has attained internal tranquility of awareness, but not insight into phenomena through heightened discernment, should approach an individual who has attained insight into phenomena through heightened discernment...and ask him: 'How should fabrications be regarded? How should they be investigated? How should they be seen with insight?' The other will answer in line with what he has seen & experienced: 'Fabrications should be regarded in this way...investigated in this way...seen in this way with insight.' Then eventually he [the first] will become one who has attained both internal tranquility of awareness & insight into phenomena through heightened discernment.

As for the individual who has attained insight into phenomena through heightened discernment, but not internal tranquility of awareness, he should approach an individual who has attained internal tranquility of awareness... and ask him, 'How should the mind be steadied? How should it be made to settle down? How should it be unified? How should it be concentrated?' The other will answer in line with what he has seen & experienced: 'The mind should be steadied in this way...made to settle down in this way... unified in this way...concentrated in this way.' Then eventually he [the first] will become one who has attained both internal tranquility of awareness & insight into phenomena through heightened discernment.

As for the individual who has attained neither internal tranquility of awareness nor insight into phenomena through heightened discernment, he should approach an individual who has attained both internal tranquility of awareness & insight into phenomena through heightened discernment...and ask him, 'How should the mind be steadied? How should it be made to settle down? How should it be unified? How should it be concentrated? How should fabrications be regarded? How should they be investigated? How should they be seen with insight?' The other will answer in line with what he has seen & experienced: 'The mind should be steadied in this way...made to settle down in this way...unified in this way...concentrated in this way. Fabrications should be regarded in this way...investigated in this way...seen in this way with insight.' Then eventually he [the first] will become one who has attained both internal tranquility of awareness & insight into phenomena through heightened discernment.

As for the individual who has attained both internal tranquility of awareness & insight into phenomena through heightened discernment, his duty is to make an effort in establishing ('tuning') those very same skillful qualities to a higher degree for the ending of the effluents.

A.IV.94

§ 166. Ven. Ananda: Whenever a monk or nun declares the attainment of Arahantship in my presence, they all do it by means of one or another of four paths. Which four?

There is the case of a monk who has developed insight preceded by tranquility. As he develops insight preceded by tranquility, the path is born. He follows that path, develops it, pursues it. As he follows the path, developing it & pursuing it—his fetters are abandoned, his latent tendencies abolished.

Furthermore, there is the case of the monk who has developed tranquility preceded by insight. As he develops tranquility preceded by insight, the path is born. He follows that path....His fetters are abandoned, his latent tendencies abolished.

Furthermore, there is the case of the monk who has developed tranquility & insight in concert. As he develops tranquility & insight in concert, the path is born. He follows that path....His fetters are abandoned, his latent tendencies abolished.

Furthermore, there is the case where monk's mind has its restlessness concerning the Dhamma [Comm: the corruptions of insight] well under control. There comes a time when his mind grows steady inwardly, settles down, and becomes unified & concentrated. In him the path is born. He follows that path....His fetters are abandoned, his latent tendencies abolished.

Whenever a monk or nun declares the attainment of Arahantship in my presence, they all do it by means of one or another of these four paths.

A.IV.170

§ 167. Then Ven. Anuruddha went to where Ven. Sariputta was staying and, on arrival, greeted him courteously. After an exchange of friendly greetings & courtesies, he sat down to one side. As he was sitting there, he said to Ven. Sāriputta: By means of the divine eye, purified & surpassing the human, I see the thousand-fold cosmos. My persistence is aroused & unsluggish. My mindfulness is established & unshaken. My body is calm & unaroused. My mind is concentrated into singleness. And yet my mind is not released from the effluents through lack of clinging/sustenance.

Sariputta: My friend, when the thought occurs to you, 'By means of the divine eye, purified & surpassing the human, I see the thousand-fold cosmos,' that is related to your conceit. When the thought occurs to you, 'My persistence is aroused & unsluggish. My mindfulness is established & unshaken. My body is calm & unperturbed. My mind is concentrated into singleness,' that is related to your restlessness. When the thought occurs to you, 'And yet my mind is not released from the effluents through lack of clinging/sustenance,' that is related to your anxiety. It would be well if—abandoning these three qualities, not attending to these three qualities—you directed your mind to the Deathless property.'

So after that, Ven. Anuruddha—abandoning those three qualities, not attending to those three qualities—directed his mind to the Deathless property. Dwelling alone, secluded, heedful, ardent, & resolute, he in no long time reached & remained in the supreme goal of the holy life for which clansmen rightly go forth from home into homelessness, knowing & realizing it for himself in the here & now. He knew: 'Birth is ended, the holy life fulfilled, the task done. There is nothing further for the sake of this world.' And thus Ven. Anuruddha became another one of the Arahants.

A.III.128

§ 168. And what is an individual released in both ways? There is the case of the individual who remains touching with his body the peaceful liberations, the formlessnesses beyond forms; when he has seen with discernment, his effluents are totally ended. I do not say that such a monk has any duty to do with heedfulness. Why is that? Because he has done his duty with heedfulness; he is no more capable of being heedless.

And what is an individual released through discernment? There is the case of the individual who does not remain touching with his body the peaceful liberations, the formlessnesses beyond forms; but when he has seen with discernment, his effluents are totally ended. I do not say that such a monk has any duty to do with heedfulness. Why is that? Because he has done his duty with heedfulness; he is no more capable of being heedless.

M.70

§ 169. Develop concentration, monks. A concentrated monk discerns things as they actually are present. And what does he discern as it actually is present?

'This is stress,' he discerns as it actually is present. 'This is the origination of stress...This is the cessation of stress...This is the path of practice leading to the cessation of stress,' he discerns as it actually is present....

Therefore your duty is the contemplation, 'This is stress...This is the origination of stress...This is the cessation of stress...This is the path of practice leading to the cessation of stress.'

S.LVI.1

§ 170. Develop concentration, monks. A concentrated monk discerns things as they actually are present. And what does he discern as it actually is present?

The origination & disappearance of form...of feeling...of perception...of fabrications...of consciousness.

And what is the origination of form...of feeling...of perception...of fabrications...of consciousness? There is the case where one relishes, welcomes, & remains fastened. To what? One relishes form, welcomes it, & remains fastened to it. While one is relishing form, welcoming it, & remaining fastened to it, delight arises. Any delight in form is clinging. With that clinging as a condition there is becoming. With becoming as a condition there is birth. With birth as a condition then aging & death, sorrow, lamentation, pain, distress, & despair all come into play. Thus is the origination of this entire mass of suffering & stress. (Similarly with feeling, perception, fabrications, & consciousness.)

And what is the disappearance of form...feeling...perception...fabrications...consciousness? There is the case where one does not relish, welcome or remain fastened. To what? One does not relish form, welcome it, or remain fastened to it. While one is not relishing form, welcoming it, or remaining fastened to it, one's delight in form ceases. From the cessation of that delight, clinging ceases. From the cessation of clinging, becoming ceases. From the cessation of becoming, birth ceases. From the cessation of birth, then aging & death, sorrow, lamentation, pain, distress, & despair all cease. Thus is the cessation of this entire mass of suffering & stress [§211]. (Similarly with feeling, perception, fabrications, & consciousness.)

S.XXII.5

§ 171. There is no jhana
for one without discernment,
 no discernment
 for one not in jhana.
One who has both jhana & discernment
is truly in the presence
 of Unbinding.

DHP.372

§ 172. Monks, Sariputta is wise, of great discernment, deep discernment, wide...joyous...rapid...quick...penetrating discernment....There is the case where Sariputta...enters & remains in the first jhana. Whatever qualities there are in the first jhana—applied thought, evaluation, rapture, pleasure, singleness of mind, contact, feeling, perception, intention, consciousness *(vl.* intent), desire, decision, persistence, mindfulness, equanimity, & attention—he ferrets them out one by one. Known to him they arise, known to him they remain, known to him they subside. He discerns, 'So this is how these qualities, not having been, come into play. Having been, they vanish.' He remains unattracted & unrepelled with regard to those qualities, independent, detached, released, dissociated, with an awareness rid of barriers. He understands, 'There is a further escape,' and pursuing it, he confirms that 'There is.' (Similarly with the levels of jhana up through the sphere of nothingness.)

Furthermore, completely transcending the sphere of nothingness, he enters & remains in the sphere of neither perception nor non-perception. He emerges mindful from that attainment. On emerging...he regards the past qualities that have ceased & changed: 'So this is how these qualities, not having been, come into play. Having been, they vanish.' He remains unattracted & unrepelled with regard to those qualities, independent, detached, released, dissociated, with an awareness rid of barriers. He understands, 'There is a further escape,' and pursuing it, he confirms that 'There is.'

Furthermore, completely transcending the sphere of neither perception nor non-perception, he enters & remains in the cessation of feeling & perception. When he sees with discernment, his effluents are totally ended. He emerges mindful from that attainment. On emerging...he regards the past qualities that have ceased & changed: 'So this is how these qualities, not having been, come into play. Having been, they vanish.' He remains unattracted & unrepelled with regard to those qualities, independent, detached, released, dissociated, with an awareness rid of barriers. He understands, 'There is no further escape,' and pursuing it, he confirms that 'There isn't.'

If someone, rightly describing a person, were to say, 'He has attained mastery & perfection in noble virtue...noble concentration...noble discernment...noble release,' he would be rightly describing Sāriputta.... Sariputta takes the unexcelled wheel of Dhamma set rolling by the Tathagata, and keeps it rolling rightly.

M.111

§ 173. I tell you, the ending of the effluents depends on the first jhāna...the second jhāna...the third...the fourth...the sphere of the infinitude of space...the sphere of the infinitude of consciousness... the sphere of nothingness...the sphere of neither perception nor non-perception.

'I tell you, the ending of the effluents depends on the first jhāna.' Thus it has been said. In reference to what was it said?... Suppose that an archer or archer's apprentice were to practice on a straw man or mound of clay, so that after a while he would become able to shoot long distances, to fire accurate shots in rapid succession, and to pierce great masses. In the same way, there is the case where a monk...enters & remains in the first jhana: rapture & pleasure born of withdrawal, accompanied by directed thought & evaluation. He regards whatever phenomena there that are connected with form, feeling, perceptions, fabrications, & consciousness, as inconstant, stressful, a disease, a cancer, an arrow, painful, an affliction, alien, a disintegration, a void, not-self. He turns his mind away from those phenomena, and having done so, inclines his mind to the property of deathlessness: 'This is peace, this is exquisite—the resolution of all fabrications; the relinquishment of all the paraphernalia [of becoming]; the ending of craving; dispassion; cessation; Unbinding.'

Staying right there, he reaches the ending of the mental effluents. Or, if not, then—through passion & delight for this very property [the discernment inclining to deathlessness] and from the total wasting away of the first of the five Fetters [self-identity views, grasping at precepts & practices, uncertainty, sensual passion, and irritation]—he is due to be reborn [in the Pure Abodes], there to be totally unbound, never again to return from that world.

'I tell you, the ending of the effluents depends on the first jhana.' Thus it was said, and in reference to this was it said.

(Similarly with the other levels of jhana up through the sphere of nothingness.)

Thus, as far as the perception-attainments go, that is as far as gnosis-penetration goes. As for these two spheres—the attainment of the sphere of neither perception nor non-perception & the attainment of the cessation of feeling & perception—I tell you that they are to be rightly explained by those monks who are meditators, skilled in attaining, skilled in attaining & emerging, who have attained & emerged in dependence on them.

A.IX.36

§ 174. Then Dasama the householder from the city of Aṭṭhaka went to where Ven. Ananda was staying and on arrival, having bowed down, sat to one side. As he was sitting there, he said to Ven. Ananda, 'Is there, venerable sir, any one condition explained by the Blessed One...whereby a monk—dwelling heedful, ardent, & resolute—releases his mind that is as yet unreleased, or whereby the effluents not yet brought to an end come to an end, or whereby he attains the unsurpassed security from bondage that he has not yet attained?

Ananda: Yes, householder, there is....There is the case where a monk...enters & remains in the first jhana....He notices that 'This first jhana is fabricated & willed.' He discerns, 'Whatever is fabricated & willed is inconstant & subject to cessation.' Staying right there, he reaches the ending of the effluents. Or, if not, then—through passion & delight for this very phenomenon [of discernment] and from the total ending of the first five Fetters—he is due to be reborn [in the Pure Abodes], there to be totally unbound, never again to return from that world. (Similarly with the other levels of jhana up through the sphere of nothingness and the four releases of awareness based on good will, compassion, appreciation, & equanimity.)

A.XI.17

§ 175. Sariputta: This Unbinding is pleasant, friends. This Unbinding is pleasant.

Udayin: But what is the pleasure here, my friend, where there is nothing felt?

Sariputta: Just that is the pleasure here, my friend: where there is nothing felt. There are these five strands of sensuality. Which five? Forms cognizable via the eye—agreeable, pleasing, charming, endearing, fostering desire, enticing; sounds...smells...tastes...tactile sensations cognizable via the body—agreeable, pleasing, charming, endearing, fostering desire, enticing. Whatever pleasure or joy arises in dependence on these five strands of sensuality, that is sensual pleasure.

Now there is the case where a monk—quite withdrawn from sensuality, withdrawn from unskillful qualities—enters & remains in the first jhana....If, as he remains there, he is beset with attention to perceptions dealing with *sensuality,* that is an illness for him. Just as pain arises as an affliction in a healthy person for his affliction, even so the attention to perceptions dealing with sensuality that beset the monk is an affliction for him. Now the Blessed One has said that whatever is an affliction is stress. So by this line of reasoning it may be known how pleasant Unbinding is.

Furthermore, there is the case where a monk...enters & remains in the second jhana....If, as he remains there, he is beset with attention to perceptions dealing with *directed thought,* that is an affliction for him....

Furthermore, there is the case where a monk...enters & remains in the third jhana....If, as he remains there, he is beset with attention to perceptions dealing with *rapture,* that is an affliction for him....

Furthermore, there is the case where a monk...enters & remains in the fourth jhana....If, as he remains there, he is beset with attention to perceptions dealing with *equanimity,* that is an affliction for him....

Furthermore, there is the case where a monk...enters & remains in the sphere of the infinitude of space. If, as he remains there, he is beset with attention to perceptions dealing with *form,* that is an affliction for him....

Furthermore, there is the case where a monk...enters & remains in the sphere of the infinitude of consciousness. If, as he remains there, he is beset with attention to perceptions dealing with *the sphere of the infinitude of space,* that is an affliction for him....

Furthermore, there is the case where a monk...enters & remains in the sphere of nothingness. If, as he remains there, he is beset with attention to perceptions dealing with *the sphere of the infinitude of consciousness,* that is an affliction for him....

Furthermore, there is the case where a monk...enters & remains in the sphere of neither perception nor non-perception. If, as he remains there, he is beset with attention to perceptions dealing with *the sphere of the infinitude of consciousness,* that is an affliction for him...whatever is an affliction is stress. So by this line of reasoning it may be known how pleasant Unbinding is.

Furthermore, there is the case where a monk...enters & remains in the cessation of perception & feeling. And, having seen [that] with discernment, his effluents are completely ended. So by this line of reasoning it may be known how pleasant Unbinding is.

A.IX.34

§ 176. Ananda: It is amazing, my friend, it is marvelous, how the Blessed One has attained & recognized the opportunity for the purification of beings...and the direct realization of Unbinding, where the eye will be, and forms, and yet one will not be sensitive to that sphere; where the ear will be, and sounds...where the nose will be, and smells... where the tongue will be, and tastes...where the body will be, and tactile sensations, and yet one will not be sensitive to that sphere.

Udayin: Is one insensitive to that sphere with or without a perception in mind?

Ananda: ...with a perception in mind....

Udayin: ...what perception?

Ananda: There is the case where with the complete transcending of perceptions dealing with form, with the disappearance of perceptions of resistance, and not heeding perceptions of diversity, thinking, 'infinite space,' one remains in the sphere of the infinitude of space: Having this perception in mind, one is not sensitive to that sphere.

Further, with the complete transcending of the sphere of the infinitude of space, thinking, 'infinite consciousness,' one remains in the sphere of the infinitude of consciousness: Having this perception in mind, one is not sensitive to that sphere.

Further, with the complete transcending of the sphere of the infinitude of consciousness, thinking, 'There is nothing,' one remains in the sphere of nothingness: Having this perception in mind, one is not sensitive to that sphere.

Once, friend, when I was staying in Sāketa at the Game Refuge in the Black Forest, the nun Jaṭilā Bhāgikā went to where I was staying, and on arrival—having bowed to me—stood to one side. As soon as she had stood to one side, she said to me: 'The concentration whereby—neither pressed down nor forced back, nor with mental fabrications kept blocked or suppressed—still as a result of release, contented as a result of stillness, and as a result of contentment one is not agitated: This concentration is said by the Blessed One to be the fruit of what?'

I said to her, '...This concentration is said by the Blessed One to be the fruit of gnosis [the knowledge of Awakening].' Having this sort of perception, friend, one is not sensitive to that sphere.

A.IX.37

§ 177. The Buddha: Sandha, practice the absorption (jhāna) of a thoroughbred horse, not the absorption of an unbroken colt. And how is an unbroken colt absorbed? An unbroken colt, tied to the feeding trough, is absorbed with the thought, 'Barley grain! Barley grain!' Why is that? Because as he is tied to the feeding trough, the thought does not occur to him, 'I wonder what task the trainer will have me do today? What should I do in response?' Tied to the feeding trough, he is simply absorbed with the thought, 'Barley grain! Barley grain!'

In the same way, there are cases where an unbroken colt of a man, having gone to the wilderness, to the foot of a tree, or to an empty dwelling, dwells with his awareness overcome by sensual passion, obsessed with sensual passion. He does not discern the escape, as it actually is present, from sensual passion once it has arisen. Making that sensual passion the focal point, he absorbs himself with it, besorbs, resorbs, & supersorbs himself with it.

He dwells with his awareness overcome by ill will...sloth & drowsiness... restlessness & anxiety...uncertainty, obsessed with uncertainty. He does not discern the escape, as it actually is present, from uncertainty once it has arisen. Making that uncertainty the focal point, he absorbs himself with it, besorbs, resorbs, & supersorbs himself with it.

He is absorbed dependent on earth...liquid...fire...wind...the sphere of the infinitude of space...the sphere of the infinitude of consciousness... the sphere of nothingness...the sphere of neither perception nor non-perception...this world...the next world...whatever is seen, heard, sensed, cognized, attained, sought after, pondered by the intellect. That is how an unbroken colt of a man is absorbed.

And how is a thoroughbred absorbed? An excellent thoroughbred horse tied to the feeding trough, is not absorbed with the thought, 'Barley grain! Barley grain!' Why is that? Because as he is tied to the feeding trough, the thought occurs to him, 'I wonder what task the trainer will have me do today? What should I do in response?' Tied to the feeding trough, he is not absorbed with the thought, 'Barley grain! Barley grain!' The excellent thoroughbred horse regards the feel of the spur as a debt, an imprisonment, a loss, a piece of bad luck.

In the same way, an excellent thoroughbred of a man, having gone to the wilderness, to the foot of a tree, or to an empty dwelling, dwells with his awareness not overcome by sensual passion, not obsessed with sensual passion. He discerns the escape, as it actually is present, from sensual passion once it has arisen. He dwells with his awareness not overcome by ill will...sloth & drowsiness... restlessness & anxiety...uncertainty, obsessed with uncertainty. He discerns the escape, as it actually is present, from uncertainty once it has arisen.

He is absorbed dependent neither on earth, liquid, heat, wind, the sphere of the infinitude of space, the sphere of the infinitude of consciousness, the sphere of nothingness, the sphere of neither perception nor non-perception, this world, the next world, nor on whatever is seen, heard, sensed, cognized, attained, sought after, or pondered by the intellect—and yet he is absorbed. And to this excellent thoroughbred of a man, absorbed in this way, the gods, together with Indra, the Brahmas, & Pajapati, pay homage even from afar:

'Homage to you, O thoroughbred man.
Homage to you, O superlative man—
of whom we have no direct knowledge
even by means of that with which
you are absorbed.'

Sandha: But in what way is the excellent thoroughbred of a man absorbed when he is absorbed...?

The Buddha: There is the case, Sandha, where for an excellent thoroughbred of a man the perception (mental note or label) of earth with regard to earth has ceased to exist; the perception of liquid with regard to liquid...the perception of fire with regard to fire...the perception of wind with regard to wind...the perception of the sphere of the infinitude of space with regard to the sphere of the infinitude of space...the perception of the sphere of the infinitude of consciousness with regard to the sphere of the infinitude of consciousness...the perception of the sphere of nothingness with regard to the sphere of nothingness...the perception of the sphere of neither perception nor non-perception with regard to the sphere of neither perception nor non-perception...the perception of this world with regard to this world...the next world with regard to the next world...and whatever is seen, heard, sensed, cognized, attained, sought after, or pondered by the intellect: the perception of that has ceased to exist.

Absorbed in this way, the excellent thoroughbred of a man is absorbed dependent neither on earth, liquid, fire, wind, the sphere of the infinitude of space, the sphere of the infinitude of consciousness, the sphere of nothingness, the sphere of neither perception nor non-perception, this world, the next world, nor on whatever is seen, heard, sensed, cognized, attained, sought after, or pondered by the intellect—and yet he is absorbed. And to this excellent thoroughbred of a man, absorbed in this way, the gods, together with Indra, the Brahmas, & Pajapati, pay homage even from afar:

"Homage to you, O thoroughbred man.
Homage to you, O superlative man—
of whom we have no direct knowledge
even by means of that with which
you are absorbed."

A.XI.10

§ 178. Knowledge of the ending of the effluents, as it is actually present, occurs to one who is concentrated, I tell you, and not to one who is not concentrated. So concentration is the path, monks. Non-concentration is no path at all.

A.VI.64

G. EQUANIMITY IN CONCENTRATION & DISCERNMENT

We have pinpointed the fifth, reflective level of noble right concentration [§150] as the mental state in which transcendent discernment can arise. A look at how equanimity functions in this process will help to flesh out our account of this state.

The word "equanimity" is used in the Canon in two basic senses: 1) a neutral feeling in the absence of pleasure and pain, and 2) an attitude of even-mindedness in the face of every sort of experience, regardless of whether pleasure and pain are present or not. The attitude of even-mindedness is what is meant here.

Passage §179 gives an outline of the place of equanimity in the emotional life of a person on the path of practice. This outline is interesting for several reasons. To begin with, contrary to many teachings currently popular in the West, it shows that there is a skillful use for the sense of distress that can come to a person who longs for the goal of the practice but has yet to attain it. This sense of distress can help one to get over the distress that comes when one feels deprived of pleasant sensory objects, for one realizes that the goal unattained is a much more serious lack than an unattained sensual pleasure. With one's priorities thus straightened out, one will turn one's energy to the pursuit of the path, rather than to sensual objectives. As the path thus matures, it results in the sense of joy that comes on gaining an insight into the true nature of sensory objects—a joy that in turn matures into a sense of equanimity resulting from that very same insight. This is the highest stage of what is called equanimity "dependent on multiplicity"—i.e., equanimity in the face of multiple objects.

Passages §180 and §181 go into more detail on how to foster this sort of equanimity. Passage §181 describes three stages in the process: 1) *development,* or a conscious turning of the mind to equanimity in the face of agreeable or disagreeable objects; 2) a state of *being in training,* in which one feels a spontaneous disillusionment with agreeable or disagreeable objects; and 3) *fully developed faculties,* in which one's even-mindedness is so completely mastered that one is in full control of one's thought processes in the face of agreeable or disagreeable objects. Because the first of these three stages is a conscious process, both §180 and §181 illustrate it with a series of graphic metaphors to help "tune" the mind to the right attitude and to help keep that attitude firmly in mind.

However, the cultivation of equanimity does not stop with equanimity dependent on multiplicity. Formless jhana, if one is able to attain it, functions as a basis for equanimity dependent on singleness [§179], i.e., the singleness of jhana. The next stage is to use this equanimity to bring on the state of equipoise called non-fashioning *(atammayata),* although §183 shows that non-fashioning can be attained directly from any of the stages of jhana, and not just the formless ones. Exactly what non-fashioning involves is shown in §182: one perceives the fabricated and willed nature of even one's refined state of jhana, and becomes so dispassionate toward the whole process that one "neither fabricates nor wills for the sake of becoming or un-becoming." In this state of non-fashioning, the mind is so balanced that it contributes absolutely no present input into the conditioning of experience at all. Because the process of conditioned or fabricated experience, on the unawakened level, requires present input together with input from the past in order to continue functioning, the entire process then breaks down, and all that remains is the Unfabricated.

After this experience, the processes of worldly experience resume due to the kammic input from the past, but one's attitude toward these processes is changed, in line with the mental fetters [II/A] that have been cut by the Awakening. If the Awakening was total, one continues to deal on an awakened level with the world until the time of one's total Unbinding with an attitude of perfect even-mindedness, illustrated by the three "frames of reference" described at the end of §179 [see also II/B]. One feels sympathy for others and seeks their well-being, experiencing a sense of satisfaction when they respond to one's teachings, but otherwise one stays equanimous, untroubled, mindful, and alert. This passage shows that the even-mindedness of a fully awakened person is not an attitude of cold indifference, but rather of mental imperturbability. Such a person has found true happiness and would like others to share that happiness as well, but that happiness is not dependent on how others respond. This is the ideal state of mind for a person who truly works for the benefit of the world.

§ 179. 'The thirty-six emotions should be known by experience.' Thus it was said. And in reference to what was it said? Six kinds of household joy & six kinds of renunciation joy; six kinds of household distress & six kinds of renunciation distress; six kinds of household equanimity & six kinds of renunciation equanimity.

And what are the six kinds of household joy? The joy that arises when one regards as an acquisition the acquisition of forms cognizable by the eye—agreeable, pleasing, charming, endearing, connected with worldly baits—or when one recalls the previous acquisition of such forms after they have passed, ceased, & changed: That is called household joy. (Similarly with sounds, smells, tastes, tactile sensations, & ideas.)

And what are the six kinds of renunciation joy? The joy that arises when—experiencing the inconstancy of those very forms, their change, fading, & cessation—one sees with right discernment as it actually is that all forms, past or present, are inconstant, stressful, subject to change: That is called renunciation joy. (Similarly with sounds, smells, tastes, tactile sensations, & ideas.)

And what are the six kinds of household distress? The distress that arises when one regards as a non-acquisition the non-acquisition of forms cognizable by the eye—agreeable, pleasing, charming, endearing, connected with worldly baits—or when one recalls the previous non-acquisition of such forms after they have passed, ceased & changed: That is called household distress. (Similarly with sounds, smells, tastes, tactile sensations, & ideas.)

And what are the six kinds of renunciation distress? The distress coming from the longing that arises in one who is filled with longing for the unexcelled liberations when—experiencing the inconstancy of those very forms, their change, fading, & cessation—he sees with right discernment as it actually is that all forms, past or present, are inconstant, stressful, subject to change and he is filled with this longing: 'O when will I enter & remain in the sphere that the noble ones now enter & remain in?' This is called renunciation distress. (Similarly with sounds, smells, tastes, tactile sensations, & ideas.)

And what are the six kinds of household equanimity? The equanimity that arises when a foolish, deluded person—a run-of-the-mill, untaught person who has not conquered his limitation or the results of action & who is blind to danger—sees a form with the eye. Such equanimity does not go beyond the form, which is why it is called household equanimity. (Similarly with sounds, smells, tastes, tactile sensations, & ideas.)

And what are the six kinds of renunciation equanimity? The equanimity that arises when—experiencing the inconstancy of those very forms, their change, fading, & cessation—one sees with right discernment as it actually is that all forms, past or present, are inconstant, stressful, subject to change: This equanimity goes beyond the form, which is why it is called renunciation equanimity. (Similarly with sounds, smells, tastes, tactile sensations, & ideas.)

'Thirty-six emotions should be known by experience.' Thus it was said. And in reference to this was it said.

'With regard to them, depending on this, abandon that.' Thus it was said. And in reference to what was it said?

Here, by depending & relying on the six kinds of renunciation joy, abandon & transcend the six kinds of household joy. Such is their abandoning, such is their transcending. By depending & relying on the six kinds of renunciation distress, abandon & transcend the six kinds of household distress. Such is their abandoning, such is their transcending. By depending & relying on the six kinds of renunciation equanimity, abandon & transcend the six kinds of household equanimity. Such is their abandoning, such their transcending.

By depending & relying on the six kinds of renunciation joy, abandon & transcend the six kinds of renunciation distress. Such is their abandoning, such is their transcending. By depending & relying on the six kinds of renunciation equanimity, abandon & transcend the six kinds of renunciation joy. Such is their abandoning, such their transcending.

There is equanimity coming from multiplicity, dependent on multiplicity; and there is equanimity coming from singleness, dependent on singleness.

And what is equanimity coming from multiplicity, dependent on multiplicity? There is equanimity with regard to forms, equanimity with regard to sounds...smells...tastes...tactile sensations [& ideas: this word appears in one of the recensions]. This is equanimity coming from multiplicity, dependent on multiplicity.

And what is equanimity coming from singleness, dependent on singleness? There is equanimity dependent on the sphere of the infinitude of space, equanimity dependent on the sphere of the infinitude of consciousness...dependent on the sphere of nothingness... dependent on the sphere of neither perception nor non-perception. This is equanimity coming from singleness, dependent on singleness.

By depending & relying on equanimity coming from singleness, dependent on singleness, abandon & transcend equanimity coming from multiplicity, dependent on multiplicity. Such is its abandoning, such its transcending.

By depending & relying on non-fashioning, abandon & transcend the equanimity coming from singleness, dependent on singleness. Such is its abandoning, such its transcending.

'Depending on this, abandon that.' Thus it was said. And in reference to this was it said.

'There are three frames of reference that a noble one cultivates, cultivating which he is a teacher fit to instruct a group.' Thus it was said. And in reference to what was it said?

There is the case where the Teacher—out of sympathy, seeking their well-being—teaches the Dhamma to his disciples: 'This is for your well-being, this is for your happiness.' His disciples do not listen or lend ear or apply their minds to gnosis. Turning aside, they stray from the Teacher's message. In this case the Tathāgata is not satisfied nor is he sensitive to satisfaction, yet he remains untroubled, mindful, & alert. This is the first frame of reference...

Furthermore, there is the case where the Teacher—out of sympathy, seeking their well-being—teaches the Dhamma to his disciples: 'This is for your well-being, this is for your happiness.' Some of his disciples do not listen or lend ear or apply their minds to gnosis. Turning aside, they stray from the Teacher's message. But some of his disciples listen, lend ear, & apply their minds to gnosis. They do not turn aside or stray from the Teacher's message. In this case the Tathāgata is not satisfied nor is he sensitive to satisfaction; at the same time he is not dissatisfied nor is he sensitive to dissatisfaction. Free from both satisfaction & dissatisfaction, he remains equanimous, mindful, & alert. This is the second frame of reference....

Furthermore, there is the case where the Teacher—out of sympathy, seeking their well-being—teaches the Dhamma to his disciples: 'This is for your well-being, this is for your happiness.' His disciples listen, lend ear, & apply their minds to gnosis. They do not turn aside or stray from the Teacher's message. In this case the Tathāgata is satisfied and is sensitive to satisfaction, yet he remains untroubled, mindful, & alert. This is the third frame of reference....

'There are three frames of reference that a noble one cultivates, cultivating which he is a teacher fit to instruct a group.' Thus it was said. And in reference to this was it said.

M.137

§ 180. Rahula, develop meditation in tune with earth. For when you are developing meditation in tune with earth, agreeable & disagreeable sensory impressions that have arisen will not stay in charge of your mind. Just as when people throw what is clean or unclean on the earth—feces, urine, saliva, pus, or blood—the earth is not horrified, humiliated, or disgusted by it; in the same way, when you are developing meditation in tune with earth, agreeable & disagreeable sensory impressions that have arisen will not stay in charge of your mind.

Develop meditation in tune with water. For when you are developing meditation in tune with water, agreeable & disagreeable sensory impressions that have arisen will not stay in charge of your mind. Just as when people wash what is clean or unclean in water—feces, urine, saliva, pus, or blood—the water is not horrified, humiliated, or disgusted by it; in the same way, when you are developing meditation in tune with water, agreeable & disagreeable sensory impressions that have arisen will not stay in charge of your mind.

Develop meditation in tune with fire. For when you are developing meditation in tune with fire, agreeable & disagreeable sensory impressions that have arisen will not stay in charge of your mind. Just as when fire burns what is clean or unclean—feces, urine, saliva, pus, or blood—it is not horrified, humiliated, or disgusted by it; in the same way, when you are developing meditation in tune with fire, agreeable & disagreeable sensory impressions that have arisen will not stay in charge of your mind.

Develop meditation in tune with wind. For when you are developing meditation in tune with wind, agreeable & disagreeable sensory impressions that have arisen will not stay in charge of your mind. Just as when wind blows what is clean or unclean—feces, urine, saliva, pus, or blood—it is not horrified, humiliated, or disgusted by it; in the same way, when you are developing meditation in tune with wind, agreeable & disagreeable sensory impressions that have arisen will not stay in charge of your mind.

Develop meditation in tune with space. For when you are developing meditation in tune with space, agreeable & disagreeable sensory impressions that have arisen will not stay in charge of your mind. Just as space is not established anywhere, in the same way, when you are developing meditation in tune with space, agreeable & disagreeable sensory impressions that have arisen will not stay in charge of your mind.

M.62

§ 181. And how, Ananda, in the discipline of a noble one is there the unexcelled development of the faculties? There is the case where, when seeing a form with the eye, there arises in a monk what is agreeable, what is disagreeable, what is agreeable & disagreeable. He discerns that 'This agreeable thing has arisen in me, this disagreeable thing...this agreeable & disagreeable thing has arisen in me. And that is compounded, gross, dependently co-arisen. But this is peaceful, this is exquisite, i.e., equanimity. With that, the arisen agreeable thing...disagreeable thing...agreeable & disagreeable thing ceases, and equanimity takes its stance. Just as a man with good eyes, having closed them, might open them; or having opened them, might close them, that is how quickly, how rapidly, how easily, no matter what it refers to, the arisen agreeable thing...disagreeable thing...agreeable & disagreeable thing ceases, and equanimity takes its stance. In the discipline of the noble ones, this is called the unexcelled development of the faculties with regard to forms cognizable by the eye.

Furthermore, when hearing a sound with the ear, there arises in a monk what is agreeable, what is disagreeable, what is agreeable &

disagreeable. He discerns that...and equanimity takes its stance. Just as a strong man might easily snap his fingers, that is how quickly... equanimity takes its stance. In the discipline of the noble ones, this is called the unexcelled development of the faculties with regard to sounds cognizable by the ear.

Furthermore, when smelling a smell with the nose, there arises in a monk what is agreeable, what is disagreeable, what is agreeable & disagreeable. He discerns that...and equanimity takes its stance. Just as drops of water roll off a gently sloping lotus leaf & do not remain there, that is how quickly...equanimity takes its stance. In the discipline of the noble ones, this is called the unexcelled development of the faculties with regard to smells cognizable by the nose.

Furthermore, when tasting a taste with the tongue, there arises in a monk what is agreeable, what is disagreeable, what is agreeable & disagreeable. He discerns that...and equanimity takes its stance. Just as a strong man might easily spit out a ball of saliva gathered on the tip of his tongue, that is how quickly...equanimity takes its stance. In the discipline of the noble ones, this is called the unexcelled development of the faculties with regard to tastes cognizable by the tongue.

Furthermore, when sensing a tactile sensation with the body, there arises in a monk what is agreeable, what is disagreeable, what is agreeable & disagreeable. He discerns that...and equanimity takes its stance. Just as a strong man might easily extend his flexed arm or flex his extended arm, that is how quickly...equanimity takes its stance. In the discipline of the noble ones, this is called the unexcelled development of the faculties with regard to tactile sensations cognizable by the body.

Furthermore, when sensing a idea with the intellect, there arises in a monk what is agreeable, what is disagreeable, what is agreeable & disagreeable. He discerns that 'This agreeable thing has arisen in me, this disagreeable thing...this agreeable & disagreeable thing has arisen in me. And that is compounded, gross, dependently co-arisen. But this is peaceful, this is exquisite, i.e., equanimity. With that, the arisen agreeable thing...disagreeable thing...agreeable & disagreeable thing ceases, and equanimity takes its stance. Just as a strong man might let two or three drops of water fall onto an iron pan heated all day: Slow would the falling of the drops of water, but they quickly would vanish & disappear. That is how quickly, how rapidly, how easily, no matter what it refers to, the arisen agreeable thing...disagreeable thing...agreeable & disagreeable thing ceases, and equanimity takes its stance. In the discipline of the noble ones, this is called the unexcelled development of the faculties with regard to ideas cognizable by the intellect. [§60]

And how is one a person in training, someone following the way? There is the case where, when seeing a form with the eye, there arises in a monk what is agreeable, what is disagreeable, what is agreeable & disagreeable. He feels horrified, humiliated, & disgusted with the arisen agreeable thing... disagreeable thing... agreeable & disagreeable thing. (Similarly with the other senses.)....

And how is one a noble one with developed faculties? There is the case where, when seeing a form with the eye, there arises in a monk what is agreeable, what is disagreeable, what is agreeable & disagreeable. If he wants, he remains percipient of loathsomeness in the presence of what is not loathsome. If he wants, he remains percipient of unloathsomeness in the presence of what is loathsome. If he wants, he remains percipient of loathsomeness in the presence of what is not loathsome & what is. If he wants, he remains percipient of unloathsomeness in the presence of what is loathsome & what is not. If he wants—in the presence of what is loathsome & what is not—cutting himself off from both, he remains equanimous, alert, & mindful. [§45-46; 98]

This is how one is a noble one with developed faculties.

M.152

§ 182. [On attaining the fourth level of jhāna] there remains only equanimity: pure & bright, pliant, malleable & luminous. Just as if a skilled goldsmith or goldsmith's apprentice were to prepare a furnace, heat up a crucible, and, taking gold with a pair of tongs, place it in the crucible. He would blow on it periodically, sprinkle water on it periodically, examine it periodically, so that the gold would become refined, well-refined, thoroughly refined, flawless, free from dross, pliant, malleable & luminous. Then whatever sort of ornament he had in mind—whether a belt, an earring, a necklace, or a gold chain—it would serve his purpose. In the same way, there remains only equanimity: pure & bright, pliant, malleable, & luminous. He [the meditator] discerns that 'If I were to direct equanimity as pure & bright as this toward the sphere of the infinitude of space, I would develop the mind along those lines, and thus this equanimity of mine—thus supported, thus sustained—would last for a long time. (Similarly with the spheres of the infinitude of consciousness, nothingness, & neither perception nor non-perception.)'

He discerns that 'If I were to direct equanimity as pure & bright as this toward the sphere of the infinitude of space and to develop the mind along those lines, that would be fabricated. (Similarly with the spheres of the infinitude of consciousness, nothingness, & neither perception nor non-perception.)' He neither fabricates nor wills for the sake of becoming or un-becoming. This being the case, he is not sustained by anything in the world (does not cling to anything in the world). Unsustained, he is not agitated. Unagitated, he is totally unbound right within. He discerns that 'Birth is ended, the holy life fulfilled, the task done. There is nothing further for this world.'

M.140

§ 183. A person who is not truly good...enters & remains in the first jhāna. He notices, 'I have gained the attainment of the first jhāna, but these other monks have not gained the attainment of the first jhāna.' He exalts himself for the attainment of the first jhāna and disparages others. This is the quality of a person who is not truly good.

The truly good person notices, 'The Blessed One has spoken of non-fashioning even with regard to the attainment of the first jhāna, for however they construe it, it becomes otherwise.' So, making non-fashioning his focal point, he neither exalts himself for the attainment of the first jhāna nor disparages others. This is the quality of a person who is truly good.

(Similarly with the other levels of jhāna up through the sphere of nothingness.)

A person who is not truly good...enters & remains in the sphere of neither perception nor non-perception. He notices, 'I have gained the attainment of the sphere of neither perception nor non-perception, but these other monks have not gained the attainment of the sphere of neither perception nor non-perception.' He exalts himself for the attainment of the sphere of neither perception nor non-perception and disparages others. This is the quality of a person who is not truly good.

The truly good person notices, 'The Blessed One has spoken of non-fashioning even with regard to the attainment of the sphere of neither perception nor non-perception, for however they construe it, it becomes otherwise.' So, making non-fashioning his focal point, he neither exalts himself for the attainment of the sphere of neither perception nor non-perception nor disparages others. This is the quality of a person who is truly good.

The truly good person, completely transcending the sphere of neither perception nor non-perception, enters & remains in the cessation of feeling & perception. When he sees with discernment, his effluents are ended. This is a monk who does not construe anything, does not construe anywhere, does not construe in any way.

M.113

H. DISCERNMENT: RIGHT VIEW

The texts define right view as knowledge with regard to the four noble truths. The phrase "with regard to," here (expressed by the locative case in Pali), can also mean "in terms of," and this alternative meaning is especially relevant in this case. It reflects the point that the knowledge constituting right view is not a theoretical knowledge about the truths but is a way of using the truths to categorize all of conditioned experience. Because these truths view experience in terms of function—how unskillful and skillful mental qualities play a role in the causal chain of creating suffering or bringing it to an end [D.1; MFU, p. 64]—the right way to view right view itself is not to stop with its definition but to regard it in terms of its function and then put it to its intended use.

The function of right view is to look at events in the mind in a way that gives rise to a sense of dispassion, leading the mind to a state of non-fashioning and then on to Awakening. It does this by focusing on the way in which passion and desire lead to suffering and stress. In this, it develops the mind's basic reaction to stress—the search for a way to escape from the stress [§189]—in a skillful way so that this reaction actually leads to utter release. When the mind sees, without its normal bewilderment, the actual process by which stress is caused, it will naturally let go of the causes. When it sees passion clearly enough to catch that passion in the act of leading to stress, it will naturally develop a sense of dispassion for and detachment from the passion, so that it can view it simply as a mental event, with no meaning in terms of anything else. This opens the way to the state of non-fashioning where the cause of stress is allowed to cease.

The causal connection between passion and desire on the one hand, and stress on the other, is explained in the standard formula for dependent co-arising under the factor of clinging/sustenance. A passage in the Canon [S.XII.121, MFU, pp. 44-45] analyzes this factor into four forms of passion and desire for the five aggregates: clinging to sensuality, clinging to precepts and practices, clinging to views, and clinging to theories about the self. The third form of clinging listed here points to one of the paradoxes about right view: it is a form of view that has to loosen attachment to all views, ultimately including itself. Passage §187 shows how this happens. When faced with a variety of views about the world and the self, right view looks at the views, not in terms of their content, but simply as events in the mind, in and of themselves. It sees them as part of a causal chain: fabricated, inconstant, stressful, and thus not-self, not worthy of attachment. In this way it makes the mind dispassionate to all other views: dispassionate toward the terms they use, dispassionate toward their claims to truth. Right view then turns on itself to see itself as part of a similar causal chain. This loosens any sense of attachment even for right view so that the mind can see the view simply as an event: "there is this." This entry into the perceptual mode of emptiness leads straight to the "higher escape"—the state of non-fashioning—that then becomes present to awareness.

Because right view is the only form of view that contains the seeds of its own transcendence in this way, it is the only form of knowing that is skillful enough to lead to Awakening. The Canon gives no room for any alternative "skillful means" that would contradict right view. After the experience of Awakening, the texts tell us [S.XXII.122], one continues to make use of right view, without any sense of clinging, as a pleasant abiding for the mind and for mindfulness and alertness, much as one would use jhana for the same purpose [III/E]. This process of transcending right view even as one makes use of it shows that non-attachment to views does not mean agnosticism or an openness to all views. Instead, non-attachment is a skillful way of making use of one's discerning faculties, seeing through to the causal function of all views, so that one may attain Awakening and then maintain a pleasant and mindfully alert abiding after one has become awakened.

The steps in the functioning of right view correspond to the three stages of frames-of-reference meditation [II/B]. The first step, in which one focuses on events in and of themselves—and not in reference to anything they might mean outside of the range of immediate experience—corresponds to the first stage of frames-of-reference meditation, in which one stays focused on the body, etc., in and of itself, putting aside all greed and distress with reference to the world. The second step of right view, in which one focuses on events in terms of their role in the causal chain—fabricated, inconstant, stressful, and not-self—corresponds to the second stage of frames-of-reference meditation, in which one remains focused on the phenomenon of origination and passing away. The third step of right view, in which one sees even right view simply as an event, corresponds to the third stage of frames-of-reference meditation in which one moves to the perceptual mode of "entry into emptiness," noting simply, "There is this"—without being caught up in the "this"—and from there on to non-fashioning and Awakening. Because the practice of jhana is also implicated in these three steps—steadying the mind in the first step, sensitizing it to causality in the second, and providing the basis for the fifth factor of noble concentration in the third—mindfulness, concentration, and discernment are thus inextricably intertwined as they develop along the path to Awakening.

It is important to note that right view functions in two time frames: small and large. Its primary frame is in the small frame, dealing exclusively with the immediate present. As it focuses on the phenomenon of origination and passing away, it reduces its terms of analysis to more and more basic levels until reaching the point where it sees even such simple categories as "being" and "non-being" as extraneous, inappropriate, and irrelevant to the simple flow of events arising and passing away in the present [§186]. As a result, it strips everything down to the most basic categories of experience—the presence and absence of stress—without adding anything further. This phenomenological mode of perception, or "entry into emptiness," sees things simply in terms of what is present and what is not [M.121; MFU, pp. 82-85]. Here, realizations are expressed merely as pointers to present phenomena without any content that would point to anything outside of direct experience: "There is this," [M.102; MFU, pp. 81-82] "Such is form, such is feeling," [§149] etc. The Pali name for this/that conditionality, *idappaccayata,* points to the fact that not only the phenomena but also their relationships are a matter of immediate, "right here-and-now" insight.

Once these insights are gained on the level of radically immediate experience, one realizes that they have implications for the larger time frame of the whole process of transmigration, and one's entire experience of the cosmos as well [§211-15]. The process of stress arising and passing away in the present is precisely the same process as that of living beings arising and passing away on the cosmic scale. One sees that one has participated in this process from an inconceivable beginning in time; one knows—now that the process has been disbanded—that one has found the end of the cycle of rebirth. This is because, in entering radically into the present moment by stripping away all clinging, one ultimately steps out of the dimensions of time and the present; having done so, one can see the totality of what it means to be in those dimensions.

This point is illustrated in two passages [§§74, 64] that express the content of right view immediately before and after the experience of the Deathless:

> 'From an inconceivable beginning comes transmigration. A beginning point is not evident, though beings hindered by ignorance and fettered by craving are transmigrating & wandering on. The total fading & cessation of ignorance, of this mass of darkness, is this peaceful, exquisite state: the resolution of all fabrications; the relinquishment of all the paraphernalia of becoming; the ending of craving; dispassion; cessation; Unbinding.'

> 'This is stress....This is the origination of stress....This is the cessation of stress....This is the way leading to the cessation of stress....These are effluents....This is the origination of efflu-

> ents.... This is the cessation of effluents....This is the way leading to the cessation of effluents.' His heart, thus knowing, thus seeing, is released from the effluent of sensuality, released from the effluent of becoming, released from the effluent of ignorance. With release, there is the knowledge, 'Released.' He discerns that 'Birth is ended, the holy life fulfilled, the task done. There is nothing further for this world.'

The first passage depicts the act of discernment that verifies the principles of conviction. The second passage depicts the act of discernment that confirms the fact that the five faculties, when fully developed, do lead to the Deathless [§89]. Notice that both passages follow a similar pattern, even though they deal with vastly different time scales. Transmigration and darkness, in the first passage, correspond to stress in the second. Ignorance and craving are the origination of stress, and the sentence, "The total fading & cessation of ignorance...Unbinding," describes the cessation of stress. The act of discernment that sees all these things is the way leading to the cessation of stress.

This repetition of the same pattern on two different frames of space and time in non-linear systems is called scale invariance: the same process on two different scales [I/B]. It is one of the most distinctive features of the Buddha's teachings, for it shows how an insight into a present moment in the mind can have repercussions on one's entire involvement in the cosmos. The principle behind the scale invariance of right view is this/that conditionality: the fact that one's continued participation in the cosmos is kept going by one's present contribution to the causal stream initiated over the long course of the past. By reaching the state of non-fashioning, one stops contributing to the present, and thus can bring the totality of one's participation to an end, leaving the utter freedom of Unbinding. In this sense, the principle of this/that conditionality explains the possibility of attaining the Deathless, while the actuality of the Deathless—once it is attained through skillful mastery of kamma—is what proves the principle of this/that conditionality as an adequate description of the causal process that fabricates conditioned experience and provides an opening to the Unfabricated.

§ 184. I do not envision any one other quality by which unarisen unskillful qualities arise, and arisen unskillful qualities go to growth & proliferation, like wrong view. When a person has wrong view, unarisen unskillful qualities arise, and arisen unskillful qualities go to growth & proliferation.

I do not envision any one other quality by which unarisen skillful qualities arise, and arisen skillful qualities go to growth & proliferation, like right view. When a person has right view, unarisen skillful qualities arise, and arisen skillful qualities go to growth & proliferation.

Just when a nimb-tree seed, a bitter creeper seed, or a bitter melon seed is placed in moist soil, whatever nutriment it takes from the soil & the water, all conduces to its bitterness, acridity, & distastefulness. Why is that? Because of the evil nature of the seed.

In the same way, when a person has wrong view, whatever bodily deeds he undertakes in line with that view, whatever verbal deeds...whatever mental deeds he undertakes in line with that view, whatever intentions, whatever determinations, whatever vows, whatever fabrications, all lead to what is disagreeable, unpleasing, unappealing, unprofitable, & stressful. Why is that? Because of the evil nature of the view....

Just when a sugar cane seed, a rice grain, or a grape seed is placed in moist soil, whatever nutriment it takes from the soil & the water, all conduces to its sweetness, tastiness, & unalloyed delectability. Why is that? Because of the auspicious nature of the seed.

In the same way, when a person has right view, whatever bodily deeds he undertakes in line with that view, whatever verbal deeds... whatever mental deeds he undertakes in line with that view, whatever intentions, whatever vows, whatever determinations, whatever fabrications, all lead to what is agreeable, pleasing, charming, profitable, & easeful. Why is that? Because of the auspicious nature of the view.

A.I.181-82, 189-90

§ 185. Right view, when assisted by these five factors, has release of awareness as its fruit & reward, has release of discernment as its fruit & reward. Which five?

There is the case where right view is assisted by virtue, assisted by learning, assisted by discussion, assisted by tranquility, & assisted by insight *(vipassanā).*

When assisted by these five factors, right view has release of awareness & release of discernment as its fruit & reward.

A.V.25

§ 186. Kaccayana: 'Lord, "Right view, right view," it is said. To what extent is there right view?'

The Buddha: 'By & large, Kaccāyana, this world is supported by (takes as its object) a polarity, that of existence & non-existence. But when one sees the origination of the world as it actually is with right discernment, "non-existence" with reference to the world does not occur to one. When one sees the cessation of the world as it actually is with right discernment, "existence" with reference to the world does not occur to one.

'By & large, Kaccayana, this world is in bondage to attachments, clingings (sustenances), & biases. But one such as this does not get involved with or cling to these attachments, clingings, fixations of awareness, biases, or latent tendencies; nor is he resolved on "my self." He has no uncertainty or doubt that, when there is arising, only stress is arising; and that when there is passing away, only stress is passing away. In this, one's knowledge is independent of others. It is to this extent, Kaccāyana, that there is right view.'

S.XII.15

§ 187. Then Anāthapiṇḍika the householder went to where the wanderers of other persuasions were staying. On arrival he greeted them courteously. After an exchange of friendly greetings & courtesies, he sat down to one side. As he was sitting there, the wanderers said to him, 'Tell us, householder, what views the contemplative Gotama has.'

'Venerable sirs, I don't know entirely what views the Blessed One has.' [§188]

'Well, well. So you don't know entirely what views the contemplative Gotama has. Then tell us what views the monks have.'

'I don't even know entirely what views the monks have.'

'So you don't know entirely what views the contemplative Gotama has or even that the monks have. Then tell us what views you have.'

'It wouldn't be difficult for me to expound to you what views I have. But please let the venerable ones expound each in line with his position, and then it won't be difficult for me to expound to you what views I have.'

When this had been said, one of the wanderers said to Anāthapiṇḍika the householder, *'The cosmos is eternal.* Only this is true; anything otherwise is worthless. This is the sort of view I have.'

Another wanderer said to Anāthapiṇḍika, *'The cosmos is not eternal.* Only this is true; anything otherwise is worthless. This is the sort of view I have.'

Another wanderer said, *'The cosmos is finite...'...'The cosmos is infinite...'...'The soul & the body are the same...'...'The soul is one thing and the body another...'...'After death a Tathāgata exists...'...'After death a Tathāgata does not exist...'...'After death a Tathāgata both does & does not exist...'...'After death a Tathāgata neither does nor does not exist.* Only this is true; anything otherwise is worthless. This is the sort of view I have.'

When this had been said, Anathapiṇḍika the householder said to the wanderers, 'As for the venerable one who says, "*The cosmos is eternal.* Only this is true; anything otherwise is worthless. This is the sort of view I have," his view arises from his own inappropriate attention or in dependence on the words of another. Now this view has been brought into being, is fabricated, willed, dependently co-arisen. Whatever has been brought into being, is fabricated, willed, dependently co-arisen, that is inconstant. Whatever is inconstant is stress. This venerable one thus adheres to that very stress, submits himself to that very stress.' (Similarly for the other positions.)

When this had been said, the wanderers said to Anāthapiṇḍika the householder, 'We have each & every one expounded to you in line with our own positions. Now tell us what views you have.'

'Whatever has been brought into being, is fabricated, willed, dependently co-arisen, that is inconstant. Whatever is inconstant is stress. Whatever is stress is not mine, is not what I am, is not my self. This is the sort of view I have.'

'So, householder, whatever has been brought into being, is fabricated, willed, dependently co-arisen, that is inconstant. Whatever is inconstant is stress. You thus adhere to that very stress, submit yourself to that very stress.'

'Venerable sirs, whatever has been brought into being, is fabricated, willed, dependently co-arisen, that is inconstant. Whatever is inconstant is stress. Whatever is stress is not mine, is not what I am, is not my self. Having seen this well with right discernment as it actually is present, I also discern the higher escape from it as it actually is present.'

When this had been said, the wanderers fell silent, abashed, sitting with their shoulders drooping, their heads down, brooding, at a loss for words. Anathapiṇḍika the householder, perceiving that the wanderers were silent, abashed...at a loss for words, got up & left.

A.X.93

i. The Four Noble Truths

In §139, the Buddha refers to himself as a doctor, treating the spiritual illnesses of his students. This metaphor is useful to keep in mind as we discuss the basic categories of right view: the four noble truths. Many people have charged Buddhism with being pessimistic because the four truths start out with stress and suffering, but this charge misses the fact that the first truth is part of a strategy of diagnosis and therapy focusing on the basic problem in life so as to offer a solution to it. This is the sense in which the Buddha was like a doctor, focusing on the disease he wanted to cure. The total cure he promised as a result of his course of therapy shows that, in actuality, he was much less pessimistic than the vast majority of world, for whom wisdom means accepting the bad things in life with the good, assuming that there is no chance in this life for unalloyed happiness. The Buddha was an extremely demanding person, unwilling to bend to this supposed wisdom or to rest with anything less than absolute happiness. We are fortunate that he was so demanding and succeeded in his aim, for otherwise we would have to undertake the uncertain task of trying to discover the way to that happiness ourselves.

Although the four noble truths constitute the most basic categories of the Buddha's teaching, he did not discuss them unless he felt that his listeners were ready for them. To understand and accept them requires a basic shift in the framework of one's awareness, and only a mind that has been thoroughly prepared is in a position to make such a shift. Often the Buddha would prepare his listeners with what he called a gradual discourse: discussing step by step the joy of generosity; the joy of living a virtuous life; the long-term sensory rewards of generosity and virtue in heaven; the drawbacks and impermanence of sensory pleasures and conditioned phenomena in general; and finally the rewards of renunciation. Then, if he sensed that his listeners were ready to look favorably on renunciation as a means of true happiness, he would discuss the four truths, beginning with suffering and stress. In this, he followed the sequence of his own Awakening: beginning with insight into the punishments of bad kamma, the rewards of good kamma, and the limitations of all kamma, and then proceeding to insight into the origination of stress and its cessation through the cessation of kamma [§9].

Once the problem of stress and suffering is solved, he said, there are no more problems. This is why he limited his teaching to this issue, even though his own Awakening encompassed much more [§188]. The vicious cycle that operates between suffering and ignorance—with ignorance underlying the craving that causes suffering, and suffering causing the bewilderment that leads people to act in ignorant and unskillful ways [§189]—can be broken only when one focuses on understanding suffering and stress and the causal network that surrounds them. Most people are so bewildered by the complexities of suffering and stress that they do not even know what the true problem is. Thus they may deny that they are suffering, or may imagine that something stressful can actually be a solution to their problems. The genius of the Buddha is that he recognized the most elegant and comprehensive way to deal with every variety of dissatisfaction in life. When suffering and stress are seen with clear knowledge, they no longer can cause bewilderment, and the cycle that underlies all the problems of experience can be disbanded for good.

As §195 states, this clear knowledge is based on knowledge of the four noble truths. These truths are best understood not as the content of a belief, but as categories for viewing and classifying the processes of immediate experience. In §51, the Buddha refers to them as categories of "appropriate attention," a skillful alternative to the common way that people categorize their experience in terms of two dichotomies: being/non-being, and self/other. For several reasons, these common dichotomies are actually problem-causing, rather than problem-solving. The being/non-being dichotomy, for instance, comes down to the question of whether or not there exist actual "things" behind the changing phenomena of experience. This type of questioning deals, by definition, with possibilities that cannot be directly experienced: If the things in question could be experienced, then they wouldn't be lying behind experience. Thus the being/non-being dichotomy pulls one's attention into the land of conjecture—"a thicket of views, a wilderness of views, a contortion of views, a writhing of views, a fetter of views" [M.72]—and away from the area of direct awareness where the real problem and its solution lie [§186].

As for the self/other dichotomy, there is the initial difficulty of determining what the self is. Any true self would have to lie totally under one's own control, and yet nothing that one might try to identify as one's self actually meets this criterion. Although the sense of self may seem intuitive enough, when carefully examined it shows itself to be based on confused perceptions and ideas. If one's basic categories for understanding experience are a cause for confusion in this way, they can lead only to confused, unskillful action, and thus to more suffering and stress. For example, when people view the source of their problems as poor relationships between themselves and others, or inadequate integration of the self, they are trying to analyze their problems in terms of categories that are ultimately uncertain. Thus there is a built-in uncertainty in the efforts they make to solve their problems in terms of those categories.

A second problem, no matter how one might define a self, is the question of how to prove whether or not it actually exists. This question entangles the mind in the unresolvable problems of the being/non-being dichotomy mentioned above: Because the problem is phrased in terms that cannot be directly experienced, it forces the solution into a realm that cannot be experienced, either. This fact probably explains the Buddha's statement in §230 to the effect that if one even asks the question of whether there is someone standing outside the processes of dependent co-arising to whom those processes pertain, it is impossible to lead the life that will bring about an end to suffering. Regardless of whether one would answer the question with a yes or a no, the terms of the question focus on an area outside of direct experience and thus away from the true problem—the direct experience of suffering—and actually make it worse. If one assumes the existence of a self, one must take on the implicit imperative to maximize the self's well-being through recourse to the "other." This recourse may involve either exploiting the "other" or swallowing the "other" into the self by equating one's self with the cosmos as a whole. Either approach involves clinging and craving, which lead to further suffering and stress. On the other hand, if one denies any kind of self, saying that the cosmos is totally "other," then one is assuming that there is nothing with any long-term existence whose happiness deserves anything more than quick, short-term attempts at finding pleasure. The imperative here is to pursue immediate pleasure with as little effort as possible. This imperative aborts any sustained effort to bring about an end to suffering.

These problems explain why the Buddha regarded questions of existence and non-existence, self and no-self, as unskillful, inappropriate ways of attending to experience.

Stress and its cessation, on the other hand, are categories that avoid these problems. To begin with, they are immediately present and apparent. Even babies recognize stress and pain, well before they have any concept of "self" or "being." If one pays close attention to one's actual experience, there is no question about whether or not stress and its cessation are present. Finally, because these categories don't require that one fashion notions of "self" or "other"—or "no-self" or "no-other"—on top of one's immediate awareness [§228-230], they allow one to reach the mode of "entry into emptiness" on the verge of non-fashioning, in which, as we mentioned in III/H, the mind simply notes, "There is this...." Thus they are ideal categories for analyzing experience in a way that (1) reduces the confusion that causes people to act in unskillful ways and (2) brings the mind to a point where it can disengage and transcend all suffering and stress by ending the mental fabrication that provides input into the causal web.

As for the imperatives implicit in the four categories of the noble truths, they are very different from the imperatives implicit in the notion that there is a self or that there isn't. Stress, the first category, should be comprehended. In practice, this means admitting its presence, recognizing it as a problem, and then observing it with patient mindfulness so as to understand its true nature. One comes to realize that the problem is not with the stress and discomfort of external conditions, but with the stress and discomfort in the mind. One also sees how stress is part of a causal process, and that it is always accompanied by craving, its point of origination.

The second category—craving, the origination of stress—should be abandoned. Here we must note that the word "craving" covers not all desire, but only the desire leading to further becoming. The desire to escape from that becoming, as we have noted [II/D] is part of the path. Without such a desire, no one would have the motivation to follow the path or reach Unbinding. When Unbinding is reached, though, even this desire is abandoned, just as a desire to walk to a park is abandoned on arriving there [§67].

As for the third category, the cessation of stress, it should be realized. The definition of this truth as the abandoning of craving means that it denotes the successful performance of the duty appropriate to the second noble truth. This introduces a double tier into the practice, in that one must not only abandon craving but also realize what is happening and what is uncovered in the process of that abandoning. This, in turn, accounts for two of the major themes covered so far in this book: the switch from "object" (craving) to "approach" (abandoning) as the focal point in one's meditation as one moves from the first to the second stage in frames-of-reference meditation [II/B]; and the need for sensitivity to one's present input into the causal network in order to nurture the mind's skillful mastery of this/that conditionality [I/A]. The feedback loop created by this combination of abandoning and knowing is what eventually short-circuits the process of this/that conditionality, cutting dependent co-arising at the links of craving and ignorance, and leading on to the state of non-fashioning that forms the threshold to the Deathless.

The fourth category, the way to the cessation of stress, is defined as the noble eightfold path, which we have already discussed in detail [II/H]. This truth must be developed. In general terms, this development involves two processes: nurturing the conditions for clear knowing; and abstaining from acts of body, speech, and mind that involve craving and would obstruct knowledge. These two processes correspond to the two layers we have just noted in the duties associated with the cessation of stress; this correspondence shows the intimate relation between the third and fourth noble truths, and explains the Buddha's insistence that the noble eightfold path is the only way to the goal.

Taken together, the four categories of the noble truths, along with their imperatives, follow a basic problem-solving approach: one solves the problem of stress by following a path of practice that directly attacks the cause of the problem. The noble eightfold path develops the qualities of mind needed to see that all the possible objects of craving—the five aggregates—are stressful, inconstant, and not-self. As a result, one grows dispassionate toward them. With nothing left to focus on, craving disbands. When one experiences the "remainderless fading & cessation, renunciation, relinquishment, release, & letting go of that very craving" [§210], the problem is solved.

Although the texts list four separate duties appropriate to each of the truths, in actual practice these duties are four aspects of a single process. When stress is comprehended, the second noble truth—craving—has no object to latch onto and so can be abandoned. The full realization of what is happening in the process of that abandoning constitutes the realization of the third noble truth, the cessation of stress. Both the abandoning and the realization are accomplished by developing the path, which destroys any trace of ignorance concerning the four noble truths at the same time that it abandons craving. This is how the practice cuts the chain of dependent co-arising simultaneously at its two most crucial factors [§210-211], thus unraveling the causal chain and opening the way for an experience of the Unfabricated.

Passage §195 lists three steps in this process, which take the form of three levels of knowledge concerning each of the four truths: recognizing the truth for what it is, recognizing the duty appropriate to the truth, and realizing that the duty has been completed. These levels of knowledge correspond to the three stages in right view that we mentioned in the preceding section. The first level corresponds to the stage of seeing events in and of themselves for what they actually are. The relationship between the second level of knowledge—realizing the duty appropriate to the truth—and the second stage of right view—viewing things as part of a causal chain—is somewhat less obvious, but more revealing once it is understood. The word "duty" makes the point that, in order to understand the process of origination and passing away, one must become involved in the process in an active way. This understanding does not come from a passive state of simply watching things arise and disappear. Instead, one must participate in the process, becoming sensitive to pre-existing causal conditions and the impact of one's present activity on those conditions, if one wants truly to understand them. The only way to know a causal relationship is to tamper with it and see what happens as a result. The more precise and skillful one's tampering, and the more properly attuned one's powers of observation, the more precise the knowledge that can be gained. This active participation corresponds to the second stage of frames of reference meditation [II/B] and the process of gaining mastery in the practice of concentration [III/E]. Ultimately, it comes down to the issues of acquiring skillfulness and understanding the connection between skillfulness and this/that conditionality. The meditator can gain escape from the confines of the causal process, not by simply watching it, but by developing the sensitivity to causal factors that comes from learning how to explore and manipulate them with skill.

The third level of knowledge—that the duty appropriate to the truth has been completed—corresponds to the mode of "entry into emptiness" on the verge of non-fashioning, when one realizes that nothing more needs to be contributed to the present moment. In fact, nothing more *can* be contributed to the present moment. As noted in the preceding section, this is the point where right view transcends itself. In terms of the four noble truths, this is where simple distinctions among the four truths begin to break down. As a modern teacher has put it, the meditator sees that all four truths are ultimately identical. After having used jhana and discernment, which form the heart of the path, to gain understanding of pain and to abandon clinging and craving, one comes to see that even jhana and discernment are composed of the same aggregates as stress and pain [§173], and that one's attitude toward them involves subtle levels of clinging and craving as well. Thus the path is simply a refined version of the first three noble truths, in which one has taken suffering, craving, and ignorance, and turned them into tools for pleasure, detachment, and insight. Without these tools, one could not have begun the process of release; were it not for one's attachment to jhana and discernment, one could not have liberated oneself from the more obvious levels of stress, and one could not have developed the sensitivity enabling one to appreciate the value of cessation and release when they finally come. Now, however, that these tools have performed their functions, they become the last remaining obstacle to full release. The approach to the problem of stress has now become, in and of itself, the only problem left. As the four truths become one in this way, their respective duties reach the point where any further activity would mean that they would cancel one another out. This is where the mind attains the state of non-fashioning, as there is nothing more it can do or know in terms of any of these duties. This lack of input into the present moment forms a breach in this/that conditionality, opening the way beyond the four truths and on to the Unfabricated.

This coalescing of the truths coincides with a movement noted earlier [II/H], in which jhana and discernment become one and the same thing. This union of jhana and discernment solves the riddle of how one can come to know the end of the intention that keeps the round of rebirth in motion. As the path nears its end, the intentional activity underlying jhana becomes the sole remaining element of intention in the mind; while the activity of discernment, as appropriate attention aimed at understanding jhana, becomes the sole function of knowledge. As they reach culmination and coalesce, the attention focused on the intention and the intention behind the act of attention short-circuit one another. All that can follow on this point is the state of non-fashioning, in which all present input into the cycle of rebirth ends, and all experience of the cycle falls away. As we explained in the Introduction, the experience of this falling away at Awakening confirms not only the Buddha's teachings on the present function of kammic input in this/that conditionality, but also on the functioning of kamma in the round of rebirth in the larger dimensions of time.

The wheel, the traditional symbol of the Dhamma, expresses these points in a visual form. The Buddha states [§195] that when he gained full knowledge of all four truths on all three levels—recognizing the truth, recognizing the duty appropriate to it, and realizing that he had fully completed that duty—he knew that he had attained full Awakening. He elaborates on his assertion by setting out a table of two sets of variables—the four noble truths and the three levels of knowledge appropriate to each—listing all twelve permutations of the two sets. This sort of table, in Indian legal and philosophical traditions, is called a wheel. This is why the discourse in which he makes this statement is called "Setting the Wheel of Dhamma in Motion," and why the wheel used as a symbol of the Dhamma has twelve spokes, uniting at the hub, symbolizing the twelve permutations that merge into a singularity—knowledge and vision of things as they actually are—at the still point of non-fashioning in the midst of the cycle of kamma.

§ 188. Once the Blessed One was staying at Kosambī in the Siṁsapa tree grove. Then, picking up a few Siṁsapa leaves with his hand, he asked the monks, 'How do you construe this, monks: Which are more numerous, the few Siṁsapa leaves in my hand or those overhead in the Siṁsapa grove?'

'The leaves in the hand of the Blessed One are few in number, lord. Those overhead in the grove are far more numerous.'

'In the same way, monks, those things that I have known with direct knowledge but have not taught are far more numerous [than what I have taught]. And why haven't I taught them? Because they are not connected with the goal, do not relate to the rudiments of the holy life, and do not lead to disenchantment, to dispassion, to cessation, to calm, to direct knowledge, to self-awakening, to Unbinding. That is why I have not taught them.

And what have I taught? 'This is stress...This is the origination of stress...This is the cessation of stress...This is the path of practice leading to the cessation of stress.' This is what I have taught. And why have I taught these things? Because they are connected with the goal, relate to the rudiments of the holy life, and lead to disenchantment, to dispassion, to cessation, to calm, to direct knowledge, to self-awakening, to Unbinding. This is why I have taught them.

Therefore your duty is the contemplation, 'This is stress...This is the origination of stress...This is the cessation of stress...This is the path of practice leading to the cessation of stress.'

S.LVI.31

§ 189. 'Stress should be known. The cause by which stress comes into play should be known. The diversity in stress should be known. The result of stress should be known. The cessation of stress should be known. The path of practice for the cessation of stress should be known.' Thus it has been said. Why was it said?

Birth is stress, aging is stress, death is stress; sorrow, lamentation, pain, distress, & despair are stress; association with what is not loved is stress, separation from what is loved is stress, not getting what is wanted is stress. In short, the five aggregates for sustenance are stress.

And what is the cause by which stress comes into play? Craving is the cause by which stress comes into play.

And what is the diversity in stress? There is major stress & minor, slowly fading & quickly fading. This is called the diversity in stress.

And what is the result of stress? There are some cases in which a person overcome with pain, his mind exhausted, grieves, mourns, laments, beats his breast, & becomes bewildered. Or one overcome with pain, his mind exhausted, comes to search outside, 'Who knows a way or two to stop this pain?' I tell you, monks, that stress results either in bewilderment or in search.

And what is the cessation of stress? From the cessation of craving is the cessation of stress; and just this noble eightfold path is the path of practice leading to the cessation of stress: right view, right resolve, right speech, right action, right livelihood, right effort, right mindfulness, right concentration.

Now when a noble disciple discerns stress in this way, the cause by which stress comes into play in this way, the diversity of stress in this way, the result of stress in this way, the cessation of stress in this way, & the path of practice leading to the cessation of stress in this way, then he discerns this penetrative holy life as the cessation of stress.

'Stress should be known. The cause by which stress comes into play...The diversity in stress...The result of stress...The cessation of stress...The path of practice for the cessation of stress should be known.' Thus it has been said, and this is why it was said.

A.VI.63

§ 190. These four things are real, not unreal, not other than what they seem. Which four?

'This is stress,' is real, not unreal, not other than what it seems. 'This is the origination of stress...This is the cessation of stress...This is the path of practice leading to the cessation of stress,' is real, not unreal, not other than what it seems.

These are the four things that are real, not unreal, not other than what they seem.

Therefore your duty is the contemplation, 'This is stress...This is the origination of stress...This is the cessation of stress...This is the path of practice leading to the cessation of stress.'

S.LVI.20

§ 191. Suppose that a man were to cut down all the grass, sticks, branches, & leaves in India and to gather them into a heap. Having gathered them into a heap, he would make stakes from them, and having made stakes he would impale all the large animals in the sea on large stakes, all the medium-sized animals in the sea on medium-sized stakes, & all the minute animals in the sea on minute stakes. Before he had come to the end of all the sizable animals in the sea, he would have used up all the grass, sticks, branches, & leaves here in India. It would not be feasible for him to impale on stakes the minute animals in the sea, which are even more numerous [than the sizable ones]. Why is that? Because of the minuteness of their bodies. So great is the plane of deprivation *(apāya,* the lower realms of being).

Freed from this great realm of deprivation is the individual who is consummate in his views. He discerns, as it is actually present, that 'This is stress...This is the origination of stress...This is the cessation of stress...This is the path of practice leading to the cessation of stress.'

S.LVI.36

§ 192. 'Monks, there is a between-the-worlds space of impenetrable darkness, and in the murk of that darkness not even the sun & moon, so mighty, so powerful, can spread their light.'

When this was said, a certain monk addressed the Blessed One: 'What a great darkness, lord! What a very great darkness! Is there another darkness greater & more fearsome than that?'

'Yes, there is....'

'What darkness...?'

'Any priests or contemplatives who do not discern, as it is actually present, that "This is stress...This is the origination of stress...This is the cessation of stress...This is the path of practice leading to the cessation of stress," cherish the fabrications leading to birth, cherish the fabrications leading to aging...death...sorrow, lamentation, pain, distress, & despair. Cherishing the fabrications leading to birth...aging... death...sorrow, lamentation, pain, distress, & despair, they fashion fabrications leading to birth...aging...death...sorrow, lamentation, pain, distress, & despair, and so they fall into the darkness of birth...

aging...death...sorrow, lamentation, pain, distress & despair. They are not released from birth...aging...death... sorrows, lamentations, pains, distresses, & despairs. They are not released, I tell you, from stress.

However, those priests or contemplatives who discern, as it is actually present, that "This is stress...This is the origination of stress...This is the cessation of stress...This is the path of practice leading to the cessation of stress," do not cherish the fabrications leading to birth... aging...death. They do not cherish the fabrications leading to sorrow, lamentation, pain, distress, & despair. They do not fashion fabrications leading to birth...aging...death...sorrow, lamentation, pain, distress, & despair, and so do not fall into the darkness of birth...aging...death... sorrow, lamentation, pain, distress, & despair. They are released from birth...aging...death...sorrows, lamentations, pains, distresses, & despairs. They are released, I tell you, from stress.

Therefore your duty is the contemplation, 'This is stress...This is the origination of stress...This is the cessation of stress...This is the path of practice leading to the cessation of stress.'

S.LVI.46

§ 193. Suppose that people would say to a man whose life span was 100 years: 'Look here, fellow. They will stab you at dawn with 100 spears, at noon with 100 spears, & again at evening with 100 spears. You, thus stabbed every day with 300 spears, will live to be 100, and at the end of 100 years you will realize the four noble truths that you have never realized before.'

If the man desired his own true benefit, he would do well to take them up on their offer. Why is that? From an inconceivable beginning comes transmigration. A beginning point is not evident for the [pain of] blows from spears, swords, & axes. Even if this [offer] were to occur, I would not say that the realization of the four noble truths would be accompanied by pain & distress. Instead, I would say that the realization of the four noble truths would be accompanied by pleasure & joy.

S.LVI.35

§ 194. Gavampati: Face to face with the Blessed One did I hear this, face to face did I learn it: Whoever sees stress also sees the origination of stress, the cessation of stress, & the path of practice leading to the cessation of stress.

Whoever sees the origination of stress also sees stress, the cessation of stress, & the path of practice leading to the cessation of stress.

Whoever sees the cessation of stress also sees stress, the origination of stress, & the path of practice leading to the cessation of stress.

Whoever sees the path of practice leading to the cessation of stress also sees stress, the origination of stress, & the cessation of stress.

S.LVI.20

§ 195. Awakening. Vision arose, clear knowing arose, discernment arose, knowledge arose, illumination arose within me with regard to things never heard before: 'This is the noble truth of stress....This noble truth of stress is to be comprehended....This noble truth of stress has been comprehended....This is the noble truth of the origination of stress....This noble truth of the origination of stress is to be abandoned....This noble truth of the origination of stress has been abandoned....This is the noble truth of the cessation of stress....This noble truth of the cessation of stress is to be realized....This noble truth of the cessation of stress has been realized....This is the noble truth of the path of practice leading to the cessation of stress....This noble truth of the path of practice leading to the cessation of stress is to be developed....This noble truth of the path of practice leading to the cessation of stress has been developed.'

And, monks, as long as this knowledge & vision of mine—with its three rounds & twelve permutations concerning these four noble truths as they actually are—was not pure, I did not claim to have directly awakened to the unexcelled right self-awakening....But as soon as this knowledge & vision of mine—with its three rounds & twelve permutations concerning these four noble truths as they actually are—*was* truly pure, only then did I claim to have directly awakened to the unexcelled right self-awakening...The knowledge & vision arose in me: 'Unshakable is my release. This is the last birth. There is now no further becoming.'

S.LVI.11

ii. The First Truth

The first noble truth is that of *dukkha,* translated here as stress and suffering. The term has a wide range of other meanings as well, including distress, dis-ease, and—what is probably its most elemental meaning—pain. People learn their most basic strategies for dealing with pain in very early childhood, when their powers of observation are undeveloped and they cannot learn from the verbal lessons of others. Being in such a stage, they are in a poor position to understand pain, and it often leaves them bewildered. This means that they develop unskillful ways of handling it. Even when their minds later develop verbal and higher logical skills, many of the unskillful strategies and attitudes toward pain that they developed in early childhood persist on a subconscious level.

One of the most important insights leading up to the Buddha's Awakening was his realization that the act of comprehending pain lay at the essence of the spiritual quest. In trying to comprehend pain—instead of simply trying to get rid of it in line with one's habitual tendencies—one learns many valuable lessons. To begin with, one can end any sense of bewilderment in the face of pain. In seeing pain for what it truly is, one can treat it more effectively and skillfully, thus weakening the process by which pain and ignorance feed on each other. At the same time, as one learns to resist one's habitual reactions to pain, one begins to delve into the non-verbal, subconscious levels of the mind, bringing to light many ill-formed and hidden processes of which one was previously unaware. In this sense, pain is like a watering hole where all the animals in the forest—all the mind's subconscious tendencies—will eventually come to drink. Just as a naturalist who wants to make a survey of the wildlife in a particular area can simply station himself near a watering hole to wait for the animals that will eventually have to come there for water; in the same way, a meditator who wants to understand the mind can simply keep watch right at pain in order to see what subconscious reactions will appear. Thus the act of trying to comprehend pain leads not only to an improved understanding of pain itself, but also to an increased awareness of the most basic processes at work in the mind. As one sees the way in which the lack of skill in these processes, and in particular in one's reactions to pain, leads only to more pain, one's mind opens to the possibility that more skillful reactions will not only alleviate specific pains but also lead way from pain altogether. Passage §238 shows how conviction in this possibility—which is nothing other than the principle of kamma—leads from the experience of stress and pain into a causal chain that cuts the bewilderment leading to further pain and ends in total release.

Although pain is the best vantage point for observing the processes of the mind, it is also the most difficult, simply because it is so unpleasant and hard to bear. This is why discernment needs the faculties of conviction, persistence, mindfulness, and concentration to give it the detached assurance and steady focus needed to stick with pain in and of itself, in the phenomenological mode, and not veer off into the usual narratives, abstract theories, and other unskillful defenses the mind devises against the pain. Only through the development of the five faculties into right concentration does discernment have the basis of pleasure and equanimity it needs to probe into pain without feeling threatened by it, thus being able to arrive at an unbiased understanding of its true nature.

Passage §198 shows the direction this understanding should take, ultimately analyzing the wide variety of stress and pain down to five categories: the five aggregates of clinging/sustenance. Many of the remaining passages in this section give more detailed analysis of these categories. Taken together, these passages provide a useful conceptual framework for taking on the duty of trying to comprehend the issues surrounding stress, suffering, and pain. Here we will first discuss the aggregates, and then their connection with clinging and sustenance.

The five aggregates are form, feeling, perception, fabrications, and consciousness. These five categories cover the entire range of experience that can be adequately described [§231]. "Form" covers all physical phenomena, both within one's own body and without. The remaining four categories cover all mental events. "Feeling" covers feelings of pleasure, pain, and neither pleasure nor pain, regardless of whether they are based on physical or mental sensations. "Perception" denotes the mental act of applying labels or names to physical or mental events. "Fabrications" here covers the verbal and mental processes of concocting thoughts, questions, urges, or intentions in the mind. "Consciousness" covers the act of consciousness at any of the six senses: eyes, ears, nose, tongue, body, and intellect. A few texts [§§235-36] discuss a separate type of consciousness that does not partake of any of the six senses or their objects. This type of consciousness is said to lie beyond the range of describable experience and so is not included under the five aggregates. In fact, it is equivalent to the Unfabricated and forms the goal at the end of the path.

The five aggregates, on their own, do not constitute suffering or stress. They are stressful only when functioning as objects of clinging/sustenance. This hybrid word—clinging/sustenance—is a translation of the Pali term *upadana. Upadana* has a hybrid meaning because it is used to cover two sides of a physical process metaphorically applied to the mind: the act of clinging whereby a fire takes sustenance from a piece of fuel, together with the sustenance offered by the fuel. On the level of the mind, *upadana* denotes both the act of clinging and the object clung to, which together give sustenance to the process whereby mental pain arises. In terms of this metaphor, pain is hot and unstable like fire, whereas the mental act of clinging to the five aggregates is what keeps the fire burning. These images are part of a larger complex of imagery contained in the Pali discourses, likening the processes of pain and its cessation to the physical processes of fire and its extinguishing. An understanding of this imagery helps to give a graphic, intuitive sense for the ways in which the Pali texts analyze the problem of stress and pain.

Many of the texts explicitly liken pain to a fever or to a burning, unstable fire [§221; Thig.VIII.1]. Others deal more in indirect imagery, in which the terminology for explaining fire is applied to the mind. The word *upadana* is one instance of this type of indirect imagery. Others include *khandha,* or aggregate, which also means the trunk of a tree;

and *nibbana,* the most common name for the Buddhist goal, which also means the extinguishing of a fire. According to the physics of the Buddha's time, fire was "seized' when it was ignited. Burning, it was in a state of unstable agitation, entrapped by the fuel to which it clung for sustenance. On going out, it was "freed." Letting go of its sustenance, it grew cool, calm, and unbound. According to the commentaries, "unbound' is what *nibbana* literally means. Thus the study of pain is like the study of a raging fire: one tries to comprehend it in order to find the source of the burning, bondage, and entrapment so as to put the fire out and gain freedom from it for good.

There are four types of clinging to the aggregates that give sustenance to the processes of suffering and stress: desire and passion for

- the *sensuality* found in the aggregates,
- *views* regarding the aggregates,
- *practices and precepts* involving the aggregates, and
- *theories about the self* involving the aggregates.

M.44 [MFU, pp. 44-45] makes the point that the act of clinging is not the same as the aggregates, and yet it is not entirely separate from them. If clinging were identical with the aggregates, there would be no way to experience the aggregates without clinging, and thus there would be no way for an awakened person to return to the conditioned level of experience after Awakening. If clinging and the aggregates were totally separate, clinging could exist independently of the aggregates and would count as a separate part of describable experience. If this were so, the transcending of the aggregates at the moment of Awakening would not constitute the transcending of the fabricated realm, and thus the task of comprehending suffering would not yet be finished. Thus the nature of the actual interdependence between clinging and the aggregates means that a full comprehension of the aggregates is enough to bring about Awakening, at the same time that it leaves an opening for the continued experience of the fabricated realm after Awakening has occurred.

What this interdependence means in practical terms is that one must examine the aggregates in such a way as to realize fully that they are not worth clinging to. One does this by focusing on two of their common characteristics: their instability and their complexity. In seeing their inherent instability, one realizes that they are inconstant. Because they are inconstant, any attempt to base happiness on them is inherently stressful, just as there is inherent stress in trying to sit comfortably on a wobbling chair. Because the aggregates offer no basis for true happiness, they lie beyond one's control, and thus do not deserve to be viewed as "me" or "mine." Focusing further on the aggregates, one perceives the complexity of their interrelationships. Passage §201 indicates some of this complexity in its discussion of the relationship among feeling, perception, and sensory consciousness. Although these aggregates function in different ways, in actual experience they can occur only as parts of an interrelated cluster of mental events surrounding a common object. In fact, they are so closely related to one another that ordinary awareness assumes them to be a single whole. One of the tasks of discernment in comprehending pain is to see these aggregates as interrelated events. Because their interrelationships follow complex, invariable laws, one's comprehension of their true behavior brings with it the oppressive realization—oppressive as long as one is still regarding the causal network in part or in whole in terms of "self" or "other"—that they ultimately do not lie under one's control. At best, one can explore and manipulate them to the extent of understanding them to gain freedom from them, but in and of themselves they do not offer any stable kind of happiness.

Observing and understanding the complex interrelationships among feeling, perception, and consciousness leads one into the area of dependent co-arising, which forms the essence of the second truth. As one's understanding grows more sensitive, it drives home the point that all clinging to these interrelated phenomena should be abandoned. This understanding—that phenomena taking part in such relationships are unworthy of clinging—forms the essence of the path. The full pursuit of this path, in which one abandons all passion and desire for the five aggregates, brings about knowledge of the cessation of stress. All of this bears out Ven. Gavampati's comment [§194] that knowledge of the first noble truth inherently involves knowledge of the remaining three.

§ 196. And what is the noble truth of stress? The six internal sense media, should be the reply. Which six? The medium of the eye...the ear...the nose... the tongue...the body...the intellect. This is called the noble truth of stress.

S.LVI.14

§ 197. The All is aflame. Which All is aflame? The eye is aflame. Forms are aflame. Eye consciousness is aflame. Eye contact is aflame. And whatever there is that arises in dependence on eye contact, experienced as pleasure, pain or neither-pleasure-nor-pain, that too is aflame. Aflame with what? Aflame with the fire of passion, the fire of aversion, the fire of delusion. Aflame, I tell you, with birth, aging, & death, with sorrows, lamentations, pains, distresses, & despairs.

The ear is aflame. Sounds are aflame....
The nose is aflame. Smells are aflame....

The tongue is aflame. Tastes are aflame....
The body is aflame. Tactile sensations are aflame....

The intellect is aflame. Ideas are aflame. Intellect consciousness is aflame. Intellect contact is aflame. And whatever there is that arises in dependence on intellect contact, experienced as pleasure, pain or neither-pleasure-nor-pain, that too is aflame. Aflame with what? Aflame with the fire of passion, the fire of aversion, the fire of delusion. Aflame, I tell you, with birth, aging, & death, with sorrows, lamentations, pains, distresses, & despairs.

S.XXXV.28

§ 198. Sariputta: Now what, friends, is the noble truth of stress? Birth is stress, aging is stress, death is stress; sorrow, lamentation, pain, distress, & despair are stress; not getting what is wanted is stress. In short, the five aggregates for sustenance are stress.

Now what is *birth?* Whatever birth, taking birth, descent, coming-to-be, coming-forth, appearance of aggregates, & acquisition of [sense] media of the various beings in this or that group of beings, that is called birth.

And what is *aging?* Whatever aging, decrepitude, brokenness, graying, wrinkling, decline of life-force, weakening of the faculties of the various beings in this or that group of beings, that is called aging.

And what is *death?* Whatever deceasing, passing away, breaking up, disappearance, dying, death, completion of time, break up of the aggregates, casting off of the body, interruption in the life faculty of the various beings in this or that group of beings, that is called death.

And what is *sorrow?* Whatever sorrow, sorrowing, sadness, inward sorrow, inward sadness of anyone suffering from misfortune, touched by a painful thing, that is called sorrow.

And what is *lamentation?* Whatever crying, grieving, lamenting, weeping, wailing, lamentation of anyone suffering from misfortune, touched by a painful thing, that is called lamentation.

And what is *pain?* Whatever is experienced as bodily pain, bodily discomfort, pain or discomfort born of bodily contact, that is called pain.

And what is *distress?* Whatever is experienced as mental pain, mental discomfort, pain or discomfort born of mental contact, that is called distress.

And what is *despair?* Whatever despair, despondency, desperation of anyone suffering from misfortune, touched by a painful thing, that is called despair.

And what is the stress of not getting what one wants? In beings subject to birth, the wish arises, 'O, may we not be subject to birth, and may birth not come to us.' But this is not be achieved by wishing. This is the stress of not getting what one wants. In beings subject to aging...illness...death...sorrow, lamentation, pain, distress, & despair, the wish arises, 'O, may we not be subject to aging...illness...death... sorrow, lamentation, pain, distress, & despair, and may aging...illness... death...sorrow, lamentation, pain, distress, & despair not come to us.' But this is not be achieved by wishing. This is the stress of not getting what one wants.

And what are the five aggregates for sustenance that, in short, are stress? Form as an aggregate for sustenance, feeling as an aggregate for sustenance, perception as an aggregate for sustenance, fabrications as an aggregate for sustenance, consciousness as an aggregate for sustenance: These are called the five aggregates for sustenance that, in short, are stress.

This is called the noble truth of stress.

M.141

§ 199. The Buddha: These are the five aggregates for sustenance: form as an aggregate for sustenance, feeling as an aggregate for sustenance, perception as an aggregate for sustenance, fabrication as an aggregate for sustenance, consciousness as an aggregate for sustenance....These five aggregates for sustenance are rooted in desire....

A certain monk: Is it the case that sustenance and the five aggregates for sustenance are the same thing, or are they separate?

The Buddha: Sustenance is neither the same thing as the five aggregates for sustenance, nor are they separate. Whatever desire & passion there is with regard to the five aggregates for sustenance, that is the sustenance there....

The monk: To what extent does the term 'aggregates' apply to the aggregates?

The Buddha: Any form whatsoever—past, present, or future; internal or external; gross or subtle; inferior or superior; near or far—that is the form aggregate. Any feeling whatsoever—past, present, or future... near or far—that is the feeling aggregate. Any perception whatsoever—past, present, or future...near or far—that is the perception aggregate. Any fabrications whatsoever—past, present, or future... near or far—those are the fabrication aggregate. Any consciousness whatsoever—past, present, or future; internal or external; gross or subtle; inferior or superior; near or far—that is the consciousness aggregate.

The monk: What is the cause, what is the condition, for the discernibility (manifesting) of the form aggregate...feeling aggregate...perception aggregate... fabrication aggregate...consciousness aggregate?

The Buddha: The four great existents [the properties of earth, liquid, fire, & wind] are the cause & condition for the discernibility of the form aggregate. Contact is the cause & condition for the discernibility of the feeling...perception...fabrication aggregate. Name-&-form is the cause & condition for the discernibility of the consciousness aggregate.

M.109

§ 200. What do you call 'form' *(rūpa)?* Because it is afflicted *(ruppati)*, thus it is called 'form.' Afflicted with what? With cold & heat & hunger & thirst, with the touch of flies, mosquitoes, wind, sun, & reptiles. Because it is afflicted, it is called form.

What do you call feeling? Because it feels, thus it is called feeling. What does it feel? It feels pleasure, it feels pain, it feels neither-pleasure-nor-pain. Because it feels, it is called feeling.

What do you call perception? Because it perceives, thus it is called perception. What does it perceive? It perceives blue, it perceives yellow, it perceives red, it perceives white. Because it perceives, it is called perception.

What do you call fabrications? Because they fabricate fabricated things, thus they are called fabrications. What do they fabricate into a fabricated thing? From form-ness, they fabricate form into a fabricated thing. From feeling-ness, they fabricate feeling into a fabricated thing. From perception-hood...From fabrication-hood...From consciousness-hood, they fabricate consciousness into a fabricated thing. Because they fabricate fabricated things, they are called fabrications.

What do you call consciousness? Because it cognizes, thus it is called consciousness. What does it cognize? It cognizes what is sour, bitter, pungent, sweet, alkaline, non-alkaline, salty, & unsalty. Because it cognizes, it is called consciousness.

S.XXII.79

§ 201. Maha Koṭṭhita: Feeling, perception, & consciousness: are these qualities conjoined or disjoined? And is it possible, having divided them, to describe their separateness?

Sariputta: Feeling, perception, & consciousness are conjoined, not disjoined, and it is impossible, having divided them, to describe their separateness. What one feels, one perceives; and what one perceives, one cognizes....'

M.43

§ 202. Form. Sariputta: And what, friends, is form as an aggregate of sustenance? The four great existents and the form derived from them. And what are the four great existents? They are the earth property, the liquid property, the fire property, & the wind property.

And what is the earth property? The earth property can be either internal or external. What is the internal earth property? Whatever internal, within oneself, is hard, solid, & sustained [by craving]: head hairs, body hairs, nails, teeth, skin, flesh, tendons, bones, bone marrow, kidneys, heart, liver, pleura, spleen, lungs, large intestines, small intestines, contents of the stomach, feces, or whatever else internal, personal, is hard, solid, & sustained: This is called the internal earth property. Now both the internal earth property and the external earth property are simply earth property. And that should be seen as it actually is present with right discernment: 'This is not mine, this is not me, this is not my self.' When one sees it thus as it actually is present with right discernment, one becomes disenchanted with the earth property and makes the earth property fade from the mind....

And what is the liquid property? The liquid property may be either internal or external. What is the internal liquid property? Whatever internal, belonging to oneself, is liquid, watery, & sustained: bile, phlegm, pus, blood, sweat, fat, tears, skin-oil, saliva, mucus, oil-of-the-joints, urine, or whatever else internal, within oneself, is liquid, watery, & sustained: This is called the internal liquid property. Now both the internal liquid property and the external liquid property are simply liquid property. And that should be seen as it actually is present with right discernment: 'This is not mine, this is not me, this is not my self.' When one sees it thus as it actually is present with right discernment, one becomes disenchanted with the liquid property and makes the liquid property fade from the mind....

And what is the fire property? The fire property may be either internal or external. What is the internal fire property? Whatever internal, belonging to oneself, is fire, fiery, & sustained: that by which [the body] is warmed, aged, & consumed with fever; and that by which what is eaten, drunk, chewed, & savored gets properly digested, or whatever else internal, within oneself, is fire, fiery, & sustained: This is called the internal fire property. Now both the internal fire property and the external fire property are simply fire property. And that should be seen as it actually is present with right discernment: 'This is not mine, this is not me, this is not my self.' When one sees it thus as it actually is present with right discernment, one becomes disenchanted with the fire property and makes the fire property fade from the mind....

And what is the wind property? The wind property may be either internal or external. What is the internal wind property? Whatever internal, belonging to oneself, is wind, windy, & sustained: up-going winds, down-going winds, winds in the stomach, winds in the intestines, winds that course through the body, in-&-out breathing, or whatever else internal, within oneself, is wind, windy, & sustained: This is called the internal wind property. Now both the internal wind property and the external wind property are simply wind property. And that should be seen as it actually is present with right discernment: 'This is not mine, this is not me, this is not my self.' When one sees it thus as it actually is present with right discernment, one becomes disenchanted with the wind property and makes the wind property fade from the mind....

M.28

§ 203. Sariputta: There comes a time, my friends, when the external liquid property is provoked, and at that moment the external earth property vanishes [e.g., in a flood]. And so, in the external earth property—so vast—inconstancy will be discerned, the principle of decay, passing-away, & change will be discerned. So do 'me,' 'mine,' or 'I am' pertain to this body—fleeting & sustained [by craving]? All that pertains there is a 'no'....

There comes a time when the external liquid property is provoked and it carries away village, town & city, country-side & rural area. There comes a time when the waters of the ocean recede one hundred leagues, two hundred... seven hundred leagues. There comes a time when the water in the ocean stands only seven palm trees deep, six... one palm tree deep. There comes a time when the water in the ocean stands only seven fathoms deep, six fathoms...one fathom deep. There comes a time when the water in the ocean stands only half a fathom deep, hip deep, knee deep, ankle deep. There comes a time when the water in the ocean is not enough to wet even the joint of a finger. And so, in the external liquid property—so vast—inconstancy will be discerned, the principle of decay, passing away, & change will be discerned....

There comes a time when the external fire property is provoked and consumes village, town & city, country-side & rural area, and then, coming to the edge of a green district, the edge of a road, the edge of a rocky district, to the water's edge, or to a lush, well-watered area, it goes out from lack of sustenance. There comes a time when people try to make (lit. 'search for') fire even with a wing bone & tendon parings. And so, in the external fire property—so vast—inconstancy will be discerned....

There comes a times a time when the external wind property is provoked, and carries off village, town & city, country-side & rural area. There comes a time when, in the last month of the hot season, they make ('search for') wind with a fan or a bellows, and even the grasses hanging in the drip-fringe of the thatch do not stir. And so, in the external wind property—so vast—inconstancy will be discerned, the principle of decay, passing-away, & change will be discerned. So do 'me,' 'mine,' or 'I am' pertain to this body—fleeting & sustained [by craving]? All that pertains there is a 'no'....

M.28

§ 204. Feeling. Sister Dhammadinnā: There are three kinds of feeling: pleasant feeling, painful feeling, & neither-pleasant-nor-painful feeling....Whatever is experienced physically or mentally as pleasant & gratifying is pleasant feeling. Whatever is experienced physically or mentally as painful & hurting is painful feeling. Whatever is experienced physically or mentally as neither gratifying nor hurting is neither-pleasant-nor-painful feeling....Pleasant feeling is pleasant in remaining and painful in changing. Painful feeling is painful in remaining and pleasant in changing. Neither-pleasant-nor-painful feeling is pleasant when conjoined with knowledge and painful when devoid of knowledge.

M.44

§ 205. Fabrications. And what are fabrications? There are these six classes of intention: intention aimed at sights, sounds, smells, tastes, tactile sensations, & ideas. These are called fabrications.

S.XXII.56

§ 206. Three kinds of fabrications: meritorious fabrications [ripening in pleasure], demeritorious fabrications [ripening in pain], & imperturbable fabrications [the formless states of jhāna].

D.33

§ 207. Consciousness. Consciousness is classified simply by the condition in dependence on which it arises.

When consciousness arises in dependence on eye & forms, it is classified simply as eye-consciousness.
When consciousness arises in dependence on ear & sounds, it is classified simply as ear-consciousness.
When consciousness arises in dependence on nose & smells, it is classified simply as nose-consciousness.
When consciousness arises in dependence on tongue & tastes, it is classified simply as tongue-consciousness.

When consciousness arises in dependence on body & tactile sensations, it is classified simply as body-consciousness.
When consciousness arises in dependence on intellect & ideas, it is classified simply as intellect-consciousness.

Just as fire is classified simply by the condition in dependence on which it burns—a fire burning in dependence on logs is classified simply as a log fire...a fire burning in dependence on rubbish is classified simply as a rubbish fire; in the same way, consciousness is classified simply by the condition in dependence on which it arises.

M.38

iii. The Second & Third Truths

As noted under III/H/i, the third noble truth is identical with the successful performance of the duty appropriate to the second. Thus these two truths are best discussed together.

Passage §210 gives the short definition of the second noble truth:

> Now what is the noble truth of the origination of stress? The craving that makes for further becoming—accompanied by passion & delight, relishing now here & now there—i.e., craving for sensuality, craving for becoming, craving for non-becoming.

Craving for sensuality, here, means the desire for sensual objects. Craving for becoming means the desire for the formation of states or realms of being that are not currently happening, while craving for non-becoming means the desire for the destruction or halting of any that are. "Passion and delight," here, is apparently a synonym for the "desire and passion" for the five aggregates that constitutes clinging/sustenance [III/H/ii].

Passage §210 also gives the short definition of the third noble truth:

> And what is the noble truth of the cessation of stress? The remainderless fading & cessation, renunciation, relinquishment, release, & letting go of that very craving.

The extended passages that make up the remainder of §210 make the point that craving must be brought to cessation right at the objects where it arises, i.e., by realizing that those objects are unworthy of craving.

The longer definitions of the second and third noble truths center on dependent co-arising, a detailed map of how craving arises and how it can be brought to cessation by undercutting its preconditions. This map is the most complex teaching in the Canon. In a famous passage [§231],

Ven. Ananda comments on how clear the doctrine of dependent co-arising seems to him, and the Buddha replies:

> Don't say that, Ananda. Don't say that. Deep is this dependent co-arising, and deep its appearance. It's because of not understanding & not penetrating this Dhamma that this generation is like a tangled skein, a knotted ball of string, like matted rushes & reeds, and does not go beyond the cycle of the planes of deprivation, woe, & bad destinations.

Nevertheless, although no explanations can be expected to give a full and final understanding of the process of dependent co-arising, they can provide tools that the meditator can use to probe the process in the course of training the mind and come to an understanding for him or herself. The passages in this section help to provide that set of tools.

A few general points about dependent co-arising are important to understand before going into the details. To begin with, dependent co-arising is often presented in the texts as an expansion of the general principle of this/that conditionality [§211], which we have already discussed in the Introduction. Here we will recapitulate some of the essential points. This/that conditionality is expressed in a simple formula:

"(1) When this is, that is.
(2) From the arising of this comes the arising of that.
(3) When this isn't, that isn't.
(4) From the stopping of this comes the stopping of that."

This formula is non-linear, an interplay of linear and synchronic principles. The linear principle—taking (2) and (4) as a pair—connects events over time; the synchronic principle—(1) and (3)—connects objects and events in the present moment. The two principles intersect, so that any given event is influenced by two sets of conditions, those acting from the past and those acting from the present. Because this is the pattern underlying dependent co-arising, it is a mistake to view dependent co-arising simply as a chain of causes strung out over time. Events in any one category of the list are affected not only by past events in the categories that act as their conditions, but also by the ongoing, interacting presence of whole streams of events in those categories. All categories can be present at once, and even though two particular conditions may be separated by several steps in the list, they can be immediately present to each other. Thus they can create the possibility for unexpected feedback loops in the causal process. *Feeling,* for instance, keeps reappearing at several stages in the process, and *ignorance* can contribute to any causal link at any time. The importance of these points will become clear when we examine how to disengage the causal network so as to realize the third noble truth.

Because new input into the causal stream is possible at every moment, the actual working out of this/that conditionality and dependent co-arising can be remarkably fluid and complex. This point is borne out by the imagery used in the Canon to illustrate these teachings. Although some non-canonical texts depict dependent co-arising as a circle or a wheel of causes—implying something of a mechanical, deterministic process—the Canon never uses that image at all. Instead it likens dependent co-arising to water flowing over land: lakes overflow, filling rivers, which in turn fill the sea [§238]; while the tides of the sea rise, swelling the rivers, which in turn swell the lakes [S.XII.69]. This imagery captures something of the flow of give and take among the factors of the process. A more modern pattern that might be used to illustrate dependent co-arising is the "strange attractor": an intricate, interwoven pattern that chaos theory uses to describe complex, fluid systems containing at least three feedback loops. As we will see below, the number of feedback loops in dependent co-arising is far more than three.

The fluid complexity of dependent co-arising means that it is inherently unstable, and thus stressful and not-self. Although some non-Theravadin Buddhist texts insist that happiness can be found by abandoning one's smaller, separate identity and embracing the interconnected identity of all interdependent things, this teaching cannot be found in the Pali Canon. The instability of conditioned processes means that they can never provide a dependable basis for happiness. The only true basis for happiness is the Unfabricated. The Pali discourses are quite clear on the point that the fabricated and Unfabricated realms are radically separate. In M.1 the Buddha strongly criticizes a group of monks who tried to develop a theory whereby the fabricated was derived out of the Unfabricated or somehow lay within it. Stress, he says, is inherent in the interdependent nature of conditioned phenomena, while the Unfabricated is totally free from stress. Stress could not possibly be produced by absolute freedom from stress. Because the nature of conditioning is such that causes are in turn influenced by their effects, the Unfabricated could not itself function as a cause for anything. The only way the Unfabricated can be experienced is by using fabricated, conditioned processes (the Wings to Awakening) to unravel the network of fabricated, conditioned processes (dependent co-arising) from within. To do so, one needs to know the individual factors of dependent co-arising and the patterns in which they depend on one another.

These factors come down to the five aggregates. In fact, the entire pattern of dependent co-arising is a map showing how the different aggregates group, disband, and regroup in one another's presence in a variety of configurations, giving rise to stress and to the cosmos at large [§212]. As we have mentioned earlier, one of the most basic features of the Buddha's teachings is his confirmation that the knowable cosmos, composed of old kamma [§15], is made up of the same factors that make up the personality [§213]; and that the interaction of the aggregates, as immediately present to awareness in the here and now, is the same process that underlies the functioning of the knowable cosmos as a whole [§§212-15]. As a result, the descriptions of dependent co-arising slip easily back and forth between two time scales—events in the present moment and events over the vast cycle of time. It is important to remember, though, that the Buddha discovered this principle by observing events in the immediate present, which is where the individual meditator will have to discover them as well. Thus the practice takes the same approach as phenomenology: exploring the processes of conditioning from the inside as they are immediately experienced in the present moment. This is why the pattern of dependent co-arising lists factors of consciousness—such as ignorance, attention, and intention—as prior conditions for the experience of the physical world, for if we take as our frame of reference the world as it is directly experienced—rather than a world conceived somehow as separate from our experience of it—we have to see the processes of the mind as prior to the objects they process. References in the texts to the larger frame of space and time provide examples to illustrate particularly subtle points in the immediate present and serve as reminders that the pattern of events observed in the present moment has implications that cover the entire cosmos.

Given the fluid, complex nature of the basic causal principle, it should come as no surprise that the Canon contains several variations on the list of basic factors and configurations in dependent co-arising. Like the seven sets in the Wings to Awakening, these different lists offer the meditator a variety of ways to approach the complexities of the causal stream and to gain a handle on mastering them. The most basic list is found in §228 and §231, which give the factors—starting with the stress of aging and death, and then working backwards—as follows:

Aging and death require birth (i.e., rebirth). If there were no birth, there would be nothing to set in motion the processes of aging and death. Here and in the following causal links, "birth," "aging," and "death" denote not only the arising, decay, and passing away of the body, but also the repeated arising, decay, and passing away of mental states, moment-by-moment in the present. In fact, during the third watch on the night of his Awakening, the Buddha probably focused on present mental states as his primary examples of birth, aging, and death. From them he gained insight into how these processes functioned in the cosmos as a whole.

Birth depends on becoming. If there were no coming-into-being of a sensual realm, a realm of form, or a formless realm, there would be no locus for rebirth. Again, these realms refer not only to levels of being on the cosmic scale, but also to levels of mental states. Some mental states are concerned with sensual images, others with forms (such as form jhana), and still others with formless abstractions, such as the formless jhanas. The relationship between birth and becoming can be compared to the process of falling asleep and dreaming. As drowsiness makes the mind lose contact with waking reality, a dream image of another place and time will appear in it. The appearance of this image is called becoming. The act of entering into this image and taking on a role or identity within it—and thus entering the world of the dream and falling asleep—is birth. The commentaries maintain that precisely the same process is what enables rebirth to follow the death of the body. At the same time, the analogy between falling asleep and taking birth explains why release from the cycle of becoming is called Awakening.

Becoming requires clinging/sustenance. The image here is of a fire staying in existence by appropriating sustenance in the act of clinging to its fuel. The process of becoming takes its sustenance from the five aggregates, while the act of taking sustenance is to cling to these aggregates in any of four forms of passion and delight mentioned in III/H/ii: sensual intentions, views, precepts and practices, or theories about the self. Without these forms of clinging, the realms of sensuality, form, and formlessness would not come into being.

Sustenance requires craving. If one did not thirst (the literal meaning of *tanha,* or craving) for sensuality, for becoming, or for non-becoming, then the process would not appropriate fuel.

Craving requires feeling. If there were no experience of pleasant, painful, or neither-pleasant-nor-painful feelings, one would not thirst for continuing experience of the pleasant or for cessation of the unpleasant.

Feeling requires contact. Without contact there would be no feelings of pleasure, pain, or neither-pleasure-nor-pain.

Contact requires name-and-form. "Form" covers all physical phenomena. "Name" here is defined as feeling, perception, contact, attention, and intention. Without these phenomena, there would be nothing to make contact.

Name-and-form requires consciousness of the six sense fields. Without this kind of consciousness, the physical birth of the individual composed of the aggregates would abort, while on the level of momentary mental birth there would be nothing to activate an experience of the aggregates.

Consciousness of the six sense fields requires name-and-form. Without name-and-form, there would be no object for this type of consciousness.

In §228, Ven. Sariputta points out that the entire process of dependent co-arising relies on the mutual dependency of name-and-form on the one hand, and sensory consciousness on the other. This mutual dependency is actually composed of many feedback loops, which can get quite complex. If either of the two factors is pulled away from the other, the whole edifice falls down. For this reason, as we shall see when we discuss the cessation of stress, this mutual dependency is one of the primary points for focusing attention in disbanding the causal process.

Other lists of the factors in dependent co-arising expand on this basic list. The most common list adds the factors of the six sense fields between contact and name-and-form, and then states that *sensory consciousness requires the three types of fabrication*—bodily, verbal, and mental—while *these fabrications in turn require ignorance* of the four noble truths [§§211, 218]. There is some disagreement over the meaning of the three types of fabrication in this list. One passage in the Canon [§223], which seems to treat fabrications as they are immediately experienced in the present, defines bodily fabrication as the breath, verbal fabrication as directed thought and evaluation, and mental fabrication as feeling and perception. Other passages [such as §225], which seem to regard fabrications as they function over time, simply class these three types of fabrication as to whether they are meritorious, demeritorious, or imperturbable (i.e., pertaining to the four levels of formless jhana). If we regard these two definitions as typical of the dual time frame of dependent co-arising, there is no conflict between them.

Another point of disagreement is over the question of how the factors of fabrication and ignorance came to be added to the basic list. Some scholars maintain that this was the result of a temporal development in the Buddha's teachings, either during his lifetime or after his passing away. However, if we examine the content of the added factors, we find that they are simply an elaboration of the mutual dependence between name-and-form and sensory consciousness, and do not add anything substantially new to the list. The three fabrications are simply another way of presenting name-and-form in their active role as shapers of consciousness. Bodily fabrication, the breath, is the active element of "form"; verbal fabrications, directed thought and evaluation, are the active element in the attention and intention sub-factors of "name"; while mental fabrications, feeling and perception, are identical with the feeling and perception under "name." Ignorance, on the other hand, is the type of consciousness that actively promotes inappropriate questioning in the verbal fabrication of evaluation, which in turn can lead to inappropriate attention in the factor of name-and-form.

It may seem redundant to have the factors of name-and-form on the one hand, and fabrications on the other, covering the same territory in two different configurations, but these configurations serve at least two practical purposes. First, the connection between ignorance and inappropriate questioning helps to pinpoint precisely what is wrong in the typical relationship between name-and-form and consciousness. As one modern teacher has put it, the verbal fabrications are the ones to watch out for. Second, the relationship between verbal fabrications on the one hand, and attention and intention on the other, mediated by consciousness, diagrams the double-tiered (and sometimes multi-tiered) relationships among mental events as they breed and feed on one another in the presence of consciousness. In the course of giving rise to suffering and stress, this incestuous interbreeding can fly out of hand, leading to many complex and intense patterns of suffering. However, its double-tiered quality can also be used—as we will see below—to help bring that suffering to an end.

Passage §227 adds yet another factor to the list, pointing out another way of looking at the mutually dependent relationships that feed the process of dependent co-arising: *ignorance requires the effluents (asava)* of sensuality, becoming, views, and ignorance, while *these effluents in turn require ignorance* of the four noble truths. These added factors point to one of the ways in which the process of dependent co-arising is self-sustaining. Sensuality and views are forms of clinging/sustenance, while becoming is a result of clinging/sustenance. Ignorance as an effluent is nowhere defined in the discourses to differentiate it from simple ignorance, and in fact the distinction may simply be one of role, with both forms of ignorance denoting a state of awareness out of touch with the four noble truths. When ignorance is entwined with the feelings that result from contact, it forms the requisite condition for clinging/sustenance and becoming; together, all of these factors act as impulses that "flow out" of the process and then return to reinforce the ignorance that provides the requisite condition for fabrications, consciousness, and name-and-form, thus fueling another round in the process leading to further becoming and stress.

The self-sustaining nature of dependent co-arising makes it easy to see why many non-canonical texts explain it as a wheel. However, the many openings for feedback loops among the various factors—creating smaller cycles within the larger cycle—make the process exceedingly complex. This explains why stress and suffering are so bewildering. If they were a simple cycle, there would be little or no variety to the sufferings of living beings, and the process of suffering would be easy for everyone to predict and understand.

Some of the feedback loops that make stress so complex are explicitly mentioned in the texts [§227-28]. Others are implicit in the fact that particular factors—such as feeling and contact—keep re-appearing at different points of the process of dependent co-arising. Feeling is perhaps the most important of these. The stress that forms the final factor of dependent co-arising counts as a feeling, which can then re-enter the causal stream at the factor of fabrications (as a mental fabrication), name-and-form (as an instance of name), or at feeling itself. If it re-enters at feeling, it would then directly condition further craving, which in turn would create a positive feedback loop, leading to increased stress and pain. On the other hand, if the stress re-enters the stream at name-and-form, it could be subjected either to unskillful intentions and inappropriate attention, or to skillful intentions and appropriate attention. The former pair would simply aggravate the stress and pain, whereas the latter pair would weaken the tendency to craving, and thus act as a negative feedback loop, alleviating the conditions that would lead to further stress and pain or eliminating them altogether.

This shows that these feedback loops, instead of being a mere curiosity in the formal structure of dependent co-arising, actually help to explain the wide variations in the way living beings experience stress. They also help explain the possibility of the cessation of stress. The elements of contact, intention, and attention under the factor of "name" are especially important in opening up this latter possibility. As we noted in I/A, this is the factor of dependent co-arising that intersects with the teachings on kamma and skillfulness. Contact—here, apparently, meaning contact with consciousness—forms the precondition for kamma [§9]. Intention lies at the essence of the kamma that keeps the cycle of rebirth in motion. Through appropriate attention—the right way of looking at things and focusing on appropriate questions about them—kamma can be trained to be skillful and thus lead away from stress rather than toward it. For this reason, any feedback loop that does not pass through the factor of name-and-form will tend simply to continue the problem of stress and pain, whereas any loop that does lead through this factor allows for the possibility for using appropriate attention to weaken the process or disband it entirely.

In feeding the loops of dependent co-arising through the factor of name-and-form, the factor of fabrication plays an especially important role. As we have noted in III/E, the practice of jhana focused on the breath gathers all three forms of fabrication—bodily, verbal, and mental—into a single whole. In doing so, it takes all the aggregates that play a variety of roles in the pattern of dependent co-arising, and gathers them into a configuration where appropriate attention can conveniently focus on all their interactions at once. To express this in terms of the four noble truths, it takes the aggregates that make up the first noble truth and gives them a role in the fourth [III/H/i]. In this way, the double-tiered relationship mentioned above—between name-and-form on the one hand, and fabrications on the other—can be put to use in disbanding, rather than compounding, the causal network leading to suffering and stress. In terms of meditation practice, this double-tiered relationship corresponds to the five factors of noble right concentration [§150]. The three types of fabrication cover the same ground as the four levels of jhana, while the sub-factor of attention under "name" forms a separate tier of mental activity that allows one to monitor one's practice of jhana and to develop it as a skill [II/G].

As the process of developing skill becomes more and more refined, this tier of attention turns into the fifth, reflective level of noble concentration that allows one to analyze the state of jhana while it is present, and thus to develop a sharpened discernment of its fabricated nature. As passage §172 shows, one begins to see that jhana is composed not only of such "fabrication" sub-factors as directed thought, evaluation, feeling, and perception, but also of sensory consciousness and such "name" factors as attention, intention, and contact. In other words, the boundary line between the different tiers of mental activity begins to break down. This allows for the conflation of discernment and concentration noted in II/H and III/H, in which concentrated discernment begins to take its own workings as its object. As discernment in the role of "object" short-circuits with discernment in the role of "approach" [II/B], then contact between the factors of name-and-form on the one hand, and sensory consciousness on the other, ceases in a state of clear knowing. In the image of Ven. Sariputta [§228], one of the two sheaves of reeds is pulled away, and the entire edifice of suffering based on them comes tumbling down.

Another crucial point to note in understanding how to disband the workings of dependent co-arising is that the relationships between particular factors and their neighbors in the list are not all the same. In some cases, factor *x* is a *sufficient* cause for factor *y*. What this means is that whenever *x* occurs, *y* will always have to follow. An example is the relationship between contact and feeling, or between clinging and the remaining factors leading up to stress. Whenever there is contact in the presence of consciousness, there will have to be feeling. Whenever there is clinging, there will have to be becoming and stress. Thus it is impossible to cut the process at these links. However, there are other cases where *x* is a *necessary* cause, but not a sufficient one, for *y*. In other words, *x* has to be present for *y* to occur, but *y* does not have to follow every time there is *x*. Examples would include the link between consciousness and name-and-form, between feeling and craving, and between craving and clinging. In each of these cases there has to be an added factor—the presence of ignorance, the most subtle and basic of the roots of unskillfulness—for *x* to give rise to *y*.

This fact is what opens the way for appropriate attention to bring about the end of suffering and stress. At the same time it determines precisely what that way must be. An analysis of how this happens will reveal in a nutshell the convergence of many of the themes of this book: the role of the three levels of frames-of-reference practice [II/B], and by extension the three levels in the development of concentration [III/E] and discernment [III/H]; the way in which the principles of this/that conditionality and skillfulness [I/A] apply to the practice; and the way in which the duties appropriate to the four noble truths—comprehending stress, abandoning its origination, realizing its cessation, and developing the path [III/H/i]—in practice are one.

The nutshell is this: If each factor in dependent co-arising were a sufficient cause for the following factor, the pattern would be absolutely deterministic and there would be no way out. However, in cases where the link between *x* and *y* is necessary but not sufficient, then in terms of this/that conditionality, the *x* factor is input from the past—even if only a split-second past—whereas ignorance is the input from the present needed to give rise to *y*. Thus the strategy of the practice must be to use appropriate attention to eliminate ignorance in the presence of *x*. To do this, one must focus on comprehending the aggregate that functions as *x*—or, in the case of the craving/clinging link, that functions as the potential object of *x*. At first this means learning to focus on the aggregate in and of itself. Then, to overcome the unskillfulness inherent in ignorance, one must gain practical familiarity with the aggregate in its role as a factor in the skillful practice of jhana [§173]. As this approach attains a state of mastery, one turns one's powers of discernment on the "how" of the approach to the practice, taking it as the "what" or object of investigation, until one can see the aggregate even in this role in terms of the four noble truths [III/H/i]. The more precise and comprehensive this knowing, the less craving is produced; the less craving produced, the fewer the effluents that cloud one's knowing. With the culmination of totally clear knowing, ignorance is totally wiped out, together with its attendant craving, and thus the present input that maintained the cycle is ended. This forms the point of non-fashioning at which the cycle breaks down, and where stress and suffering cease.

Modern practice traditions differ as to which links in dependent co-arising they focus on in order to bring about the cessation of craving and thus realize the third noble truth. For the purposes of this essay, we will discuss three of these links as they relate to the three different lists of factors mentioned above. These different points of focus are best regarded as alternative options for tackling the problem of stress and its cessation. All are equally valid, and so it is up to the individual meditator to choose whichever focus seems most congenial and comprehensible, and to follow it through.

The first list of the factors of dependent co-arising, which takes the process down to the mutual dependence of consciousness and name-and-form, emphasizes precisely that link: how name-and-form depends on consciousness, and how consciousness relates to name-and-form. Passage §233 treats this point in detail, using the term "fabrication" to cover attention, intention, and contact. In practical terms this approach focuses on the question of how consciousness relates to its objects, making use of skillful intention and appropriate attention (in terms of the four noble truths) as the approach to help peel away any sense of passion or desire for name-and-form. Once the more blatant forms of passion and desire have been eliminated, this approach then peels away passion and desire even for the approach of skillful intentions and appropriate attention themselves. Consciousness—thus deprived of its support in name-and-form either in terms of objects or approaches [II/B]—has no basis for proliferation and so is released. Passages related to this perspective on Awakening include §§233, 234, and 239.

As for the second list, which traces the pattern of dependent co-arising down to fabrication and ignorance, we have already noted that this is simply an explanation of a particular type of relationship between consciousness and name-and-form. We have also noted [III/E] that all three types of fabrication, in their present aspect, are brought together in the experience of jhana based on the breath. Thus the question here is how to master jhana to the point where one can step back in the fifth factor of five-factored noble concentration [§150] so as to overcomes one's ignorance of the willed and fabricated nature of jhana or of any views and assumptions—based on inappropriate attention—that might underlie the attainment of jhana [§237]. With the cessation of ignorance, there is nothing willed or fabricated to form a station of consciousness. At this point of non-fashioning—where there is no sense of one's doing anything, or of anyone else's doing anything [§229]—nothing is created for the sake of further becoming or non-becoming. As a result, consciousness is released. Passages related to this perspective on Awakening include §§225-26.

In the third list of dependent co-arising, which traces the pattern to the mutual dependence of ignorance and the effluents, the focus is on the acts of clinging/sustenance and the resultant states of becoming that, conditioned by ignorance, breed more ignorance. The difficulty in focusing on becoming is that its apparent opposite, non-becoming—the suppression or prevention of the change inherent in becoming—can also act as an object of craving leading to further becoming [§221-22]. Thus the question is how to focus on the drawbacks of sensuality and becoming without falling into the reverse trap of willing non-becoming. As §182 shows, this requires seeing the drawbacks of all willed states, regardless of whether the will is aimed at fostering change or preventing it. Once the mind has abandoned all such states, the only alternative left open is the equipoise of non-fashioning, the threshold to the Unfabricated. Passages related to this perspective on Awakening include §§221-22.

Although these three points of focus differ in emphasis, in essence they come down to different aspects of the same approach. In every case, one must use skillful intentions and appropriate attention to undercut craving and ignorance regarding the five aggregates so that no fabrications will be activated for the sake of further becoming. This lack of activation—the moment of non-fashioning—releases consciousness from the aggregates, both in their role as objects of consciousness and in their role as the intention and attention that served as the approaches to release. The differences among the points of focus lie primarily in the questions they ask in framing a view of the problem at hand. In this we see the true function of the teaching of dependent co-arising in practice: as a guide to appropriate attention. Not only does the teaching provide a direct way of viewing experience that avoids useless questions of being and non-being [§186], self and other [§228-230], it also gives a framework for inspiring alternative ways of asking appropriate questions about the crucial junctures in the conditioned flow of phenomena in and of themselves. As with all of the Buddha's teachings, once the processes of discernment inspired by the teaching of dependent co-arising have fully performed their function, the teaching itself is transcended in the release of consciousness.

Once consciousness is released from the objects that bring sensory consciousness into play [§232], all that remains is "consciousness without feature, without end, luminous all around" [§235]. This consciousness—which lies beyond "the extent to which there are means of designation, expression, & description...the extent to which the sphere of discernment extends, the extent to which the cycle revolves for the manifesting (discernibility) of this cosmos" [§231]—is the experience of the goal. There is some question as to whether the goal can be equated with the third noble truth. Some passages in the Canon [S.XLIII.1-44; S.XXII.86] would seem to indicate yes; others [such as Sn.V.6; MFU, p. 28; and especially the ending to M.27], no. This contradiction can be resolved by noting that the full realization of the third noble truth and the experience of the goal are two different things so intimately related that the one can not be experienced without the other. Their relationship can be compared to noticing a long-overlooked valuable in the course of cleaning one's yard. The act of cleaning is not the same as the valuable, but only in the course of doing the former thoroughly and attentively can the latter be found. As one modern teacher has said, the fact that the third noble truth involves a duty means that it is part of fabricated reality, whereas the goal at the end of the path is absolutely unfabricated. Free from all acting and doing, it pertains to an entirely different dimension, and thus—although found in the same spot as the truth of cessation—it is something utterly beyond and unbound.

From the time of Awakening to that of death, there remains a sense of dissociated contact between the inner and outer sense media that comprise the Awakened One's old kamma [§15] and his/her only remaining experience of the stress inherent in the dimensions of time and the present: contact, in that there is sensitivity to pain and pleasure in these things; dissociated, in that the passion and delight, the fetters, defilements, and attachments in between the inner and outer sense media are totally severed by discernment [M.146; MFU, p. 113]. Old kamma thus runs through the pattern of dependent co-arising from name-and-form and consciousness up through feeling, but—without the fashioning factors of ignorance and craving—the feeling of pain and pleasure does not feed back into any causal patterns that would lead to further becoming [§219] or any renewed kamma. The texts liken this state to a fire that has gone out, but whose embers are still glowing and warm [Thag.XV.2; MFU, p. 34]. Eventually, old kamma runs out at the death of the Awakened One, and there is a total Unbinding like that of a fire so completely released from its fuel that the embers have grown thoroughly cold. Although this analogy may sound negative in terms of modern ideas about the workings of fire, in the Buddha's time it was recognized as an image, not of extinction or annihilation, but of freedom so unlimited and irreversible that it cannot be described.

§ 208. If its root remains
undamaged & strong,
a tree, even if cut,
will grow again.
So too if latent craving
is not rooted out,
this suffering returns

again
&
again.

DHP.338

§ 209. Gandhabhaka: It would be good, lord, if the Blessed One would teach me the origination & ending of stress.

The Buddha: If I were to teach you the origination & ending of stress with reference to the past, saying, 'Thus it was in the past,' you would be doubtful and perplexed. If I were to teach you the origination & ending of stress with reference to the future, saying, 'Thus it will be in the future,' you would be doubtful and perplexed. So instead, I—sitting right here—will teach you sitting right there the origination & ending of stress. Listen & pay close attention. I will speak."

Gandhabhaka: As you say, lord.

The Buddha: Now what do you think: Are there any people in Uruvelakappa who, if they were murdered or imprisoned or fined or censured, would cause sorrow, lamentation, pain, distress, or despair to arise in you?

Gandhabhaka: Yes, there are....

The Buddha: And are there any people in Uruvelakappa who, if they were murdered or imprisoned or fined or censured, would cause no sorrow, lamentation, pain, distress, or despair to arise in you?

Gandhabhaka: Yes, there are....

The Buddha: Now what is the cause, what is the reason, why the murder...of some would cause you sorrow...and the murder...of others would cause you no sorrow...?

Gandhabhaka: Those...whose murder...would cause me sorrow...are those for whom I feel desire & passion. Those...whose murder...would cause me no sorrow...are those for whom I feel no desire or passion.

The Buddha: Now, from what you have realized, attained, plunged into right now in the present, without regard to time, you may draw an inference with regard to the past and future: Whatever stress, in arising, arose for me in the past, all of it had desire as its root, had desire as its cause. Thus desire is the cause of stress. And whatever stress, in arising, will arise for me in the future, all of it will have desire as the root, will have desire as its cause. Thus desire is the cause of stress.

Gandhabhaka: Amazing, lord. Stupendous. How well the Blessed One has put it: Whatever stress, in arising, arose for me in the past, all of it had desire as its root, had desire as its cause. Thus desire is the cause of stress. And whatever stress, in arising, will arise for me in the future, all of it will have desire as the root, will have desire as its cause. Thus desire is the cause of stress. I have a son, lord, named Ciravasi, who lives far away from here. When I get up in the morning, I send a man, saying, 'Go, learn how Ciravāsi is doing.' And as long as that man has not returned, I am simply beside myself, [thinking], 'Don't let Ciravāsi be sick!'

The Buddha: Now, what do you think: If Ciravāsi were to be murdered or imprisoned or fined or censured, would you feel sorrow, lamentation, pain, distress, & despair?

Gandhabhaka: If my son Ciravāsi were to be murdered or imprisoned or fined or censured, my very life would be altered. So how could I not feel sorrow, lamentation, pain, distress, & despair?

The Buddha: ...And what do you think: Before you had seen or heard of Ciravāsi's mother, did you feel desire, passion, or love for her?

Gandhabhaka: No, lord.

The Buddha: And after you had seen or heard of Ciravāsi's mother, did you feel desire, passion, or love for her?

Gandhabhaka: Yes, lord.

The Buddha: Now, what do you think: If Ciravāsi's mother were to be murdered or imprisoned or fined or censured, would you feel sorrow, lamentation, pain, distress, & despair?

Gandhabhaka: If Ciravasi's mother were to be murdered or imprisoned or fined or censured, my very life would be altered. So how could I not feel sorrow, lamentation, pain, distress, & despair?

The Buddha: Thus by this line of reasoning it may be realized how stress, when arising, arises: All of it has desire as its root, has desire as its cause. Thus desire is the cause of stress.

S.XLII.11

§ 210. Craving & Its Cessation. Now what is the noble truth of the origination of stress? The craving that makes for further becoming—accompanied by passion & delight, relishing now here & now there—i.e., craving for sensuality, craving for becoming, craving for non-becoming.

And where does this craving, when arising, arise? And where, when dwelling, does it dwell? Whatever is endearing & alluring in terms of the world: that is where this craving, when arising, arises. That is where, when dwelling, it dwells.

And what is endearing & alluring in terms of the world? The eye is endearing & alluring in terms of the world. That is where this craving, when arising, arises. That is where, when dwelling, it dwells.

The ear....The nose....The tongue....The body....The intellect....Forms.... Sounds....Smells....Tastes....Tactile sensations....Ideas....

Eye-consciousness....Ear-consciousness....Nose-consciousness.... Tongue-consciousness....Body-consciousness.... Intellect-consciousness....

Eye-contact....Ear-contact....Nose-contact....Tongue-contact....Body-contact.... Intellect-contact....

Feeling born of eye-contact....Feeling born of ear-contact....Feeling born of nose-contact....Feeling born of tongue-contact....Feeling born of body-contact.... Feeling born of intellect-contact....

Perception of forms....Perception of sounds....Perception of smells.... Perception of tastes....Perception of tactile sensations....Perception of ideas....

Intention for forms....Intention for sounds....Intention for smells.... Intention for tastes....Intention for tactile sensations....Intention for ideas....

Craving for forms....Craving for sounds....Craving for smells.... Craving for tastes....Craving for tactile sensations....Craving for ideas....

Thought directed at forms....Thought directed at sounds....Thought directed at smells....Thought directed at tastes....Thought directed at tactile sensations....Thought directed at ideas....

Evaluation of forms....Evaluation of sounds....Evaluation of smells.... Evaluation of tastes....Evaluation of tactile sensations....Evaluation of ideas is endearing & alluring in terms of the world. That is where this craving, when arising, arises. That is where, when dwelling, it dwells.

This is called the noble truth of the origination of stress.

And what is the noble truth of the cessation of stress? The remainderless fading & cessation, renunciation, relinquishment, release, & letting go of that very craving.

And where, when being abandoned, is this craving abandoned? And where, when ceasing, does it cease? Whatever is endearing & alluring in terms of the world: that is where, when being abandoned, this craving is abandoned. That is where, when ceasing, it ceases.

And what is endearing & alluring in terms of the world? The eye is endearing & alluring in terms of the world. That is where, when being abandoned, this craving is abandoned. That is where, when ceasing, it ceases.

The ear....The nose....The tongue....The body....The intellect....Forms.... Sounds....Smells....Tastes....Tactile sensations....Ideas....

Eye-consciousness....Ear-consciousness....Nose-consciousness.... Tongue-consciousness....Body-consciousness.... Intellect-consciousness....

Eye-contact....Ear-contact....Nose-contact....Tongue-contact....Body-contact.... Intellect-contact....

Feeling born of eye-contact....Feeling born of ear-contact....Feeling born of nose-contact....Feeling born of tongue-contact....Feeling born of body-contact.... Feeling born of intellect-contact....

Perception of forms....Perception of sounds....Perception of smells.... Perception of tastes....Perception of tactile sensations....Perception of ideas....

Intention for forms....Intention for sounds....Intention for smells.... Intention for tastes....Intention for tactile sensations....Intention for ideas....

Craving for forms....Craving for sounds....Craving for smells.... Craving for tastes....Craving for tactile sensations....Craving for ideas....

Thought directed at forms....Thought directed at sounds....Thought directed at smells....Thought directed at tastes....Thought directed at tactile sensations....Thought directed at ideas....

Evaluation of forms....Evaluation of sounds....Evaluation of smells.... Evaluation of tastes....Evaluation of tactile sensations....Evaluation of ideas is endearing & alluring in terms of the world. That is where, when being abandoned, this craving is abandoned. That is where, when ceasing, it ceases.

This is called the noble truth of the cessation of stress.

D.22

§ 211. And what is the noble method that is rightly seen & rightly ferreted out by discernment? There is the case where a noble disciple notices:

> *When this is, that is.*
> *From the arising of this comes the arising of that.*
> *When this isn't, that isn't.*
> *From the cessation of this comes the cessation of that.*

In other words:

From ignorance as a requisite condition come fabrications.
From fabrications as a requisite condition comes consciousness.
From consciousness as a requisite condition comes name-&-form.
From name & form as a requisite condition come the six sense media.
From the six sense media as a requisite condition comes contact.
From contact as a requisite condition comes feeling.
From feeling as a requisite condition comes craving.
From craving as a requisite condition comes clinging/sustenance.
From clinging/sustenance as a requisite condition comes becoming.

From becoming as a requisite condition comes birth.
From birth as a requisite condition, then old age & death, sorrow, lamentation, pain, distress, & despair come into play. Such is the origination of this entire mass of stress & suffering.

Now from the remainderless fading & cessation of that very ignorance comes the cessation of fabrications. From the cessation of fabrications comes the cessation of consciousness. From the cessation of consciousness comes the cessation of name-&-form. From the cessation of name & form comes the cessation of the six sense media. From the cessation of the six sense media comes the cessation of contact. From the cessation of contact comes the cessation of feeling. From the cessation of feeling comes the cessation of craving. From the cessation of craving comes the cessation of clinging/ sustenance. From the cessation of clinging/sustenance comes the cessation of becoming. From the cessation of becoming comes the cessation of birth. From the cessation of birth, then old age & death, sorrow, lamentation, pain, distress, & despair all cease. Such is the cessation of this entire mass of stress & suffering.

This is the noble method that is rightly seen & rightly ferreted out by discernment.

A.X.92

§ 212. Monks, I will teach you the origination & disappearance of the world. Listen & pay close attention. I will speak.

What is the origination of the world? In dependence on the eye & forms there arises eye consciousness. The coming together of these three is contact. From contact as a requisite condition comes feeling. From feeling as a requisite condition comes craving. From craving as a requisite condition comes clinging/sustenance. From clinging/ sustenance as a requisite condition comes becoming. From becoming as a requisite condition comes birth. From birth as a requisite condition, then aging & death, sorrow, lamentation, pain, distress, & despair come into play. This is the origination of the world. (Similarly with ear, nose, tongue, body, & intellect.)

And what is the disappearance of the world? In dependence on the eye & forms there arises eye consciousness. The coming together of these three is contact. From contact as a requisite condition comes feeling. From feeling as a requisite condition comes craving. Now from the remainderless fading & cessation of that very craving comes the cessation of clinging/ sustenance. From the cessation of clinging/sustenance comes the cessation of becoming. From the cessation of becoming comes the cessation of birth. From the cessation of birth, then aging & death, sorrow, lamentation, pain, distress, &

despair all cease. Such is the cessation of this entire mass of stress & suffering. This is the disappearance of the world. (Similarly with ear, nose, tongue, body, & intellect.)

S.XXXV.107

§ 213. A certain monk: The world, the world *(loko)*, it is said. To what extent does the word 'world' apply?

The Buddha: It disintegrates *(lujjati)*, therefore it is called the 'world.' Now what disintegrates? The eye disintegrates. Forms disintegrate. Eye consciousness disintegrates. Eye contact disintegrates. And whatever there is that arises in dependence on eye contact, experienced as pleasure, pain or neither-pleasure-nor-pain, that too disintegrates.

The ear disintegrates. Sounds disintegrate....
The nose disintegrates. Smells disintegrate....
The tongue disintegrates. Tastes disintegrate....
The body disintegrates. Tactile sensations disintegrate....

The intellect disintegrates. Ideas disintegrate. Intellect consciousness disintegrates. Intellect contact disintegrates. And whatever there is that arises in dependence on intellect contact, experienced as pleasure, pain or neither-pleasure-nor-pain, that too disintegrates.

It disintegrates, therefore it is called the 'world.'

S.XXXV.82

§ 214. Ananda: Concerning the brief statement made by the Blessed One, after which he entered his dwelling without expounding the detailed meaning—i.e., 'I do not say that the end of the world is to be known, seen, & reached by traveling. But neither do I say that there is a making an end of stress without having reached the end of the world'—I understand the detailed meaning of this statement to be this:

That by means of which one has a perception of world, a concept of world with regard to the world: that, in the discipline of a noble one, is called the 'world.' Now, by means of what does one have a perception of world, a concept of world with regard to the world?
By means of the eye...the ear...the nose...the tongue...the body...the intellect one has a perception of world, a concept of world with regard to the world.

S.XXXV.116

§ 215. Now what, monks, are the 44 bases for knowledge?
Knowledge with regard to aging & death, knowledge with regard to the origination of aging & death, knowledge with regard to the cessation of aging & death, knowledge with regard to the path of

practice leading to the cessation of aging & death. (Similarly with birth, becoming, sustenance/clinging, craving, feeling, contact, the sixfold sense media, name-&-form, consciousness, & fabrications.)

And what is aging & death? Whatever aging, decrepitude, brokenness, graying, wrinkling, decline of life-force, weakening of the faculties of the various beings in this or that group of beings, that is called aging. Whatever deceasing, passing away, breaking up, disappearance, dying, death, completion of time, break up of the aggregates, casting off of the body, interruption in the life faculty of the various beings in this or that group of beings, that is called death. From the origination of birth comes the origination of aging & death. From the cessation of birth comes the cessation of aging & death. And just this noble eightfold path is the path of practice leading to the cessation of aging & death....

Now when the noble disciple discerns aging & death in this way, discerns the origination of aging & death in this way, discerns the cessation of aging & death in this way, discerns the path of practice leading to the cessation of aging & death in this way, that is his knowledge of the Dhamma (principle). By means of this principle—seen, understood, not limited to time, attained, plunged into—he draws out inferences with regard to the past & future: 'Whatever priests & contemplatives in the past comprehended aging & death... the origination of aging & death...the cessation of aging & death...the path of practice leading to the cessation of aging & death, all comprehended them as I do now; whatever priests & contemplatives in the future will comprehend aging & death...the origination of aging & death...the cessation of aging & death...the path of practice leading to the cessation of aging & death, all will comprehend them as I do now.' This is his knowledge of consistency.

Now, when these two knowledges of the noble disciple—knowledge of principle & knowledge of consistency—are pure & clear, he is called a noble disciple, consummate in view, consummate in vision, attained to this true Dhamma. He is said to see this true Dhamma, to be endowed with the knowledge of one in training, endowed with the clear knowing of one in training, attained to the stream of the Dhamma, a person of penetrating noble discernment who stands knocking at the door to the Deathless.

(Similarly with the remaining links down to fabrications.)

S.XII.33

§ 216. Sariputta: Now, the Blessed One has said, 'Whoever sees dependent co-arising sees the Dhamma; whoever sees the Dhamma sees dependent co-arising.'

M.28

§ 217. I will teach you dependent co-arising & dependently co-arisen phenomena. Listen & pay close attention. I will speak....

Now what is dependent co-arising? From birth as a requisite condition comes aging & death. Whether or not there is the arising of Tathagatas, this property stands—this regularity of the Dhamma, this orderliness of the Dhamma, this this/that conditionality. The Tathagata directly awakens to that, breaks through to that. Directly awakening & breaking through to that, he declares it, teaches it, describes it, sets it forth. He reveals it, explains it, makes it plain, & says, 'Look.' From birth as a requisite condition comes aging & death.

(Similarly down through the causal stream to:)

From ignorance as a requisite condition come fabrications. Whether or not there is the arising of Tathāgatas, this property stands—this regularity of the Dhamma, this orderliness of the Dhamma, this this/that conditionality. The Tathāgata directly awakens to that, breaks through to that. Directly awakening & breaking through to that, he declares it, teaches it, describes it, sets it forth. He reveals it, explains it, makes it plain, & says, 'Look.' From ignorance as a requisite condition come fabrications. What's there in this way is a reality, not an unreality, not other than what it seems, conditioned by this/that. This is called dependent co-arising.

And what are dependently co-arisen phenomena? Aging & death are dependently co-arisen phenomena: inconstant, compounded, dependently co-arisen, subject to ending, subject to passing away, subject to fading, subject to cessation. (Similarly down through the causal stream to:)

Ignorance is a dependently co-arisen phenomenon: inconstant, compounded, dependently co-arisen, subject to ending, subject to passing away, subject to fading, subject to cessation. These are called dependently co-arisen phenomena.

When a noble disciple has seen well with right discernment this dependent co-arising & these dependently co-arisen phenomena as they are actually present, it is not possible that he would run after the past, thinking, 'Was I in the past? Was I not in the past? What was I in the past? How was I in the past? Having been what, what was I in the past?' or that he would run after the future, thinking, 'Shall I be in the future? Shall I not be in the future? What shall I be in the future? How shall I be in the future? Having been what, what shall I be in the future?' or that he would be inwardly perplexed about the immediate present, thinking, 'Am I? Am I not? What am I? How am I? Where has this being come from? Where is it bound?' [§51]

Such a thing is not possible. Why is that? Because the noble disciple has seen well with right discernment this dependent co-arising & these dependently co-arisen phenomena as they are actually present.

S.XII.20

§ 218. Now what is *becoming?* These three are becomings: sensual becoming, form becoming, & formless becoming. This is called becoming.

And what is *clinging/sustenance?* These four are clingings: sensuality clinging, view clinging, precept & practice clinging, and doctrine of self clinging. This is called clinging.

And what is *craving?* These six are classes of craving: craving for forms, craving for sounds, craving for smells, craving for tastes, craving for tactile sensations, craving for ideas. This is called craving.

And what is *feeling?* These six are classes of feeling: feeling born from eye-contact, feeling born from ear-contact, feeling born from nose-contact, feeling born from tongue-contact, feeling born from body-contact, feeling born from intellect-contact. This is called feeling.

And what is *contact?* These six are classes of contact: eye-contact, ear-contact, nose-contact, tongue-contact, body-contact, intellect-contact. This is called contact.

And what are *the six sense media?* These six are sense media: the eye-medium, the ear-medium, the nose-medium, the tongue-medium, the body-medium, the intellect-medium. These are called the six sense media.

And what is *name-&-form?* Feeling, perception, intention, contact, & attention: This is called name. The four great elements, and the form dependent on the four great elements: This is called form. This name & this form are called name-&-form.

And what is *consciousness?* These six are classes of consciousness: eye-consciousness, ear-consciousness, nose-consciousness, tongue-consciousness, body-consciousness, intellect-consciousness. This is called consciousness.

And what are *fabrications?* These three are fabrications: bodily fabrications, verbal fabrications, mental fabrications. These are called fabrications.

And what is *ignorance?* Not knowing stress, not knowing the origination of stress, not knowing the cessation of stress, not knowing the way of practice leading to the cessation of stress: This is called ignorance.

S.XII.2

§ 219. When a fool is obstructed by ignorance and conjoined with craving, this body thus results. Now there is both this body and external name-&-form. Here, in dependence on this duality, there is contact at the six senses. Touched by these, or one or another of them, the fool is sensitive to pleasure & pain. When a wise person is obstructed by ignorance and conjoined with craving, this body thus results. Now there is both this body and external name-&-form. Here, in dependence on this duality, there is contact at the six senses. Touched by these, or one or another of them, the wise person is sensitive to pleasure & pain. Now what is the difference...here between the wise person & the fool?...

In the wise person that ignorance has been abandoned and that craving has been destroyed. Why is that? The wise person has practiced the holy life for the right ending of stress. Therefore, at the break-up of the body, he is not headed for a [new] body. Not headed for a body, he is entirely freed from birth, aging, death, sorrow, lamentation, pain, distress, & despair. I tell you, he is entirely freed from stress.

S.XII.19

§ 220. **Becoming.** Ananda: This word, 'becoming, becoming'—to what extent is there becoming?

The Buddha: If there were no kamma ripening in the property of sensuality, would sensual becoming be discerned?

Ananda: No, lord.

The Buddha: Thus kamma is the field, consciousness the seed, and craving the moisture. The consciousness of living beings hindered by ignorance & fettered by craving is established in (tuned to) a lower element. Thus there is the production of renewed becoming in the future. If there were no kamma ripening in the property of form, would form-becoming be discerned?

Ananda: No, lord.

The Buddha: Thus kamma is the field, consciousness the seed, and craving the moisture. The consciousness of living beings hindered by ignorance & fettered by craving is established in (tuned to) a middling element. Thus there is the production of renewed becoming in the future. If there were no kamma ripening in the property of formlessness, would formless becoming be discerned?

Ananda: No, lord.

The Buddha: Thus kamma is the field, consciousness the seed, and craving the moisture. The consciousness of living beings hindered by ignorance & fettered by craving is established in (tuned to) a refined element. Thus there is the production of renewed becoming in the future. This is how there is becoming.

A.III.76

(The discourse immediately following this is identical to this except that the phrase, 'the consciousness of living beings...is established,' changes to, 'the intention & determination of living beings...is established.')

A.III.77

§ 221. I have heard that on one occasion, when the Blessed One was newly Awakened—living at Uruvelā by the banks of the Nerañjarā River in the shade of the Bodhi tree, the tree of Awakening—he sat in the shade of the Bodhi tree for seven days in one session, sensitive to the bliss of release. At the end of seven days, after emerging from that concentration, he surveyed the world with the eye of an Awakened One. As he did so, he saw living beings burning with the many fevers and aflame with the many fires born of passion, aversion, & delusion. Then, on realizing the significance of that, he on that occasion exclaimed:

> This world is burning.
> Afflicted by contact,
> it calls disease a 'self.'
> By whatever it construes [things],
> that is always otherwise.
> Becoming otherwise,
> the world is
>   held by becoming
>   afflicted by becoming
> and yet delights
>   in that very becoming.
> Where there's delight,
>   there is fear.
> What one fears
>   is stressful.
> This holy life is lived
> for the abandoning of becoming.

Whatever priests or contemplatives say that liberation from becoming is by means of becoming, all of them are not released from becoming, I say.

And whatever priests or contemplatives say that escape from becoming is by means of non-becoming, all of them have not escaped from becoming, I say.

This stress comes into play
in dependence on all the paraphernalia of becoming.
With the ending of all clinging/sustenance,
there is no stress
coming into play.

Look at this world:
Beings, afflicted with thick ignorance,
are unreleased
from delight in what has come to be.
All levels of becoming,
anywhere,
in any way,
are inconstant, stressful, subject to change.
Seeing this—as it actually is present—
with right discernment,
one abandons craving for becoming,
without delighting in non-becoming.
From the total ending of craving
comes fading & cessation without remainder:

Unbinding.

For the monk unbound,
from lack of clinging/sustenance,
there is no further becoming.
He has vanquished Māra,
won the battle.
Having gone beyond all levels of being,

he is Such.

UD.III.10

§ 222. Overcome by two viewpoints, some human & divine beings adhere, other human & divine beings slip right past, while those with vision see.

And how do some adhere? Human & divine beings delight in becoming, enjoy becoming, are satisfied with becoming. When the Dhamma is being taught for the sake of the cessation of becoming, their minds do not take to it, are not calmed by it, do not settle on it, or become resolved on it. This is how some adhere.

And how do some slip right past? Some, feeling horrified, humiliated, & disgusted with that very becoming, delight in non-becoming: 'When this self, at the break-up of the body, after death, perishes & is destroyed, and does not exist after death, that is peaceful, that is exquisite, that is sufficiency!' This is how some slip right past.

And how do those with vision see? There is the case where a monk sees being as being. Seeing being as being, he practices for disenchantment with being, dispassion toward being, cessation of being. This is how those with vision see....

> One who, having seen
> what has come to be
> as what has come to be,
> has gone beyond being,
> and is released in line
> with things as they are,
> through the exhaustion of craving for becoming.
> The monks who have comprehended being—
> free from the craving to go
> from becoming to becoming;
> with the non-becoming
> of what has come to be—
> come to no further becoming.

ITI.49

§ 223. Fabrications. Visakha: And what, lady, are bodily fabrications, what are verbal fabrications, what are mental fabrications?

Sister Dhammadinna: In-&-out breathing is bodily, bound up with the body, therefore is it called a *bodily fabrication.* Having directed one's thought and evaluated [the matter], one breaks into speech. Therefore directed thought & evaluation are called *verbal fabrications.* Perception & feeling are mental, bound up with the mind. Therefore perception & feeling are called *mental fabrications.*

M.44

§ 224. When there is a body, pleasure & pain arise internally with bodily intention as the cause; or when there is speech, pleasure & pain arise internally with verbal intention as the cause; or when there is intellect, pleasure & pain arise internally with intellectual intention as the cause.

From ignorance as requisite condition, then either of one's own accord one fabricates the bodily fabrication on account of which that pleasure & pain arise internally, or because of others one fabricates the bodily fabrication on account of which that pleasure & pain arise internally. With alertness...or without alertness one fabricates the bodily fabrication on account of which that pleasure & pain arise internally. (Similarly with verbal & intellectual fabrications.)

Now, ignorance is bound up in these things. From the remainderless fading & cessation of that very ignorance, there no longer exists [the sense of] the body...the speech...the intellect on account of which that pleasure & pain internally arise. There no longer exists the field, the site, the dimension, or the issue on account of which that pleasure & pain internally arise.

S.XII.25

§ 225. If a person immersed in ignorance fabricates a meritorious fabrication, his consciousness goes on to merit. If he fabricates a demeritorious fabrication, his consciousness goes on to demerit. If he fabricates an imperturbable fabrication, his consciousness goes on to the imperturbable. When ignorance is abandoned by a monk, clear knowing arises. From the fading of ignorance and the arising of knowledge, he neither fabricates a meritorious fabrication nor a demeritorious fabrication nor an imperturbable fabrication. Neither fabricating nor willing, he is not sustained by anything in the world. Unsustained, he is not agitated. Unagitated, he is totally unbound right within. He discerns that 'Birth is ended, the holy life fulfilled, the task done. There is nothing further for this world.'

Sensing a feeling of pleasure, he discerns that it is fleeting, not grasped at, not relished. Sensing a feeling of pain....Sensing a feeling of neither-pleasure-nor-pain, he discerns that it is fleeting, not grasped at, not relished. Sensing a feeling of pleasure, he senses it disjoined from it. Sensing a feeling of pain....Sensing a feeling of neither-pleasure-nor-pain, he senses it disjoined from it. When sensing a feeling limited to the body, he discerns that 'I am sensing a feeling limited to the body.' When sensing a feeling limited to life, he discerns that 'I am sensing a feeling limited to life.' He discerns that 'With the break-up of the body, after the termination of life, all that is experienced, not being relished, will grow cold right here, while the corpse will remain.'

Just as if a man, having removed a heated jar from a kiln, were to place it on level ground: Whatever heat in the jar would subside right there, while the fired clay would remain. In the same way, when sensing a feeling limited to the body, he discerns that 'I am sensing a feeling limited to the body.' When sensing a feeling limited to life, he discerns that 'I am sensing a feeling limited to life.' He discerns that 'With the break-up of the body, after the termination of life, all that is experienced, not being relished, will grow cold right here, while the corpse will remain.'

How do you construe this, monks? Would a monk whose effluents were ended fabricate a meritorious or a demeritorious or an imperturbable fabrication?

No, lord.

With the total non-existence of fabrications, from the cessation of fabrications, would consciousness be discernible (manifest)?

No, lord.

(And similarly down to:) With the total non-existence of birth, from the cessation of birth, would aging & death be discernible?

No, lord.

Very good, monks. Just so should you construe it. Just so should you be convinced. Just so should you believe. Do not be doubtful, do not be uncertain. This, just this, is the end of stress.

S.XII.51

§ 226. What is willed, what is arranged, and what lies latent: This is a support for the stationing of consciousness. There being a support, there is a landing of consciousness. When that consciousness lands and grows, there is the production of renewed becoming in the future. When there is the production of renewed becoming in the future, there is future birth, aging & death, sorrow, lamentation, pain, distress, & despair. Such is the origination of this entire mass of stress.

If nothing is willed, if nothing is arranged, but something lies latent: This is a support for the stationing of consciousness....Such [too] is the origination of this entire mass of stress.

But when nothing is willed, arranged, or lies latent, there is no support for the stationing of consciousness. There being no support, there is no landing of consciousness. When that consciousness does not land & grow, there is no production of renewed becoming in the future. When there is no production of renewed becoming in the future, there is no future birth, aging & death, sorrow, lamentation, pain, distress, or despair. Such is the cessation of this entire mass of stress.

S.XII.38

§ 227. Sariputta: Now what is ignorance, what is the origination of ignorance, what is the cessation of ignorance, and what is the way of practice leading to the cessation of ignorance?

Not knowing stress, not knowing the origination of stress, not knowing the cessation of stress, not knowing the way of practice leading to the cessation of stress: This is called ignorance. From the origination of effluents comes the origination of ignorance. From the cessation of effluents comes the cessation of ignorance. And just this noble eightfold path is the way of practice leading to the cessation of ignorance....

Now when a noble disciple discerns ignorance in this way, discerns the origination of ignorance in this way, discerns the cessation of ignorance in this way, & discerns the way of practice leading to the cessation of ignorance in this way, then—having entirely abandoned the latent tendency to passion, having abolished the latent tendency to irritation, having uprooted the latent tendency to the view & conceit 'I am,' having abandoned ignorance, having given rise to clear knowing—he puts an end to stress in the here & now. It is to this extent that the noble disciple is a person of right view, his views straightened, endowed with perfect confidence in regard to the Dhamma, having arrived at this true Dhamma....

Now what are effluents, what is the origination of effluents, what is the cessation of effluents, and what is the way of practice leading to the cessation of effluents?

These three are effluents: the effluent of sensuality, the effluent of becoming, the effluent of ignorance. From the origination of ignorance comes the origination of effluents. From the cessation of ignorance comes the cessation of effluents. And just this noble eightfold path is the way of practice leading to the cessation of effluents....

Now when a noble disciple discerns the effluents in this way, discerns the origination of effluents in this way, discerns the cessation of effluents in this way, & discerns the way of practice leading to the cessation of effluents in this way, then—having entirely abandoned the latent tendency to passion, having abolished the latent tendency to irritation, having uprooted the latent tendency to the view & conceit 'I am,' having abandoned ignorance, having given rise to clear knowing—he puts an end to stress in the here & now. It is to this extent that the noble disciple is a person of right view, his views straightened, endowed with perfect confidence in regard to the Dhamma, having arrived at this true Dhamma.

M.9

§ 228. Maha Koṭṭhita: Now tell me, Sariputta my friend: Are aging & death self-made or other-made or both self-made & other-made, or—without self-making or other-making—do they arise spontaneously?

Sariputta: It's not the case, Koṭṭhita my friend, that aging & death are self-made, that they are other-made, that they are both self-made & other-made, or that—without self-making or other-making—they arise spontaneously. However, from birth as a requisite condition comes aging & death.

(Similarly with birth, becoming, sustenance/clinging, craving, feeling, the six sense media down to:)

Maha Koṭṭhita: Now tell me: Is name-&-form self-made or other-made or both self-made & other-made, or—without self-making or other-making—does it arise spontaneously?

Sariputta: It's not the case that name-&-form is self-made, that it is other-made, that it is both self-made & other-made, or that—without self-making or other-making—it arises spontaneously. However, from consciousness as a requisite condition comes name-&-form.

Maha Koṭṭhita: Now tell me: is consciousness self-made or other-made or both self-made & other-made, or—without self-making or other-making, does it arise spontaneously?

Sariputta: It's not the case that consciousness is self-made, that it is other-made, that it is both self-made & other-made, or that—without self-making or other-making—it arises spontaneously. However, from name-&-form as a requisite condition comes consciousness.

Maha Koṭṭhita: Just now I understood what you said as...from consciousness as a requisite condition comes name-&-form...from name-&-form as a requisite condition comes consciousness. Now how is the meaning of what you said to be understood?

Sariputta: Very well then, my friend, I will give you an analogy; for there are cases where it is through the use of an analogy that intelligent people can understand the meaning of what is being said. It is as if two sheaves of reeds stood leaning against one another. In the same way, from name-&-form as a requisite condition comes consciousness, from consciousness as a requisite condition comes name-&-form. From name-&-form as a requisite condition come the six sense media....Thus is the origination of this entire mass of stress.

If one were to pull away one of those sheaves of reeds, the other would fall; if one were to pull away the other, the first one would fall. In the same way, from the cessation of name-&-form comes the cessation of consciousness, from the cessation of consciousness comes the cessation of name-&-form. From the cessation of name-&-form comes the cessation of the six sense media....Thus is the cessation of this entire mass of stress.

S.XII.67

§ 229. People are intent on the idea of
'made by me'
and attached to the idea of
'made by another.'
Some do not realize this,
nor do they see it as a thorn.
But to one who sees,
having extracted this thorn,

[the thought] 'I am doing,' doesn't occur;
'Another is doing,' doesn't occur.

This human race is possessed by conceit
bound by conceit,
tied down by conceit.
Speaking hurtfully because of their views
they do not go beyond transmigration.

UD.VI.6

§ 230. The Buddha: "From ignorance as a requisite condition come fabrications....From birth as a requisite condition, then old age & death, sorrow, lamentation, pain, distress, & despair come into play. Such is the origination of this entire mass of stress & suffering."

When this was said, a certain monk said to the Blessed One: "Which aging & death, lord? And to whom does this aging & death belong?"

"Not a valid question," the Blessed One said. If a monk were to ask, 'Which aging & death? And to whom does this aging & death belong?' and if a monk were to ask, 'Is aging & death one thing, and does it belong to someone/something else?' both of them would have the same meaning, even though their words would differ. When a monk is of the view that the soul is the same as the body, there is no leading the holy life. And when a monk is of the view that the soul is one thing and the body another, there is no leading the holy life. Avoiding these two extremes, the Tathāgata points out the Dhamma in between them: From birth as a requisite condition comes aging & death."

"Which birth, lord? And to whom does this birth belong?"

"Not a valid question," the Blessed One said.

(Similarly with all the requisite conditions down to fabrications.)

"....Avoiding these two extremes, the Tathāgata points out the Dhamma in between them: From ignorance as requisite condition come fabrications. Now from the remainderless fading & cessation of that very ignorance, every one of these writhings & wrigglings & wigglings—'Which aging & death? And to whom does this aging & death belong?' or 'Is aging & death one thing, and does it belong to someone/something else?' or 'The soul is the same as the body,' or 'The soul is one thing and the body another'—are abandoned, their root destroyed, like an uprooted palm tree, deprived of the conditions of existence, not destined for future arising."

(Similarly with all the requisite conditions down to fabrications.)

S.XII.35

§ 231. Ananda: It is amazing, lord, it is astounding, how deep this dependent co-arising is, & how deep its appearance, and yet to me it seems as clear as clear can be.

The Buddha: Don't say that, Ānanda. Don't say that. Deep is this dependent co-arising, and deep its appearance. It's because of not understanding & not penetrating this Dhamma that this generation is like a tangled skein, a knotted ball of string, like matted rushes & reeds, and does not go beyond the cycle of the planes of deprivation, woe, & bad destinations....

'From birth as a requisite condition come aging & death.' Thus it has been said. And this is the way to understand how from birth as a requisite condition come aging & death. If there were no birth at all, in any way, of anything anywhere...in the utter absence of birth from the cessation of birth, would aging & death be discerned?'

Ananda: No, lord.

The Buddha: Thus this is a cause, this is a reason, this is an origination, this is a requisite condition for aging & death, i.e., birth. (Similarly for the rest of the stream of requisite conditions down to contact.)

'From name-&-form as a requisite condition comes contact. Thus it has been said. And this is the way to understand how, from name-&-form as a requisite condition comes contact. If the qualities, traits, themes, & indicators by which there is a description of name-group (mental activity) were all absent, would designation-contact with regard to the form-group (the physical body) be discerned?

Ānanda: No, lord.

The Buddha: If the permutations, signs, themes, & indicators by which there is a description of form-group were all absent, would resistance-contact with regard to the name-group be discerned?

Ananda: No, lord.

The Buddha: If the permutations, signs, themes, & indicators by which there is a description of name-group & form-group were all absent, would designation-contact or resistance-contact be discerned?

Ananda: No, lord.

The Buddha: Thus this is a cause, this is a reason, this is an origination, this is a requisite condition for contact, i.e., name-&-form.

'From consciousness as a requisite condition comes name-&-form.' Thus it has been said. And this is the way to understand how from consciousness as a requisite condition comes name-&-form. If consciousness were not to descend into the mother's womb, would name-&-form take shape in the womb?

Ananda: No, lord.

The Buddha: If, after descending into the womb, consciousness were to depart, would name-&-form be produced for this world?

Ananda: No, lord.

The Buddha: If the consciousness of the young boy or girl were to be cut off, would name-&-form ripen, grow, & reach maturity?

Ananda: No, lord.

The Buddha: Thus this is a cause, this is a reason, this is an origination, this is a requisite condition for name-&-form, i.e., consciousness.

'From name-&-form as a requisite condition comes consciousness.' Thus it has been said. And this is the way to understand how from name-&-form as a requisite condition comes consciousness. If consciousness were not to gain a foothold in name-&-form, would a coming-into-play of the origination of birth, aging, death, & stress in the future be discerned?

Ananda: No, lord.

The Buddha: Thus this is a cause, this is a reason, this is an origination, this is a requisite condition for consciousness, i.e., name-&-form.

This is the extent to which there is birth, aging, death, passing away, & re-arising. This is the extent to which there are means of designation, expression, & description. This is the extent to which the sphere of discernment extends, the extent to which the cycle revolves for the manifesting (discernibility) of this world—i.e., name-&-form together with consciousness.

D.15

§ 232. It is in dependence on a pair that consciousness comes into play. And how does consciousness come into play independence on a pair? In dependence on the eye & forms there arises eye-consciousness. The eye is inconstant, changeable, of a nature to become otherwise. Forms are inconstant, changeable, of a nature to become otherwise. Thus this pair is both fleeting & unsettled—inconstant, changeable, of a nature to become otherwise. Eye-consciousness is inconstant, changeable, of a nature to become otherwise. Whatever is the cause, the requisite condition, for the arising of eye-consciousness, that is inconstant, changeable, of a nature to become otherwise. Having arisen in dependence on an inconstant factor, how could eye-consciousness be constant? (Similarly with the ear, nose, tongue, body, & intellect.)

S.XXXV.93

§ 233. One attached is unreleased; one unattached is released. Should consciousness, when taking a stance, stand attached to [a physical] form, supported by form [as its object], established on form, watered with delight, it would exhibit growth, increase, & development. Should consciousness, when taking a stance, stand attached to feeling...to perception...to fabrications... it would exhibit growth, increase, & development. Were someone to say, 'I will describe a coming, a going, a passing away, an arising, a growth, an increase or a development of consciousness apart from form, from feeling, from perception, from fabrications,' that would be impossible.

If a monk abandons passion for the property of form...feeling... perception... fabrications...consciousness, then owing to the abandoning of passion, the support is cut off, and consciousness is unestablished. Consciousness, thus unestablished, undeveloped, not performing any function, is released. Owing to its release, it stays firm. Owing to its staying firm, it is contented. Owing to its contentment, it is not agitated. Not agitated, he [the monk] is totally unbound right within himself. He discerns that, 'Birth is ended, the holy life fulfilled, the task done. There is nothing further for this world.'

S.XXII.53

§ 234. There are these four nutriments for the establishing of beings who have taken birth or for the support of those in search of a place to be born. Which four? Physical food, gross or refined; contact as the second, consciousness the third, and intellectual intention the fourth. These are the four nutriments for the establishing of beings or for the support of those in search of a place to be born.

Where there is passion, delight, & craving for the nutriment of physical food, consciousness lands there and grows. Where consciousness lands and grows, name-&-form alights. Where name-&-form alights, there is the growth of fabrications. Where there is the growth of fabrications, there is the production of renewed becoming in the future. Where there is the production of renewed becoming in the future, there is future birth, aging, & death, together, I tell you, with sorrow, affliction, & despair.

Just as—when there is dye, lac, yellow orpiment, indigo, or crimson—a dyer or painter would paint the picture of a woman or a man, complete in all its parts, on a well-polished panel or wall, or on a piece of cloth; in the same way, where there is passion, delight, & craving for the nutriment of physical food, consciousness lands there & grows...together, I tell you, with sorrow, affliction, & despair.

(Similarly with the other three kinds of nutriment.)

Where there is no passion for physical nutriment, where there is no delight, no craving, then consciousness does not land there or grow.... Name-&-form does not alight....There is no growth of fabrications.... There is no production of renewed becoming in the future. Where there is no production of renewed becoming in the future, there is no future birth, aging, & death. That, I tell you, has no sorrow, affliction, or despair.

Just as if there were a roofed house or a roofed hall having windows on the north, the south, or the east. When the sun rises, and a ray has entered by way of the window, where does it land?

On the western wall, lord.

And if there is no western wall...?

On the ground, lord.

And if there is no ground...?

On the water, lord.

And if there is no water...?

It does not land, lord.

In the same way, where there is no passion for physical nutriment... consciousness does not land or grow....That, I tell you, has no sorrow, affliction, or despair.

(Similarly with the other three kinds of nutriment.)

S.XII.64

§ 235. Consciousness without feature,
without end,
luminous all around:
Here water, earth, fire, & wind have no footing.
Here long & short
coarse & fine
fair & foul
name & form
are, without remnant,
brought to an end.
From the cessation
of [the activity of] consciousness,
each is here brought to an end.

D.11

§ 236. Where water, earth, fire, & wind
have no footing:
There the stars do not shine
the sun is not visible,
the moon does not appear,
darkness is not found.

And when a sage, an honorable one,
through sagacity
has known [this] for himself,
then from form & formless,
from pleasure & pain,
he is freed.

Ud.I.10

§ 237. Then Ven. Ananda, together with a group of monks, went to where the Blessed One was staying in Palileyyaka, at the root of the Auspicious Sal Tree, and on arrival, after bowing down to him, sat down to one side. As they were sitting there, the Blessed One instructed, urged, roused, & encouraged them with a talk on Dhamma.

Then this train of thought appeared in the awareness of one of the monks: 'Now I wonder—knowing in what way, seeing in what way, does one without delay put an end to the effluents?'

The Blessed One, perceiving with his awareness the train of thought in the monk's awareness, said to the monks, 'I have analyzed & taught you the Dhamma, monks. I have analyzed & taught you the four frames of reference, the four right exertions, the four bases of power, the five faculties, the five strengths, the seven factors of awakening, & the noble eightfold path....And yet still there appears this train of thought in the awareness of one of the monks: "Now I wonder—knowing in what way, seeing in what way, does one without delay put an end to the effluents?"

Well then—knowing in what way, seeing in what way, *does* one without delay put an end to the effluents? There is the case where an uninstructed, run-of-the-mill person...assumes form (the body) to be the self. That assumption is a fabrication. Now what is the cause, what is the origination, what is the birth, what is the coming-into-existence of that fabrication? To an uninstructed, run-of-the-mill person, touched by that which is felt born of contact with ignorance, craving arises. That fabrication is born of that. And that fabrication is inconstant, compounded, dependently co-arisen. That craving... That feeling...That contact...That ignorance is inconstant, compounded, dependently co-arisen. It is by knowing & seeing in this way that one without delay puts an end to the effluents.

Or he doesn't assume form to be the self, but he assumes the self as possessing of form...form as in the self...self as in form... or feeling to be the self...the self as possessing feeling...feeling as in the self...self as in feeling...or perception to be the self...the self as possessing perception...perception as in the self...self as in perception...or fabrications to be the self...the self as possessing fabrications...fabrications as in the self...self as in fabrications...or consciousness to be the self...the self as possessing consciousness...consciousness as in the self...self as in consciousness.

Now that assumption is a fabrication. What is the cause...of that fabrication? To an uninstructed, run-of-the-mill person, touched by the feeling born of contact with ignorance, craving arises. That fabrication is born of that. And that fabrication is inconstant, compounded, dependently co-arisen. That craving...That feeling... That contact...That ignorance is inconstant, compounded, dependently co-arisen. It is by knowing & seeing in this way that one without delay puts an end to the effluents.

Or...he may have a view such as this: 'This self is the same as the cosmos. This I will be after death, constant, lasting, eternal, not subject to change.' This eternalist view is a fabrication....Or...he may have a view such as this: 'I would not be, neither would there be what is mine. I will not be, neither will there be what is mine.' This annihilationist view is a fabrication....Or...he may be doubtful & uncertain, having come to no conclusion with regard to the true Dhamma. That doubt, uncertainty, & coming-to-no-conclusion is a fabrication.

What is the cause...of that fabrication? To an uninstructed, run-of-the-mill person, touched by what is felt born of contact with ignorance, craving arises. That fabrication is born of that. And that fabrication is inconstant, compounded, dependently co-arisen. That craving...That feeling...That contact...That ignorance is inconstant, compounded, dependently co-arisen. It is by knowing & seeing in this way that one without delay puts an end to the effluents.

S.XXII.81

§ 238. The ending of the effluents is for one who knows & sees, I tell you, not for one who does not know & does not see. For one who knows what & sees what?...'Such is form, such its origination, such its disappearance. Such is feeling.... Such is perception....Such are fabrications....Such is consciousness, such its origination, such its disappearance.' The ending of the effluents is for one who knows in this way & sees in this way. [§30; 149; 170; 173; 199-207]

The knowledge of ending in the presence of ending has its prerequisite, I tell you. It is not without a prerequisite. And what is its prerequisite? Release... Release has its prerequisite, I tell you. It is not without a prerequisite. And what is its prerequisite? Dispassion.... Disenchantment....Knowledge & vision of things as they actually are present....Concentration....Pleasure....Serenity.... Rapture....Joy.... Conviction....Stress....Birth....Becoming....Clinging....Craving.... Feeling....Contact....The six sense media....Name-&-form.... Consciousness....Fabrications....Fabrications have their prerequisite, I tell you. They are not without a prerequisite. And what is their prerequisite? Ignorance....

Just as when the gods pour rain in heavy drops & crash thunder on the upper mountains: The water, flowing down along the slopes, fills the mountain clefts & rifts & gullies. When the mountain clefts & rifts & gullies are full, they fill the little ponds. When the little ponds are full, they fill the big lakes...the little rivers...the big rivers. When the big rivers are full, they fill the great ocean. In the same way:

> fabrications have ignorance as their prerequisite,
> consciousness has fabrications as its prerequisite,
> name-&-form has consciousness as its prerequisite,
> the six sense media have name-&-form as their prerequisite,
> contact has the six sense media as its prerequisite,
> feeling has contact as its prerequisite,
> craving has feeling as its prerequisite,
> clinging has craving as its prerequisite,
> becoming has clinging as its prerequisite,
> birth has becoming as its prerequisite,
> stress & suffering have birth as their prerequisite,
> conviction has stress & suffering as its prerequisite,
> joy has conviction as its prerequisite,
> rapture has joy as its prerequisite,
> serenity has rapture as its prerequisite,
> pleasure has serenity as its prerequisite,
> concentration has pleasure as its prerequisite,
> knowledge & vision of things as they actually are present has concentration as its prerequisite,
> disenchantment has knowledge & vision of things as they actually are present as its prerequisite,
> dispassion has disenchantment as its prerequisite,
> release has dispassion as its prerequisite,
> knowledge of ending has release as its prerequisite.

S.XII.23

iv. The Fourth Truth

§ 239. Before my Awakening, when I was just an unawakened Bodhisatta, the realization came to me: 'How this world has fallen on difficulty! It is born, it ages, it dies, it falls away & rearises, but it does not discern the escape from this stress, from this aging & death. O when will it discern the escape from this stress, from this aging & death?'

Then the thought occurred to me, 'Aging & death exist when what exists? From what as a requisite condition is there aging & death?' From my appropriate attention there came the breakthrough of discernment: 'Aging & death exist when birth exists. From birth as a requisite condition comes aging & death.' Then the thought occurred to me, 'Birth exists when what exists? From what as a requisite condition comes birth?' From my appropriate attention there came the breakthrough of discernment: 'Birth exists when becoming exists. From becoming as a requisite condition comes birth...'Name-&-form exists when what exists? From what as a requisite condition is there name-&-form?' From my appropriate attention there came the breakthrough of discernment: 'Name-&-form exists when consciousness exists. From consciousness as a requisite condition comes name-&-form.' Then the thought occurred to me, 'Consciousness exists when what exists? From what as a requisite condition comes consciousness?' From my appropriate attention there came the breakthrough of discernment: 'Consciousness exists when name-&-form exists. From name-&-form as a requisite condition comes consciousness.'

Then the thought occurred to me, 'This consciousness turns back at name-&-form, and goes no farther. It is to this extent that there is birth, aging, death, falling away, & re-arising, i.e., from name-&-form as a requisite condition comes consciousness, from consciousness as a requisite condition comes name-&-form. From name-&-form as a requisite condition come the six sense media....Thus is the origination of this entire mass of stress. Origination, origination.' Vision arose, clear knowing arose, discernment arose, knowledge arose, illumination arose within me with regard to things never heard before.

Then the thought occurred to me, 'Aging & death don't exist when what doesn't exist? From the cessation of what comes the cessation of aging & death?' From my appropriate attention there came the breakthrough of discernment: 'Aging & death don't exist when birth doesn't exist. From the cessation of birth comes the cessation of aging & death.'...'Name-&-form doesn't exist when what doesn't exist? From the cessation of what comes the cessation of name-&-form?'

From my appropriate attention there came the breakthrough of discernment: 'Name-&-form doesn't exist when consciousness doesn't exist. From the cessation of consciousness comes the cessation of name-&-form.' Then the thought occurred to me, 'Consciousness doesn't exist when what doesn't exist? From the cessation of what comes the cessation of consciousness?' From my appropriate attention there came the breakthrough of discernment: 'Consciousness doesn't exist when name-&-form doesn't exist. From the cessation of name-&-form comes the cessation of consciousness.'

The thought occurred to me, 'I have attained this path to awakening, i.e., from the cessation of name-&-form comes the cessation of consciousness, from the cessation of consciousness comes the cessation of name-&-form. From the cessation of name-&-form comes the cessation of the six sense media....Thus is the cessation of this entire mass of stress. Cessation, cessation.' Vision arose, clear knowing arose, discernment arose, knowledge arose, illumination arose within me with regard to things never heard before.

It is just as if a man, traveling along a wilderness track, were to see an ancient path, an ancient road, traveled by people of former times. He would follow it. Following it, he would see an ancient city, an ancient capital inhabited by people of former times, complete with parks, groves, & ponds, walled, delightful. He would go to address the king or the king's minister, saying, 'Sire, you should know that while traveling along a wilderness track I saw an ancient path.... I followed it....I saw an ancient city, an ancient capital...complete with parks, groves, & ponds, walled, delightful. Sire, rebuild that city!' The king or king's minister would rebuild the city, so that at a later date the city would become powerful, rich, & well-populated, fully grown & prosperous.

In the same way I saw an ancient path, an ancient road, traveled by the Rightly Self-awakened Ones of former times. And what is that ancient path...? Just this noble eightfold path: right view, right resolve, right speech, right action, right livelihood, right effort, right mindfulness, right concentration....I followed that path. Following it, I came to direct knowledge of aging & death, direct knowledge of the origination of aging & death, direct knowledge of the cessation of aging & death, direct knowledge of the path leading to the cessation of aging & death. I followed that path. Following it, I came to direct knowledge of birth...becoming...clinging...craving...feeling... contact...the six sense media...name-&-form...consciousness, direct knowledge of the origination of consciousness, direct knowledge of the cessation of consciousness, direct knowledge of the path leading to the cessation of consciousness. I followed that path.

Following it, I came to direct knowledge of fabrications, direct knowledge of the origination of fabrications, direct knowledge of the cessation of fabrications, direct knowledge of the path leading to the cessation of fabrications. Knowing that directly, I have revealed it to monks, nuns, male lay followers, & female lay followers, so that this holy life has become powerful, rich, detailed, well-populated, widespread, proclaimed among celestial & human beings.

S.XII.65

§ 240. Now at that time Subhadda the Wanderer was staying in Kusinara. He heard, 'Tonight, in the last watch of the night, the total Unbinding of Gotama the contemplative will take place.' Then this thought occurred to him: 'I have heard the elder wanderers, teachers of teachers, saying that only once in a long, long time do Tathagatas—worthy ones, rightly self-awakened—appear in the world. Tonight, in the last watch of the night, the total Unbinding of Gotama the contemplative will take place. Now there is a doubt that has arisen in me, but I have faith that he could teach me the Dhamma in such a way that I might abandon that doubt.'

So he went to the Mallan Sal Tree grove and, on arrival, said to Ven. Ananda, 'I have heard the elder wanderers, teachers of teachers, saying that only once in a long, long time do Tathagatas—worthy ones, rightly self-awakened—appear in the world. Tonight, in the last watch of the night, the total Unbinding of Gotama the contemplative will take place. Now there is a doubt that has arisen in me, but I have faith that he could teach me the Dhamma in such a way that I might abandon that doubt. It would be good, Ven. Ananda, if you would let me see him.'

When this was said, Ven. Ananda said to him, 'Enough, friend Subhadda. Do not bother the Blessed One. The Blessed One is tired.'

For a second time...For a third time, Subhadda the Wanderer said to Ven. Ananda, '...It would be good, Ven. Ananda, if you would let me see him.'

For a third time, Ven. Ananda said to him, 'Enough, friend Subhadda. Do not bother the Blessed One. The Blessed One is tired.'

Now, the Blessed One heard the exchange between Ven. Ananda & Subhadda the Wanderer, and so he said to Ven. Ananda, 'Enough, Ananda. Do not stand in his way. Let him see the Tathāgata. Whatever he asks me will all be for the sake of knowledge, and not to be bothersome. And whatever I answer when asked, he will quickly understand.'

So Ven. Ananda said to Subhadda the Wanderer, 'Go ahead, friend Subhadda. The Blessed One gives you his leave.'

Then Subhadda went to the Blessed One and exchanged courtesies, and after the exchange of courtesies sat down to one side. As he was sitting there, he said to the Blessed One, 'Venerable sir, these priests & contemplatives, each with his group, each with his community, each the teacher of his group, an honored leader, well-regarded by people at large—i.e., Pūraṇa Kassapa, Makkhali Gosāla, Ajita Kesakambalin, Pakudha Kaccāyana, Sañjaya Belaṭṭhitaputta, & Nigaṇṭha Naṭaputta: Do they all have direct knowledge as they themselves claim, or do they all not have direct knowledge, or do some of them have direct knowledge and some of them not?'

'Enough, Subhadda. Put this question aside. I will teach you the Dhamma. Listen and pay close attention. I will speak.'

'Yes, lord,' Subhadda answered, and the Blessed One said, 'In any doctrine & discipline where the noble eightfold path is not found, no contemplative of the first...second...third...fourth order [stream-winner, once-returner, non-returner, or Arahant] is found. But in any doctrine & discipline where the noble eightfold path *is* found, contemplatives of the first...second...third...fourth order *are* found. The noble eightfold path is found in this doctrine & discipline, and right here there are contemplatives of the first...second...third...fourth order. Other teachings are empty of knowledgeable contemplatives. And if the monks dwell rightly, this world will not be empty of Arahants.

At age twenty-nine I went forth,
seeking what might be skillful,
and since my going forth
more than fifty years have past.

Outside of the realm
of methodical Dhamma,
there is no contemplative.

And no contemplative of the second...third...fourth order. Other teachings are empty of knowledgeable contemplatives. And if the monks dwell rightly, this world will not be empty of Arahants.'

Then Subhadda the Wanderer said, 'Magnificent, lord, magnificent! In many ways has the Blessed One made the Dhamma clear—just as if one were to place upright what has been overturned, to reveal what has been hidden, to point out the way to one who is lost, or to set out a lamp in the darkness so that those with eyes might see forms. I go to the Blessed One for refuge, and to the Dhamma and to the community of monks. Let me obtain the going forth in the Blessed One's presence, let me obtain admission.'

'Anyone, Subhadda, who has previously belonged to another sect and who desires the going forth & admission in this doctrine & discipline, must first undergo probation for four months. If, at the end of four months, the monks feel so moved, they give him the going forth & admit him to the monk's state. But I know distinctions among individuals in this matter.'

'Lord, if that is so, I am willing to undergo probation for four years. If, at the end of four years, the monks feel so moved, let them give me the going forth & admit me to the monk's state.'

Then the Blessed One said to Ven. Ananda, 'Very well then, Ananda, give Subhadda the going forth.'

'Yes, lord,' Ananda answered.

Then Subhadda said to Ven. Ananda, 'It is a gain for you, Ananda, a great gain, that you have been anointed here in the Teacher's presence with the pupil's anointing.'

Then Subhadda the Wanderer received the going forth & the admission in the Blessed One's presence. And not long after his admission—dwelling alone, secluded, heedful, ardent, & resolute—he in no long time reached & remained in the supreme goal of the holy life, for which clansmen rightly go forth from home into homelessness, knowing & realizing it for himself in the here & now. He knew: 'Birth is ended, the holy life fulfilled, the task done. There is nothing further for the sake of this world.' And thus Ven. Subhadda became another one of the Arahants, the last of the Blessed One's face-to-face disciples.

D.16

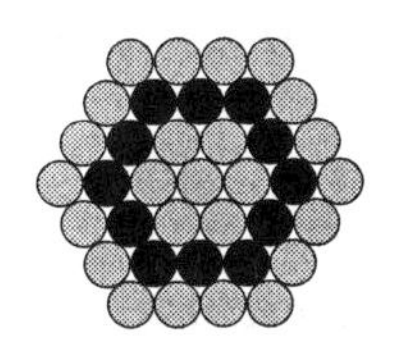

Glossary

Pali-English

Abhidhamma: (1) In the discourses of the Pali Canon, this term simply means "higher Dhamma," a systematic attempt to define the Buddha's teachings and understand their interrelationships. (2) A later collection of analytical treatises based on lists of categories drawn from the teachings in the discourses, added to the Canon several centuries after the Buddha's life.

Apaya: Realm of destitution. One of the four lower realms of existence, in which beings suffer because of their bad kamma: hell, the realm of hungry shades, the realm of angry demons, and level of common animals. In the Buddhist cosmology, a person reborn in any of these realms may stay there for long or short periods of time, but never for an eternity. After the bad kamma has worked out, the person will return to the higher realms.

Arahant: A "worthy one" or "pure one;" a person whose mind is free of defilement and thus is not destined for further rebirth. A title for the Buddha and the highest level of his noble disciples.

Āsava: Effluent; fermentation. Four qualities—sensuality, views, becoming, and ignorance—that "flow out" of the mind and create the flood of the round of death and rebirth.

Bodhisatta: "A being (striving) for Awakening;" a term used to describe the Buddha before he actually become Buddha, from his first aspiration to Buddhahood until the time of his full Awakening. Sanskrit form: *Bodhisattva.*

Deva: Literally, "shining one." An inhabitant of the heavenly realms.

Dhamma: (1) Event; a phenomenon in and of itself; (2) mental quality; (3) doctrine, teaching; (4) nibbāna. Sanskrit form: *Dharma.*

Hīnayāna: "Inferior Vehicle," a pejorative term, coined by a group who called themselves followers of the Mahāyāna, the "Great Vehicle," to denote the path of practice of those who adhered only to the earliest discourses as the word of the Buddha. Hīnayānists refused to recognize the later discourses, composed by the Mahāyānists, that claimed to contain teachings that the Buddha felt were too deep for his first generation of disciples, and which he thus secretly entrusted to underground serpents. The Theravāda school of today is a descendent of the Hīnayana.

Idappaccayata: This/that conditionality. This name for the causal principle the Buddha discovered on the night of his Awakening emphasizes the point that, for the purposes of ending suffering and stress, the processes of causality can be understood entirely in terms of conditions in the realm of direct experience, with no need to refer to forces operating outside of that realm.

Jhāna: Mental absorption. A state of strong concentration focused on a single sensation or mental notion.

Kamma: Intentional act. Sanskrit form: *karma.*

Maṇḍala: Microcosmic diagram, used as a power circle and object of contemplation in the rituals of Tantric Buddhism.

Māra: The personification of evil and temptation.

Nibbana: Literally, the "unbinding" of the mind from passion, aversion, and delusion, and from the entire round of death and rebirth. As this term also denotes the extinguishing of a fire, it carries connotations of stilling, cooling, and peace. "Total nibbāna" in some contexts denotes the experience of Awakening; in others, the final passing away of an Arahant. Sanskrit form: *nirvāṇa.*

Pali: The canon of texts preserved by the Theravāda school and, by extension, the language in which those texts are composed.

Paṭimokkha: Basic code of monastic discipline, composed of 227 rules for monks and 310 for nuns.

Samaṇa: Contemplative. Literally, a person who abandons the conventional obligations of social life in order to find a way of life more "in tune" *(sama)* with the ways of nature.

Saṁsara: Transmigration; the round of death and rebirth.

Saṅgha: On the conventional *(sammati)* level, this term denotes the communities of Buddhist monks and nuns; on the ideal *(ariya)* level, it denotes those followers of the Buddha, lay or ordained, who have attained at least stream-entry.

Stupa: Originally, a tumulus or burial mound enshrining relics of a holy person—such as the Buddha—or objects associated with his life. Over the centuries this has developed into the tall, spired monuments familiar in temples in Thailand, Sri Lanka, and Burma; and into the pagodas of China, Korea, and Japan.

Tadı: "Such," an adjective to describe one who has attained the goal. It indicates that the person's state is indefinable but not subject to change or influences of any sort.

Tathagata: Literally, "one who has become authentic *(tatha-āgata),*" an epithet used in ancient India for a person who has attained the highest religious goal. In Buddhism, it usually denotes the Buddha, although occasionally it also denotes any of his Arahant disciples.

Theravada: The "Teachings of the Elders"—the only one of the early schools of Buddhism to have survived into the present; currently the dominant form of Buddhism in Thailand, Sri Lanka, and Burma.

Vinaya: The monastic discipline, whose rules and traditions comprise six volumes in printed text.

English-Pali

Although I have tried to be as consistent as possible in rendering Pali terms into English, there are a few cases where a single English term will not do justice to all the meanings of a Pali term. The rule of one English equivalent per one Pali word may make for consistency, but any truly bilingual person knows that such a rule can create ludicrous distortions of meaning in translation. Thus, while I have not consciously used one English term to translate two different Pali terms, there are cases where I have found it necessary to render a single Pali term with one or more English terms, depending on context. *Citta* in some cases is rendered as mind, in others as intent. Similarly, *loka* is rendered either as cosmos or world, *manas* as intellect or heart, *āyatana* as medium or sphere, *upādāna* as clinging or sustenance, and *dhamma* as phenomenon, quality, or principle.

Also, with some of the Pali terms that are central to the teaching, I have chosen equivalents that do not follow general usage. In the following list I have indicated these equivalents with asterisks; explanations for these choices are provided at the end of the list.

aggregate — *khandha*
alertness — *sampajañña*
appropriate attention — *yoniso manasikāra*
Awakening — *bodhi*
awareness — *cetas*
becoming — *bhava*
clear knowing — *vijjā*
clinging — *upādāna*
concern — *ottappa*
conscience — *hiri*
contemplative — *samaṇa*
conviction — *saddhā*
cosmos — *loka*
craving — *taṇhā*
dependent co-arising — *paṭicca samuppāda*
desire — *chanda*
directed thought — *vitakka*
discern — *pajānāti*
discernment — *paññā*
discrimination — *vimaṁsā*
disenchantment — *nibbidā*
dispassion — *virāga*
effluent — *āsava*
emptiness — *suññatā*
evaluation — *vicāra*
fabricated — *saṅkhata*

fabrication — *saṅkhāra*
fetter — *saṅyojana*
frame of reference* — *satipaṭṭhāna*
gnosis — *añña*
good will — *mettā*
heart — *manas*
inconstant* — *anicca*
insight — *vipassanā*
intellect — *manas*
intent — *citta*
intention — *cetanā*
letting go — *vossagga*
medium — *āyatana*
mind — *citta*
non-fashioning — *atammayatā*
not-self — *anattā*
origination — *samudaya*
paraphernalia — *upadhi*
perception — *saññā*
persistence — *viriya*
pertinent — *opanayika*
phenomenon — *dhamma*
prerequisite — *upanisā*
property — *dhātu*
quality — *dhamma*
release — *vimutti*
relinquishment — *paṭinissagga*
requisite condition — *paccaya*
resolve — *saṅkappa*
self-awakening — *sambodhi*
sensuality — *kāma*
skillful — *kusala*
sphere — *āyatana*
stream-entry — *sotapatti*
stress* — *dukkha*
Such — *tādī*
sustenance — *upādāna*
theme — *nimitta*
this/that conditionality — *idappaccayatā*
tranquility — *samatha*
transcendent — *lokuttara*
transmigration — *saṁsāra*
Unbinding* — *nibbāna*
Unfabricated — *asaṅkhata*
world — *loka*

Fabrication: *Saṅkhāra* literally means "putting together," and carries connotations of jerry-rigged artificiality. It is applied to physical and to mental processes, as well as to the products of those processes. Various English words have been suggested as renderings for *saṅkhāra*—such as "formation," "determination," "force," and "construction"—but "fabrication," in both of its senses, as the process of fabrication and the fabricated things that result, seems the best equivalent for capturing the connotations as well as the denotations of the term.

Frame of reference: The literal rendering of *satipaṭṭhāna* is "foundation of mindfulness" or "application of mindfulness," both of which require a great deal of explanation to make them intelligible in English. However, the actual function of *satipaṭṭhāna* in practice is precisely that of the English idiom, frame of reference. Although adopting this rendering requires some inconsistency in translating *sati*—using "reference" here, and "mindfulness" otherwise—this seems a small price to pay for instant intelligibility in an otherwise obscure term.

Inconstant: The usual rendering for *anicca* is "impermanent." However, the antonym of the term, *nicca,* carries connotations of constancy and dependability; and as *anicca* is used to emphasize the point that conditioned phenomena cannot be depended on to provide true happiness, this seem a useful rendering for conveying this point.

Stress: The Pali term *dukkha,* which is traditionally translated in the commentaries as, "that which is hard to bear," is notorious for having no truly adequate equivalent in English, but stress—in its basic sense as a strain on body or mind—seems as close as English can get. In the Canon, *dukkha* applies both to physical and to mental phenomena, ranging from the intense stress of acute anguish or pain to the innate burdensomeness of even the most subtle mental or physical fabrications.

Unbinding: Because *nibbāna* is used to denote not only the Buddhist goal, but also the extinguishing of a fire, it is usually rendered as "extinguishing" or, even worse, "extinction." However, a study of ancient Indian views of the workings of fire (see *The Mind Like Fire Unbound)* will reveal that people of the Buddha's time felt that a fire, in going out, did not go out of existence but was simply freed from its agitation and attachment to its fuel. Thus, when applied to the Buddhist goal, the primary connotation of *nibbāna* is one of release and liberation. According to the commentaries, the literal meaning of the word *nibbāna* is "unbinding," and as this is a rare case where the literal and contextual meanings of a term coincide, this seems to be the ideal English equivalent.

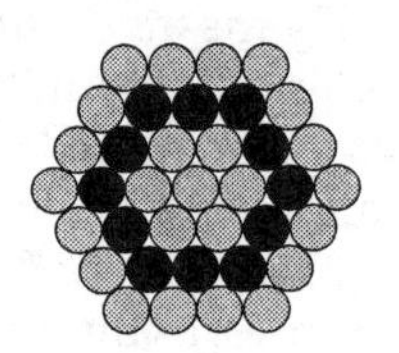

Index

Similes

Persons

Subjects

Bibliography

The following secondary sources were useful in placing the teachings of the Pali Canon in their historical context, both social and intellectual:

Bhattacharya, Arun. *A Treatise of Ancient Hindu Music.* Columbia, Missouri: South Asian Books, 1978.
Jayatilleke, K. N. *Early Buddhist Theory of Knowledge.* London: George Allen & Unwin Ltd., 1963.
McClain, Ernest G., *The Myth of Invariance: The Origin of the Gods, Mathematics and Music from the Ṛg Veda to Plato.* New York: Nicholas-Hays, 1976.
______. *The Pythagorean Plato.* York Beach, Maine: Nicholas-Hays, 1978.
Warder, A. K. *Indian Buddhism,* 2d. ed. Delhi: Motilal Banarsidass, 1980.
______. *Indian Kavya Literature. Volume One: Literary Criticism.* Delhi: Motilal Banarsidass, 1989.
______. *Outline of Indian Philosophy.* Delhi: Motilal Banarsidass, 1971.
______. *Pali Metre.* London: Pali Text Society, 1967.
______. "Prologomena to a History of Indian Science" in *New Paths in Buddhist Research,* edited by A. K. Warder. Durham, N. C.: Acorn Press, 1985.
Weiss, Mitchell G. "Caraka Samhita on the Doctrine of Karma" in *Karma and Rebirth in Classical Indian Traditions,* edited by Wendy Doniger O'Flaherty. Berkeley: University of California Press, 1980.